Innovation in Environmental Policy?

Innovation in Environmental Policy?

Integrating the Environment for Sustainability

Edited by

Andrew J. Jordan

Professor of Environmental Politics, School of Environmental Sciences, University of East Anglia, UK

Andrea Lenschow

Professor of European Integration and Policy, Department of Social Science, University of Osnabrück, Germany

Edward Elgar

Cheltenham, UK • Northampton, MA, USA

Published by
Edward Elgar Publishing Limited
The Lypiatts
15 Lansdown Road
Cheltenham
Glos GL50 2JA
UK

Edward Elgar Publishing, Inc.
William Pratt House
9 Dewey Court
Northampton
Massachusetts 01060
USA

A catalogue record for this book
is available from the British Library

Library of Congress Control Number: 2008932873

ISBN 978 1 84720 490 5 (cased)

Printed and bound in Great Britain by MPG Books Ltd, Bodmin, Cornwall

Contents

PART III   NATIONAL EXPERIENCES AND
PROSPECTS

PART IV   COMPARATIVE CONCLUSIONS

Figures

Tables

Boxes

Contributors

David Benson is an ESRC Postdoctoral Fellow at the Centre for Social and Economic Research on the Global Environment (CSERGE), University of East Anglia, Norwich, UK.

Olivia Bina is a Research Fellow at the Centre of Philosophy (University of Lisbon) and the Centre of Urban and Regional Systems (Instituto Superior Técnico, Lisbon), Portugal.

Julia Hertin is a Research Fellow at the Environmental Policy Research Centre, Freie Universität Berlin, Germany.

John Hoornbeek serves as Director of the Center for Public Administration and Public Policy, and is an Assistant Professor of Political Science at Kent State University, USA.

Klaus Jacob is the Research Director of the Environmental Policy Research Centre, Freie Universität, Berlin, Germany.

Andrew Jordan is Professor of Environmental Politics at the School of Environmental Sciences, University of East Anglia, Norwich, UK.

William M. Lafferty is Professor of Political Science and Director of ProSus at the Centre for Development and the Environment (SUM), University of Oslo, Norway; he is also Professor of Strategic Research for Sustainable Development in Europe at the Centre for Clean Technology and Environmental Policy, University of Twente, the Netherlands.

Olav Mosvold Larsen was a researcher at ProSus/SUM until 2007. He is now Senior Executive Adviser on Sustainable Development at Avinor AS, the company responsible for air traffic control and airport management in Norway.

Andrea Lenschow is Professor of European Integration and Policy and Jean Monnet Chair at the Department of Social Science at the University of Osnabrück, Germany.

Måns Nilsson is Research Fellow at the Stockholm Environment Institute (SEI), Sweden, and a Director of SEI's Policy and Institutions Programme.

Åsa Persson is a Research Associate at the Stockholm Environment Institute, Stockholm, Sweden.

Andrew Ross is a Researcher at the Fenner School of Environment and Society, Australian National University, Canberra, Australia.

Duncan Russel is an ESRC Postdoctoral Fellow at the Centre for Social and Economic Research on the Global Environment (CSERGE), University of East Anglia, Norwich, UK.

Audun Ruud is Senior Research Fellow at ProSus/SUM, University of Oslo, Norway.

Adriaan Schout is a Senior Researcher at the European Studies Programme, Netherlands Institute for International Relations (Clingendael) in the Hague, the Netherlands.

Reinhard Steurer is Principal Researcher and Lecturer at the Research Institute for Managing Sustainability (RIMAS), Vienna University of Economics and Business Administration, Vienna, Austria.

Martin Unfried is a Senior Lecturer at the European Institute of Public Administration, Maastricht, the Netherlands.

Axel Volkery is Project Manager for Policy and Scenario Analysis at the European Environment Agency, Copenhagen, Denmark.

David Wilkinson is currently Principal Specialist in European Relations at Natural England. His chapter was written when he was a Senior Research Fellow at the Institute for European Environmental Policy (IEEP), London, UK.

Rüdiger K. Wurzel is Reader in Politics and Jean Monnet Chair in European Union Studies at the University of Hull, UK. He is also the Director of the Centre for European Union Studies (CEUS) in Hull.

Abbreviations

ABB	Activity-Based Budgeting (EU)
BAT	Best Available Technology
BMI	Bundesministerium des Innern (Federal Interior Ministry) (Germany)
BML	Bundesministerium für Landwirtschaft (Federal Agricultural Ministry) (Germany)
BMU	Bundesministerium für Umwelt, Naturschutz und Reaktorsicherheit (Federal Ministry for the Environment, Nature and Nuclear Safety) (Germany)
BMWi	Bundesministerium für Wirtschaft (Economics Ministry) (Germany)
CAP	Common Agricultural Policy (EU)
CDU	Christian Democratic Union (Germany)
CEQ	Council on Environmental Quality (USA)
CSU	Christian Social Union (Germany)
DEFRA	Department of the Environment, Food and Rural Affairs (UK)
DETR	Department for the Environment, Transport and Regions (UK)
DG	Directorate General (EU)
DUX	German Environment Index
EA	Environmental Assessment
EAC	Environmental Audit Committee (UK)
EAGGF	European Agricultural Guidance and Guarantee Fund (EU)
EAP	Environmental Action Programme (EU)
EEA	European Environment Agency (EU)
EIA	Environmental Impact Assessment
EIS	Environmental Impact Statement
EMS	Environmental Management System(s)
EPA	Environmental Protection Agency (USA)
EPA	Environmental Policy Appraisal
EPI	Environmental Policy Integration
EPR	Environmental Policy Review (EU)
EPSB	Environmental Profile of the State Budget (Norway)
EU	European Union
FDP	Free Democratic Party (Germany)
GDR	German Democratic Republic

IA	Impact Assessment (EU)
IIA	Integrated Impact Assessment
ISTEA	Inter-modal Surface Transportation Efficiency Act (USA)
ITPS	Institute for Growth Policy Studies (Sweden)
MoE	Ministry of Environment (Norway)
NAPSD	National Action Plan for Sustainable Development (Norway)
NCSD	National Committee for Sustainable Development (Norway)
NCSD	National Council(s) for Sustainable Development
NEMS	National Environmental Monitoring System (Norway)
NEP	National Environmental Plan
NEPA	National Environmental Policy Act (USA)
NEPI	'New' Environmental Policy Instrument
NEQO	National Environmental Quality Objectives (Sweden)
NGO	Non-governmental Organization
NIM	Committee for International Environmental Issues (Norway)
NOU	Official Norwegian Reports (Norway)
NPM	New Public Management
NSESD	National Strategy for Ecologically Sustainable Development (Australia)
NSSD	National Strategy/ies for Sustainable Development
OECD	Organisation for Economic Cooperation and Development
PEIS	Programmatic Environmental Impact Statements (USA)
PMCs	Programme Monitoring Committees
PPP	Policies, Plans and Programmes
PSA	Public Service Agreements (UK)
RDS	Results and Documentation System (Norway)
RIA	Regulatory Impact Assessment
SD	Sustainable Development
SDC	Sustainable Development Commission (UK)
SDS	Sustainable Development Strategy (EU)
SDU	Sustainable Development Unit (UK)
SEA	Strategic Environmental Assessment
SEAP	Sectoral Environmental Action Plan (Norway)
SER	State of the Environment Report (Norway)
SFT	Pollution Control Authority (Norway)
SIA	Sustainability Impact Assessment
SPD	Social Democratic Party (Germany)
SRU	Sachverständigenrat für Umweltfragen (German Advisory Council on the Environment, (Germany)
TEN-T	Trans-European Transport Networks
UGB	Unified Environmental Act (Germany)
UK	United Kingdom

UN	United Nations
UNCED	United Nations Conference on Environment and Development
UNEP	United Nations Environment Programme
US/USA	United States of America
WCED	World Commission on Environment and Development
WHG	Water Management Act (Germany)

Foreword

In 1963 David Braybrooke and Charles Lindblom coined the phrase 'disjointed incrementalism' to characterise the way that decisions are made in a world of imperfect knowledge. No sooner had the phrase entered into circulation than it came to be used in descriptive and analytical studies of governmental decision making. Decision making is incremental, because it only advances slowly away from its existing commitments. It is disjointed because more often than not the right hand of government does not know what the left hand is doing.

A good case can be made for the proposition that this feature of government poses special problems for any policy goal that requires high levels of co-ordination and foresight across many branches of government, whether it be community care for mentally ill people, protection of individuals from discrimination or the reduction of crime. However, for the achievement of sustainable development, the barriers to implementation created by disjointed incrementalism are particularly severe, for policy making has to cope not only with the difficulties of disjointed political organisations but also with the cognitive problems created by the complexity of natural systems.

Good empirical social science may not raise our spirits, but it should improve our understanding. Andrew Jordan and Andrea Lenschow have produced a volume that provides a subtle and empirically informed understanding of the issues in question, using a design that looks both at the policy cycle and at cross-national comparisons.

Among their conclusions, the following stand out. No country has succeeded in institutionalising sustainable development in a strong sense, that is in a way that gives environmental protection a trump card in respect of other policies. Such institutionalisation as there is produces a balancing of environmental against other concerns, but no more.

Secondly, communicative integration – in the form of declaratory documents and strategies – is stronger than organisational and procedural integration. In short, the easy things have been done first and further integration is then stalled. Thirdly, whatever may be true of governments generally, distinctive national styles persist. Consensual Sweden manages more integration than most; German ministries are still compartmentalised; and UK governments continue to reorganise departments rather than develop the integrated policies. Fourthly, politics matters, whether in the form of the composition of governments or the commitment of individual leaders.

Sustainable development was never going to be easy. The merit – the depressing merit – of this book is that it shows the many different ways in which it is difficult.

Professor Albert Weale FBA
University of Essex, UK

Preface

In 1999, we were asked to submit evidence to a parliamentary inquiry on environmental policy organized by the UK Environmental Audit Committee. With hindsight, this was a time of high hopes amongst those advocating something new known as 'environmental policy integration' – a policy principle first established by the Brundtland Commission in 1987. The principle of environmental policy integration (or EPI) is not a hard and fast decision rule, but broadly speaking it suggests that environmental thinking should be integrated into sectoral policy making at the earliest available opportunity in order to make human development more sustainable. Traditionally, the core task of environmental policy makers has been to remedy the environmental damage generated by cognate sectors (such as agriculture, transport and energy) by regulating their activities. Brundtland's motive for pushing for EPI was to institutionalize a more anticipatory approach to environmental problem solving, which would aim to 'design out' environmental damage from policies before they were formally adopted and implemented.

The Environmental Audit Committee had been established by Tony Blair's new Labour government in 1997 and given the task of monitoring the UK's implementation of EPI and sustainable development. In 1998, the European Union (EU) had launched a high-level initiative at EU level known as the Cardiff Process, and the Audit Committee was eager to understand how well this had performed and how it might impact on national policy making in the UK, where a similar initiative ('Greening Government') had been running since 1997. The Audit Committee's principal finding was that Brundtland was right: the 'post hoc' approach had had its day and that henceforth 'the emphasis [must] shift towards creating a more integrated framework for a preventative approach to environmental protection' (House of Commons 1999: v). In Europe, this implied that the EU institutions should make every effort to 'coordinate their policies and working practices under strong leadership and strategic direction to achieve real change' (ibid.).

Were such a change ever fully to occur it would, as the title of this book makes clear, represent a profound innovation in the orientation and structures of environmental policy making. In our evidence (Jordan and Lenschow 1999), we sought to draw the committee's attention to some of the barriers to successful integration, particularly those in multi-level political systems such as the EU, in which high-level principles (such as EPI) that enjoy political support have a tendency to be differentially interpreted and applied in the everyday 'grind' of policy making (see also Jordan and Lenschow 2000).

Ten years on, it is apparent that most of the European countries that pledged to 'integrate the environment for sustainable development' have not made nearly as much progress as they had declared when the European Commission launched the Cardiff Process. This book seeks to document and assess what has been done in the name of EPI. It does so by drawing together a series of studies of the most common implementing instruments and the varied experiences of applying them in six OECD states and the EU. Written by a team of international experts using a common analytical framework, it seeks to draw together insights into the broad patterns and dynamics of EPI at different spatial scales and in a variety of policy sectors.

As with many books, this one has been a rather long time in the writing. The team of authors first met in Norwich in March 2005 principally to share experiences, reflect on the state of knowledge (as it then was) and agree upon a common approach. We met again in Cambridge in October 2005 to discuss first drafts of the chapters and deepen our mutual understanding of the links between EPI and sustainable development. Then we met once again in Stockholm in December 2006. At this third and final meeting, we identified and debated the main findings of our collective analysis.

We firmly believe that by organizing ourselves in this way, we have been able to produce a genuinely integrated book which represents much more than a jumble of individual chapters prefaced with an introductory essay by us, the two editors. On the contrary, the structure and the key messages to emerge from this book are the outcome of a joint enterprise.

We have accumulated a large number of debts during the production of this book. First and foremost, we would like to thank the contributors for their enormous enthusiasm and enduring commitment. By forging strong bilateral links with one another and with us, they have powerfully confirmed that there is such a thing as 'self-organizing governance'.

Most of the funding for the three workshops was kindly provided by the UK Economic and Social Research Council Programme on Environmental Decision Making, which was managed by CSERGE (the Centre for Social and Economic Research on the Global Environment) between 2001 and 2007. We are indebted to Dawn Turnbull and Emily Sheldon for their efficient administrative support and kind hospitality, particularly during the first workshop in Norwich. Måns Nilsson – one of the authors of the chapter on EPI in Sweden – kindly co-organized the third seminar in

Sweden that not only allowed us to discuss the conclusions of our comparative analysis of EPI measures, but also provided an important opportunity to share insights with a larger network of researchers (PINTS – Policy Integration for Sustainability) that had just successfully completed a study of EPI in Sweden.

We would also like to thank Ingmar von Homeyer, Anthony Zito and Henrik Gudmundsson, who agreed to participate in the first seminar in Norwich, at which the broad outline of the project was established. Subsequently, David Benson, David Wilkinson, Andrew Ross and John Hoornbeek agreed to join the team. Their contributions (on green budgeting, and EPI in Australia and the USA respectively) helped to extend greatly the coverage of the project – and hence this volume – to areas that are barely covered by the existing literature. We are extremely grateful to all of them for their time and effort. We would also like to thank Ingmar for subsequently inviting us to participate in an EU-funded network on EPI (EPIGOV – Environmental Policy Integration and Multi-level Governance), generously supported by the 6th Research Framework Programme (Contract no. 028661). This network has enabled us to refine our ideas and share them with a much larger audience. The European Commission's financial support is gratefully acknowledged. Finally, we would like to thank Catherine Elgar and her team at Edward Elgar for supporting our work and guiding it to publication, and Sylvia Potter, the copy editor.

Andrew Jordan, Norwich
Andrea Lenschow, Osnabrück

BIBLIOGRAPHY

House of Commons (Environmental Audit Committee) (1999), *EU Policy and the Environment: An Agenda for the Helsinki Summit*, HC 44, Session 1999–2000, London: The Stationery Office.

Jordan, A.J. and A. Lenschow (1999), 'Memorandum submitted by Dr Andrew Jordan and Dr Andrea Lenschow', in House of Commons (Environmental Audit Committee), *EU Policy and the Environment: An Agenda for the Helsinki Summit*, HC 44, Session 1999–2000, London: The Stationery Office.

Jordan, A.J. and A. Lenschow (2000), ' "Greening" the European Union: what can be learned from the leaders of EU environmental policy?' *European Environment*, 10 (3): 109–120.

Lenschow, A. (ed.) (2002), *Environmental Policy Integration: Greening Sectoral Policies in Europe*, London: Earthscan.

PART I

The conceptual and institutional context

1. Integrating the environment for sustainable development: an introduction

Andrew Jordan and Andrea Lenschow

At a public hearing organized by the World Commission on Environment and Development (WCED) in May 1986, the former Canadian federal minister of the environment, Charles Caccia, asked a deceptively simple question: 'How long can we go on and safely pretend that the environment is not the economy, is not health, is not the prerequisite to development, is not recreation?' (quoted in WCED 1987: 38). He firmly believed that new ways had to be found to ensure that environmental thinking was a part of all these things, if society genuinely wanted to develop more sustainably. But how could and, just as importantly, should this be achieved?

This line of thinking evidently influenced the WCED because in the first few pages of its landmark report – *Our Common Future* – it remarked that:

> Those responsible for managing natural resources and protecting the environment are institutionally separated from those responsible for managing the economy. *The real world of interlocked economic and ecological systems will not change; the policies and institutions concerned must* (ibid.: 9) (emphasis added).

In a later section, it tried to explain more precisely how 'policies and institutions' should change:

> The major central economic and sectoral agencies of governments should now be made directly responsible and fully accountable for ensuring that their policies, programmes and budgets support development that is ecologically, as well as economically sustainable (ibid.: 314).

Although the WCED did not use the term 'environmental policy integration' (or EPI), these paragraphs effectively introduced it to a global audience. Since 1987, EPI has received widespread political backing internationally, but especially in the European Union (EU), where it now has a prominent legal status in the founding Treaties. At EU level and in many Member

States, EPI is regarded as a key element of the transition to sustainability (Jordan 2008). In fact, one of us has referred to EPI as a 'first-order operational principle to implement and institutionalize the idea of sustainable development' in the manner popularized by Gro Harlem Brundtland's World Commission (Lenschow 2002a: 6).[1]

The verb 'to innovate' means to introduce something new, or to change fundamentally something that is already well established. In the past, environmental policy has tended to be a rather reactive exercise in remedying the environmental damage generated by sectoral policies such as the intensification of agricultural production or the construction of new transport infrastructure. If EPI was implemented in the manner described by Charles Caccia or Brundtland's World Commission, it would – as the title of this book suggests – represent a very significant innovation in the way in which environmental policy has traditionally been thought about and implemented. Liberatore (1997: 107) made this point very succinctly over a decade ago:

> The relevance of [EPI] for moving towards sustainable development is straightforward: if environmental factors are not taken into consideration in the formulation and implementation of the policies that regulate economic activities and other forms of social organization, a new model of development that can be environmentally and socially sustainable in the long term cannot be achieved.

EPI – at least as the Brundtland Report perceived it – aims to turn the policy status quo on its head, so that in future, environmental protection involves a much more holistic and, above all, proactive search early on in the policy process for opportunities to prevent environmental damage from occurring. Lafferty and Hovden (2003: 2) argue that such a change would be innovative in the sense that it would constitute 'a relatively strong revision of the traditional hierarchy of policy objectives, where environmental goals and values historically have tended to be at the lower end of the scale'.

But more than twenty years after the publication of *Our Common Future*, the majority of political systems seem no closer to institutionalizing EPI in the manner elegantly set out by Mrs Brundtland or Mr Caccia. In many respects, they appear to have moved further away, even in Europe. In 2003, the European Environment Agency (EEA) (EEA 2003: 7) concluded that 'the implementation of more integrated approaches to policy making needs to be accelerated if Europe is . . . to meet its aspirations on sectoral integration and sustainable development'.[2] In 2007, the European Commission conceded that 'progress has been mixed' and as a consequence 'Europe is not yet on the path towards a genuinely sustainable development' (COM (2007) 225 final, 30-4-07: 15, 4). Some commentators have gone even further, claiming that '[t]he recent overriding concern for growth and jobs has been used to call into question the very legitimacy of [EU] regulatory action in many fields, including the environment' (Pallemaerts *et al.* 2006: ii). In short, integration has not yet reached the degree of normality envisioned by Mrs Brundtland or Mr Caccia. In fact, as policy goals, sustainable development and EPI appear more remote and more politically contested today than they did twenty years ago.

Those looking for a detailed assessment of what has – or has not – been achieved with respect to EPI, can now consult a growing corpus of academic papers and at least two edited books (Lenschow 2002b; Nilsson and Eckerberg 2007). In the 2000s, these were supplemented with a series of policy reviews conducted by the Organisation for Economic Cooperation and Development (OECD) and the European Environment Agency (EEA). Nonetheless, the evidence base underpinning both the concept and the everyday practice of EPI remains relatively fragmented. Considering that the focus on the environmental pillar of sustainable development appears to be a European 'speciality', it is no coincidence that the available literature on EPI has a distinctly European – and, dare we say, even an EU – bias. Unfortunately, detailed country-based research on EPI remains very scarce.[3] Although there are some excellent overviews (for example, OECD 2002; Jacob and Volkery 2004; EEA 2005a), unlike the literature on governance for sustainable development (Jordan 2008), systematic comparative analyses of EPI are still relatively thin on the ground. Studies of how EPI has been interpreted and implemented in non-European contexts are extremely rare. Similarly, while there are potentially many instruments that can be used to implement EPI, most have either been studied in isolation and/or for other (that is, non-EPI) purposes.

This book aims to address these gaps by bringing together the state of the art in research on EPI conducted at national and supranational levels. It does so by charting the numerous instruments that have been introduced at these two administrative levels since 1987, and analysing the conditions for their effectiveness. In order to do this, we first explore EPI in terms of its conceptual meaning, then we scrutinize the various processes and instruments that can be – or have been – used to put it into effect, and assess the cumulative outcomes of these activities 'on the ground' in different jurisdictions. Thus in Section 2 of this chapter, we begin by discussing the conceptual meaning of EPI that can be inferred from the 'mother document' of sustainable development, namely the Brundtland Report. We also note that in the public discourse in relation to EPI and sustainable development as well as in the application of these concepts, the basic principle of EPI still invites a great variety of different interpretations and, consequently, instruments of implementation. In an early analysis, Weale and Williams (1992: 46) concluded that there was 'no canonical statement of precisely what it might involve'. In its stocktaking report, the EEA (2005a: 12) also detected 'little agreement' on its core meaning. In order to permit more systematic analysis, we therefore adopt the economist Keynes's famous distinction between normative and positive definitions, this being a 'pre-requisite for further empirical work' (Lafferty and Hovden 2003: 8–9).

Having done this, Section 3 turns to explore EPI as a governing process. Existing studies identify several factors that influence the scope and the effectiveness of different implementing instruments. Yet little systematic knowledge has emerged. In this book, we identify three broad types of instrument: communicative, organizational and procedural. We set out systematically to investigate them both from a conceptual (or 'textbook') perspective (Part II of this book), and as they have actually been used 'in action' in several key OECD countries (Part III of this book). These instruments, both individually and in combination, delineate the 'game' of EPI in the sense that they define the 'who, when and where' of how different policy choices impact on behaviour. We do so by studying the deployment of different combinations of EPI instruments (namely, administrative instruments, green budgeting, sustainable development strategies, policy appraisal and Strategic Environmental Assessment) and tracking their overall performance in five countries that are generally considered to be pioneers in environmental policy – namely Germany, Norway, Sweden, the UK and the USA – and the European Union (EU). The USA has been remarkably under-studied with regard to EPI, although it was very much a model environmental state in the 1960s and 1970s (Vogel 2005). By contrast, Australia provides another political and institutional setting in which to explore the contemporary processes of EPI.

In Section 3, we suggest two basic perspectives to order our knowledge: a political systems approach and a policy analysis approach. We focus on the European experience, as this is – so far – the main context in which EPI (as opposed to sustainable development) has received serious attention. This is, of course, a gap in the literature that we are also hoping to address in this book (see especially the chapters on the USA and Australia). By proceeding in this way, we try to hold the general political context constant – namely, the fundamental acceptance of environmental protection as a goal of policy making – and focus on the strengths and weaknesses of individual instruments from a comparative perspective, as well as taking account of the interplay between different instruments in the context of different political systems.

Finally, Section 4 explains that EPI can also be interpreted as the cumulative outcome of implementing relevant instruments in different policy systems. Although an outcome perspective is not, for reasons that we elaborate upon more fully below, the main focus of this book, given our analysis of various policy instruments that have been developed to accomplish EPI, we do have a unique opportunity to begin the process of linking these various EPI instruments to the policy outcomes they have generated 'on the ground' in different jurisdictions. Section 5 concludes this chapter and looks forward to the rest of the book.

Before proceeding any further, we would like to point out that the main purpose of this chapter is not to develop a tight analytical framework and impose it on the empirical chapters, but rather to present a range of standpoints and questions to guide the 'instrument' and 'country' studies respectively. In other words, in this chapter we will pose questions and give analytical direction; answers are expected in the empirical chapters and in Chapter 15.

EPI: NORMATIVE AND POSITIVE CONCEPTUAL MEANINGS

Many academics and policy makers consider EPI to be a policy-making 'principle' without reflecting too much on precisely what this implies. This may seem like a matter of mere semantics to some, but – especially for lawyers – it is far from trivial as it raises the tricky issues of legal commitment and enforceability (see Hession and Macrory 1998; Nollkaemper 2002). In the EU, the political and legal salience of the principle suggests that the perceived need for clarity is especially important (Nollkaemper 2002: 25–29). If EPI is primarily a policy objective whose role in international, EU and national government documents is to inspire either concrete legal rules or political programmes and activities, it does not form a suitable foundation for legal decisions. Consequently, the EU's commitment will be as enforceable as a United Nations declaration or have the same degree of compulsion as one of the OECD's benchmarks of 'good practice'. If, however, EPI is deemed to have an autonomous meaning and is thus a 'standard to be observed', then a clear definition of the principle's substantive meaning needs to be developed in order for it to be enforceable. But do we actually have agreement on what EPI means?

Lafferty and his colleagues (Lafferty and Hovden 2003; Lafferty 2004; Lafferty and Knudsen 2007) have made the most systematic effort to pin down the core meaning of EPI. Based on a close textual analysis of the international document in which it was first brought to the world's attention – the Brundtland Report – they argue that the WCED's 'mother concept' – sustainable development – attributed 'principled priority' to environmental objectives in the process of 'balancing' economic, social and environmental concerns. In other words, the three should not be simply blended together, as this would be little more than 'policy integration'; EPI on the other hand, demands that the environment consistently receives 'special recognition' or 'principled priority' in the decision-making process (Lafferty and Hovden 2003: 9). According to them (ibid.):

> The whole point of EPI is . . . to avoid situations where environmental degradation becomes subsidiary; and in the context of sustainable development, to ensure that the long-term carrying capacity of nature becomes a *principal or overarching societal objective* (emphasis added).

In thinking about sustainable development (and thus the view one adopts of how to balance the three concerns), Lafferty and his co-workers designate 'environmental objectives as "trump" in the policy game' (Lafferty and Knudsen 2007: 22) vis-à-vis other policy objectives. The metaphor of 'trump card' in a game called policy, indicates that environmental concerns may lose in individual decisions (that is, if the trump card is not played), but according to a set of more basic 'rules of the game' which prioritize the environment in the sense of 'guarantee[ing] that every effort is made to assess the impact of the [sectoral] policy on the life-sustaining capacities of the affected ecosystem' (ibid.: 25).

This particular reading of EPI implies that it should not mean merely the search for synergy effects and 'win-win' solutions in making sectoral policy choices (that is, the consideration of environmental concerns at no expense to sectoral policy). Nor should it be reduced to a search for a middle ground between three equally valued objectives. Rather, EPI should amount to a deliberate attempt to prioritize the protection of the environment before any trade-offs are made between environmental, economic and/or social objectives. Hence, EPI does not call on environmental policy makers to assess the economic or social impact of environmental policy, but vice versa; the merits of general policy integration notwithstanding, environmental policy integration refers to one-, rather than two-way integration (EEA 2005a: 13). In this perspective, environmental impacts of sectoral decisions may be ignored only if – metaphorically speaking – (environmental) policy makers choose not to use their environmental trump card and instead reserve it for a future decision. Such leeway provided by the rules of the game ensures that trade-off decisions are made in a proportional manner (justifying the otherwise misleading term of 'balancing' in the Brundtland text).

But how has the conceptual link between sustainable development and EPI, with its normative core of prioritizing environmental objectives, been translated into political practice? This chapter will briefly look at the global level before turning to the EU and several individual countries which are all covered in the remainder of this book. At a global level, we can observe a (re-) introduction of ambiguity when studying closely Agenda 21, the UN's blueprint for sustainable development. This was the institutional follow-up to the Brundtland Report and was extensively debated prior to being adopted at the 1992 UN Conference on Environment and Development (UNCED). It clearly reflects the political character of the process of implementing sustainable development and hints at the political reluctance to prioritize the environment. '[E]nvironment *and* development is to be put at the centre of economic and political decision-making' (UNCED 1992: Chapter 8.2, emphasis in original).[4] Agenda 21 identified four fields of activity to improve the integration of environment and development: (1) integration in policy, planning and at management level (involving the adjustment of institutional structures and procedures as well as the use of data and information instruments); (2) integration by establishing appropriate legal and regulatory frameworks (implying judicial and administrative capacity building to ensure the formulation of effective laws and regulations and their enforcement as well as ongoing monitoring); (3) integration through the use of economic instruments (aiming at a reversal of the tendency to treat the environment as a 'free good' and to ignore the environmental and social cost of economic activity); and (4) integration into environmental and economic accounting (in order to take note more effectively of natural resource use).

But when it came to implementing these activities, Agenda 21 repeatedly emphasized the need to recognize that 'countries will develop their own priorities in accordance with their prevailing conditions, needs, national plans, policies and programmes' (UNCED 1992: Chapters 8.3, 8.4, 8.5, 8.16, 8.31), contradicting Brundtland's argument – summarized in Section 1 of this chapter – that policies and institutions must be changed. Thus, according to Agenda 21, market instruments and information instruments (allowing for flexible national solutions) should aim, among other things, at reducing the 'severe economic and social costs' that environmental standards could impose 'if they are uniformly applied in developing countries' (UNCED 1992: Chapter 8.2). Finally and perhaps most crucially of all, Agenda 21 pointedly refers not to EPI, but to the integration of environmental *and* developmental concerns into decision making (Chapter 8.2). Later on, it goes one step further by referring to the need to 'improve the processes of decision making so as to achieve the progressive integration of economic, social and environmental issues in the pursuit of development that is economically efficient, socially equitable and responsible and environmentally sound' (UNCED 1992: Chapter 8.4). Notably absent, therefore, was the clear pledge found in *Our Common Future* to 'integrate the environment for sustainable development'.

Hence, EPI has not been elaborated as a single concept at the global level; we are missing the explicit global pronouncement of rhetorical and operational commitment. On the contrary, Agenda 21 appears to accept that EPI can have a normative meaning and what Keynes would recognize as a series of more positive meanings. The fact that the conceptual meaning of the EPI principle is still contested frustrates lawyers, but it represents an interesting point of departure for comparative policy and political research.

That is to say, we believe that there is value in keeping the debate about the normative meaning of EPI (that is, what kinds of change to existing policy systems it should seek to achieve), apart from but in constant dialogue with the more positive question of how it is actually conceptualized in discourse and implemented in everyday political and policy settings. It is here that we will engage with the issue of priority setting that has attracted a great deal of academic comment, particularly amongst scholars of sustainable development. We will seek to show that while it is necessary to define EPI in normative terms (that is, in terms of the simultaneous pursuit of environmental, economic and social concerns: sustainable development), in the heat of everyday political processes, these interpretations tend to mutate, according to the push and pull of political forces.

Moreover, when and why they mutate should be of great interest to scholars of politics and public policy. Understanding how and why EPI is read in different ways by different actors in different jurisdictions and/or different stages of the policy cycle, is important, as these readings will inform different organizational or policy reforms which – we might reasonably expect – generate different policy outcomes. Analytically, comparative systems and policy-analytical approaches are well equipped to shed light on the interpretation and implementation of EPI.

This book will focus on a set of countries that are reputed to be pioneers in environmental policy, and on the EU, where we might expect that the normative core of EPI would be most likely to meet a high level of acceptance among policy makers and in society. Hence, here we may expect a high level of coherence between the normative definition of EPI and the positive meanings the concept is given in day-to-day political practice. Failure to achieve such coherence over time or compared to other jurisdictions should highlight the operational challenges implied in the concepts of sustainable development and EPI.

EPI AS A GOVERNING PROCESS

Different Analytical Perspectives

Understood as a governing process, EPI refers to the development and application of different communicative, organizational and procedural instruments. In Chapter 2, these three sub-types are explained more fully. Essentially, communicative instruments set out visions and longer-term objectives which are supposed to guide more detailed reform efforts, while leaving it to individual governments and targeted sectors to develop concrete 'operations' for policy integration. Organizational instruments, by contrast, alter the context (for example, the rules and frameworks) in which policy decisions are made. Typically, these might seek to strengthen some actors (for example, environmental departments) at the expense of others, open up existing networks or even create completely new actors to push forward environmental concerns. Finally, procedural reforms seek to alter decision-making procedures (for example, law making, appraisal and budgeting).

Those working with a process interpretation of EPI (for example, Schout and Jordan 2005; Jordan and Schout 2006; Nilsson and Eckerberg, 2007: 3) are concerned less with pinning down the normative core of EPI in an abstract or conceptual sense, and more with describing and explaining the ways in which different actors interact to develop and implement positive interpretations of it in everyday policy-making situations. According to this view, EPI is 'a process through which "non" environmental sectors consider the overall environmental consequences of their policies, and take active and early steps to incorporate an understanding of them into policy making at all relevant levels of governance' (Jordan and Schout 2006: 66). What counts here is the political struggle between different normative conceptions. Hence the EEA's point about EPI being an 'ongoing process, not something that is simply "achieved"' (EEA 2005b: 9).

Those that work with this interpretation distinguish between two broad understandings (or positive meanings) of EPI which may emerge in the heat of political decision making: a strong one and a weak one (Hill and Jordan 1993; Jordan and Schout 2006). 'Weak' EPI occurs when the sectors simply take environmental considerations 'into account', without giving them the 'principled priority' sought by Lafferty and his colleagues. The core of sectoral policies therefore remains essentially untouched, although some new routines may be added and the information upon which sectoral policy decisions are founded may be broadened. For example, the transport sector might discuss different ways of reducing the environmental burden of car transport (for example, by fitting catalytic converters or adopting alternative fuel sources), without radically challenging the underlying societal demand for more cars or more travel. 'Strong' EPI, by contrast, corresponds much more to Lafferty's (2004) reading of the normative core of the Brundtland Report, which would correspond to placing 'environmental considerations at the heart of decision making in other sectoral policies' (Haigh 2005, section 3.1-1). The commitment to minimize any contradictions between environmental and sectoral policies in the framework of EPI results 'giv[es] priority to the former over the latter' (Lafferty 2004: 13).[5] A strong reading of EPI builds on an important insight with regard to the application of sustainable development: synergies between economic, social and environmental objectives (that is, the much emphasized 'win-win' solutions) may be constructed at an aggregate level over long periods, but may not be so obvious in everyday decision-making situations (compare Lenschow 2002c: 227ff), where harder choices may have to be made and priorities set.

This process of pulling and hauling (Dunsire 1993) amongst the various sectoral actors can be studied from different analytical perspectives. In this book we probe two of them: one which proceeds by comparing political systems; and another which is derived from a policy analysis approach and distinguishes between distinct phases of the policy-making process (for example, agenda setting, initiation, decision making, implementation, evaluation, revision) or between the different manifestations of policy instruments (for example, as ideas/text/speech, organization and procedure). Both of these can, in turn, be studied from an institutional, a political (that is actor-centred) and a cognitive perspective. The next two sub-sections discuss these in some detail.

A Comparative Political Systems Perspective

In our case studies (the chapters in Part III), we view EPI as a process: that is anchored in a political system; needs to be decided by political majorities; must be organized and managed; and finally, should be maintained (either through enforcement or through persuasion). The structure of the prevailing political system (institutions), the political context (politics) and the legal and administrative tradition of a polity (cognitive predispositions) are looked at 'in concert' in order (hopefully) to recognize the relevant dynamics for (effective) EPI. In this section we take stock of our knowledge of EPI processes from a political systems perspective. While the case studies in Part III analyse EPI processes in single political settings, Chapter 15 adopts a more comparative perspective.

As indicated above, our existing knowledge of EPI is very much limited to single, relatively isolated accounts of some instruments in the EU and some of its Member States. In the absence of more systematic analysis, these studies nonetheless suggest that there is considerable variation in terms of the national motivations for pursuing EPI, the implementing instruments adopted and the obstacles encountered. First, it reveals that EPI has been interpreted differently according to the way it has been embedded in national political discourses and legal systems. For instance, in the Netherlands, EPI is seen to require a deep-seated change in societal attitudes and the development of policy commitments between the state and civil society; Germany, on the other hand, focuses on its economic dimension and emphasizes the need to market environmental technologies and correct market failures; meanwhile, the UK initially approached it from a governance perspective, seeing it as a further impetus to strive for more coordinated and efficient government (Jordan and Lenschow 2000; Lenschow 2002a). In Sweden, EPI has mostly been interpreted in the wider, social context of sustainability (see Chapter 11). Meanwhile, the country studies in Lenschow (2002b) focused on Germany, Italy and the UK, and identified several obstacles to greater EPI. These range from the institutional structure of government (Germany), to administrative and legal culture (Italy and Germany), and high-level political will and leadership (Italy and the UK). These patterns suggest a great deal of path-dependency in terms of developing and implementing national strategies.

From an institutional perspective, the challenge of EPI, namely coordination across both horizontal and vertical boundaries in policy-making processes, is presumably compounded in political systems with a very high level of fragmentation. Hence, disintegrated policy making might be particularly evident in federal jurisdictions (like the USA, Germany, Australia and the EU in our sample). Implicit in this view is the notion that centralized (and strong) states are better able to ensure the successful implementation of sustainable development and EPI policies. A variant of this notion – in the sense of also focusing on the number of veto points in the decision-making system – follows from a comparison of Westminster-type systems (for example, the UK and Australia) and presidential systems (USA), or of single-party versus coalition governments (as these are typical in most parliamentary systems with proportional voting systems, for example, Germany, Sweden, Norway in our sample). A contrary position is adopted by parts of the implementation literature that suggest that decentralized systems may lead to stronger EPI as these are more capable of developing a feeling of 'ownership' at the grassroots level and hence bottom-up support for EPI. In short, from a comparative political systems perspective – distinguishing centralized and decentralized systems – we will be able to make a link to the 'top-down' versus 'bottom-up' debate that is ongoing in discussions of effective (environmental) policy making and governance. The conceptual discourse on EPI tends towards a 'top-down' approach, assuming in particular that an institutionalized normative anchor such as a constitutional commitment is required to ensure the prioritizing of the environment. The comparative country studies should contribute empirical evidence with which to test this claim.

By contrast, a political perspective focuses on political will and leadership. These are already recurring themes in the existing literature on EPI (OECD 2001; EEA 2005a; Jordan and Schout 2006). In this book, we deliberately look at states and political systems that are considered to be frontrunners in environmental policy, as we may assume that these countries have developed some response to the sustainable development and EPI discourse. More analytically, this allows us to investigate the impact of political leadership within a fairly homogeneous group.

Furthermore, differences in legal and administrative traditions affecting the third – or cognitive – dimension of policy making can be explored in explaining: (1) different approaches or strategies in adapting administrative practices to the task of EPI; and (2) different normative constraints in achieving EPI. The EEA (2005b)[6] distinguishes between: the German-speaking systems, which rely heavily on legislation and law-obeying bureaucrats in administrations; the Anglo-Saxon system, where flexibility, adaptive capacity and the use of generalists is supposed to contribute to policy coordination and reform; the Nordic system, with its tendency towards consensual and cooperative governance; southern European systems, with highly legalistic, hierarchical and expert-based administrations; and finally, the former communist countries, where administrative tasks tend to rely heavily on external (party) control. By studying countries from the first three categories of legal and administrative culture, this book will be able to provide some insights with regard to the relevance of this factor.

To summarize, the existing literature suggests that EPI can be linked to a large bundle of institutional, political and cultural or cognitive issues. What has actually flowed from this research by way of suggesting concrete policy changes in the driving force sectors is by no means clear, however. One of the main purposes of the empirical chapters of this book is to review and compare systematically the experiences of implementing particular instruments (Part II) and bundles of instruments in particular political jurisdictions (Part III).

A Policy Analysis Perspective

From a policy analysis perspective, several analytical devices could be adopted. The phases of the policy cycle model are (despite some well-known weaknesses) a useful heuristic to investigate the level of commitment to EPI. EPI – if taken seriously – should shape every stage of decision making: sectoral policy makers would set the policy agenda with the environmental implications in mind; decision making would then be informed by environmental assessments; and policy feedback would cover any intended or unintended environmental consequences. Documenting the distribution of instruments empirically, within and across individual countries, will hopefully allow us to distinguish countries that establish a clear agenda for policy integration from countries that adopt EPI instruments in a more post hoc fashion. In order to ensure 'strong' EPI, the policy cycle model suggests that attention to environmental objectives needs to be given at the very start, that is, the credo of EPI should permeate the agenda-setting stage in sectoral policy making. Isolated EPI measures at later stages of the policy-making process may be capable of raising awareness and correcting individual decisions in the light of their negative environmental effects, but are very unlikely to give environmental thinking sufficient access to the 'mainstream' of sectoral policy to deliver greater EPI. At the same time, we should be able to distinguish systematic EPI efforts (that is, linked through the entire policy cycle) from more ad hoc attempts.

EPI instruments may also be ordered according to the way in which they manifest themselves. Communicative ones are relatively easy to implement but may not be followed up by action. Hence, they may be used for rhetorical purposes only. Organizational and (especially) procedural ones tend to intervene more actively in political and administrative routines; following an institutional logic, they should be adopted with greater reluctance. While this appears to correspond with the picture painted by existing studies, the chapters in Parts II and III will seek to reveal a much fuller picture. While the policy cycle perspective allows us to analyse the commitment of EPI over time, a systematic focus on the type of instrument alerts us to different forms of intervening in the process of EPI (forms that may be more or less deeply felt by the policy makers).

Also of analytical interest is the distinction between the institutional, political and cognitive impact of policy instruments, that is, our focus shifts from the form to the logic of change that is implied by them. This allows a direct link to be made with the political systems perspective and, more generally, to governance structures. The institutional and cognitive analytical interpretations relate to the need to embed EPI in the organizational set-up of government, and in the minds of policy makers and other relevant stakeholders. The crucial analytical distinction between the two explanations lies in the role attributed to political actors (and the degrees of freedom available for political choices). We will see that the institutional and cognitive logics often interact (for example, in governance frameworks that aim to facilitate communicative interaction). The governance structure that is most frequently associated with institutionalized communication is of course a network, which relies on there being an atmosphere of trusting collaboration between its members to be effective. In contrast, the political perspective tends to be less optimistic with regard to the effects of a stable institutional framework and the emergence of a normative framework for EPI. The presence of winners and losers and the resulting conflicts of interest call for powerful political interventions and a more hierarchical mode of governing. Such analysis of the institutional, political and cognitive factors in explaining the level of effectiveness of EPI requires a careful – case by case – approach, as policy instruments are not easily categorized in these terms. However, the existing literature does at least offer some guidance.

An institutional perspective

From an institutional perspective, EPI can be understood as a problem of policy coordination. The challenge of EPI arises from the fragmented nature of governmental systems, where policy sectors are institutionally separated (horizontal fragmentation) and where the coordination across different levels of government (vertical fragmentation) poses an additional problem, particularly in federal states like Germany, the USA, Australia and the EU. Here, the value of institution-building and organizational instruments or reforms would seem to be obvious. Building on an impressive body of research, Peters (1998: 296) defines coordination as a situation 'in which the policies and programmes of government are characterized by minimal redundancy, incoherence and lacunae'. But this headline definition can in turn be broken down into different coordination tasks. The influential Metcalfe scale (Metcalfe 1994), for instance, distinguishes nine tasks ranging from different sectors communicating with one another right through to a joint strategy. Chapter 3 shows how certain institutional and procedural arrangements can be associated with different levels or forms of coordination. Such arrangements may focus on the high level (cabinet, prime ministerial office) or on the lower, street levels of governments; they may also have a more strategic or a more operational character. Schout and Jordan argue that institutional (or 'administrative') change was a key element of Brundtland's prescription (see also Schout and Jordan 2005). They show that very many EPI instruments could be placed under this heading and explain why the existing literature is far from clear about how they could or should fit together.

A political perspective

While policy coordination via institutional and organizational means resonates well with the current discourse on 'good governance', the implementation of 'rational' structures and procedures can be a highly contentious matter, hence the importance of a political perspective. The bureaucratic politics literature[7] sees political conflict arising from the development of distinct cultures and routines in the bureaucratic segments of an administration and from the 'rational' inclination of each part to protect its competences (and resources) as well as ways of doing things from the intervention of other parts.[8] Such an inherently competitive structure poses a serious problem for those seeking to achieve greater policy integration. The obvious routes to achieving this involve lobbying the sectors from the outside and/or by exerting political leadership from above (hence the discussion of 'political will', 'commitment' and 'vision', particularly in the EEA's thinking – EEA 2005a/b). The extent to which political pressure from the apex of government and/or from society (whether as voters, activists or in other roles) are necessary prerequisites for EPI is an empirical question which is addressed in Parts II and III.

A cognitive perspective
A cognitive perspective searches for the source of the actor interests which stimulate the political conflicts noted above. According to Lenschow (2002a: 17), policy interests are often embedded in a 'frame of reference' or set of ideas 'which pre-structures the thinking within a policy sector'. The gradual, longer-term acceptance of new ideas can lead to a modification of actor interests and, possibly, also a reduction in the political conflicts noted above. Such ideas might relate to the economic and technological benefits of environmental protection, the potentially synergistic (win-win-win) relationship between the three pillars of sustainability, or – more deeply – to the life-sustaining role of environmental resources and hence their principled priority (most recently, Lafferty and Knudsen 2007). Those that adopt a learning perspective (for example, Hertin and Berkhout 2001; Nilsson 2005; Nilsson and Eckerberg 2007) are particularly interested in understanding the circumstances under which cognitive learning takes place within and across different 'frames of reference' (for example, sudden, unforeseen crises; exogenous shocks from outside the policy system; the gradual accumulation of worrying evidence, or – more manipulable – the accumulation of relevant knowledge in the early decision-making phase).

EPI AS A POLICY OUTCOME

Many environmentalists and, we suspect, Gro Harlem Brundtland, might well argue that concepts are only concepts, and process is only process; policy outcomes (that is, the influence of any EPI activity on the state of the environment and, ultimately, the sustainability or otherwise of human development) are what really matter in life. However, the measurement of outcome effectiveness is a very difficult task, and one which is not helped by the relative immaturity of this particular sub-field of evaluation research (but see Knaap and Kim 1998).

First, one needs to decide what counts as a 'good' or 'satisfactory' outcome and what outcome lies 'below standard'. In other words, are there certain basic benchmarks – that is, certain basic environmental quality standards or ecological support functions – that must be addressed regardless of the social and environmental cost (Lafferty and Knudsen 2007), before the policy 'game' of trading off begins? Knowing that the setting of benchmarks can be a scientifically complex and highly politicized process, it cannot be assumed that securing them actually promotes long-term sustainability, however. In other words, the measuring rod for assessing outcome effectiveness lies in the eyes of the beholder, and this causes serious methodological problems.

In the case of EPI, the main 'subject' – that is, the state of the environment now and in the long run – is a highly complex matter, affected by a multitude of factors. Objective and reliable data is hard to come by (Scruggs 2003: 205). Moreover, as we will see in this book, there are many different instruments which could be applied to deliver EPI, and these may well interact with one another, as well as background factors like economic and technological development, basic features of democracy (for example, veto points, democratic style), the prevailing regulatory culture and levels of public opinion, to name just a few. From an analytical perspective, the existence of so many potential causal factors and implementing instruments implies that causality cannot easily be determined.

From a policy maker's perspective, this creates a situation where the outcome of any single instrument can hardly be known with any degree of certainty. To address this requires inter alia a highly sophisticated understanding of: (1) the way in which any single EPI instrument operates and what behavioural impacts it generates within 'non' environmental sectors; (2) the manner in which different EPI instruments interact; (3) how instruments that were adopted at various levels of governance cohere (for example, strategic plans decided in the prime minister's office and consultation practices at sub-national level); (4) the manner in which all the instruments used are embedded in a larger political, economic and social context; and (5) how well all the instruments and interrelations effectively translate into policy outcomes.

In order to develop such a sophisticated understanding, two different approaches are potentially available: complex forms of decomposition analysis and detailed case studies of individual policy interventions. In this book, we will take the middle ground, whilst remaining cognisant of the difficulty of arriving at causal explanations. First, we will investigate the merits of a range of different EPI instruments[9] (Part II). In order to isolate these merits we will approach them from a comparative angle. Based on a review of the existing literature, we also aim to identify some of the conditions under which these instruments work. Second, we then look at how these instruments have been applied (both individually and together) in different political contexts. In order to control for too much complexity, this contextual analysis is done in single jurisdictions (Part III). When taken together, we hope they will offer some comparative insights into the extent to which each jurisdiction has considered EPI from an outcome perspective, what steps (if any) it has taken to measure and evaluate outcome effectiveness, and what it has learned from such activities. We shall report on the outcome of this approach in our concluding chapter.

THE STRUCTURE OF THE BOOK

The concept of EPI achieved far greater prominence and much greater conceptual coherence after it had been highlighted in the 1987 Brundtland Report. There can be no denying that the potential scope of EPI is very wide indeed, with a vertical (multi-level governance) and a horizontal (cross-sectoral) dimension on the one hand, and a continuing relevance right across the policy cycle on the other. In a sense, EPI is very much like its 'mother concept' – sustainable development – in that it seeks to be 'everywhere' in the policy system. However, this is a rather precarious position to be in when the firewalls between sectors are strong and political leadership from politicians and prime ministers is relatively ephemeral.

Were EPI ever to be implemented in the manner sought by Brundtland, it would involve a profound innovation in the orientation and structures of environmental policy making. So, to what extent have our seven jurisdictions managed to engineer such an innovation in their policy-making structures and decision-making systems? The literature on sustainable development is already voluminous and that on EPI is growing fast. Despite their obvious conceptual interconnectedness, these two literatures are relatively poorly integrated, both due to their spatial appeal (EPI seems to be a particularly European concern, whereas sustainable development has a much broader application) and distinct levels of analysis (many empirical accounts of EPI tend to be relatively narrow, covering it from the perspective of particular sectors and/or countries).

Our approach is to inspect the toolbox of available instruments and then investigate how they have – or have not – been adopted to implement EPI. Our analysis commences in Chapter 2, with a panoramic analysis of the deployment of the main implementing instruments in 30 OECD countries. This chapter seeks to highlight the most important geographical and temporal patterns in a manner which is absent from the existing literature. In Part II we delve further into the toolbox by looking at five main instruments. Each of the five chapters follows the same format, namely a brief introduction to and historical summary of the instrument in question, a description of its conceptual underpinnings and then an assessment of its performance.[10] In Part III, we present the national experience of deployment. Again, these seven chapters have been written to fit a standard format which includes a brief historical summary, a review of how each instrument has been implemented and an assessment of its performance. Finally, in Part IV we attempt to identify broad patterns and future research needs in this new and important area of environmental policy analysis.

NOTES

1. The Brundtland committee's report did not invent the phrase 'sustainable development'; the interdependence of ecological and developmental goals had been discussed as long ago as the 1972 UN conference in Stockholm (Alker and Haas 1993: 5–6; Lenschow 2002a: 5). Brundtland's greatest contribution was to bring together the (now very well known) triad of economic, social and environmental issues under the umbrella of sustainable development.
2. See also EEA (2007) and UNEP (2007).
3. But see Nilsson and Eckerberg (2007) on Sweden, Hovden and Torjussen (2002) on Norway and Jordan (2002) on the UK.
4. The way in which 'development' is used here is broadly synonymous with 'social'. This highlights another source of terminological confusion, as neither 'social' nor 'development' are entirely separate from the 'economic' as all economic activities are a special form of social interactions (which may go through a process of development or change). Hence the notion that there are 'pillars' of activity that can be (and have been) kept apart is itself a political and social construction.
5. Elsewhere, Lafferty (2002: 2) argues that 'the general environmental . . . element [that is, pillar] of sustainable development is *the most fundamental* – the one without which the concept loses its distinctive meaning' (emphasis added).
6. The EEA report (EEA 2005b) speaks of 'administrative *cultures*' (our emphasis), which is broadly synonymous with our term 'tradition'.
7. For the classical view, see Allison (1971). For an application to EPI in the EU, see Schout and Jordan (2005) and Jordan and Schout (2006).
8. As Allison (1971) was at great pains to point out, where you stand (on an issue) depends on where you sit (in an organization).
9. It is instructive that recent comparative studies of the policy determinants of environmental performance have tended to analyse performance at an aggregate level (that is, of all policy and non-policy interventions), rather than in terms of individual policies or policy instruments. For good summaries of why the latter might be very difficult to produce, see Parsons (1995: 600–613), Weale (1992) and Knaap and Kim (1998).
10. Given obvious space constraints, we decided not to include a separate chapter on 'new' environmental policy instruments (NEPIs) (for example, voluntary agreements, eco-taxes and environmental management systems), because these are already extensively addressed in the existing literature (Jordan *et al.* 2003; Jordan *et al.* 2005).

BIBLIOGRAPHY

Alker, H. and P. Haas (1993), 'The rise of global ecopolitics', in N. Coucri (ed.), *Global Accord: Environmental Challenges and International Responses*, Cambridge, MA and London: MIT Press.

Allison, G. (1971), *Essence of Decision: Explaining the Cuban Missile Crisis*, Boston, MA: Little Brown.

Dunsire, A. (1993), 'Modes of governance', in J. Kooiman (ed.), *Modern Governance: New Government–Society Interaction*, London: Sage.

EEA (European Environment Agency) (2003), *Europe's Environment: The Third Assessment (Full report)*, Copenhagen: European Environment Agency.

EEA (European Environment Agency) (2005a), *Environmental Policy Integration in Europe: State of Play and an Evaluative Framework*, Technical Report, No. 2/2005, Copenhagen: European Environment Agency.

EEA (European Environment Agency) (2005b), *Environmental Policy Integration in Europe: Administrative Culture and Practices*, Technical Report, No 5/2005, Copenhagen: European Environment Agency.

EEA (European Environment Agency) (2007), *Europe's Environment: The Fourth Assessment (Full report)*, Copenhagen: European Environment Agency.

Haigh, N. (ed.) (2005), *Manual of European Environmental Policy: The EU and Britain*, Leeds: Maney Publishing.

Hertin, J. and F. Berkhout (2001), 'Ecological modernization and EU environmental policy integration', *Journal of Environmental Policy and Planning*, 5 (1): 39–56.

Hession, M. and R. Macrory (1998), 'The legal duty of environmental integration: commitment and obligation or enforceable right?' in T. O'Riordan and H. Voisey (eds), *The Transition to Sustainability: The Politics of Agenda 21 in Europe*, London: Earthscan.

Hill, J. and A.J. Jordan (1993), 'The greening of government: lessons from the White Paper process', *ECOS*, 14 (3–4): 3–9.

Hovden, E. and S. Torjussen (2002), 'Environmental policy integration in Norway', in W. Lafferty, M. Nordskag and H. Aakre (eds), *Realizing Rio in Norway: Evaluative Studies of Sustainable Development*, Oslo: ProSus.

Jacob, K. and A. Volkery (2004), 'Institutions and instruments for government self-regulation: environmental policy integration in a cross-country comparison', *Journal of Comparative Policy Analysis*, 6 (3): 291–309.

Jordan, A.J. (2002), 'Efficient hardware and light green software? Environmental policy integration in the UK', in A. Lenschow (ed.), *Environmental Policy Integration: Greening Sectoral Policies in Europe*, London: Earthscan.

Jordan, A.J. (2008), 'The governance of sustainable development: taking stock and looking forwards', *Environment and Planning C*, 26 (1): 17–33.

Jordan, A. and A. Lenschow (2000), 'Greening the European Union: What can be learned from the "leaders" of EU environmental policy?' *European Environment*, 10 (3): 109–120.

Jordan, A.J. and A. Schout (2006), *The Coordination of the European Union: Exploring the Capacities for Networked Governance*, Oxford: Oxford University Press.

Jordan, A.J., Wurzel, R. and Zito, A. (eds) (2003), *'New' Instruments of Environmental Governance? National Experiences and Prospects*, London: Frank Cass.

Jordan, A., Wurzel, R. and A. Zito (2005), 'The rise of "new" policy instruments in comparative perspective: has governance eclipsed government?' *Political Studies*, 53 (3): 477–496.

Knaap, G. and T. Kim (eds) (1998), *Environmental Program Evaluation*, Urbana: University of Illinois Press.

Lafferty, W. (2002), Adapting Governance Practice to the Goals of Sustainable Development, paper presented at an *OECD PUMA seminar on Improving Governance for Sustainable Development*, 22–23 November, Paris: OECD.

Lafferty, W. (2004), 'From environmental protection to sustainable development: the challenge of decoupling through sectoral integration', in W. Lafferty (ed.), *Governance for Sustainable Development: The Challenge of Adapting Form to Function*, Cheltenham: Edward Elgar.

Lafferty, W. and E. Hovden (2003), 'Environmental policy integration: towards an analytical framework', *Environmental Politics*, 12 (3): 1–22.

Lafferty, W. and J. Knudsen (2007), *The Issue of 'Balance' and Trade-offs in EPI: How Will We Know EPI When We See It?* EPIGOV Working Paper, 31 January, Berlin: Ecologic.

Lenschow, A. (2002a), 'Greening the European Union: an introduction', in A. Lenschow (ed.), *Environmental Policy Integration: Greening Sectoral Policies in Europe*, London: Earthscan.

Lenschow, A. (ed.) (2002b), *Environmental Policy Integration: Greening Sectoral Policies in Europe*, London: Earthscan.

Lenschow, A. (2002c), 'Conclusion: what are the bottlenecks and where are the opportunities for greening the EU?' in A. Lenschow (ed.), *Environmental Policy Integration: Greening Sectoral Policies in Europe*, London: Earthscan.

Liberatore, A. (1997), 'The integration of sustainable development objectives into EU policy making', in S. Baker, M. Kousis, D. Richardson and S. Young (eds), *The Politics of Sustainable Development*, London: Routledge.

Metcalfe, L. (1994), 'International policy coordination and public management reform', *International Review of Administrative Studies*, 60: 271–290.

Nilsson, M. (2005), 'Learning, frames, and environmental policy integration: the case of Swedish energy policy', *Environment and Planning C*, 23: 207–226.

Nilsson, M. and K. Eckerberg (eds) (2007), *Environmental Policy Integration in Practice*, London: Earthscan.

Nollkaemper, André (2002), 'Conceptions of the integration principle in international environmental law', in A. Lenschow (ed.), *Environmental Policy Integration: Greening Sectoral Policies in Europe*, London: Earthscan.

OECD (Organisation for Economic Cooperation and Development) (2001), *Governance For Sustainable Development: Five OECD Case Studies*, Paris: OECD.

OECD (Organisation for Economic Cooperation and Development) (2002), *Improving Policy Coherence and Integration For Sustainable Development: A Checklist*, Paris: OECD

Pallemaerts, M., D. Wilkinson, C. Bowyer, J. Brown *et al.* (2006), *Drowning in Process? The Implementation of the EU's 6th Environmental Action Programme*, Report for the European Environmental Bureau, London: IEEP.

Parsons, W. (1995), *Public Policy*, Aldershot: Edward Elgar.

Peters, G.B. (1998), *Managing Horizontal Government: The Politics of Coordination*, Research paper No. 21, Ottawa: Canadian Centre for Management Development.

Schout, A. and A.J. Jordan (2005), 'Coordinated European governance: self-organizing or centrally steered?' *Public Administration*, 83 (1): 201–220.

Scruggs, L. (2003), *Sustaining Abundance*, Cambridge: Cambridge University Press.

UNCED (United Nations Commission on Environment and Development) (1992), *Agenda 21*, New York: United Nations.

UNEP (United Nations Environment Programme) (2007), *Global Environmental Outlook: GEO 4*, Nairobi: UNEP.

Vogel, D. (2005), 'The hare and the tortoise revisited', in A. Jordan (ed.), *Environmental Policy in the European Union*, 2nd edn, London: Earthscan.

WCED (World Commission on Environment and Development) (1987), *Our Common Future*, Oxford: Oxford University Press.

Weale, A. (1992), 'Implementation failure: a suitable case for review?' in E. Lykke (ed.), *Achieving Environmental Goals*, London: Belhaven Press.

Weale, A. and A. Williams (1992), 'Between economy and ecology? The single market and the integration of environmental policy', *Environmental Politics*, 1 (4): 45–64.

2. Instruments for environmental policy integration in 30 OECD countries

Klaus Jacob, Axel Volkery and Andrea Lenschow

INTRODUCTION: THE UPS AND DOWNS OF EPI

The integration of environmental concerns into decision-making processes in other policies (that is, EPI) has been a long-standing challenge for many OECD countries. But precisely what kinds of actions have been taken to implement the EPI principle? This chapter presents an overview of the most important instruments that have emerged for this task and analyses their application within 30 OECD countries.

Since the early 1970s, many OECD countries have experimented with instruments to 'mainstream' environmental policy concerns into other domains of policy making such as industry, energy, transport, housing, agriculture and other sectors. The environment's cross-cutting nature was prominently mentioned, for example, in the first environmental programme in Germany, which dates back to 1971. The EU declared in its very first Environmental Action Programme in 1973 that all policies should take the environment into account (see also Chapter 8). These policy commitments were subsequently reflected in more concrete institutional and administrative changes. In Germany, for example, a Green Cabinet was formed in 1971, and in 1975 an obligation was placed on all departments to consult the responsible minister if their legislative proposals were likely to be environmentally relevant (see Chapter 9). The USA introduced environmental assessment for policy proposals as early as 1969 (see Chapters 7 and 13); Canada followed in 1973. Several countries introduced requirements to report on the environmental performance of different policy domains, and a few countries set up independent bodies to provide advice and evaluation as early as the 1970s.

In this initial phase, EPI was perceived as a task to be overseen by environment departments, which were made responsible for developing integration strategies for other departments and coordinating the various integration activities and instruments. However, the results were rather disappointing. The core of many sectoral policies remained largely unchanged; only incremental changes were accepted that could be handled at reasonable economic cost. Furthermore, the economic crisis in the second half of the 1970s and the early 1980s weakened the position of environmental actors within government in many countries. As a result, the enforcement and implementation of the EPI principle tended to be quite poor (OECD 2002a).

It took a long time for the integration principle to climb back up the political agenda. The refinement of existing approaches and the development of new ones was also a cumbersome process that only really regained speed in the late 1980s, triggered by the growing importance of the sustainable development paradigm (see Chapter 1 for details). The 1987 Single European Act, amending the Treaty base of the European Community, for example, stated that 'environmental protection requirements shall be a component of the community's other policies'. At the international level, the Brundtland Report (WCED 1987) and Agenda 21 (United Nations 1992) also called for a strengthening of the integration principle. A whole chapter – number 8 – of Agenda 21 was devoted to the integration challenge. In this context, new approaches and instruments for EPI were promoted in many OECD countries, such as national plans and strategies (Chapter 5), various administrative instruments such as environmental correspondents (Chapter 3), green budgeting (Chapter 4), and Strategic Environmental Assessment (SEA) (Chapter 7).

Since the middle of the 1990s, a number of front-runner countries have implemented some innovations. As part of a more decentralized strategic approach (see Jacob and Volkery (2007) for a more detailed discussion of centralized and decentralized strategies), they requested relevant departments such as agriculture, energy or transport to adopt a strategy for incorporating environmental objectives in their portfolio of activities and to report on the progress they had made. These processes were backed by high-level commitments from the cabinet, head of government or parliament; clear objectives, indicators and benchmarks for monitoring were also set (Lafferty 2001; Jänicke *et al.* 2002; OECD 2002a; SRU 2004; see also the contributions in Lenschow 2002).

One example of such an innovation was the EU's Cardiff Process. As part of this process, responsibility for EPI was passed from the European Commission's DG Environment to the European Council. Meanwhile, individual Councils of Ministers were put in charge of sectoral reforms. Similar shifts in responsibility from the environment sector to the 'driving force' sectors also occurred at the national level, with central institutions (such as parliament, the prime minister) playing a supervisory role.

However, this process came to an end only few years later (Jordan and Schout 2006). The EU Lisbon strategy was perceived by many observers as a shift in political priorities from sustainable development issues towards economic competitiveness concerns (see Chapter 8 for details). The implementation of the EU's strategy for sustainable development subsequently lost momentum, a development which was mirrored across many other EU Member States.

More recently, the debate on climate change has brought a shift in the terms of the debate about policy integration. Mitigation of climate change is perceived both as an environmental and an economic imperative (for example, the Stern Review in the UK) (Jordan and Lorenzoni 2007). Accordingly, new attempts can be observed to develop joint policy programmes and to mainstream climate policies into economic policies, for example, the integrated energy and climate change policy that the European Council adopted at its Spring meeting in 2007 (Presidency Conclusions, European Council, Brussels, 8–9 March 2007).

This brief historical review reveals that the ambitiousness of the commitment to EPI has moved up and down over time, depending on the political preferences of key actors and the nature of economic framework conditions. It has not been a one-way modernization process with an ever-improving performance; rather EPI has been fiercely debated, with phases of successful integration as well as phases of retreat.

A careful empirical analysis of the instruments that have been used in these attempts to implement EPI should shed some light on the question of why it has not yet gained a sufficiently robust support base to prevent rollbacks. In the remainder of this chapter we provide an overview of the different instruments for EPI distilled from the empirically oriented literature on environmental policy analysis. We first develop a simple typology of EPI instruments, distinguishing three categories: communicative, organizational and procedural. Then, for each instrument, we discuss its basic purposes and mechanisms. Given the many different forms in which a given instrument can be implemented in practice, we are only able to make general observations about their popularity. Readers requiring more detailed observations about their mode of operation should refer to the chapters in Parts II and III of this book.

EPI INSTRUMENTS: THREE CATEGORIES OF DEPLOYMENT

The main instruments to achieve greater EPI can be categorized in various ways. In this chapter, which looks at EPI instruments from an aggregate level, we adopt an institutional perspective in ordering EPI initiatives and reviewing their deployment in the OECD.[1] We distinguish between three general categories of operation. First, EPI instruments may focus on communicating visions, objectives, strategies and the accumulation of knowledge that are supposed to frame reform efforts, while leaving it to individual governments and targeted sectors to develop concrete 'operations' for policy integration. From an institutional perspective, these EPI instruments constitute a relatively 'easy' challenge as they do not directly require significant changes to existing structures or routines. Such instruments add to the existing institutional setting rather than intervene in or replace other institutions and procedures of policy making. However, EPI instruments in this category may structure and coordinate subsequent instruments (that is, they may be a prerequisite for future action) and at the very least should communicate (political) commitment.

In summary, communicative instruments (at a greater or lesser aggregate level of policy making) include:

- the inclusion of environmental provisions in the constitution;[2]
- national environmental plans and/or strategies;
- sustainable development strategies;
- requirements to develop sectoral environmental strategies;
- obligations to report on environmental performance; and
- external and independent reviews of environmental performance (scientific bodies, parliamentary committees or court of auditor).

At a more operational level, we distinguish between, secondly, changes to the organizational set-up and, thirdly, reforms of a more procedural nature. Organizational reforms often frame procedural changes in political and administrative decision making by rearranging the relevant actors involved. They include:

- the amalgamation of departments;
- green cabinets;
- environmental units and correspondents within the various sectoral departments;
- interdepartmental working groups.

Potentially, they may strengthen environmental departments, open up existing networks or even create entirely new actors with an environment brief. Yet organizational reforms may also amount to 'window dressing' whilst policy making in the sectors continues as usual.

Finally, procedural instruments include:

- extended rights for the department of the environment (for example, veto, consultation);
- green budgeting;
- strategic environmental assessments (SEA); and
- the inclusion of environmental aspects in the assessment of new policies and regulations.

These can be assumed to be the most immediately consequential for EPI as they affect the substance of policy decisions. They are meant to alter the core procedures for decision making (for example, law making, budgeting). From an institutional perspective we would therefore expect that EPI at a procedural level poses the greatest challenge to decision makers.[3]

Against this background, it is interesting to see how EPI has been institutionalized in different OECD countries and how the balance between communicative, organizational and procedural instruments has evolved over time. Is there a trend to integrate EPI in the decision-making process? Precisely which instruments are most popular? And is there a shift from quite symbolic action to more substantive instruments? These questions are tackled in the next section.

PATTERNS OF INSTRUMENT DEPLOYMENT IN 30 OECD COUNTRIES

In this section, we describe all the instruments mentioned above and chart their spread in 30 OECD countries. The database for the analysis is derived mainly from the OECD Environmental Performance reviews. These are complemented with the country reports submitted to the 2002 Earth Summit, and various academic studies of environmental policy. Our database has some limitations. It is, for example, not possible to obtain exact data about the year of introduction for all instruments. This is partly because some instruments are inconsistently reported and named; sometimes the relevant data sources provide contradictory information on the introduction of particular EPI instruments. Furthermore, our quantitative data ignore the quality and continuity of implementation (that is, some instruments may exist on paper only or have been abandoned in the meantime). It is attractive for governments to announce the introduction of new EPI instruments. However, it is very rare for them to acknowledge publicly their non-use and/or abandonment. Hence, our figures showing the cumulative introduction of EPI instruments over time may provide an impression of steady improvement, when the reality may be far less smooth and optimistic.

These shortcomings are, of course, typical of large 'n' studies of policy outputs. However, the analysis of the spread of policies over time does allow some broad conclusions to be drawn about developments over space (for example, who are the EPI pioneers?) and through time, as well as between the three categories of instrument (for example, which are spreading more rapidly?), as a precursor to the more detailed analyses in subsequent chapters.

Communicative Instruments

Constitutional provisions
Constitutional provisions to protect the environment require that all governmental action is consistent with the imperative of protecting the environment. Potentially, a constitutional provision constitutes a powerful political commitment – possibly even with legal consequences – that seeks to empower pro-environmental actors. Overall, seventeen countries in our sample of thirty have adopted them (Busch and Jörgens 2005). Most of these were formulated before 1986; some were introduced as long ago as the early 1970s. However, they vary considerably regarding their content. Mostly, they refer broadly to the goal of environmental protection and do not give the environment 'principled priority'. As such, the provisions contribute to the dissemination of a vision, but they neither change the performance of sectoral departments with regard to EPI nor raise the political status of environmental actors in sectoral policy making. One of the most clearly formulated provisions can be found in the treaties of the EU (see Chapter 8).

National Environmental Plans
A National Environmental Plan (NEP) and/or strategies should comprehensively define priorities and objectives of environmental policy over a long-term perspective. Twenty out of the 30 OECD countries in our sample have a National Environmental Plan in place (Busch and Jörgens 2005). Typically, they identify relevant target groups and related instruments, and propose indicators for monitoring and evaluation purposes. Such plans are often drawn up on the basis of extensive inter-administrative consultation and wide societal participation (SRU 2000).

National Strategies for Sustainable Development
National Strategies for Sustainable Development (NSSD) should be distinguished from environmental planning (see Chapter 5 for details). They

usually have a broader focus, covering economic, social *and* environmental policy. The vast majority of countries (26) in our sample have adopted NSSDs. But more often than not, they only contain a few highly aggregated environmental objectives and indicators. Despite the central role that EPI is thought to play in the transition to sustainable development empirically (see Chapter 1 on the vexed question of prioritization), sustainable development strategies cover a very wide range of long-term social and economic issues. Crucially, they do not normally prioritize environmental concerns in a way which is fully supportive of EPI. Unlike National Environmental Plans, NSSDs are often coordinated by a central institution such as the office of the prime minister. Potentially, if there is political commitment to implement EPI, such a centralized organization strengthens the capacity for cross-sectoral policy steering (Volkery *et al.* 2006).

The success of both types of planning can be mainly assigned to the relevant provisions of Agenda 21 (United Nations 1992), which called for the establishment of national plans and strategies for sustainable development. The first plans were introduced in the Netherlands, Canada, UK, Denmark, Sweden and Norway towards the end of the 1980s. In the 1990s, a much more rapid spread of these particular instruments could be observed (Tews *et al.* 2003). However, the different strategies and plans vary considerably regarding scope and content (Jänicke and Jörgens 2000; SRU 2000; Volkery *et al.* 2006).

Sectoral strategies

Sectoral strategies are supposed to reshape departmental agenda setting and decision making by merging sectoral and environmental objectives and describing instruments for the incorporation of environmental concerns. The respective departments are normally responsible for drafting and implementing those strategies, but ideally they should contain quantified objectives, timetables and indicators so that performance can be audited by an independent central body. The call for sectoral strategies signifies a political interest in EPI. But as the development of sectoral strategies typically does not affect the position of environmental actors in the political process, their impact on EPI is all too easily undermined.

As of 2004, seven countries had made use of sectoral strategies, with a great divergence regarding their concrete scope, institutional settings and procedural aspects. Most countries do have an environmental strategy for one or the other sector. However, in our sample of 30, we only count those countries where parliament or government has issued a general obligation requiring the different departments to develop such plans as well as those countries where most of the departments have developed such strategies (that is, regardless of any formal obligation). The countries which systematically make use of sectoral strategies are Canada, Denmark, Finland, Mexico, Norway, Poland and the UK.

The first country to introduce sectoral integration strategies was Norway in 1989. Denmark also became well known for requesting elaborate sectoral strategies. The instrument was pioneered by the Danish Ministry of Agriculture, but it was soon followed by the Departments of Energy and Transport. Recently, Denmark has also established a multidimensional strategy for sustainable development (Danish Government 2002). Another innovator is Canada, where a *Guide to Green Government* issued in 1995 committed a large number of departments and agencies to report on their environmental policy, to develop sectoral strategies and to update these strategies every three years. An independent Commissioner of the Environment and Sustainable Development in the General Accounting Office reviews these strategies (Environment Canada 1995; Canadian Environmental Assessment Agency 2004). In spite of the fact that the EU is not in our sample of OECD countries, its Cardiff Process is equivalent to a sectoral integration strategy (see Chapter 8 for details).

Reporting obligations are a standard procedure of government and ought to make evaluation and monitoring of EPI possible. In anticipation of this, environmental concerns are expected to be considered in the earliest stages. However, there are different ways of organizing the reporting procedure, indicating also different levels of commitment: reporting may be on a merely voluntary basis; it may be linked to individual legislative acts (that is, be limited in scope); or it may be standard practice and involve strong, independent evaluation procedures, for example, by parliament. In our survey, we focused on obligations to report to institutions like the cabinet, parliament or a specialized institution or agency to check the environmental performance of departments. Fourteen out of the 30 countries sampled report on the existence of such provisions. These are Austria, Belgium, Canada, Germany, Hungary, Italy, Japan, Mexico, Netherlands, Norway, Poland, Portugal, the UK and the USA.

Independent evaluation

An independent institution that evaluates and monitors is often, but not necessarily, linked to an obligation to report: the external evaluation can be performed by parliamentary committees, independent experts, units that are affiliated with the national court of auditors or other governmental agencies. Most of the OECD countries in our sample have introduced independent institutions that are in one way or another responsible for pushing EPI forward, such as advisory bodies, bodies responsible for monitoring and evaluation or parliamentary committees. To take the national commissions and councils for sustainable development as an example, 23 out of

30 OECD countries have reported the introduction of such institutions (Busch and Jörgens 2005). These committees come in a variety of shapes and sizes, ranging from scientific advisory councils that provide non-binding advice, through to councils for sustainable development with members from science, civil society and sometimes also the government (which then may hamper their independence). Furthermore, their mandates as well as their resources vary considerably (see Niestroy 2007 for an empirical analysis). Only a case-by-case analysis can reveal if these institutions have a mandate to assess governmental policies regarding their environmental performance. Very few countries have established independent governmental or parliamentary institutions to evaluate the environmental performance of different departments. A prominent example is the Canadian Commissioner for Sustainable Development, who is located in the General Auditor's Office. The Commissioner evaluates the overall activities for EPI within the Canadian government and has on several occasions provided critical, in-depth analyses of what has been achieved. New Zealand's General Auditor performs a similar function. Another interesting example is the UK Parliament's Environmental Audit Committee (see Chapter 12). Figure 2.1 provides an overview of these trends in 30 OECD countries.

Conclusions

A number of conclusions flow from this overview. First, there was little activity before the second half of the 1980s, with one exception: constitutional provisions. The introduction of other communicative instruments was limited to a few front-runner countries. Second, a surge in the adoption of such instruments can be observed in the late 1980s and early 1990s. Only the national strategies for sustainable development and the councils for sustainable development were introduced after this date, hinting at the possible causal influence of international factors (for example, the adoption of Agenda 21 in 1992). Third, with the exception of sectoral strategies, all the instruments in our typology have been introduced in at least one country and some are present in the majority of countries. The EU's Cardiff Process, which was widely praised for its ambitiousness, has not triggered a self-sustaining process of strategy writing and reviewing at Member State level (see Chapter 8).

Organizational Instruments

In this section, we analyse the extent to which organizational arrangements have been redesigned to follow up on political pronouncements and general strategies to ensure EPI (see Figure 2.2). The amalgamation

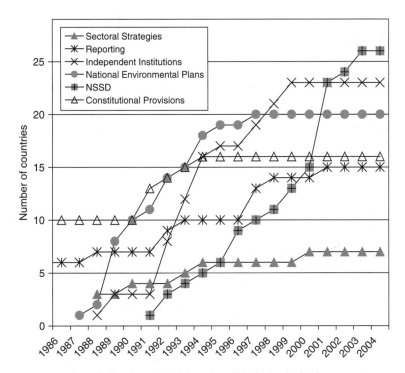

Notes: Reporting: missing dates for Belgium, the USA, the Netherlands.
Sectoral strategies: missing dates for Finland and Poland.

Sources: Various OECD Environmental Performance Reviews; Country reports to the
2002 Earth Summit (http://www.un.org/esa/sustdev/natlinfo/natlinfo.htm); Busch and
Jörgens (2005), Swanson et al. (2004)

*Figure 2.1 The uptake of communicative instruments to achieve EPI in
          OECD countries*

of departments is a possible way of enhancing the relative power of the
environment department as it gains immediate access to policy making
in other sectors (for example, transport, agriculture, spatial planning).
Furthermore, the relative importance of the environment department
compared to the other departments is increased. However, amalgamation
(understood as a two-way relationship) may lead to a dilution of environmental influence if environmental policy makers become marginalized
in their new – amalgamated – department, particularly if the partners are
much larger.

Four countries in our sample have experimented with this approach.
For example, Denmark merged its Ministries for Energy and Environment

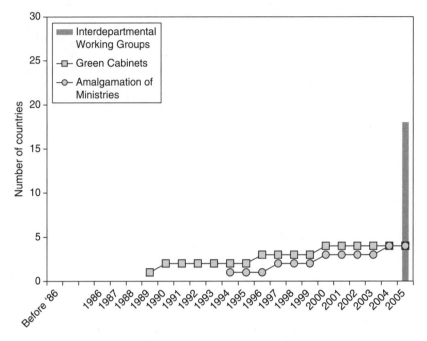

Sources: Various OECD Environmental Performance Reviews; country reports to the 2002 Earth Summit (http://www.un.org/esa/sustdev/natlinfo/natlinfo.htm)

Figure 2.2   The uptake of organizational instruments to achieve EPI in OECD countries

in 1994, but this was revoked by the new conservative government in 2002. In the UK, the merger of the Departments of Transport and of the Environment occurred in 1997. The selection of the then Deputy Prime Minister, John Prescott, as its head was interpreted as a considerable boost for EPI efforts (see Chapter 12 for details). In 2000, Austria merged its Ministries for Agriculture and the Environment. This was not a response to EPI, but corresponds to the structure discussed here. In 2004, Sweden formed a new Ministry for Sustainable Development as well as energy issues, climate change, construction and housing (see Chapter 11). With the change in government in 2006, this move was reversed and the responsibilities for housing and energy transferred to other departments.

There have been many efforts to strengthen EPI by creating interdepartmental coordination committees, by institutionalizing working groups both on the cabinet level ('green cabinets') and the departmental level ('interdepartmental working groups') (see Chapter 3 for details). Green cabinets usually consist of secretaries of state or junior ministers and are typically assisted by working committees that comprise the relevant heads of directorates or units of the departments involved. Green cabinets are reported for four countries: Germany, Hungary, Norway and the UK. Norway introduced a State Secretary Committee for Environmental Issues as early as 1989 (Sverdrup 1998). In the UK, such a committee was introduced in 1990 (Jordan and Lenschow 2000). More recently, Hungary (1996) and Germany (2000) also introduced such committees. More often, the interdepartmental negotiations take place in working groups of high-ranking civil servants. Currently, 18 OECD countries claim to have established interdepartmental working groups to further EPI. However, it is not always possible to identify precisely their date of creation without more detailed, case study analysis.

The establishment of different departmental units for the environment is a well-known coordinating device (see Chapter 3). Such units are meant to oversee the environmental performance of their host departments. Furthermore, they are expected to coordinate relevant proposals for new policies with their opposite numbers in cognate departments. Evaluation studies reveal, however, slightly disappointing results (Wilkinson 1997; Kraack *et al.* 2001). Many have been unwilling or unable to influence the overall policy orientation of their respective departments. There are also strong indications (see Chapter 3) that officials are wary of jeopardizing their own status or career opportunities when they try to lobby for environmental proposals that are not part of their departments' core business. Data on the introduction of such units is not readily available from OECD sources. However, such units appear to be relatively common.

The analysis reported in Figure 2.2 reveals that – compared to the introduction of communicative instruments for EPI – countries are a lot more hesitant about initiating major governmental reforms (for example, the amalgamation of departments or the creation of green cabinets): the merger between departments of the environment and more powerful sectoral departments was reversed in Denmark, Sweden and the UK (see above). Interdepartmental coordination units on the political level are rare. At the administrative level, we do, however, note numerous interdepartmental working groups (in 18 out of the 30 countries sampled). The establishment of environmental units is also relatively widespread. In this case, it is questionable whether these organizational changes have had a significant impact on the policy-making routines in the sectoral departments, however. The more detailed country studies in this book will seek to investigate whether these organizational innovations are actually put into practice or not.

Procedural Instruments

Department of the Environment

The extension of the competences of the Department of the Environment has been proposed as a instrument for EPI (Müller 2002). This concerns the procedural rights and rules that are relevant for inter-administrative coordination (see Chapter 3 for further details). It is difficult, however, to define precise criteria capable of measuring the strength of environment departments in relation to sectoral departments.[4] The most far-reaching provision is possibly the right to veto legislative proposals made by other departments (this is a merely hypothetical provision, as nowhere in the OECD is it actually implemented). Another – weaker – instrument is the obligation to consult the environment department if legislative instruments with probable environmental impacts are drafted; this is a standard device in many countries.

Green budgeting

Green budgeting, understood as in-depth environmental evaluation as part of the annual budgeting procedure, can reveal spending that is contradictory to environmental objectives (see Chapter 4 for further details). By highlighting environmentally harmful spending and offering alternatives by, for example, shifting resources to more environmental-friendly policies and programmes, it represents a strong political commitment to improving the environmental performance of all departments.

Green budgeting is applied in 4 of our 30 countries, namely Denmark, Norway, the Netherlands and the UK.[5] Norway introduced it for the first time in 1988, when an environmental profile requirement was added to the state budget proposal (see Chapter 10). This was further elaborated in 1992 and 1996 with the development of more detailed categories of spending that have environmental effects. The Netherlands implemented the measure only on an experimental basis. Denmark applied the instrument temporarily but dropped it in 2001. Green budgeting is also undertaken in the EU and the UK (see Chapter 4 for a general discussion and Chapters 8 and 12 for the EU and the UK respectively).

Strategic Environmental Assessment

Strategic Environmental Assessment (SEA) is a procedural instrument for evaluating the probable environmental impacts of a programme or a plan. SEA focuses on the early stages of the decision-making process (see Chapter 7 for some of the difficulties which emerge in practice). The actual procedures may of course amount to very different depths of environmental integration: SEA may be limited to developing simple checklists or it may extend to running modelling exercises; it may be conducted in a technocratic fashion or it may involve participatory processes. Furthermore, SEA may be applied by the sectoral departments, but it can also be designed as a mechanism that routinely brings the environmental department into sectoral decision making, thereby strengthening its overall role in pursuing EPI.

Twelve countries in our sample introduced Strategic Environmental Assessment before 2004.[6] It was introduced in the USA as long ago as 1969, but it was seldom applied (Andrews 1997). Canada introduced a similar Environmental Assessment Review Process in 1973, but it was only applied to a few policies. In Europe, the Netherlands can be regarded as the clear forerunner. Denmark, Finland and Norway also belong to a group of pioneers. Since all EU Member States must now implement an EU Directive on SEA, this number has increased considerably. As of early 2007, some kind of SEA is conducted in 25 of the 30 countries in our sample (Busch *et al.* 2007). Nevertheless, countries differ considerably regarding the form and scope of SEA. In some countries, it is applied on an experimental basis in pilot studies. There is also a considerable variation in the institutional design (ranging from it being a formal, legal requirement through to just an example of 'best practice').

Impact Assessment
Impact Assessment aims at an *ex ante* assessment of possible impacts of new legislative proposals. It is typically performed by the lead department (see Chapter 6 for details). Originally, it aimed to reduce the costs of regulation. It was only later that social and environmental aspects were included in the purview of the assessment process. Compared to SEA, Impact Assessment is not limited to plans and programmes that are expected to be environmentally relevant. On the contrary, it is commonly applied to all new policy proposals. Having said that, the level of detail is not normally as high as in SEA (especially for elaborate plans and programmes covering new infrastructure developments).

The consideration of environmental aspects in prevailing systems of Impact Assessment is difficult to count (see Chapter 6 for details). On the one hand, regulatory impact assessments (RIAs) are a standard procedure in all OECD countries (Radaelli 2004). On the other hand, it is not always clear whether these procedures comprise an assessment of environmental aspects, how the instruments are actually applied and whether or not they support EPI. We therefore only include those countries that explicitly identify EPI as a main concern of their respective procedures. These are the USA, Canada, the UK and the Netherlands (that is, just 4 out of the 30 countries in our sample). The USA and Canada introduced a requirement to assess policy proposals in the late 1960s and early 1970s. However, these procedures were hardly ever applied (Bartolomeo *et al.* 2005). The instrument was

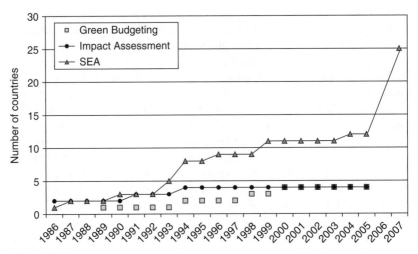

Notes: No data for consultation of MOE.
2006 and 2007 data only for SEA.

Sources: Various OECD Environmental Performance Reviews; country reports to the
2002 Earth Summit (http://www.un.org/esa/sustdev/natlinfo/natlinfo.htm); Busch and
Jörgens (2005); Swanson *et al.* (2004); Busch *et al.* (2007)

Figure 2.3   *The uptake of procedural instruments to achieve EPI in OECD
countries*

'rediscovered' by the UK in the late 1980s, when it developed a system of environmental policy appraisal (Russel and Jordan 2007). The Netherlands developed similar instruments (the E- and B-tests) for appraising new legislation in 1994 (Marsden 1999). Switzerland has also experimented with Sustainability Assessment (Federal Office for Spatial Development 2004). A decision on a mandatory application will be made after the evaluation of practical experiences (Berger 2007). In the EU, DG Environment of the European Commission developed an appraisal system (termed 'green star') in 1993 to evaluate the effects of policy proposals with significant effects on the environment (see Chapter 8 for details), but very few appraisals were ever conducted (Wilkinson 1998: 120). Since then, the European Commission has introduced a new and more integrated assessment procedure for all legislative proposals, known as Impact Assessment (see Chapter 6 for details). Figure 2.3 provides an overview of the application of procedural instruments for EPI.

The use of procedural instruments
We find only very few examples of the introduction of procedural instruments. There are even indications that the few cases of green budgeting

were limited to short-term experiments; only in Norway, the UK and the EU is this procedure applied on a routine basis. The sharp increase in SEAs was due to the adoption of the EU Directive in 2001, which obliges all EU Member States to introduce it. In practice, SEAs are often designed to operate in a fairly undemanding fashion (that is, not significantly challenging the main thrust of sectoral policy making). Generally, neither organizational nor procedural arrangements have been influenced by any of the waves of interest in EPI noted in the introduction to this chapter – not the first (the 1970s), the second (in the second half of the 1980s) or the most recent (in the late 1990s with the Cardiff Process).

Overview: the Use of EPI Instruments

Table 2.1 presents a comparison of the use of EPI instruments in all 30 OECD countries under the three categories noted above – namely communicative, organizational and procedural. As indicated above, each instrument aims at slightly different entry points into the policy process. Thus, while some instruments seek to change the configuration of actors, others aim to influence the agenda-setting process, mobilize new knowledge, improve the coordination between sectors and issues, influence the distribution of resources during decision making and implementation, or create new opportunities for evaluation and monitoring. Ideally, utilizing as many instruments for EPI as possible in a complementary manner furthers the cause of EPI, because the number of entry points in the policy process is maximized. However, our empirical analysis reveals that there is a pronounced tendency to use instruments based on information gathering and issue raising, while few countries make use of approaches that aim to redistribute resources or that significantly empower environmental departments in the decision-making process. Furthermore, most countries prefer instruments that add to the existing institutions rather than intervening and changing existing institutions. The UK, Canada, Norway and the Netherlands are the most active when it comes to introducing the more operational EPI instruments. The UK in particular can be regarded as a pioneer, both concerning the restructuring of government and the assessment of new policy proposals. Nearly all countries have introduced general strategic approaches such as sustainability strategies or environmental plans, and the majority of countries have introduced constitutional provisions, interdepartmental working groups and independent bodies for advising and evaluation. The introduction of SEA procedures is now relatively widespread.

Table 2.1 *The distribution of EPI instruments within and across 30 OECD countries*

	General Framing and Communicative Tools					
	Constitutional provision	NEP	NSSD	Sectoral strategies	Reporting obligation	Independent institutions
Australia		•	•			•
Austria	•	•	•		•	•
Belgium	•		•		•	•
Canada		•	•	•	•	•
Czech Rep	•	•	•			•
Denmark		•	•	•		
Finland	•	•	•	•		•
France		•	•			•
Germany	•		•		•	•
Greece	•		•			
Hungary	•	•	•		•	•
Iceland		•				
Ireland			•			•
Italy			•		•	•
Japan		•	•		•	•
Korea	•	•	•			•
Luxembourg			•			
Mexico		•	•	•	•	•
Netherlands	•	•	•		•	•
New Zealand		•				
Norway	•		•	•	•	•
Poland	•	•	•	•	•	•
Portugal	•	•	•		•	•
Slovakia	•	•	•			•
Spain	•		•			
Sweden	•	•	•			•
Switzerland	•		•			•
Turkey	•	•				
United Kingdom		•	•	•	•	•
United States					•	•
Count	17	20	26	7	14	23

Sources: Various OECD Environmental Performance Reviews; country reports to the 2002 Earth Summit (http://www.un.org/esa/sustdev/natlinfo/natlinfo.htm); Busch and Jörgens (2005); Swanson *et al.* (2004); Busch *et al.* (2007)

Organizational EPI Measures			Procedural EPI Tools		
Amalgamation of departments	Green cabinet	Interdepartmental working groups	Green budgeting	SEA (data until 2007)	Impact assessment
				•	
		•		•	
		•		•	
		•		•	•
				•	
• (dismissed in 2002)			• (dismissed in 2002)	•	
				•	
		•		•	
	•	•		•	
	•	•		•	
				•	
		•		•	
				•	
		•		•	
		•			
		•			
		•	• (experimental)	•	•
		•		•	
	•	•	•	•	
				•	
		•		•	
				•	
				•	
• (dismissed in 2006)		•		•	
•	•	•	•	•	•
		•		•	•
4	4	18	4	25	4

Yet there are some countries that show almost no activity with regard to EPI instruments and strategies. These are small countries like Luxembourg and Iceland, but also Switzerland and Turkey. If we concentrate on EPI pronouncements at the general level and ignore the organizational and procedural arrangements, some countries would catch up with the group of front-runners (for example, Austria, Hungary, Finland, Poland and Portugal). However, these countries have some way to go in developing their repertoire of EPI instruments.

SUMMARY AND CONCLUSIONS

Our analysis shows that OECD countries diversified their mix of EPI instruments in the late 1980s and the 1990s. Although our figures should be treated with some caution (see above), they do indicate that there has been no clear shift towards making the integration of environmental concerns a standard procedure of decision making. Instead, most countries seem to prefer to develop policy objectives and frameworks that flag the importance of EPI, without developing operational structures and procedures that significantly alter the distribution of power among the various actors involved or decisively change the prevailing political and administrative routines of policy making. Put differently, the emphasis lies on 'soft' and often 'symbolic' action. Harder and more consequential instruments that make the environment a main concern of all (sectoral) policy makers are adopted less frequently and with far less enthusiasm. So while a rich institutional landscape of EPI instruments has emerged, EPI is far from being mainstreamed into everyday decision making processes. This is in line with our observation (see the introduction to this chapter) that interest in EPI has oscillated through a number of cycles. Thus the general framing and communicative instruments may work well when interest is swinging up, but they may quickly lose momentum as attention slides away.

Admittedly, our overview says little about the effect of different EPI instruments, either singly or in combination. While our three-category typology seems to confirm the notion that EPI has entered the political rhetoric in most countries but – so far – failed to trigger the reforms to the 'policies and the institutions' that Brundtland referred to in 1987 (see Chapter 1), we need to learn about country experiences and the precise operation of individual instruments to come to a definitive conclusion. The following chapters seek to address this gap.

ACKNOWLEDGEMENTS

We are extremely grateful to Andrew Jordan, John Hoornbeek and the authors of the other chapters of this volume for their valuable comments on earlier drafts.

NOTES

1. Chapter 1 distinguishes the cognitive, institutional and political perspectives that may be used to analyse EPI processes.
2. In grouping constitutional provisions in the communicative category, we are potentially downplaying the legal nature of this instrument. However, there are clear limits to the enforceability of such commitments, suggesting that they play a 'softer' role in the political discourse.
3. It is true, however, that procedural instruments may reach different depths of reform (merely adjust or completely transform policy-making procedures). Hence the concrete institutional challenge will vary from case to case.
4. Liberatore (1997) stresses this point in her study of DG Environment: its workforce and budget are small compared to many other DGs, but its regulatory output has been and still is of considerable importance for their activities.
5. Importantly, we counted only those countries that reported performing an environmental assessment of their annual budgets (see Chapter 4 for a discussion of other interpretations).
6. Our database of all EPI instruments is only complete for the period up to 2004. After that, data is available only for some countries and instruments. To keep the results comparable, our analysis therefore terminates at 2004.

BIBLIOGRAPHY

Andrews, R.N.L. (1997), 'United States', in M. Jänicke and H. Weidner (eds), *National Environmental Policies: A Comparative Study of Capacity Building*, Berlin: Springer.

Bartolomeo, M., P. Giugni, J. Hertin, K. Jacob, K. Rennings, A. Volkery, D. Wilkinson and D. Zanoni (2005), *Approaches to Impact Assessment in Six OECD Countries and at the European Commission: Findings and Recommendations for the European Commission*, Unpublished Report, Milan: Avanzi.

Berger, G. (2007), 'Sustainability impact assessment: approaches and applications in Europe', *ESDN Quarterly Report*, June 2007. Available at: http://www.sd-network.eu/?k=quarterly%20reports&report_id=5 (accessed 23 December 2007).

Busch, P.-O., K. Jacob and N. Künkel (2007), Modelling Environmental Capacities of Nation States: Path Dependencies and Policy Domains, paper given at the *Amsterdam Conference on the Human Dimension of Global Environmental Change*, 24–26 May 2007.

Busch, P.-O. and H. Jörgens (2005), *The Diffusion of Environmental Policy Innovations*, Berlin: Environmental Policy Research Centre.

Canadian Environmental Assessment Agency (2004), *Sustainable Development Strategy 2004–2006*. Available at: http://www.ceaa-acee.gc.ca/017/0004/001/SDS2004_e.pdf (accessed 9 October 2007).

Danish Government (2002), *A Shared Future: Balanced Development: Denmark's National Strategy for Sustainable Development*, Copenhagen: Danish Government.

Environment Canada (1995), *A Guide to Green Government*, Ottawa: Government of Canada. Available at: http://www.sdinfo.gc.ca/reports/en/ggg/Default.cfm (accessed 9 October 2007).

Federal Office for Spatial Development (2004), *Sustainability Assessment: Conceptual Framework and Basic Methodology*, Zurich: Federal Office for Spatial Development. Available at: http://www.ecologic-events.de/eu-impact-assessment/en/documents/Are_Admin.pdf (accessed 9 October 2007).

Jacob, K. and A. Volkery (2007), 'Umweltpolitikintegration und Selbstregulierung: ein Vergleich von Instrumenten der Umweltpolitikintegration in den OECD Ländern', in K. Jacob, F. Biermann, P.-O. Busch and P.H. Feindt (eds), *Politik und Umwelt*, Wiesbaden: VS Verlag. (PVS Sonderheft 39/2007).

Jänicke, M. and H. Jörgens (eds) (2000), *Umweltplanung im Internationalen Vergleich: Strategien der Nachhaltigkeit*, Berlin: Springer.

Jänicke, M., H. Jörgens, K. Jörgensen and R. Nordbeck (2002), 'Governance for sustainable development in Germany', in OECD (eds), *Governance for Sustainability: Five Case Studies*, Paris: OECD.

Jordan, A. and A. Lenschow (2000), ' "Greening" the European Union: what can be learned from the "leaders" of EU environmental policy?' *European Environment*, 10, 109–120.

Jordan, A.J. and I. Lorenzoni (2007), 'Is there now a political climate for policy change? Policy and politics after the Stern Review', *Political Quarterly*, 78, 2 (April–June), 310–319.

Jordan, A.J. and A. Schout (2006), *The Coordination of the European Union: Exploring the Capacities of Networked Governance*, Oxford: Oxford University Press.

Kraack, M., H. Pehle and P. Zimmermann-Steinhart (2001), *Umweltintegration in der Europäischen Union: Das Umweltpolitische Profil der EU im Politikfeldvergleich*, Baden-Baden: Nomos.

Lafferty, W.B. (2001), Adapting Government Practice to the Goals of Sustainable Development, paper presented at an *OECD/PUMA Seminar on Improving Governance for Sustainable Development*, 22–23 November, Paris: OECD.

Lenschow, A. (ed.) (2002), *Environmental Policy Integration: Greening Sectoral Policies in Europe*, London: Earthscan.

Liberatore, A. (1997), 'The integration of sustainable development objectives into EU policy-making: barriers and prospects', in S. Baker, M. Kousis, D. Richardson and S. Young (eds), *The Politics of Sustainable Development: Theory, Policy and Practice within the European Union*, London and New York: Routledge.

Marsden, S. (1999), 'Legislative EA in the Netherlands: the e-test as a strategic and integrative instrument', *European Environment*, 9, 90–100.

Müller, E. (2002), 'Environmental policy integration as a political principle: the German case and the implications for European policy', in A. Lenschow (ed.), *Environmental Policy Integration: Greening Sectoral Policies in Europe*, London: Earthscan.

Niestroy, I. (2007), Stimulating Informed Debate: Sustainable Development Councils in EU Member States – A Compilation of Tasks, Capacities and Best Practice, paper given at the *EEAC conference European Sustainability Berlin 07*, Berlin, 3 June 2007.

OECD (2002a), *Policies to Enhance Sustainable Development: Critical Issues*, Paris: OECD.
OECD (2002b), *Sustainable Development: Critical Issues*, Paris: OECD.
Radaelli, C. (2004), 'The diffusion of regulatory impact analysis: best-practice or lesson drawing?' *European Journal of Political Research*, 43 (5), 723–747.
Russel, D. and A. Jordan (2007), 'Gearing up governance for sustainable development: patterns of policy appraisal in UK central government', *Journal of Environmental Planning and Management*, 50 (1), 1–22.
SRU (2000), *Umweltgutachten 2000: Schritte ins nächste Jahrtausend*, Stuttgart: Metzler-Poeschel.
SRU (2004), *Umweltgutachten 2004: Umweltpolitische Handlungsfähigkeit sichern*, Baden-Baden: Nomos.
Sverdrup, L.A. (1998), 'The Norwegian experience of the transition to sustainability', in T. O'Riordan and H. Voisey (eds), *The Transition to Sustainability: The Politics of Agenda 21 in Europe*, London: Earthscan.
Swanson, D., P. Pintér, F. Bregha, A. Volkery and K. Jacob (2004), *National Strategies for Sustainable Development: Challenges, Approaches and Innovations in Strategic and Co-ordinated Action*. Winnipeg: International Institute for Sustainable Development.
Tews, K., P.-O. Busch and H. Jörgens (2003), 'The diffusion of new policy instruments', *European Journal of Political Research*, 42 (4), 569–600.
United Nations (1992), *United Nations Conference on Environment and Development: Agenda 21*, New York: United Nations. Available at: http://www.un.org/esa/sustdev/documents/agenda21/index.htm (accessed 12 October 2007).
Volkery, A., D. Swanson, K. Jacob, F. Bregha and L. Pintér (2006), 'Coordination, challenges and innovations in 19 national sustainable development strategies', *World Development*, 34 (12), 2047–2063.
WCED (World Commission on Environment and Development) (1987), *Our Common Future*, Oxford: Oxford University Press.
Wilkinson, D. (1997), 'Towards sustainability in the European Union? Steps within the European Commission towards integrating the environment into other European Union policy sectors', *Environmental Politics*, 6 (1), 153–173.
Wilkinson, D. (1998), 'Steps towards integrating the environment into other EU policy sectors', in T. O'Riordan and H. Voisey (eds), *The Transition to Sustainability: The Politics of Agenda 21 in Europe*, London: Earthscan.

PART II

The toolbox of implementing instruments

3. Administrative instruments

Adriaan Schout and Andrew Jordan

INTRODUCTION

The very old idea that governmental systems should somehow be reoriented and reshaped to 'fit' the integrated functioning of the environment (Lenschow 2002a: 17), only achieved wider political attention following the publication of the Brundtland Report in 1987. Since then, the idea that 'the major central economic and sectoral agencies of governments should . . . be made directly responsible . . . for ensuring that their policies, programmes, and budgets support development that is . . . sustainable' (WCED 1987: 314) has been continually reiterated by many international bodies (OECD 1996; OECD 2002a/b; EEA 2005b).

Many states have taken active steps to reorientate their 'policies and institutions' (WCED 1987: 9), but our overall understanding of the extent and effect (or 'outcome') of these patterns of change remains surprisingly limited in at least two different respects. First, the empirical stock of knowledge is rather weak in comparison to some of the other instruments of EPI such as appraisal. Second (and more fundamentally), there is a lack of agreement on the most appropriate terms to describe these instruments, which are variously referred to as being 'administrative', 'bureaucratic' or 'organizational', let alone an understanding their impacts and effectiveness. Most accounts of policy coordination do, of course, make some references to governmental structures, but they are not organized around a set of consistent definitions and are often highly descriptive, which combine to impede comparative analysis. In a panoramic survey of different 'coordination devices', Peters (1998b: 27) refers inter alia to: the core executive (that is, the centre of government – the cabinet and the prime minister's office); ministerial organizations (that is, vesting coordination tasks in one super-ministry); inter-ministerial organizations; task forces and working groups; interdepartmental committees; various informal coordination devices organized around the delivery of services at street level; policy processes (such as budgeting, appraisal and evaluation); and coordination through interest groups and political parties. Clearly, some of these devices are covered in other chapters in Part II of this book. Meanwhile, in a checklist for improving policy coherence and integration, the OECD (2002b: 5) mentions 'institutional mechanisms to steer integration' as one of five 'good governance preconditions' for sustainable development. Under 'institutional mechanisms', it includes budgeting, evaluating, reporting and catalysing (that is, putting something in charge 'of enforcing sustainable development strategies') (OECD 2002b: 6). Elsewhere, the OECD (2001: 107; see also OECD 1996: 16–18) refers to several broad types of 'organizational approach' to embedding EPI in the executive, including inter-ministerial working groups, cabinet-level committees, mega-ministries and integration strategies.

To make what is evidently an unclear picture much clearer, in this chapter we use the shorthand term 'administrative instruments' to refer to those governmental structures and processes which seek to achieve greater policy integration, and hence, cross-sectoral coordination. We attempt to take stock of what is – and is not – known about these different elements and ground them in relevant theories. Section 2 sets out the broad history of this particular instrument or set of instruments. Section 3 describes the conceptual background to our analysis by unpacking three theoretical interpretations. It then analyses what each has to say about issues such as effectiveness and the link with the more political dimensions of coordination discussed in Chapter 1, namely political leaders, pressure groups and parliamentary bodies. Section 4 draws upon Mintzberg's review of relevant theories to set out the main types of administrative instrument relevant to EPI. In Section 5 we summarize our discussion, and in Section 6 we bring together the main threads of our argument and draw some broader conclusions.

HISTORY

It is fair to say that governments have struggled mightily hard to implement Brundtland's plea for more coherent and holistic administrative systems. They have struggled for several reasons. First, governments have spent the last 50 years steadily compartmentalizing their activities into different sectoral ministries in order to achieve a clearer focus and reap efficiency savings (OECD 2002a: 11; OECD 2002b: 3). The compartmentalization of the state arguably accelerated in the 1980s and 1990s, in response to a succession of new public management initiatives as well as public demands for more devolved and publicly accountable policy making (OECD 2001: 106). But 'as the "ship of state" becomes a flotilla', coordination and cooperation have arguably become 'even more difficult than in the past' (Peters 1998b: 12).

Second, there is still a surprising level of confusion about what counts as administrative and institutional change. Recent comparative assessments (for example, OECD 2001; Jacob and Volkery 2004: 302; EEA 2005b) seem to use it as a rather broad 'catch-all' category covering everything from constitutional changes (Jacob and Volkery 2004: 302) and changes to the machinery of government, to green purchasing and budgeting (EEA 2005b: 21–3, 28), and to the activities of much more political bodies like parliaments and advisory boards (EEA 2005b: 7). In Chapter 1 it was noted that the Brundtland Report provides little by way of definitions; it simply referred to 'policies and institutions'.

In a recent review, the EEA (2005b: 13) defined administrations as the 'machinery of government' and bureaucrats (that is, the civil servants) as supporting the government 'in its executive tasks, operating in an apolitical manner'. This is not significantly different from a very simple definition of bureaucracy (Olsen 2005: 4). But of course administrative systems are not apolitical – they are enmeshed in party and interest-group politics – and no amount of administrative reform is ever likely to deliver EPI on its own (EEA 2005b: 13). To differentiate this chapter from others in Part II of this book, we therefore restrict our focus to the machinery of government as defined above, while at the same time searching for better ways of conceptualizing and typologizing the links with the more political aspects of EPI, which have been variously referred to as 'political will', 'political leadership' and 'political commitment'.

Third, the evidence base – especially that addressing the effectiveness of administrative instruments – remains surprisingly thin (EEA 2005b: 38). Many of the existing studies describe the presence or absence of particular instruments (see for example the regular OECD environmental performance reviews), or they look at different combinations of administrative instruments in one state (for example, Jordan 2002) or a small sample of states (Jacob and Volkery 2004: 306; Jordan and Schout 2006). Of course, without 'knowing the effectiveness of a particular mechanism, it is difficult to define suitable combinations of EPI mechanisms' (EEA 2005b: 38). In order to make the existing literature a little more useful for comparative analysis, we identify three broad schools of theory. We show that these provide different ways of thinking about and measuring effectiveness, as well as understanding the relationship between politics and administration.

To conclude, even though administrative reform is not and is unlikely ever to be a panacea, there are good reasons to believe that it plays an especially important role in the achievement of greater EPI. After all, EPI is chiefly concerned with ensuring that environmental thinking is adequately integrated into all stages of policy making, but especially the early ones (see Chapter 1). As administrative systems – be they national or (increasingly) supranational – are the main locus within which policy formulation takes place (Jordan and Liefferink 2004), they are likely to be the prime setting for EPI decisions (EEA 2005b: 13). Furthermore, this administrative and political setting is where many of the other instruments of EPI covered in this book are designed, adopted and implemented. Therefore, it is an important instrument to understand because of its immediate and contingent impacts on policy-making activities.

CONCEPTUAL BACKGROUND

Unlike some of the other chapters in Part II of this book, there is no settled definition of 'an administrative instrument'. One way to impose a little more order is to go back to the existing literature on organizational science and public administration, where coordination has been an enduring issue of debate for decades. There we find at least three different, but potentially complementary, ways of thinking about administrative instruments. These are: (1) the bureaucratic politics view; (2) the organizational process view; and (3) the symbolic politics view.

The Bureaucratic Politics View

Within political science, policy coordination is often presented as an exercise in informal relations (that is, bureaucratic politics) between the various parts of the state (Allison 1971; Palumbo 1975; Pressman and Wildavsky 1984; Wildavsky 1979). A key assumption of this work is that coordination emerges spontaneously as actors realize their interdependence in particular issues and take steps to address it. Hierarchical coordination from above or allocating specific coordinating roles to actors is generally assumed to be unnecessary. Typically, these steps add extra layers of bureaucracy, slow down decision making, stifle creativity and drag the core executive into the tedious and very time-consuming task of micro-managing the line ministries (e.g., OECD 2000: 28–9). This thinking is expressed in Lindblom's (1965) concept of 'partisan mutual adjustment'. It is also apparent in the titles of other classic works by (among others) Wildavsky – *Coordination Without a Coordinator* (in Wildavsky 1979: 90) and Chisholm (1989) – *Coordination Without Hierarchy*.

In the view of these and many other authors, coordination takes place by means of bargaining, competition, turf battles, and sharing or deliberately not sharing information. If everything was coordinated from above, there would be a confusing multiplicity of different coordinating rules and routines (Palumbo 1975). The creative tension that arises when sectors vie for political attention and resources might also be lost, as might the direct link to clients (OECD 1996: 20, 31).

The dangers of relying solely upon bureaucratic politics to deliver EPI are well known. First, environmental quality has a strongly public good character, so no single actor (apart from perhaps the environment ministry) is likely to have a sufficiently strong incentive routinely to take the environment into account. Very often, sector ministries will not openly conflict with one another on environmental matters because they do not believe the environmental aspects are relevant (or important) enough to fight over. Actors may, therefore, appear to be responding to one another's needs, but 'mutual adjustment' is not occurring because certain parties (economic ones in relation to most environmental matters) continually dominate. Second, environmental ministries tend to be rather small and weak in comparison to sector ministries, so that 'it is extremely unlikely that a ministry of environment will, with any degree of consistency, win when faced with opposition from ministries of finance, industry, transport, energy or agriculture' (Lafferty 2001: 22). One solution – which has been employed in a number of countries, including Portugal, the UK, the Netherlands and Denmark (Jacob and Volkery 2004: 302; EEA 2005a: 19; EEA 2005b: 26) – is to combine environmental and sectoral issues in one or more 'mega' ministries. However, this is often a slow and very disruptive approach to coordinating that rarely tames the forces of bureaucratic politics (OECD 1996: 20) and rarely endures (Peters 1998b: 32). It is striking that the four (out of 30 OECD countries) mega departments recorded in Chapter 2, have only had relatively short lives before being split up again.

Asking the sectors to take the environment 'into account' is also unlikely to have an enduring impact, as the ability of most ministries to achieve what Lindblom (1965) referred to as synoptic rationality 'is severely limited' and hence the extent to which the plea to integrate 'will be anything other than a distant aspiration is open to question' (Weale 1998: 24). A potentially more successful strategy might be to build up the size and budget of the environment ministry, or otherwise equip it to engage in policy learning and reframing activities (Lenschow and Zito 1998) in order to win the sectors around cognitively to its way of thinking. Otherwise, the bureaucratic politics approach suggests that the only other route to securing greater EPI lies in environmental interests finding ways to insert their demands into the political process from the outside in.

The Organizational Process View

Without denying the essentially political nature of organizations, scholars from the Carnegie School (Cyert and March 1963; Simon 1976) have

identified different devices to overcome the cognitive limitations of individual actors (Bendor and Hammond 1992). They do this by setting down
rules and supervising their implementation. These instruments can influence political behaviour, and hence, 'matter' in policy-making situations
(Egeberg 2003). Coordination is thus all about creating the right administrative conditions in which different sectors exchange their real (as opposed
to their perceived) differences and find common values and objectives
(Cyert and March 1963; Egeberg 2003). On this view, there will always be
incoherence in government; what matters 'is not simply whether contrasted
policies are being pursued, but whether they are being pursued knowingly
or unwittingly' (OECD 1996: 9).

To avoid confusion, the organizational process view does not argue that
administrative instruments determine everything, let alone eliminate
bureaucratic game playing; they simply facilitate coordination by lowering
transaction costs. They also help to determine the location and timing of
any inter-sectoral conflict, which is of course especially relevant to something like EPI, which aims to affect the very earliest phases of policy
making. Importantly, they can be more or less hierarchical in nature.

However, our understanding of the precise extent to which administrative instruments matter remains surprisingly 'modest' (Egeberg 2003: 120;
Olsen 2005: 11), due inter alia to the difficulty of organizing empirical
proof. The challenge lies in finding the right mix of coordination capacities,
which we have defined as instruments that facilitate coordination within
networks of interdependent actors (Jordan and Schout 2006). When carefully designed, these capacities – which can also be more or less hierarchical – are capable of facilitating the process of coordination.

The Symbolic Politics View

It is a commonplace that new political issues often generate a demand for
new administrative responses (OECD 2001: 108). Administrative reforms
have the attraction of being more politically palatable than new environmental regulation, in the sense that the costs are born by taxpayers, rather
than one (often quite powerful) set of polluting interests. Those who adopt
a symbolic view of politics would offer a slightly different explanation for
the reason why policy makers routinely tinker with their administrative
systems. On the one hand, they may wish to manipulate the political
agenda, to give the (misleading) impression that things are being done to
implement EPI (Edelman 1971, 1988), when in fact the status quo remains
unchanged. As Dye (1976: 21) has pointed out, much policy analysis fails
to be listened to because it focuses 'primarily upon the activities of governments, rather than the rhetoric of governments'. Crucially, if public

policy is really 'about "doing something" rather than "problem solving"' (Parsons 1995: 181), then perhaps different measures of performance and effectiveness should be added to the discussion of EPI outcomes given in Chapter 1.

On the other hand, they may simply be following international norms. It has been argued that this search process has as much to do with conforming to some accepted notion of a 'successful' environmental policy, as it is about rationally selecting the best package of instruments (Meyer and Rowan 1977; Liefferink and Jordan 2004: 17). There is evidence to suggest that emulation and mimicry have played a role in the spread of administrative instruments like environmental ministries and agencies (Busch and Joergens 2005). Again, the primary motive here is to get a new instrument in place; ensuring that it actually works is very much a secondary concern (Finnemore and Sikkink 1998).

DEPLOYMENT: PRACTICAL EXPERIENCES

Having laid out these three views, we will now use them to make sense of the bewildering array of different administrative instruments described above and extensively reviewed in the existing literature. Borrowing from Mintzberg (1979, 1989), we identify six main subtypes (for details, see Jordan and Schout 2006): (1) hierarchical instruments; (2) bureaucratic rules and standard operating procedures; (3) staff training; (4) specification of output and/or tasks; (5) horizontal instruments; and (6) mission statements. This typology is relative and somewhat eclectic, but its has the very great merit of including the traditional mode of administrative coordination – that is, hierarchy – as well as informal relations (as in the bureaucratic politics view described above) and the more formalized coordinating structures emphasized by the organizational process view.

Hierarchical Instruments

According to the classical hierarchical view, central management is in control of common tasks like coordination. Following this approach, we would typically expect tasks to be placed under a common authority such as the prime minister or president, who would then normally create a prime minister's unit, office or section. There might also be a special coordinating minister (or 'Minister without Portfolio') (Peters 1998b: 31), who coordinates broad clusters of policies that transcend sectoral boundaries (OECD 2000: 9). Some commentators have used the inherent weakness of national environmental ministries to argue that the centre should adopt greater control and exhibit greater political leadership on environmental matters:

> [T]he logic of decision making in a sustainable development value frame requires that the responsibility for promoting and overseeing environmental objectives be anchored in an overarching authority structure. This can be . . . the chief executive . . . an appropriately placed planning agency . . . the domain of the legislature . . . or placed outside of the political process in the form of a last resort judicial organ (Lafferty 2001: 22).

Other commentators (for example, EEA 2005b: 17) appear to believe that the cause of EPI would be better served by locating coordinating powers in the cabinet or executive office, rather than the environment ministry. Its work could, in turn, be supported and/or audited by an advisory council, of which there are very many in OECD countries (EEA 2005b: 29).

A number of countries have experimented with hierarchical instruments. For example, there are cabinet-level groups or committees in a wide range of countries (see Chapter 2), including Belgium, France, Japan, Germany, Spain and Sweden (OECD 2002a: 18; EEA 2005b: 28–32). Many of them were originally created to write national sustainable development strategies (Jacob and Volkery 2004: 303), only then to be retained to ensure that they are followed up on. In principle, they are supposed to provide high-level political leadership, audit progress, resolve disputes between sectors and/or ensure follow-up. In practice, they tend not to push forward EPI initiatives or get directly involved in daily policy making (EEA 2005b: 28). In fact, the EEA argues that their presence easily deflects attention from 'tougher decisions, both regarding administrations and actual policy change' (EEA 2005b: 36). For example, a green cabinet committee was established in Germany in 1971, but was disbanded shortly thereafter (Jacob and Volkery 2003: 11). Similarly, an environmental cabinet committee was instituted in the UK in 1990 (Chapter 12), but it has rarely met and is in fact not that hierarchical (it is not, for instance, chaired by the Prime Minister) (Jordan 2002). There are also more practical difficulties associated with hierarchical instruments: centralizing lots of coordination tasks, for example, can easily overload the apex, given its pre-existing commitments to deliver many other coordination goals.

Bureaucratic Rules and Standard Operating Procedures

Building new ministries or central committees is seldom enough; adequate thought also needs to be given to the way in which officials can be inculcated with a culture of better coordination (OECD 2000: para. 3). As the OECD (2000: 4) has rather nicely put it: 'all too often, administrative reforms focus on shifting the boxes of an organization chart without enough thought to the people within those structures'. Red tape is often universally reviled in liberal democracies (Olsen 2005), but procedures and rules are a powerful way to standardize behaviour (for example, when and how to apply policy appraisals) and manage information flows (OECD 1996: 15). Rules and procedures are, for example, capable of achieving significant cultural change, but are not mentioned in the existing literature on EPI.

Moving on, an important distinction can be made between procedures that encourage an active and/or a passive exchange of information (Jordan and Schout 2006; Jordan *et al.* 2008). In the case of passive information, the ministries that are not in the lead are entitled to receive the relevant information about spillover effects, but they have to hunt around to find out – and, should they desire, to influence – what the lead ministry is doing. In terms of EPI, this imposes a huge burden on environmental ministries, as most (if not all) sector ministries are involved in environmentally damaging activities. We know that the Netherlands and the European Commission are plagued by passive information flows, which hinder their attempts to deal with EPI (Jordan and Schout 2006). In her study of EPI in Germany, Müller (2002) shows that administrative rules prevent the early integration of environmental factors into decision making. In theory, the environment ministry can only initiate policies that are within its jurisdiction. If it wants to cooperate with another ministry, it must wait until it is formally invited to a meeting.

Active information, on the other hand, means that the lead department is formally obliged to ensure that other departments are informed and their views incorporated in the coordination process. Because it is a proactive way of coordination, problems are detected early on in the policy-making process, which is very much in the spirit of EPI. However, care must be taken in choosing what to share, lest it exacerbate information overload (which could, paradoxically, make coordination harder to achieve, not easier) (OECD 1996: 16).

Other rules and procedures that support EPI can, of course, be envisaged (Jacob and Volkery 2004: 302). For example, the environment ministry could be given a formal right to veto an environmentally destructive policy proposed by one of the sectors. A slightly weaker form of this rule might allow environment ministries to initiate new policy-making proposals in the sectors. In practice, Jacob and Volkery (2004: 302) could not find a single OECD state that routinely applies such rules.

Staff Training

Training (for example, on how to perform appraisal, consult with stakeholders or create 'green' budgets) is aimed at encouraging officials to work in a more coordinated way. Training and other awareness activities were meant to play a role in furthering EPI in the UK and the Netherlands (EEA 2005a: 22). Training can raise awareness of and build commitment to a particular coordination objective. However, the contribution made by training can in practice be quite limited in a world full of multiple objectives and policy procedures (Schout 1999). For example, the Civil Service College in the UK runs courses on environmental policy appraisal, but the demand for places has tended to be very low (Russel and Jordan 2007). Training is therefore probably best used to reinforce skills within the context of single (e.g., sectoral) objectives, rather than to tackle complex horizontal tasks such as EPI (Jordan and Schout 2006).

Specification of Output and/or Tasks

Telling each part of an organization what contribution it should make to the achievement of a common objective like EPI is a tried and tested mechanism of new public management (NPM) (see for example, OECD 2000: para 3; Pollitt and Bouckaert 2004). In reality, it can take many forms (that is, standardizing outputs or tasks) and be implemented in different ways (that is, more or less hierarchical). For example, the form adopted could include setting targets (e.g., embodied in environmental regulations) or specifying tasks (e.g., asking sector ministries to undertake environmental policy appraisals, produce integration strategies or adopt environmental management systems to reduce energy use or encourage recycling) (EEA 2005a: 20; EEA 2005b: 27–8). Here might be an opportunity to link administrative instruments with other EPI instruments discussed in this book. At the same time, these can (as was noted in Chapter 2) be implemented in a relatively hierarchical way (that is, the apex sets the overall priorities, which are then passed down to the line ministries to implement faithfully), or in a more bottom-up fashion (that is, where sectoral goals are formulated as part of a collective priority-setting process, led and supported by the centre of government (OECD 2000: 8). The OECD's work on sustainability seems to favour the more hierarchical route, through which the sectors are 'mandated' to develop integration strategies in conformity with an overall plan set by the apex (OECD 2002a: 33; OECD 2002b: 6). The country which has gone furthest down this road is possibly Sweden, although it has not embedded EPI nearly as deeply as was expected (see Chapter 11). By contrast, the EU asked the sectors to produce and benchmark their own 'Cardiff' integration strategies in a relatively loose and bottom-up manner (see Chapter 8).

To conclude, setting targets certainly gives the impression that things are being done in a coordinated fashion, but very often they do not tame the forces of bureaucratic politics and hence managers working at the coal face end up 'cherry picking' the most palatable ones (Jordan and Schout 2006).

Horizontal Instruments

These offer a more decentralized approach to coordination and integration, in the sense that they aim to unload hierarchical coordinating structures and permit a richer and more responsive process of communication to occur between the participating actors. They include: (1) informal relations ('bureaucratic politics'); (2) liaison officers; (3) task forces; and (4) teams (with strong and weak integrators).

Informal relations ('bureaucratic politics')

The classical bureaucratic politics view of organizations was covered above. In theory, it offers a very quick and efficient way of resolving inter-sectoral disagreements. But the sheer scale and size of most national policy systems, the pronounced lack of trust between the participating ministries and their often sharply conflicting interests, all too easily thwart the free exchange of information, hence the need (as suggested by the organizational process view) for complementary instruments.

Liaison officers

Liaison officers are people who have an overview of the whole coordination problem. Typically, they monitor developments in other fields to identify overlapping interests and remind everyone concerned that they are interdependent. Officials working in the sectors may not appreciate (or want to see – note the bureaucratic politics view) this interdependence, but the liaison officers might. According to Wilkinson (1997, 1998), liaison officials (or correspondents – see Jacob and Volkery (2003: 16) – can come in a number of different shapes and sizes. They can be:

- spies: environmental officials located in the sectors that inform the environment ministry of any 'ungreen' policy developments coming down the pipeline;
- postmen: officials located either in the sectors and/or the environment ministry who transfer information on environmentally damaging proposals;
- policemen: officials that have the ability (see the discussion of rules above) to veto 'ungreen' proposals;
- technicians: officials that provide advice on, for example, policy appraisal;

- facilitators: officials, possibly working in cross-sectoral teams (see below), that encourage and structure dialogues between cognate ministries (we term these 'integrators' – see below); or
- ambassadors: nominated officials in the sector ministries whose task it is to champion EPI.

In Italy, the UK (OECD 2001: 107) and the European Commission (Wilkinson 1997), liaison officers are placed in larger environmental (or 'mirror') units within each sector ministry, sometimes under the control of a nominated green minister. Mirror units are now a 'standard' feature in 'all' OECD countries (Jacob and Volkery 2004: 302). Table 2.1 reports that 18 out of the 30 OECD countries surveyed have interdepartmental working groups (which are functionally equivalent). Liaison officers are supposed to facilitate information flows, but they may be of limited use when differences in views are pronounced and/or when trust is lacking. It is symptomatic that in the European Commission, liaison officials have tended to take the form of technicians and ambassadors, rather than policemen or spies (Wilkinson 1997: 162; see also Jacob and Volkery 2004: 302). Usually, liaison officers need some authority within their host organizations to be effective. However, senior staff normally prefer to achieve their sector's 'core' tasks. The difficult task of liaising with other sectors (that is, coordination) tends to be passed down to more junior officials, who try not be too 'green' lest it jeopardizes their careers (Jacob and Volkery 2003: 17; Jacob and Volkery 2004: 302).

Task forces
Liaison roles seek to establish and sustain bilateral relations between two ministries. Policies (like the environment) that cut across several ministries may, however, require an even more horizontal approach, involving the creation of a task force. This is a temporary committee dealing with a specific coordination problem. Participation is normally on an equal and voluntary basis. Voluntary participation prevents participants from feeling overshadowed. However, it also constitutes their primary weakness (Peters 1998b: 35): participants may not attend; they may not share information readily; they may well join to delay or block real decision making; or their starting positions may be too dissimilar to achieve a consensus. In these situations, the risk of stalemates (and hence no coordination) can be very high.

Task forces do not feature very highly in the existing EPI literature, which is somewhat surprising given that they can facilitate policy learning and reframing activities (Peters 1998a/b). However, they may need to be buttressed by other coordination capacities – that is, a set of directions and priorities – to ensure that their 'coordinated' solutions are put into practice (Jordan and Schout 2006).

Teams

Teams are committees that meet at a higher level. They try to take a synoptic view of a problem and, where necessary, resolve conflicting values. Whereas task forces are topic-related and exist only for a short period, teams tend to have a more permanent character. Teams tend to be organized around coordinating issues, rather than permanent functions (that is, sectors). They help to build new networks of officials ('policy communities') (OECD 2000: para. 32), which span sectors and levels of governance (OECD 1996: 19). Importantly, they can also help to commit the apex to the day-to-day management of policy interdependence. Attention must, however, be paid to selecting the right mix of members. By this we mean that the right representatives have to be involved and they must be capable of making credible commitments. If not, teams can easily dissolve into 'talking shops' (Schout and Jordan 2005).

Another important factor which determines the coordinating potential of teams is the manner in which they are chaired. One way to increase the effectiveness of teams is to introduce leadership (that is, hierarchy) in the form of a chairperson or 'middleman' (Challis *et al.* 1988). The chair (or 'integrator') may have strong or weak powers. Weak integrators are the formal guardians of the coordination process but do not actually dictate the outcome. The bureaucratic power relations (see the bureaucratic politics view above) thus remain unaltered. The chairperson simply calls meetings, prepares agendas, acts as a mediator or prevents evasive behaviour. There are many examples of weakly chaired teams to be found in the EPI literature (EEA 2005b: 28). These include the green cabinets discussed above, the teams of high-level officials that prepare national sustainability (e.g., in the UK) or integration strategies, and the myriad advisory councils and groups. The EU has recently created a number of so-called High-Level Groups (of stakeholders) to coordinate areas such as competitiveness, energy and transport (Wilkinson *et al.* 2005: 18). Under Barroso, the European Commission has also established groups of Commissioners to take a more coordinated view of policy problems like economic competitiveness (Wilkinson *et al.* 2005: 17). Despite their popularity, the EEA (2005b: 28) argues that 'it is not always evident that they . . . play a strategic role in pushing forward EPI' by resolving inter-sector conflicts in the everyday grind of policy making.

By contrast, strong integrators try to take decisions that bind everyone together. The most obvious place to resolve a cross-cutting issue is the cabinet, as most if not all sectors are normally represented there (OECD 2000: para. 33). The ultimate integrator is, of course, the prime minister, but s/he rarely has the time to resolve each and every dispute, hence the need for more decentralized coordinating capacities. The real dilemma is how to involve integrators in daily policy work, without compromising their autonomy and sense of perspective (OECD 1996: 13). Several OECD countries now have environmental (or 'green') cabinets (4 out of 30 OECD countries sampled in Chapter 3), but in practice they tend to focus on broader themes like sustainable development reporting and strategizing, rather than EPI (EEA 2005b: 28–9). Crucially, they tend to be chaired by the environment department, not the prime minister, and hence are likely to lack political power. Finally, it may be very difficult to find a sufficiently powerful integrator in less hierarchical (that is, collegial) administrative systems or in multi-levelled governance systems such as the EU.

Mission Statements

These seek to influence the culture, values and symbols in an administrative system. They may not be especially hierarchical, but they can achieve a lot. After all, cultural change has the potential to bring about large organizational behaviour changes (Schein 1985), particularly in dynamic, polycentric operating environments such as the EU (March and Simon 1958). Their value is acknowledged in the existing EPI literature (EEA 2005a: 10). The EU's Article 6 could be viewed as one, as could the constitutional provisions (supporting integration, sustainability or environmental quality and so on) in many OECD countries (Jacob and Volkery 2004: 302). However, the problem with mission statements is that they often embody aspirations that are disconnected from the daily life of most policy makers, who routinely have to juggle many equally 'good' objectives. Because they often end up reflecting values that are not part of an organization's culture, they need to be buttressed with other coordinating capacities.

Finally, specification of ownership could also be placed in this category. Rather than specifying clear and precise targets (see above), this involves defining who should be responsible for cross-cutting tasks. In an EU setting, this might include implementing EPI, subsidiarity, sustainability or 'better regulation' (see Chapter 8). In Sweden, we find that the sectors have to live up to a wider responsibility principle (see Chapter 11). In practice, goals like these tend to be so widely framed that everyone (and therefore in practice no one) is responsible.

SUMMARY DISCUSSION

Having identified these six main types of coordination capacity, let us now return to the three theoretical views discussed in Section 3. The first two – namely the bureaucratic politics and the organizational process views – are not necessarily alternative ways to coordinate. The bureaucratic politics approach assumes that coordination will emerge spontaneously as and when actors realize they are interdependent. However, if they are not aware, sufficient communication (and hence, possibly coordination) may not occur. To overcome this, bureaucratic politics can, the organizational process view suggests, be proceduralized using rules and procedures (for example, by making information sharing obligatory) (Meltsner and Bellavita 1983: 37–8), or be supported by other instruments such as teams, task forces and rules. In this way, the forces of bureaucratic politics can be channelled in pursuit of more coordinated policy making.

Interestingly, our three views conceive of the relationship between politics and administration rather differently. The importance of political will and leadership – particularly from leaders at the apex – is a running theme in the EPI literature (for example, Lafferty 2001: 27; OECD 2001: 120; EEA 2005a/b). Peters (1998b: 48–9), for example, argues that administrative 'structure is important and can *facilitate* coordination, but to produce behavioural changes may require the active intervention of political leaders, often political leaders at the very top of government' (emphasis added). But this begs several questions: which political leaders need to show leadership? And what comes first – the chicken of political leadership or the egg of administrative instruments to translate it into practice? We return to these points in the final section.

Generally speaking, environmental interest groups tend to be relatively weaker than those representing producers (Peters 1998a: 300). The bureaucratic politics view therefore suggests that the political commitment has to come chiefly from the ministries, but especially the environmental ministry. The organizational process view sees will and leadership at the apex and the activities of the administrative system as being much more subtly interconnected (Wildavsky 1979), that is, the way in which coordination capacities are designed can strongly influence which issues eventually acquire public attention and hence become openly political. In other words, building the right coordination capacities provides a way to institutionalize political commitment in the administrative system, so that EPI – which tends to be a low-profile issue in the medium to long term – does not suffer when there is a downturn in the environmental issue attention cycle (EEA 2005b: 9, 37). We return to this vexed relationship between politics and administration in the final section.

Finally, the symbolic politics view offers a starkly different perspective – political leaders are seen either as highly calculating agents who adapt the administrative system to achieve their interests, or as much more passive norm followers. Either way, political motives strongly shape the selection of administrative innovations like green cabinets. However, this again begs the question of where their motivations and interests arise from in the first place.

CONCLUSIONS

Brundtland succeeded brilliantly in laying out a broad case and a general direction for institutional reform, which has never really been challenged. Indeed it is a measure of her committee's influence that the basic idea that EPI requires administrative and bureaucratic reform has become an important part of the conventional wisdom in supranational bodies as diverse as the UN, the OECD and the EEA. But unfortunately, her committee did not define a blueprint for reform, or even precisely define what it meant by 'policies and institutions'. Arguably, this has allowed (and possibly even encouraged) states to engage in a rather unstructured and eclectic process of adopting and dropping different administrative instruments, in which there are no overriding design principles. Some of the more communicative instruments (see Chapter 1 for a discussion of this term) like mission statements and obligations to report seem to have a very broad appeal (see Chapter 2), not least because they give a very obvious and high-profile signal that policy makers are committed to EPI. Although tending towards description, the EPI literature on their presence or absence is relatively well developed. Others – such as some of the horizontal instruments like rules, procedures and teams – are much less popular. Possibly because of this, the academic literature on them is a good deal sparser.

Consequently, more so than the other instruments covered in this book, the evidence base – particularly with respect to the issue of effectiveness – remains rather thin. We do, however, know from Chapter 2 that some types of administrative instrument are popular, at least in OECD countries. We also know that they provide a framework in which coordination takes place 'rather than an "iron cage" determining administrative mentality, behaviour and [policy] outcomes' (Olsen 2005: 11). We also assume that administrative reform is probably a necessary but insufficient condition for greater EPI, even though we are far from being clear about how best to 'fit' the various administrative instruments together. But to these widely shared assumptions, the science of public administration currently cannot offer that much more. Little, for example, is known about whether the current pattern of use provides an effective response to the challenge of EPI (EEA 2005a: 56).

As a result, our aims in this chapter have had to be rather modest. We have tried to capture the essence of administrative instruments, offered a typology of the main instruments, and, drawing on the work of Mintzberg, sought to show how they could fit together in pursuit of greater EPI. But in relation to many vital questions – policy effectiveness, the relationship between political and administrative factors, and the appropriate balance between hierarchical and less hierarchical interventions to name just three – we are simply not yet in a position to offer clear answers.

Often, this is because they go to the heart of profound and as yet essentially unresolved debates within the administrative and organizational sciences, such as the extent to which administrations have an independent causal effect on the behaviour of those who work within them. The three views outlined above do, however, offer useful standpoints from which to scrutinize these questions and eventually perhaps arrive at some answers. Hopefully, we have shown that looking at administrative instruments from alternative theoretical viewpoints does illuminate the complexity of the coordination *problematique*. Crucially, the choice of perspective partly depends upon what we want to understand about EPI and partly on how we think the world operates (that is, it is an implicit value choice). Thus, the bureaucratic politics view assumes that administrative systems are splintered into competing sections or sectors. But it cautions against the automatic assumption that the only way to resolve them is by adopting hierarchical interventions or brigading functions into large organizations. By contrast, the organizational process view reveals various ways in which bureaucratic conflict can and should be proceduralized. Finally, the symbolic politics view offers a useful corrective to the assumption that policy makers always adopt administrative instruments in a conscious and well-meaning manner. The fact that many of the instruments described in this chapter are deployed in a very superficial and ad hoc manner, with little attention to diagnosing underlying problems, would certainly seem to give credence to this view. There is, after all, an undeniable tendency to deploy the 'easier' instruments (mission statements, weak teams, specification of tasks and so on), than some of the more 'difficult' ones (rules, specification of output and so on).

Interestingly, the three views also suggest different routes to improving the status quo. The bureaucratic politics view suggests that states should create strong environmental ministries to politicize EPI issues in national administrative systems. As most states now have separate environmental ministries, the most obvious thing to do is to ensure that they control as many environmental policy functions as possible. Weale (1998: 30) has been a strong and consistent advocate of this view. While conceding that the intellectual case for EPI and sustainable development is impeccable, he believes that there is a practical need to strengthen (both politically and administratively) environmental ministries so they are able to bargain with the sectors on more equal terms: 'unless there are sources of countervailing power in the decision making system, progress will not take place' (ibid.).

The organizational process view on the other hand emphasizes the importance of creating the right coordination capacities. What, however, is the 'right' combination? One way to begin answering this might be to draw upon the work of Mintzberg (see above). As a general principle, the higher the level of differentiation between actors, the more coordination capacities have to be available (not just more of the same ones). Although Mintzberg (1983, 1989) argues that the six types of instrument have the potential to be mutually reinforcing, there is no obvious blueprint for organizing national administrative systems, because each faces different challenges and has different traditions (OECD 1996: 9). For example, teams with strong integrators can help to resolve conflicts that emerge from informal relations (that is, bureaucratic politics). Similarly, standardization of output can help to steer the production of policy appraisals in the sectors (that is, standardization of task). It is probably true that teams are better at implementing agreed targets and processes than engineering a sweeping redefinition of problems in the manner highlighted by those pursuing a learning perspective (Peters 1998b: 37; Jacob and Volkery 2003: 11). However, task forces do offer opportunities to engage in more open-ended processes of long-term learning (see Lenschow 2002b).

Finally, the symbolic politics view could be dismissed for offering little more than a cynical view of politics and politicians. However, it does force scholars of EPI to adopt a more critical perspective and actively question the motives of those seeking to alter administrative systems – a topic about which we still know surprisingly little. Our own view is that we should try not to think in binary terms – that is, either administrative reform or political pressure and/or leadership. The organizational process view usefully reminds us that the presence of coordination capacities helps to clarify (and hence make more openly political) cross-sectoral conflicts, which might otherwise remain latent. To an extent, they help to identify inter-sectoral conflicts (and thus help administrators to capture the relevant minister's attention). In this way, sectoral differences can be more effectively raised at an appropriately high level in order to foster the necessary political interest in and support for EPI. Politics and administration are therefore like the proverbial chicken and egg: we need both to get to grips with EPI.

BIBLIOGRAPHY

Allison, G.T. (1971), *Essence of Decision*, Boston: Harper Collins.
Bendor, J. and T.H. Hammond (1992), 'Rethinking Allison's models', *American Political Science Review*, 86 (2), 301–322.

Busch, P.-O. and H. Joergens (2005), 'The international sources of policy convergence: explaining the spread of environmental policy innovations', *Journal of European Public Policy*, 12 (5), 860–884.

Challis, L., S. Fuller, M. Henwood, P. Klein, W. Plowden, A. Webb and P. Whittingham (1988), *Joint Approaches to Social Policy: Rationality and Practice*, Cambridge: Cambridge University Press.

Chisholm, D. (1989), *Coordination without Hierarchy: Informal Structures in Multi-Organizational Systems*, Berkeley: University of California Press.

Cyert, R. and J. March (1963), *A Behavioural Theory of the Firm*, Englewood Hills: Prentice Hall.

Dye, T. (1976), *What Governments Do, Why They Do it, What Difference It Makes*, Tuscaloosa, AL: University of Alabama Press.

Edelman, M. (1971), *Politics as Symbolic Action*, Chicago: Markham Publishers.

Edelman, M. (1988), *Constructing the Political Spectacle*, Chicago: Chicago University Press.

EEA (European Environment Agency) (2005a), *Environmental Policy Integration in Europe: State of Play and an Evaluation Framework*, EEA technical report, No 2/2005, Copenhagen: European Environment Agency.

EEA (European Environment Agency) (2005b), *Environmental Policy Integration in Europe: Administrative Culture and Practices*, EEA technical report, No 5/2005, Copenhagen: European Environment Agency.

Egeberg, M. (2003) 'How bureaucratic structure matters', in: B.G. Peters and J. Pierre (eds), *Handbook of Public Administration*, London: Sage.

Finnemore, M. and K. Sikkink (1998), 'International norm dynamics and political change', *International Organisation*, 52 (4), 887–917.

Jacob, K. and A. Volkery (2003), *Instruments for Policy Integration*, Intermediate report of the RIW Project POINT, FFU report 06-2003, Berlin: Forschungsstelle Für Umweltpolitik.

Jacob, K. and A. Volkery (2004), 'Institutions and instruments for government self-regulation: environmental policy integration in a cross-country perspective', *Journal of Comparative Policy Analysis*, 6 (3), 291–309.

Jordan, A.J. (2002), 'Efficient hardware and light green software: environmental policy integration in the UK', in A. Lenschow (ed.), *Environmental Policy Integration*, London: Earthscan.

Jordan, A.J. and D. Liefferink (eds) (2004), *Environmental Policy in Europe: The Europeanization of National Environmental Policy*, London: Routledge.

Jordan, A.J. and A. Schout (2006), *The Coordination of the European Union*, Oxford: Oxford University Press.

Jordan, A.J., A. Schout, M. Unfried and A. Zito (2008), 'Coordinating environmental policy: shifting from passive to active coordination?' in H. Kassim, A. Menon and G. Peters (eds), *Co-ordinating the EU*, New York: Rowman and Littlefield.

Lafferty, W. (2001), Adapting Governance Practice to the Goals of Sustainable Development, Paper presented at an *OECD PUMA seminar Improving Governance for Sustainable Development*, 22–23 November, Paris: OECD.

Lenschow, A. (2002a), 'Greening the European Union: an introduction', in A. Lenschow (ed.), *Environmental Policy Integration*, London: Earthscan.

Lenschow, A. (2002b), 'Conclusion', in A. Lenschow (ed.), *Environmental Policy Integration*, London: Earthscan.

Lenschow, A. and A. Zito (1998), 'Blurring and shifting of policy frames', *Governance*, 11 (4), 415–441.

Liefferink, D. and A. Jordan (2004), 'Europeanization and policy convergence: a basis for comparative analysis', in A. Jordan and D. Liefferink (eds), *Environmental Policy in Europe: The Europeanization of National Environmental Policy*, London: Routledge.

Lindblom, C. (1965), *The Intelligence of Democracy*, New York: Free Press.

March, J.G. and H.A. Simon (1958), *Organizations*, New York: Wiley.

Meltsner, A.J. and C. Bellavita (1983), *The Policy Organization*, London: Sage.

Meyer, J. and B. Rowan (1977), 'Institutional organisation: formal structure as myth and ceremony', *American Journal of Sociology*, 83, 340–363.

Mintzberg, H. (1979), *The Structuring of Organizations: A Synthesis of the Research*, Englewood Cliffs, NJ: Prentice-Hall.

Mintzberg, H. (1983), *Designing Effective Organizations: Structure in Fives*, Englewood Cliffs, NJ: Prentice-Hall.

Mintzberg, H. (1989), *Mintzberg on Management: Inside Our Strange World of Organizations*, New York: The Free Press.

Müller, E. (2002), 'Environmental policy integration as a political principle: the German case and the implications for European policy', in A. Lenschow (ed.), *Environmental Policy Integration*, London: Earthscan.

OECD (Organisation for Economic Cooperation and Development) (1996), *Building Policy Coherence: Tools and Tensions*, Public Management Occasional Paper No. 12, Paris: OECD.

OECD (Organisation for Economic Cooperation and Development) (2000), *Government Coherence: the Role of the Centre of Government*, PUMA/MPM (2000) 3, Paris: OECD.

OECD (Organisation for Economic Cooperation and Development) (2001), *Sustainable Development: Critical Issues*, Paris: OECD.

OECD (Organisation for Economic Cooperation and Development) (2002a), *Governance for Sustainable Development: Five OECD Case Studies*, Paris: OECD.

OECD (Organisation for Economic Cooperation and Development) (2002b), *Improving Policy Coherence and Integration for Sustainable Development: A Checklist*, Paris: OECD.

Olsen, J.P. (2005), *Maybe it's Time to Re-discover Bureaucracy?* ARENA Working Paper, 10/2005, Oslo: ARENA (Centre for European Studies), University of Oslo.

Palumbo, D.J. (1975), 'Organization theory and political science', in F.I. Greenstein and N.W. Polsby (eds), *Handbook of Political Science, Volume 2: Micro-Political Theory*, Reading: Addison-Wesley.

Parsons, W. (1995), *Public Policy*, Aldershot: Edward Elgar.

Peters, B.G. (1998a), 'Managing horizontal government', *Public Administration*, 76, 295–311.

Peters, B.G. (1998b), *Managing Horizontal Governance: The Politics of Coordination*, Canadian Centre for Management Development, Research Paper 21, Ottawa: Canada School of Public Service.

Pollitt, C. and G. Bouckaert (2004), *Public Management Reform: A Comparative Analysis*, 2nd edn, Oxford: Oxford University Press.

Pressman, J. and A. Wildavsky (1984), *Implementation: How Great Expectations in Washington are Dashed in Oakland*, 2nd edn, Berkeley: University of California Press.

Russel, D. and A. Jordan (2007), 'Gearing up governance for sustainable development: patterns of policy appraisal in UK central government', *Journal of Environmental Planning and Management*, 50 (1), 1–22.

Schein, E.H. (1985), *Organizational Culture and Leadership*, San Francisco: Jossey-Bass.

Schout, A. (1999), *The Internal Management of External Relations*, Maastricht: European Institute of Public Administration.

Schout, A. and A.J. Jordan (2005), 'Coordinating European governance: self-organising or centrally steered?' *Public Administration*, 83 (1), 201–220.

Simon, H.A. (1976), *Administrative Behaviour*, New York: The Free Press.

WCED (World Commission on Environment and Development) (1987), *Our Common Future*, Oxford: Oxford University Press.

Weale, A. (1998), A Sceptical Look at Environmental Policy Integration, paper delivered at an EEB Conference on the *Integration of Environmental Concerns into all Policy Areas*, Brussels, 26–27 November, Brussels: European Environment Bureau.

Wildavsky, A. (1979), *Speaking Truth to Power: The Art and Craft of Policy Analysis*, New Brunswick and London: Transaction Publishers.

Wilkinson, D. (1997), 'Towards sustainability in the European Union? Steps within the European Commission towards integrating the environment into other European Union policy sectors', *Environmental Politics*, 6 (1), 153–173.

Wilkinson, D. (1998), 'Steps towards integrating the environment into other EU policy sectors', in T. O'Riordan and H. Voisey (eds), *The Transition to Sustainability*, London: Earthscan.

Wilkinson, D., C. Monkhouse, M. Herodes and A. Farmer (2005), *For Better or For Worse? The EU Better Regulation Agenda and the Environment*, London: IEEP.

4. Green budgeting

David Wilkinson, David Benson and Andrew Jordan

INTRODUCTION

Historically, budgets and their management – a process known as 'budgeting' – have been hugely important in the development of the modern state and, through their relationship to public revenue raising (typically via taxation) and spending, constitute some of the most fundamental of all the functions performed by contemporary governments. They are also highly relevant to the whole notion of EPI, because public spending, and the process of raising the revenue to support it, can have a wide range of environmental impacts – both beneficial and damaging. For example, support to intensify agricultural production or build major new infrastructure projects such as roads can have undesirable effects on biodiversity, water pollution and greenhouse gas emissions. On the other hand, different forms of expenditure may provide the infrastructure needed to treat wastes or manage critical habitats. Similarly, certain types of taxation can give the market the 'wrong' signals and therefore encourage environmentally unsustainable activities such as pollution. Finally, spending may also be earmarked explicitly for the administration of initiatives related to EPI (for example, impact assessments, training and capacity building – see Chapter 3). In short, budgeting is both a potential instrument to facilitate EPI and a means of linking together other instruments covered in this part of the book.

'Green budgeting' is in fact a convenient shorthand expression that encompasses a wide range of activities involving a diverse range of actors, institutions and instruments. The process of developing expenditure priorities, formally adopting the annual budget, implementing spending programmes, monitoring and evaluating their effectiveness and raising revenue could be said to form a kind of budgetary 'life cycle'. As each stage has potentially significant environmental implications, all of them should be brought together in any green budgeting exercise. However, this necessarily involves taking steps that cut across policy sectors and – in multi-levelled systems of governance like the EU – administrative levels. This is one of the reasons why green budgeting is far from easy to implement in practice. Another is that the *locus standi* of environment ministries in relation to setting spending priorities is weak, mainly because they are not themselves major spenders and therefore tend to be marginalised in key budgetary debates. This situation reflects the logic of the 'polluter pays principle', which means that environmental policy instruments tend to be predominantly regulatory rather than expenditure-based. At the same time, existing spending departments have occasionally sought to justify their continued control over most forms of environment-related public spending through reference to the EPI principle.

Green budgeting is clearly a very big agenda and this chapter can only provide an overview of some of the key considerations. The task is made more difficult because little research has so far been undertaken on instruments for integrating environmental considerations into the budgetary process. To make matters worse, there is also a pronounced lack of transparency in most budgetary processes which actively inhibits independent, comparative research. With that in mind, section two of this chapter develops an analytical framework for evaluating the effectiveness of green budgeting activities. The historical development of green budgeting in several jurisdictions is then outlined to show how this framework can be used to identify critical lessons. In-depth empirical evidence of green budgeting in the EU is then presented and conclusions are drawn about the future role of green budgeting as an instrument for advancing EPI.

The EU provides a particularly fruitful context in which to study the policy and politics of green budgeting. Compared to its Member States, the EU has relatively restricted budgetary powers. As discussed later in this chapter, the Member States decide how much should be spent by EU institutions, a figure currently pegged at circa 1 per cent of total EU-wide Gross National Income. In addition, the EU has only a limited capacity to raise its own revenue. The nature of budgetary spending also differs, with the EU budget dominated by just two policy sectors – agriculture and regional development – which together constitute in excess of 80 per cent of its total spending (Enderlein and Lindner 2006: 194). EU budgeting in these sectors is strongly redistributional. Thus, subsidies are paid to farmers under the Common Agricultural Policy (CAP) and financial support is provided via the structural and cohesion funds to help poorer regions develop more quickly. As such, the EU's budgeting decisions potentially have disproportionate environmental consequences, compared with Member States' public expenditure, which is dominated by sectors with less direct environmental impacts, for example health and education. For these and other reasons, the political pressure to engage in green budgeting at EU level has been particularly pronounced.

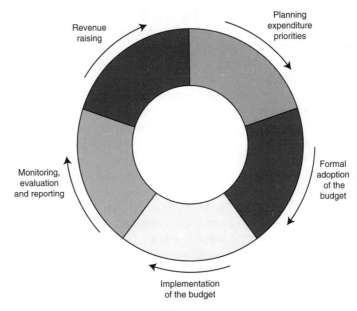

Figure 4.1   The green budgeting 'life cycle'

CONCEPTUAL BACKGROUND

The budgetary 'life cycle' within specific jurisdictions generally encompasses five interlinked stages that together constitute an integrated and adaptive fiscal process (see Figure 4.1). This process often starts with the strategic *planning of expenditure priorities*. Most EU states now engage in setting multi-annual spending priorities over the medium term. During this planning stage, the criteria for determining budgetary allocations, and the departments involved in making these decisions and determining what conditions are attached, are crucial. Multi-annual frameworks set the context for annual budget making, where decisions are still significant, albeit constrained by an overarching framework.

Secondly, medium-term planning is often accompanied by the *formal adoption of an annual budget*. Budgets are usually proposed by the finance ministry, endorsed by the cabinet and formally adopted by the legislature. Depending on national constitutional arrangements, both environmental and 'non' environmental conditions may be attached by the legislature to some forms of expenditure.

Thirdly, planning is followed by the *implementation of the budget*. Spending may be: undertaken either directly by central government departments (or – in the case of the EU – the Commission's DGs); decentralised to Member States, their regional and/or local authorities; or undertaken by EU agencies and/or other non-governmental bodies. A wide range of conditions and controls may be imposed by the centre on devolved expenditure in order to secure policy objectives such as environmental protection.

Fourthly, budgets are subject to *monitoring, evaluation and reporting*. Monitoring, *ex post* evaluation and reporting in relation to expenditure programmes may be undertaken by the spending department and/or by an external audit body. This procedure may focus narrowly on financial outputs, or ask wider questions in relation to the effects and effectiveness of expenditure from an environmental, or other, perspective.

Finally, these preceding steps inevitably feed back into the process of *raising revenue*. In relation to revenue raising, decisions as to the target and the level of taxes, charges or levies will clearly have varying environmental consequences. For example, in relation to the EU's 'own resources' (discussed below), levies on agricultural imports from developing countries are likely to be less sustainable than, for example, taxes on carbon or aviation. Similarly, from a sustainable development perspective, taxes on the use of natural resources are preferable to taxes on labour. To complete the cycle, the revenue raised by these activities determines the scope of further budgetary planning.

Figure 4.1 presents a useful analytical device for structuring an investigation into the environmental effectiveness of green budgeting. It is obvious from this model that budgetary decisions cannot be taken in isolation. They become integrated into, and are dependent on, previous steps in the cycle. Incremental adjustments in one stage can have knock-on effects on others in terms of integrating environmental considerations into policy. Effective EPI is arguably then contingent on there being a coherent consideration of environmental concerns throughout each stage of the cycle as the budgetary process gradually unfolds. Evaluating the ability of green budgeting exercises to advance EPI must therefore be undertaken through a similar analytical exercise.

HISTORY

Although only a relatively recent instrument of EPI, green budgeting has become more widespread since the early 1990s, although only 4 of the 30 OECD states sampled in Chapter 2 report performing an environmental assessment of their annual budget. Moreover, little empirical evidence exists on its effectiveness. This section therefore discusses how green budgeting has evolved in different jurisdictions, using the analytical framework described above to identify and explore broad trends.

Antecedents – the Brundtland Report and Agenda 21

An early impetus was the Brundtland Report (see also Chapter 1). Among its proposals for institutional and legal change was the recommendation that:

> the major central economic and sectoral agencies of governments should now be made directly responsible and fully accountable for ensuring that their policies, programmes and budgets support development that is ecologically as well as economically sustainable. Where resources and data permit, an annual report and an audit of changes in environmental quality and in the stock of the nation's environmental resource assets are needed to complement the traditional annual fiscal budget and economic development plan (WCED 1987: 314).

This prescription was echoed by Agenda 21 (United Nations 1992: Chapter 8.4 (c)), where it was argued that there is a need to 'ensure the coherence of sectoral, economic, social and environmental policies, plans and policy instruments, *including fiscal measures and the budget*' (ibid.) (emphasis added). Together these two documents have helped to stimulate interest in green budgeting globally, although as the next sections shows, no two jurisdictions have utilised it in exactly the same manner.

Green Budgeting – Charting its Initial Uptake

Norway was one of the very first countries to respond to the Brundtland Report. Its White Paper 46 (1988–89) introduced the Environmental Profile of the State Budget (EPSB). This required ministries to set out the main environmental challenges, targets and initiatives associated with their activities during the coming fiscal year and provide an overview of their environmentally-related expenditure and if possible its effects over the previous two years. This was principally an exercise in awareness-raising rather than exercising conditionality, and the quality of the environmental profiles proved to be rather variable (see Chapter 10). However, while the Norwegian Ministry of Finance was responsible for issuing overall guidance to ministries on the EPSB, the Environment Ministry was given a role in co-ordinating their environmental reporting. It thus established the right of the Environment Ministry to force the sectoral ministries to discuss and explain aspects of their environment-related policies.

In the UK, a commitment was made by the Blair government to consider sustainable development in its new departmental spending reviews from 1998, but the system did not become fully operational until 2002. Departments were required to produce a report assessing the sustainability implications of their spending bids. This proved to be essentially an awareness-raising procedure that most departments regarded as a simple bureaucratic step to be taken, rather than an aid to integrated decision making. However, the use of Public Service Agreements (PSAs) to impose conditions (some of them environmental) on spending, represented an important hierarchical instrument, although one that has tended to lack political bite (see Chapter 12).

In the Netherlands, the 2003 Action Programme for Sustainable Development – *Duurzame Daadkracht* – required each ministerial department in its financial statement for the coming year to explain how it would take account of the different dimensions of sustainability in preparing and implementing its policies and to undertake a sustainability impact assessment for selected major investments and new policy initiatives. The cabinet was supposed to prepare annual progress reports on these initiatives, review the level of implementation and identify good and bad practice.

By contrast, Sweden (see Chapter 11) has not adopted a systematic approach to integrating the environment into the budget. Although the Finance Ministry is required to provide a report on each budget using indicators to show broad environmental pressures, these are not linked to government spending. Yet Sweden has made use of spending programmes, taxation and green procurement to promote EPI. The government has provided funds from its budget to support local environmental projects. Public procurement has also been used to support eco-friendly products and services, with government departments and public bodies encouraged to set environmental criteria for their tendering. Less successful has been a proposed national shift towards green taxation, which was partly implemented but recently abandoned.

Germany appears to take a differing approach from other north European states (see Chapter 9). Despite the lack of formalised green budgeting at federal level, there has been a move towards some aspects of green budgeting, namely revenue-raising measures such as green taxes. Indeed, Germany has proved to be a consistent innovator in this area, having introduced a broad range of tax incentives for steering consumers towards supporting environmentally sustainable technologies. In addition, a key event was the federal ecological tax reform of 1999, aimed at shifting the tax burden on to non-renewable resource use. Another area where the federal government has focused its efforts has been in relation to the provision of subsidies for a range of eco-friendly activities, including promoting renewable energy, less polluting technologies and public transport use.

Moving further afield, the Australian government has started to adopt some green budgeting measures, although their usage is not widespread (see Chapter 14). Commonwealth government expenditure on the environment has been rising in recent years, but the country employs few environmental taxes and the revenues raised are relatively meagre (OECD/EEA 2005). The approach adopted is primarily market oriented, with various incentive arrangements employed to harness voluntary action and market forces for promoting behavioural change. It is at the state government level in Australia that the greatest advances have occurred in terms of financial management, budgeting and reporting. Nonetheless, the environmental assessment of budgets is not popular at either level of governance.

Aspects of green budgeting have been prevalent in the USA for some time (see Chapter 13). The National Environmental Policy Act (NEPA) (1969) introduced the concept of environmental assessment, with federal agencies required to prepare environmental impact statements for their proposed projects (Andrews 2006). However, this does not extend to strategic assessment of policies themselves. In contrast to the other jurisdictions noted above, the federal government in the USA has made significant use of subsidies and financial incentives in its environmental policies. Initially, grants to implement federal legislation were attached to measures such as the Clean Water Act. These have been increasingly supplemented by federal subsidies to policy sectors such as agriculture, energy and transportation. Federal subsidies are also supported by state and local expenditures, for example the 'smart' growth programme in Massachusetts.

Finally, some of the most interesting innovations have been at EU level, where a range of green budgeting initiatives have been gradually introduced. These are discussed in much greater detail below and in Chapter 8. By the late 1980s, the European Parliament had won itself a number of powers, including the right to approve (or not to approve) the way in which the Commission spends this money (Judge and Earnshaw 2003: 37). Following an environmental pressure group campaign, DG Environment and the European Parliament started to work together to turn this 'power of the purse' (Wilkinson 1997: 166) to environmental ends. One of the most obvious effects has been to ensure that all projects and programmes funded by the cohesion and structural funds now require environmental appraisal. If the Parliament feels that these are not satisfactory, it has the power to block spending (see Lenschow 1999). In a more recent development, EU approval of structural funding and financial support for agricultural projects has been tied to adequate compliance with the Habitats, Nitrates and Birds Directives (Haigh 2005: section 3.11-4), and the attainment of certain minimum environmental standards. In the agriculture sector, this environmental conditionality is known as 'cross-compliance'.

The Diffusion of Green Budgeting

Even from this necessarily brief review of existing practices and the data presented in Chapter 2, it is apparent that systematic procedures to green national (or supranational) budgets are very much the exception rather than the rule. Where they have been introduced, their effectiveness in terms of delivering greater EPI appears at best unproven. If we refer back to Figure 4.1, it is apparent that few governments have integrated environmental concerns into the strategic planning of expenditure priorities. Despite long-term financial planning being practised in many jurisdictions, multi-annual frameworks are not being widely used to pursue EPI. One notable example, however, is the EU's Multi-annual Perspective, which is outlined in further detail below.

By contrast, several governments are integrating environmental concerns into the formal adoption of their budgets, but again existing practices vary considerably. While not imposing conditionality on annual reporting, Norway's EPSB does establish a role for the Environment Ministry in overseeing this process. UK government approaches do provide a commitment for departments to consider sustainable development in their annual spending reviews but, as stated above, Public Service Agreements are not being fully utilised in this respect. Arguably, the Netherlands has the most advanced system with its Action Programme.

If we refer back to Figure 4.1, most examples of green budgeting seem to be clustered in the implementation phase, spanning a continuum from what might be termed strong to weak conditionality. Meeting environmental objectives ('strong' conditionality) has become a key condition of EU funding (see below). Although UK government departments are required to integrate sustainable development into their spending plans, implementation has been very weak (Russel 2005). Despite being the first country to introduce SEA into government decision-making processes (in the form of NEPA), the USA does not systematically integrate the environment into policy implementation. In fact, subsidies and incentives are the most widely used instruments for EPI in US federal government policy implementation. Germany has also employed subsidies to promote environmentally sustainable behaviour. Finally, federal government policy implementation in Australia has largely relied on steering consumer and producer behaviour through voluntary and market-based initiatives.

Meanwhile, the monitoring and evaluation of green budgeting is established in some jurisdictions. Although a range of measures for monitoring, both *ex ante* and *ex post*, are visible across these systems, evaluation would appear to be a critical factor in EPI. Parliamentary mechanisms for scrutinising the performance of green budgeting are a feature of the UK, and, sporadically, in the EU, but they are very much the exceptions.

Finally, EPI is also apparent at the revenue-raising stage but is not as widespread as Brundtland hoped for. Germany has made wide use of green taxes to promote environmentally sustainable behaviour. Sweden also has attempted to shift the taxation base towards green concerns. However, political pressure in Sweden has recently seen this trend reversed. A similar move away from green taxation occurred in the UK after the fuel duty escalator was suspended in 2001 due to widespread public protest (Jordan *et al.* 2003: 187). This observation is echoed by the OECD/EEA, which list environmentally-related taxes on their database. Although many such instruments exist globally, on average they only provide 6.5 per cent of total tax revenues, of which 80–90 per cent are raised from one source – transport – in the form of fuel and vehicle taxation (OECD/EEA 2005).

This section has sought to add further detail and 'colour' to the picture painted in Chapter 2 of the deployment of green budgeting. It has highlighted two main trends. Most obviously, while some elements of the 'life cycle' are apparent in existing practice, very few jurisdictions have implemented green budgeting in the holistic and integrated manner implied by Figure 4.1. In addition, different jurisdictions have specialised in certain types of green budgeting activities. However, in order to know more we need to dig deeper into particular cases of green budgeting, starting with the EU, which, for reasons outlined above, has done more than most to define and implement international best practice.

DEPLOYMENT: PRACTICAL EXPERIENCES

Before proceeding, it is important to explain that the EU is manifestly not a state in the accepted meaning of that term; its budget certainly does not conform to the principles of fiscal federalism (which would require a far more significant central budget than seems politically possible in the foreseeable future). That said, the EU does have well-established budgetary systems with an identifiable environmental component that could provide a basis for learning lessons for comparable jurisdictions. Using the 'life cycle' model set out in Figure 4.1, this section looks at each step in turn.

Strategic Planning of Expenditure Priorities

There are two contrasting models for establishing expenditure priorities. A 'bottom-up' approach would describe a process of separate, bilateral negotiations between spending departments and the central finance ministry, in which eventual budget allocations between policy priorities reflect the relative political weight of the departments involved (and possibly the other arms of government involved in setting the budget). Total expenditure therefore emerges *ex post* as the sum of these individual deals.

By contrast, a 'top-down' approach involves the prior establishment by the finance ministry (usually supported by the president or prime minister) of an overall budgetary ceiling, based on an assessment of the future spending requirements of strategic policy priorities over a number of years. Individual spending bids must be trimmed to fit into this overarching framework. Such a 'top-down' approach should in principle be more transparent. Its corporate nature in principle should also offer greater opportunities for influencing budgetary priorities.

Within the EU, the desire to control inflation and the requirement of the Stability and Growth Pact to limit budget deficits to 3 per cent of GNP, have together led to the adoption of the 'top-down' approach by most Member States and by the EU itself.

The EU's multi-annual financial perspective

The shift towards a 'top-down' approach to budgeting in the EU came with the introduction in 1988 of what was to become known as the 'Multi-annual Financial Perspective'. This sets an overall budgetary ceiling to keep expenditure within the limits of the Community's 'own resources' (see below), and determines financial allocations for the major categories of Community spending, normally over a five- or seven-year period. It thus forms an overarching framework within which the annual budgetary negotiations between the Commission, the Council and the Parliament take place. There have been four EU Financial Perspectives so far: the Delors I package (1988–1992); the 1993–1999 perspective (Delors II); and Agenda 2000 (2000–2006). The current – and fourth – financial perspective (2007–2013) (the 'Prodi Package') was tabled by the Commission in July 2004, and finally agreed by the Council and European Parliament in May 2006.

It has not always been clear what overarching principles and policy strategies are considered in the determination of multi-annual expenditure allocations, what is the machinery through which these decisions are made, and which DGs are involved. In the case of the 'Prodi Package', negotiations were led by the Budgets Commissioner, together with the Commission President and his cabinet. In an internal communication to other Commissioners in February 2003, the Budgets Commissioner proposed that the priorities for what would be the first financial perspective for a Union of 25, should be:

- 'peace' (that is, external relations and development);
- 'freedom' (that is, security, justice, health, consumer protection, the Lisbon Strategy); and
- 'solidarity' (that is, economic and social cohesion).

However, the communication made no specific reference either to the EU's Sustainable Development Strategy or to its most recent environmental policy strategy, the sixth environmental action programme.

A number of working groups, chaired by Commissioners, were established to develop each of these priorities further. Environment policy was subsumed into the working group on cohesion and solidarity, which was inevitably dominated by DG Regional Policy as a result of the size of the Structural Funds. Given DG Environment's traditionally limited budget, it is unlikely that its role was pivotal in these discussions. Moreover, it is also difficult to judge, from the draft Financial Perspective that eventually emerged, what priority was given in practice to environmental spending. The Commission's Communication noted that 'in the area of environment, the bulk of EU action comes through the mainstreaming of the environment into other policies', but the categories as set out are so broad that the extent of likely mainstreaming is unclear. Phrases such as 'sustainable growth' refer not to environmental sustainability, but principally to the Lisbon Process (covering jobs and growth – see Chapter 8) and the Structural Funds, while the 'conservation and management of natural resources' priority is dominated overwhelmingly by spending on the CAP.

In the summer and autumn of 2005, a very public row between the UK and France over the size and distribution of the post-2006 draft financial perspective forced the Commission, backed by the European Parliament, to initiate a fundamental review of EU spending and its sources of revenue. Launching a consultation paper in September 2007 (CEC 2007a), Commission President Barroso promised a 'no taboos' debate and a 'once in a generation opportunity to make a reform of the budget and also a reform of the way we work'. Concrete Commission proposals for long-term budget reform are expected in late 2008. These will then be agreed by the Member States and the European Parliament, and should determine the shape of the post-2013 financial perspective. How radical the outcome of this exercise will be depends on the success of pre-emptive attempts by the big-spending Commission DGs – agriculture and regional policy – to limit the terms of the debate through, respectively, the CAP 'Health Check' and a major public consultation on cohesion policy, both launched in 2007.

Formal Adoption of the Budget

In sovereign states, the formal adoption of the annual budget as a legal instrument is normally undertaken by the national parliament. This can be the occasion for significant amendments, although this depends on the constitutional powers of parliamentarians and the nature of the party system. Parliamentary scrutiny committees can also play a key role in the monitoring and review of the effects and effectiveness of past years' budgetary expenditure.

Greening the EU's budget

In the EU, the formal adoption of the budget is the responsibility of the Council of Ministers and the European Parliament. The Parliament's most extensive and longest-established powers have been in relation to the Community budget. In the final analysis, MEPs can reject the budget in its entirety. This was threatened on several occasions in the 1970s and 1980s.

The European Parliament's negotiations with the Council on the preliminary draft EU budget are led by the Committee on Budgets. All other committees with responsibility for policies that entail spending submit their Opinions to the Budgets Committee, with the latter finally responsible for submitting a draft Opinion for endorsement by the European Parliament meeting in plenary.

In relation to EPI, the extent of the Environment Committee's influence over the Budgets Committee is crucial. In 1995, this relationship was particularly close, partly as a result of the appointment to the Budgets Committee of the former Director-General of DG Environment, who had been elected an MEP in 1994. The Budgets Committee and the Environment Committee were jointly responsible for a remarkable process of 'greening' the 1996 EU budget, which paved the way for a similar exercise in 2000 in relation to the new wave of Structural Funds programmes for 2000–2006. In fact, the Environment Committee's rapporteur in 1995 on the budget later became the chairman of the Environment Committee in 2004.

The Environment Committee's key amendment to the draft 1996 budget threatened to put into reserve 50 per cent of the funds for the Structural and Cohesion Funds unless DG Regional Policy produced, by a given deadline, an environmental Code of Conduct governing the future use of the funds. This included the requirement for the proper environmental appraisal, monitoring and *ex post* evaluation of the environmental impacts of projects and programmes, and regular reporting to the Parliament and Council. This gained the support of the Parliament's Committee on Budgets, and as a direct result (and very rapidly), the Commission responded by:

- issuing a Communication jointly authored by the Regional Policy and Environment Commissioners entitled *Cohesion Policy and the Environment* – promising a ten-point plan for tightening environmental requirements in the use of the Structural Funds;
- writing a Letter of Intent from the Regional Affairs and the Budgets Commissioners to the chairs of the Parliament's Environment and

Budgets Committees with a further range of promises in respect of environmental integration; and

- producing a statement in the 1996 budget alongside the budget lines dealing with both the Structural Funds and the Cohesion Fund to the effect that 'appropriations for the Structural Funds cannot be implemented unless the measures financed by these Funds comply with the provisions of the Treaties and acts pursuant thereto, in particular those concerning environmental protection'.

The momentum was maintained in the following year in respect of the preliminary draft budget for 1997. The Environment and Budgets Committees organised a Joint Hearing in July 1996 at which the Commissioners for Agriculture, Transport and Energy were questioned on their proposals for mainstreaming environmental concerns in their activities.

Later – in March 2000 – as a result of sustained pressure from the Environment and Budgets Committees, the Commission made it clear to Member States that Structural Funds money would be forthcoming only if full lists of their proposed sites under the Habitats and Birds Directives were submitted by Member States. The Environment and Regional Policy Commissioners issued a joint letter to all Member States warning that the proper planning and implementation of new Structural Funds programmes was not possible in the absence of incomplete information on proposed Natura 2000 sites. A similar example of 'external conditionality' came from the Agriculture Commissioner in respect of compliance with the Nitrates Directive.

Implementation of the Budget

The horizontal integration of the environment into spending programmes at the level of central government is a necessary but not entirely sufficient condition for securing green objectives on the ground, where of course the money is spent. This is because the control of spending may be decentralised to subordinate levels of government or deconcentrated to autonomous agencies. Decentralised and deconcentrated spending present both challenges and opportunities for EPI. Instruments need to be in place to influence the pattern of such devolved expenditure – and nowhere is this more apparent than in the case of the EU.

Budget implementation in the EU
As much as 80 per cent of EU expenditure is actually spent by the governments of Member States or by regional and local authorities and partnerships – and there may be considerable discretion in how they spend it. Over

the past 20 years, an increasingly diverse range of controls has been introduced by the Commission to govern decentralised expenditure. This has been driven mainly by the need to ensure financial accountability and policy effectiveness, but among the array of required conditions, structures and procedures, a number have been introduced intended to safeguard or advance the EU's environmental policy priorities. The effectiveness of these controls ultimately depends on the political will of the Commission, and the extent of its available resources for monitoring and enforcement. Ironically, the more extensive the requirements for programming, control, monitoring, reporting and evaluation in relation to spending programmes, the more they may run counter to the prevailing political agenda in the EU, which emphasises better regulation, simplification and decentralisation.

Several key instruments are employed to control decentralised EU expenditure. Firstly, there is the 'external' sanction of conditionality. The Commission has used the threat of withholding EU funding altogether from individual Member States, in an attempt to secure EU policy objectives which may not necessarily be directly related to the expenditure in question. One example is the requirement that eligible Member States wishing to benefit from the Cohesion Fund should adhere to the Stability Pact and ensure that their public sector borrowing remains below the 3 per cent threshold. In relation to the Structural Funds and support under the Rural Development Regulation, the Commissioners for Regional Policy and Agriculture jointly informed Member States in 2000 that funding would be dependent on their compliance with key items of EU environmental legislation, including the Habitats and Nitrates Directives. As a direct result, the submission by Member States of their proposed lists of Natura 2000 protected areas to the Commission was greatly accelerated.

The Commission has not used 'external' conditionality that widely. For example, no such conditions had ever been imposed in respect of European Agricultural Guidance and Guarantee Fund (EAGGF) transfers, although this changed following the mid-term review of the CAP in 2003 that introduced 'cross-compliance'. This partly reflected the argument that it was unfair to penalise groups of potential recipients of EU funding (for example, farmers, regions or industries) for the implementation failures of their governments. Moreover, in practice it is doubtful whether the Commission would have the will to block funding indefinitely, since a major imperative for the DGs for Regional Policy and Agriculture is to be seen to be spending the large sums of money allocated to them in the EU budget.

Second, there has been a requirement to produce national and regional strategies and programmes. The introduction (from 1988) of operational programmes in contrast to a multitude of separate projects as the focus of EU structural funding, gave the Commission more leverage over the way in which Member States spent EU funds. However, programmes were still initiated by the Member States, essentially on the basis of their own national development priorities. The Commission's influence over the content of national programmes was further strengthened under Structural Funds Regulations for the period 2007–2013. For the first time, the Commission issued legally binding guidelines – the EU Strategic Cohesion Guidelines and the EU Rural Development Guidelines – which are intended to reflect the EU's policy priorities as set out in the Lisbon Strategy on growth and competitiveness. Member States have been required to respect the EU Guidelines in drawing up their National Strategic Reference Frameworks, which in turn set the framework for operational programmes at national or regional levels.

Thirdly, in relation to the existing Structural Fund Regulations, administrative structures and procedures have to be put in place in the Member States in order to manage spending. These incorporate a number of control mechanisms that constrain the discretion of national governments and give the Commission a number of opportunities to influence how the funds are spent. These include:

- the establishment of regional 'partnerships' of public authorities and relevant stakeholders to whom the management, monitoring and evaluation of Structural Fund spending is devolved;
- the inclusion in these partnerships of environmental (and other) authorities; and
- the establishment of Programme Monitoring Committees (PMCs) to oversee the implementation of programmes on which members of the partnership – and the Commission – are to be represented.

Fourthly, where Member States make EU payments to individual beneficiaries (for example, farmers), EU legislation specifies detailed requirements in relation to national systems of monitoring and control. For example, in relation to payments to farmers under the Guarantee section of the EAGGF, or in respect of 'cross-compliance' with environmental standards, Member States are required to:

- ensure regular reporting by individual farmers to the national Paying Agency;
- inspect regularly a control sample of at least 1 per cent of recipients; and
- employ aerial surveillance techniques using GIS technology.

Failure by Member States to apply such systems can lead to the recovery of funds by the Commission.

Fifthly, direct Commission intervention in the Member States to ensure that money is being spent appropriately, or that EU Regulations are being respected, can occur but is very politically sensitive. However, the Commission has the right to undertake on-the-spot checks of projects, or to undertake monitoring missions to the Member States, if there is a suspicion that national control arrangements are inadequate or are not being applied effectively. Such checks and missions average approximately 200 per year in relation to EAGGF spending, and over 20 a year in respect of Cohesion Fund projects. At the same time, the Commission has sought to develop with the Member States a more collaborative approach to inspection and control. For example, in order to improve controls on overfishing and fleet overcapacity, the Community Fisheries Control Agency will take active steps (for example, through training) to strengthen and co-ordinate national fisheries inspection systems, and participate directly with the Member States in joint control activities. On subsidiarity grounds, this is obviously easier to justify in relation to fisheries – where several Member States have a common interest – than in relation to farming practices within an individual Member State.

Sixthly, in addition to monitoring and inspection, there are financial incentives attached to EPI. In respect of the Structural Funds, programme managing authorities have discretion to increase the rate of support of EU funding to particular projects which demonstrate particular benefits, including significant contributions to environmental protection. Technical assistance can also be used to appoint 'environmental sustainability managers' to raise awareness among project proposers. At EU level, the Commission retains a significant proportion of the total Structural Funds budget (4 per cent) as a 'performance reserve' to be distributed to Member States as a reward for good practice following the mid-term review of programmes. Performance in relation to 'mainstreaming' the environment throughout all activities supported by the funds can be one criterion the Commission takes into account, although this appears not to have played an important role in the mid-term review of 2000–2006 programmes.

Finally, all Structural Fund and Rural Development programmes are subject to *ex ante*, mid-term and *ex post* evaluations, which should be conducted according to detailed Commission guidelines and should include an assessment of environmental impacts. In principle, *ex ante* evaluations should provide an opportunity to improve programmes from an environmental perspective. But hitherto, the quality of evaluations has been variable and they have often been undertaken as an afterthought rather than as an integral part of programme development. The political will of the

Commission to insist on better assessments in negotiating draft programmes has also been variable.

In addition to undertaking evaluations, a range of other reporting
requirements apply at various levels of decision making. Project managers
must submit reports every quarter to the managing authority, which in turn
must submit an Annual Implementation Report to the Commission. The
Commission then has to report regularly to the Council and European
Parliament. In practice, most of these reports focus on immediate project
and programme outputs (that is, what has been spent, on what measures),
rather than results and environmental impacts.

Monitoring, Evaluation and Reporting

Ex ante and *ex post* monitoring, evaluation and reporting are critical stages
in the overall green budgeting 'life cycle'. Appropriate monitoring procedures establish an *ex ante* baseline against which progress can be measured
through *ex post* evaluation. When properly integrated into evaluations,
reporting can provide transparency to the evaluation, while helping guide
future budgetary adjustment. To this end, the EU has a well-established
system for measuring progress within its budget procedures.

Evaluating EU expenditure: 'activity-based budgeting'
Evaluating EU expenditure is conducted through Activity-Based
Budgeting (ABB). The Financial Regulation requires both *ex ante* and
ex post evaluations of all EU programmes and activities requiring
significant spending. Results are used to inform decision making in the
annual preliminary draft budget. *Ex ante* evaluations should specify several
criteria relating to the proposal: its short- and long-term needs, its objectives, the Community 'added value', its cost-effectiveness and its monitoring procedures. *Ex post* evaluations should measure results against the
actual objectives. To this end, DGs are required to establish an evaluation
'function' or unit.

Despite these requirements, DGs enjoy considerable discretion in relation to the number and scope of evaluations they undertake. The approach
adopted is primarily 'bottom-up', with DGs supposed to learn from
each other through an evaluation network. Results published in the
Commission's *Annual Evaluation Review* for 2006, however, show that evaluation is not fully embedded in the Commission's management practices
(CEC 2007b). In 2006, the 235 completed evaluations (both *ex post* and
ex ante) covered, fully or partially, only 32 per cent of the 207 ABB activities in the budget, and only a proportion of these covered expenditure programmes. Other identified concerns relate to the need for more resources,

greater consistency in evaluations, strengthening of monitoring and better use of results in informing ABB.

Raising Revenue

All jurisdictions are reliant on revenue for their continued existence, but the EU remains unique when compared to national governments. As a trade-based international organisation, it is heavily reliant on various funding sources to finance its activities. This structure of revenue raising presents both opportunities and constraints to EPI.

The EU's 'own resources'

Revenue raising by the EU occurs through what is termed its 'own resources', although Member State sensitivity over direct taxation means that the availability of these resources remains somewhat constrained. Originally introduced in 1970, the current 'own resources' system is limited in terms of revenue raising to 1.24 per cent of EU Gross National Income. Revenues are derived from three sources. Firstly, 'Traditional own resources' are customs duties derived from the EU common external tariff and agricultural import levies. Secondly, the EU levies value-added tax across Member States. Thirdly, there are contributions from Member States, calculated on the basis of national GNI, which help 'top up' the EU budget. While for Member State governments, direct taxation is the largest source of revenue, it is not a contributor to the EU's 'own resources'.

What then, is the potential for integrating the environment into EU revenue raising? Making better use of environmental taxes coincides with the 'polluter pays' principle and therefore could, at the EU level, have positive environmental implications. The Commission has identified several additional revenue streams which could supplement the EU's 'own resources', including three environment-related areas: a CO_2/energy tax; excise duties on mineral oil and/or tobacco and alcohol; and a 'communication' tax on transport and telecommunications services (CEC 2004a). Additionally, opportunities for changes to VAT revenue raising, taxing corporate income and energy taxation have been discussed (CEC 2004b). Other revenues could be raised from an EU levy on aviation fuel or related emissions. The EU could also derive revenue from the market-based environmental policy instrument of emissions trading through auctioning future allowances.

Yet significant constraints exist on changing EU revenue raising in these environmentally positive ways, emanating primarily from national sensitivities on taxation matters. Since assigning a new resource to the EU budget requires both unanimity in the Council and ratification by all Member State parliaments, it remains problematic to introduce such initiatives. Of the specific new sources of revenue mentioned, an EU CO_2/energy tax seems unlikely given the withdrawal of previous proposals and the implementation of the energy products tax directive. Using this directive and raising taxes on fuels and electricity above the minimum rates would be an option, but would place a heavy burden on the transport sector in particular. Taxing kerosene use in aviation could potentially raise significant revenue, but barriers exist because airline companies can avoid such taxes.

SUMMARY DISCUSSION

Green Budgeting in the EU

Evidence from the EU broadly reflects the main trends detected in the other jurisdictions surveyed above: although EPI is visible at different stages, it is occurring in a too ad hoc and uncoordinated a manner to have much impact. As such, the coherent integration of environmental considerations throughout all elements of the budgetary 'life cycle' is not happening.

At the strategic level, the 'top-down' Multi-annual Financial Perspective potentially provides a powerful instrument for EPI. Since it forms a long-term, overarching frame within which budgetary negotiations take place, the integration of environmental considerations at this stage can provide a strategic steer over all EU expenditure. Despite the EU's legal commitments to EPI and sustainable development, neither forms the framing *Zeitgeist* of the Perspective. Although the prospect of opening up the financial framework process during the 2008/9 review of the EU budget provides a unique occasion to address this issue, it is uncertain whether the European Parliament will seize the opportunity to press for a greater environmental emphasis in the immediate future.

The adoption of the Annual Budget provides another access point for EPI. Here, the Parliament's Environment Committee (working with other committees) has an opportunity to scrutinise the draft budget for the following year. A range of instruments have also been introduced for controlling decentralised EU expenditure which, on paper, could help EPI.

In addition, the EU's experiences demonstrate the extent to which monitoring, evaluation and reporting can aid EPI as well as improve the transparency of green budgeting. In theory, the EU's approach (employing *ex ante* and *ex post* evaluations in ABB) can significantly enhance EPI by identifying instances of poor performance. It also allows both internal and external scrutiny. Yet one weakness is the semi-voluntary nature of the reporting, with the sectoral DGs given considerable discretion to determine the information they provide. A result has been significant variation in the quality of reporting and consequently a lack of understanding of progress in implementing EPI. One clear message which emerges from our analysis is that there is an urgent need for more systematic reporting that links into the wider budgeting 'life cycle'.

Finally, the EU has at its disposal several potentially powerful mechanisms for integrating the environment into its 'own resources' revenue raising. Most promising is the ability to employ green taxes, VAT receipts, levies and carbon trading. While these possibilities have been explored, a conspicuous constraint on their implementation is national opposition to fiscal measures at EU level. Although there appear to be considerable opportunities for green revenue raising, they may be very difficult to exploit in practice.

Critical Questions

Having looked at the integration of environmental concerns into budgeting activities at the national and EU levels: (i) what can be said about the practice of green budgeting? and (ii) what does this analysis reveal about the framework used? In relation to the first question, several points can be made. Firstly, greening the budget is a complex process involving horizontal integration of environmental objectives into centralised decision making on strategic spending priorities. Environmental objectives should also be vertically integrated in relation to spending by decentralised or deconcentrated authorities. Secondly, as discussed, EPI is then required at each stage of a multi-stage budgetary cycle. Thirdly, a broad range of EPI mechanisms exist for this purpose. These include making spending conditional on the fulfilment of environmental conditions (for example, 'cross-compliance'), promoting policy learning through impact assessment and reporting, and enhancing transparency through raising awareness among the environmental NGOs. Fourthly, a lesson from the EU and Norway is that integration depends on which departments control environment-related spending. As in most national governments, the environment ministry (in the case of the EU, DG Environment) does not control large environmental funds. Strategic decisions are largely taken by finance ministries, and environment-related spending is undertaken by non-environmental departments, such as DG Agriculture in the EU. Fifthly, another lesson from the EU is that parliaments can be a crucial force for EPI through their role in formally endorsing the annual budget, and in scrutinising the effects and effectiveness of past expenditure. The role of the UK's Parliamentary Environmental Audit Committee is worthy of mention in this regard, providing a potential model for other systems to consider. Sixthly, where spending is devolved to subordinate levels of government or agencies, an array of monitoring, reporting and auditing requirements is available which can help to secure EPI objectives. Seventhly, current monitoring and evaluation requirements in relation to spending programmes tend to focus on the rectitude of spending outputs, to the exclusion of outcomes and impacts (particularly environmental). Finally, there is a significant but as yet largely unfulfilled potential to utilise revenue raising to facilitate EPI.

In relation to the second question, the 'life cycle' framework in Figure 4.1 appears to have considerable value for guiding research into the use of green budgeting as an instrument of EPI. It provides a useful yardstick to measure the growth of green budgeting on a global scale. The framework can be used to undertake comparative studies which contrast the relative strengths and weaknesses of green budgeting in different contexts and thus provide a potentially important instrument for policy learning and transfer. It also helps identify specific challenges and opportunities within budgeting strategies, providing a measure of progress towards EPI. Using such information, the framework can help to structure a more intensive academic and political debate over the future of green budgeting and, in consequence, be employed to (re)design strategies to better account for EPI.

CONCLUSIONS

Public expenditure exerts a powerful hold over environmental quality, in terms of both benefits and impacts. Consideration of environmental concerns in budgeting strategies is therefore a critical factor in promoting sustainable development at all levels of governance. Moreover, an argument presented in this chapter is that budgeting decisions should not be viewed in isolation. Rather, they are the sum of previous decisions, which should be integrated into a holistic and constantly adapted 'life cycle'. Successful green budgeting can only be conceptualised in these terms.

In view of this argument, this chapter has constructed an analytical 'life cycle' model, which was then applied to different empirical examples of green budgeting. Although this helped identify some general trends, greater in-depth analysis of green budgeting deployment is needed to provide deeper insights into what facilitates or retards its use as an instrument of EPI. Some points, however, are apparent regarding EPI. Most significantly, few jurisdictions have considered (let alone implemented) green budgeting in the comprehensive manner suggested by Brundtland and Agenda 21.

Even in the EU, which in many respects provides a 'best practice' example, green budgeting suffers from several weaknesses. Yet significant opportunities exist for promoting EPI through budgeting procedures. In this sense, the 'life cycle' model has great potential as a way of framing future research in this fast expanding but as yet too little studied area of environmental and sustainable development policy.

BIBLIOGRAPHY

Andrews, R.N.L. (2006), *Managing the Environment, Managing Ourselves* (Second Edition), New Haven: Yale University Press.

CEC (2004a), *Communication on the Implementation of the 2003–05 Broad Economic Policy Guidelines*, COM (2004) 20, 21.1.2004, Brussels: Commission of the European Communities.

CEC (2004b), *Building Our Common Future: Policy Challenges and Budgetary Means of the Enlarged Union, 2007–2013*, COM (2004) 101, 26.02.04, Brussels: Commission of the European Communities.

CEC (2007a), *Reforming the Budget, Changing Europe: A Public Consultation Paper in View of the 2008/9 Budget Review*, SEC (2007) 1188, 12.9.2007, Brussels: Commission of the European Communities.

CEC (2007b), *Directorate-General for the Budget, Evaluation in the Commission: Reporting on Results – Annual Evaluation Review 2006*, Brussels: Commission of the European Communities.

Enderlein, H. and Lindner, J. (2006), 'The EU budgetary procedure in the constitutional debate', in J. Richardson (ed.), *European Union: Power and Policy-Making* (Third Edition), London: Routledge.

Haigh, N. (2005), *Manual of Environmental Policy: The EU and Britain*, London: Maney Publishing and Institute for European Environmental Policy.

Jordan, A., Wurzel, R.K.W., Zito A. and Brückner, L. (2003), 'Policy innovation or "muddling through"? "New" environmental policy instruments in the United Kingdom', in A. Jordan, R. Wurzel and A. Zito (eds), *'New' Instruments of Environmental Governance?* London: Frank Cass.

Judge, D. and Earnshaw D. (2003), *The European Parliament*, Basingstoke: Palgrave.

Lenschow, A. (1999), 'The greening of the EU: the Common Agricultural Policy and the Structural Funds', *Environment and Planning C: Government and Policy*, 17 (1), 91–108.

OECD/EEA (2005), *OECD/EEA Database on Instruments Used in Environmental Policy*, Paris: OECD. Available at: http://www2.oecd.org/ecoinst/queries/index.htm (Accessed 12 October 2007).

Russel, D. (2005), *Environmental Policy Appraisal in UK Central Government: A Political Analysis*, unpublished doctoral thesis, Norwich: University of East Anglia.

United Nations (1992), *United Nations Conference on Environment and Development: Agenda 21*, New York: United Nations. Available at: http://www.un.org/esa/sustdev/documents/agenda21/index.htm (Accessed 12 October 2007).

WCED (World Commission on Environment and Development) (1987), *Our Common Future*, Oxford: Oxford University Press.

Wilkinson, D. (1997), 'Towards sustainability in the European Union? Steps within the European Commission towards integrating the environment into other European Union policy sectors', in T. O'Riordan and H. Voisey (eds), *Sustainable Development in Western Europe: Coming to Terms with Agenda 21*, London: Frank Cass.

5. Sustainable development strategies

Reinhard Steurer

INTRODUCTION

EPI and sustainable development are two related concepts that have developed in parallel rather than together. The relationship between them puzzles both academics and practitioners alike (see, for example, Chapter 1 and European Environment Agency 2005b). Sustainable development strategies are strategic processes that are relevant to EPI because they aim to balance the economic, social and environmental dimensions of policy making. Both constructs are mainly concerned with how better to integrate policies across sectors. However, EPI is mainly concerned with ensuring that environmental protection is factored into all governmental decision making, whereas sustainable development is concerned with balancing economic, social and environmental issues. Chapter 1 has already addressed the tensions between the two concepts – as well as the general discourse on EPI and sustainable development – centring on priority setting. In fact, from an environmental point of view, this quest for 'balance' may appear as a conceptual justification for the dilution of environmental factors.

The question explored in this chapter is how sustainable development strategies affect the quest for EPI. We address the relationship both conceptually (regarding the idea of policy integration in sustainable development strategies in general) and in practice. Conceptually, sustainable development strategies are supposed to facilitate greater policy integration across policy sectors, spatial scales, societal sectors and time. However, this chapter also shows that, for various reasons, sustainable development strategies often fall short of these aspirations in practice.

Sustainable development strategies have witnessed a relatively rapid diffusion within the last decade (Busch and Jörgens 2005) so that nowadays, they exist at all levels of governance, from the EU (European Council 2001; European Council 2006) to the national (Steurer and Martinuzzi 2005; Volkery *et al.* 2006), regional and municipal (Berger and Steurer 2008). This chapter focuses on national sustainable development strategies in Europe. It is divided into the following sections. Section 2 provides a brief history of sustainable development strategies. Section 3 describes how sustainable development and sustainable development strategies address the notion of policy integration, and explains how both relate to the concept of EPI. Section 4 gives an overview of the policy integration instruments and mechanisms that are facilitated by sustainable development strategies (hereafter, we refer to them as strategy features) and briefly reviews how each is performing. The summary discussion in Section 5 addresses how effectively sustainable development strategies facilitate EPI. It concludes with the observation that high-level political commitment and administrative ownership are important ingredients for success, but both remain only weakly present in many European countries.

HISTORY

A key driver for introducing sustainable development strategies in Europe was the global environmental governance regime agreed at the 1992 Rio Earth Summit. Among the numerous sets of policy actions asked for in Agenda 21 (UNCED 1992a, Chapter 8) was one about adopting 'a national strategy for sustainable development'. By specifying the purpose of sustainable development strategies, Agenda 21 clearly refers to the classic Brundtlandian definition of sustainable development (see Chapter 1). Country-driven sustainable development strategies should, it claims, 'ensure socially responsible economic development while protecting the resource base and the environment for the benefit of future generations' (UNCED 1992a: para. 8.7). As Agenda 21 contains no submission date, only a few countries (notably the UK, Finland and Ireland) developed a sustainable development strategy in the 1990s. The rest already had (or were still working on) a national environmental policy plan, and assumed that this would suffice. However, since most environmental plans facilitate the old pattern of more-or-less top-down policy planning in a single policy field, they did not satisfy Agenda 21's new demand for 'a coordinated, participatory and iterative process of thoughts and actions to achieve economic, environmental and social objectives in a balanced and integrated manner' (UNDESA 2001: 8).

In June 1997, the Rio +5 summit agreed that the formulation of sustainable development strategies ought to be completed in all countries by the year 2002 (UNGASS 1997: para. 24). In June 2001, the Gothenburg European Council reiterated this call by inviting its 'Member States to draw up their own national sustainable development strategies' (European Council 2001: 4). Consequently, most EU Member States developed their sustainable development strategy rather quickly in time for the

Johannesburg World Summit for sustainable development in late 2002 (European Commission 2004; Steurer and Martinuzzi 2005). Thus, the Gothenburg European Council proved to be another major driver towards the development of sustainable development strategies in Europe, as well as various EPI initiatives within the EU (see Chapter 8).

In order to ensure that sustainable development strategies did not simply collect dust on shelves like most of the earlier environmental plans (Dalal-Clayton and Bass 2000: 20; Meadowcroft 2000: 122; IIED, UNDP and UKDFID 2002: 1), the UN and the OECD formulated sets of guidelines. Taken together, these characterize the content and governance processes of sustainable development strategies as follows (UNCED 1992a: chapter 8A; OECD-DAC 2001: 18ff; UNDESA 2001; IIED 2002: 33–36). The content should: (i) build upon existing policies, strategies and plans; (ii) be based on sound analyses of economic and environmental data; (iii) provide a long-term vision; (iv) integrate economic, social and environmental policies; and (v) provide clear, achievable objectives. The process of developing and implementing them should: (i) be transparent; (ii) build on trustful partnerships and 'the widest possible participation' (UNCED 1992a); (iii) link national and local levels, for example, by decentralizing detailed planning, implementation and monitoring; (iv) incorporate various assessment mechanisms; (v) be flexible; (vi) be backed by adequate institutional capacities and by high-level political commitment; (vii) provide clear schedules of implementation; and (viii) develop priorities and objectives to be followed in the budgetary process.[1]

According to the IIED's resource book for sustainable development strategies:

> Being strategic is about developing an underlying vision through a consensual, effective and iterative process; and going on to set objectives, identify the means of achieving them, and then monitor that achievement as a guide to the next round of this learning process. . . . More important than trying unsuccessfully to do everything at once, is to ensure that incremental steps in policy making and action are moving towards sustainability – rather than away from it, which is too frequently the case (IIED 2002: 29).

Overall, the guidelines describe sustainable development strategies as continuing strategic processes that combine aspects of formal planning and incremental learning, and that put strong emphasis on the procedural and institutional aspects of policy making (Steurer and Martinuzzi 2005). Thus sustainable development strategies 'move from developing and implementing a fixed plan, which gets increasingly out of date . . . towards operating an adaptive system that can continuously improve' (IIED 2002: 29).

Table 5.1   *Four integrative governance challenges for sustainable development*

Aspects of integration	Elements to integrate	SD governance principles
Policy sectors	Economic, social and environmental policies	Cross-sectoral (horizontal) integration/EPI
Space	Local, national and supra-national (European) levels of policy making	Cross-jurisdictional (vertical) integration
Societal sectors	State and civil society; (hierarchies and networks)	Participation
Time	Short- and long-term temporal scopes	Intergenerational equity

CONCEPTUAL BACKGROUND

A closer look at Agenda 21 (UNCED 1992a) reveals that the concept of sustainable development is a normative reform agenda not only for economic, social and environmental policies (or the integration thereof), but also for public governance and administration routines. The concept of sustainable development is concerned with the 'what' and the 'how' of public policies, and the underlying institutional structures and decision-making processes (OECD 2001; OECD 2002; World Bank 2003; European Commission 2004; European Commission 2005; Sneddon *et al.* 2006). In this sense, sustainable development puts strong emphasis on the challenge of policy integration in not one, but four related respects: policy sectors; space; societal sectors; and time (see Table 5.1). The principles agreed at Rio (see for example UNCED 1992b; OECD 2002: 11–30; Jänicke and Jörgens 2004: 307) were also reflected in the *Declaration on Guiding Principles for Sustainable Development*, which was drafted by the European Commission (2005) and later included in the renewed EU sustainable development strategy (European Council 2006). The remainder of this section explores these four integration challenges in more detail.

Integrating Sectoral Policies within Governments

The Brundtland Report famously recognized that the cross-cutting challenges of sustainable development are handled by institutions that tend to be 'independent, fragmented and working to relatively narrow mandates with closed decision-making processes' (WCED 1987: 310; see also

Chapter 3). Similarly, Agenda 21 pointed out that 'prevailing systems of decision-making in many countries tend to separate economic, social and environmental factors at the policy, planning and management levels' (UNCED 1992a: para. 8.2). Consequently, Agenda 21 requested that 'Governments . . . should strengthen national institutional capability and capacity to integrate social, economic, developmental and environmental issues at all levels of developmental decision-making and implementation' (UNCED 1992a: para. 8.12). More than a decade later, the quest to integrate different sectoral policies better seems to be more relevant than ever before.

This challenge has been addressed in a number of ways:

- in terms of the 'triple bottom line', as 'corporate sustainability' (Dyllick and Hockerts 2002) and as 'corporate social responsibility (CSR)' (ISO Advisory Group 2004) among management scholars (for a discussion of how these concepts are related to sustainable development, see Steurer *et al.* 2005: 272–276);
- as horizontal government, horizontal integration or coordination in the discourse on new aspects of public governance (Peters 1998; Steurer and Martinuzzi 2005);
- as 'coherence' in the European Commission's (2001a: 10) account of good governance, which was reiterated as one of ten 'policy guiding principles' in the renewed EU sustainable development strategy (European Council 2006: 5);
- as 'joined-up government' in the UK (Cabinet Office 2000; Jordan 2002; Ling 2002).

In accordance with Agenda 21, integrating economic, social and environmental policies plays a central role in both the guidelines for sustainable development strategies (UNDESA 2001; OECD-DAC 2001) and in most strategy processes. Regarding the strategy documents themselves, virtually all of them cover the three widely accepted dimensions of sustainable development in a balanced but not fully intertwined way (European Commission 2004: 12–17).[2] This means that the documents focus not only on environmental issues and their relationship to other policy fields (as environmental plans did and still do), but also on economic and social issues such as competitiveness, budget deficits and gender equality. Although in most countries the environment ministry coordinates the strategy process, all relevant ministries are usually involved in developing and implementing the strategy objectives (for strategy features addressing this challenge, see below).

Integrating Policies across Jurisdictions

Particular policy problems such as climate change or biodiversity not only transcend the competencies of ministries within a particular government, but also the vertical tiers of different jurisdictions. Crucially, 'the sphere of competence of authorities in charge of environmental protection or environmentally relevant matters does not always match with the boundaries of the affected environment' (Liberatore 1997: 116). Accordingly, the EU's *Declaration on Guiding Principles for Sustainable Development* (European Commission 2005: 5; European Council 2005: 30) that was incorporated in the renewed EU sustainable development strategy (European Council 2006: 2–6), also emphasizes the need to 'promote coherence between all European Union policies and coherence between local, regional, national and global actions in order to enhance their contribution to sustainable development'.

While the UN and OECD guidelines for sustainable development strategies and the sustainable development governance literature discuss the need for cross-jurisdictional policy integration, the EPI literature generally pays little attention to multi-level challenges (but see Jordan and Schout 2006). This variable focus becomes even more visible when one looks at the way EPI scholars understand the concept of vertical (environmental) policy integration. Whereas the sustainable development literature uses the term to refer to cross-jurisdictional policy integration (Jänicke *et al.* 2001; OECD 2002; European Commission 2004), the EPI literature often uses it to refer to policy integration within the purview of an individual ministry, for example, through sectoral sustainable development strategies (Lafferty 2002; Jacob and Volkery 2004; Jänicke and Jörgens 2004).

Integrating Stakeholders into Governmental Policies

The concept of sustainable development is widely acknowledged as an evolving normative model which different societies are expected to define for themselves in a deliberative and consensual manner (Reid 1995: 58; Smith 1996: 43; Rao 2000). Thus, virtually all sustainable development policy documents and strategy guidelines emphasize that '[o]ne of the fundamental prerequisites for the achievement of sustainable development is broad public participation in decision-making' (UNCED 1992a: para. 23.2). Participation is supposed to assist in at least three ways. First, it should help define the objectives of sustainable development in the first place. Second, the reconciliation of different interests in participatory arrangements should help to integrate economic, social and environmental policies. Third, integrating business and civil society stakeholders in decision making should spread and enhance the ownership of sustainable development policies in societies.

From a governance perspective, participation implies that traditional patterns of governance (most often dominated by hierarchical bureaucracies) become more open, and often linked with new, network-like arrangements. Because of the clear guidelines on participation (see above), virtually all sustainable development strategy processes in Europe try to involve civil society and business stakeholders, for example in dialogue conferences or in National Councils for Sustainable Development (NCSD).

Integrating Short- and Long-Term Perspectives

Since sustainable development seeks to balance the needs of the current generation with those in the future, the concept is essentially about the integration of a short- and long-term timescale in policy making (UNCED 1992b; OECD 2001; OECD 2002: 10; WSSD 2002: para. 26). This challenge is particularly demanding because it touches on one of the key weaknesses of Western governments, namely that their focus on short-term electoral cycles often undermines long-term decision making (at least in policy fields like the environment which do not rank that high on the political agenda) (OECD 2002: 30). Consequently, sustainable development strategies tend to have a different (that is, more symbolic) function for politicians than for administrators (for further details, see the concluding section).

DEPLOYMENT: PRACTICAL EXPERIENCES[3]

Thus far, we have argued that, unlike many of the other instruments covered in this part of the book, a sustainable development strategy does not have a clearly defined place in the policy cycle. Instead, it is a holistic attempt to reshape disjointed and incremental policy making for sustainable development into a better-integrated and systematic process so that policy making conforms with the four integrative challenges described above. By doing so, a sustainable development strategy should provide a normative sense of direction regarding both the substance and the process of policy. Regarding substance, it should identify and affirm the long-term priorities of sustainable development policies in the light of complex cross-sectoral interdependencies, trade-offs and synergies. In procedural terms, sustainable development strategies ought to introduce and orchestrate a broad variety of instruments and mechanisms (or 'strategy features') in a systematic way. This section gives a brief overview of some noteworthy strategy features in Europe.

Integrating Different Timescales

Bringing a longer-term perspective into everyday policy making is one of the key purposes of sustainable development strategies (IIED 2002: 6). The long-term focus is particularly obvious in the Netherlands. The Dutch sustainable development strategy process is framed in line with the so-called transitions management approach, which aims at a long-term transition of various environmentally relevant sectors towards sustainability (Rotmans *et al.* 2001). Other sustainable development strategies employ concrete mechanisms that link long-term visions (that often resemble vague desires rather then concrete policy objectives) (European Commission 2004) directly with short- and medium-term actions. In Austria, Ireland, Norway and Slovakia, for example, the implementation of the sustainable development strategy depends largely on the development of cyclical action programmes. The purpose of these programmes is to break down the rather general objectives of the strategy into concrete steps for relevant ministries to take.

In Austria, the creation of the working programmes was a continuous process, in which the members of the inter-ministerial committee for sustainable development were encouraged to file into a central database details of projects and measures that were in line with the objectives of the sustainable development strategy. At the end of each biennial cycle, the committee derived the consolidated work programme from the database and submitted it to the Council of Ministers for approval. Although the working programme mechanism enhanced both the implementation of the strategy and the inter-ministerial collaboration, the Austrian example shows that it can easily fail to involve reluctant (but key) ministries such as finance (Martinuzzi and Steurer 2003, 2005). In Denmark, Finland and Sweden, non-environmental ministries are required to develop sectoral sustainable development strategies in which they should demonstrate how they plan to translate the sustainable development strategy into practice (Jacob and Volkery 2004: 298ff). Since 2005, all UK government departments and their executive agencies have been required to develop sustainable development action plans (Russel 2007). These plans resemble a mixture of sustainable development working programmes and sectoral strategies, and thus address the temporal and the sectoral aspects of integration.

Integrating Stakeholders into Governmental Policies

Based on the assumption that stakeholder participation aims to reconcile conflicting interests and, in turn, facilitate policy integration across sectors, participatory mechanisms complement traditional patterns of governance in virtually all sustainable development strategy processes. In accordance with UN and OECD recommendations, many European countries have an NCSD or an equivalent institution in place (European Environment Agency 2005a: 29; Niestroy 2005). NCSDs typically bring together business leaders, academics and NGO representatives in order to discuss sustainable development policies and advise governments on sustainable development-related issues. Finland and some Eastern European countries have so-called mixed councils in which high-level politicians interact with stakeholders directly (the Finnish Council, headed by the Prime Minister until April 2007, is widely regarded as a good practice example in terms of political relevance) (European Environment Agency 2005a: 29 and 37; Berger and Steurer 2006c). Although some of the councils were established well before the appearance of sustainable development strategies, many of them were established in relation to them.

Integrating Policies across Jurisdictions

When it comes to the cross-jurisdictional aspect of policy integration, it is hard to overlook the fact that most sustainable development strategies acknowledge this challenge as important, but it is hardly tackled by any strategy features. Although many sustainable development strategies refer to regions as an important level for the delivery of sustainable development policies and the regionalization of the national strategy, the actual linkages between local and regional sustainable development policies on the one hand and national sustainable development strategies on the other are – with a few exceptions such as Switzerland – generally weak. Many countries, for example, have Local Agenda 21 initiatives at municipal and regional levels that are linked hardly at all to sustainable development strategies, although the latter could provide valuable guidance for these bottom-up activities (Berger and Steurer 2008). The fact that the linkage between national sustainable development strategies and EU policy making is also rather weak may be because, until the adoption of a revised EU sustainable development strategy in June 2006, there was no politically accepted EU strategy for sustainable development in place.[4] However, the new strategy encourages these actors to undertake future reviews of sustainable development strategies in the light of the renewed EU strategy 'to ensure consistency, coherence and mutual supportiveness, bearing in mind specific circumstances in the Member States' (European Council 2006: 28). With the exception of the recently strengthened European Sustainable Development Network (a network of public administrators that are responsible for sustainable development strategies[5]), institutional arrangements for cross-jurisdictional policy learning at the European level are rather weak.

Integrating Sectoral Policies

In the course of their sustainable development strategy process, most EU Member States have established administrative instruments (Chapter 3) such as an inter-ministerial[6] coordination body or committee (European Environment Agency 2005a). These committees bring together middle-level administrators from various ministries on a regular basis. Although their political power is often relatively limited, sustainable development strategy coordinators regard these institutional innovations as one of the key benefits of sustainable development strategies (Steurer and Martinuzzi 2005: 461).

While inter-ministerial mechanisms are quite common at the administrative level, similar arrangements are relatively rare at the political level. Germany and the UK strive for a better inter-ministerial coordination with so-called green cabinets (see also Chapters 9 and 12). The German Committee of State Secretaries for Sustainable Development was established in 2001. It is headed by the Minister of State from the Federal Chancellery and brings together politicians from ten ministries (Jänicke *et al.* 2001: 8 and 16). As Wurzel shows in Chapter 9, the Green Cabinet was a relatively strong actor in the red–green government (see also European Environment Agency 2005a: 30). In the UK, the committee of 'Green Ministers' resulted from an upgrading of an existing informal committee in 2001. It reviews policies on sustainable development and initiates reforms across ministries. However, as Russel and Jordan show in Chapter 12, various factors have hampered its effectiveness. Sweden and France on the other hand have tried to tackle the challenge of inter-ministerial coordination by creating new ministries for sustainable development which have a cross-sectoral portfolio. Time will presumably tell us what impact (if any) these changes have on the prospects for EPI.

One of the most widespread EPI mechanisms facilitated by sustainable development strategies are cyclical monitoring and reporting schemes. Drawing on UN and OECD strategy guidelines, virtually all sustainable development strategy processes in Europe monitor the government's sustainable development performance using (largely quantitative) indicators (such as GDP per capita for the economic, poverty rate for the social, and CO_2 emissions for the environmental dimension of sustainable development). Some countries also use aggregated indicators such as the ecological footprint. The NCSD or the lead ministry in the strategy process (most often the environment ministry) summarizes the monitoring results in regular progress reports. However, the indicators are not always clearly linked to the objectives in the sustainable development strategies, and the sectoral indicators do not necessarily say much about the degree of policy integration achieved.

Since monitoring is often restricted to a mere description of the sustainable development performance of a given country, some countries have begun to conduct a more analytical form of assessment. In the UK, the national Sustainable Development Commission was upgraded to an independent watchdog for sustainable development in 2005 (Berger and Steurer 2006c). In the same year, Austria and Switzerland commissioned independent evaluations. France has been a front-runner in applying the peer review mechanism whereby the strategy administrators of two to three other countries discuss the strengths and weaknesses of a sustainable development strategy process. Subsequently, Norway, the Netherlands and the Slovak Republic also initiated peer review activities but momentum quickly folded (Berger and Steurer 2006a). Since all these monitoring and evaluation mechanisms are relatively new, it is unclear how far they facilitate policy learning and integration. However, since they are *ex post* efforts that are somewhat remote from decision-making processes, it may well be that they are less effective than other, more direct assessment instruments, such as policy appraisal and Strategic Environmental Assessment (see Chapters 6 and 7).

Regarding particular policy instruments aiming at EPI (such as voluntary agreements, sustainable development research and education, regulation, fiscal reforms), sustainable development strategies tend to employ mostly voluntary instruments that emphasize cooperation and learning; they only rarely involve regulatory instruments that seek to command and control. However, since these instruments saw an upswing long before sustainable development strategies came into effect (Jordan *et al.* 2003), it is hard to assess what impact sustainable development strategies had on their development. It seems that they have reinforced the trend away from 'command and control'. For the Austrian sustainable development strategy, Martinuzzi and Steurer (2003: 273) found that 58 per cent of the first steps of implementation listed in the strategy annex were concerned with knowledge and awareness, about 35 per cent with other concepts, strategies and small-scale (pilot) projects, and 7 per cent with regulations, economic incentives or other programmes. In addition, many of these first steps of implementation did not originate in the sustainable development strategy process, but were developed independently.

The Overall Performance of Sustainable Development Strategies

If we compare the previous two sections, it is obvious that sustainable development strategy processes have mirrored the wider notion of policy integration that is typical for the concept of sustainable development. They have attempted to facilitate policy integration not only with regard to sectoral, but also with regard to temporal, governance-related (participatory) and spatial (cross-jurisdictional) aspects. However, the effectiveness of

Table 5.2   Patterns of sustainable development policy making

		Effectiveness of sustainable development policies	
		Low	High
Presence of SD strategy features	Low	I: (a) 'SD ignorance' or (b) symbolic SD strategies	III: SD through incrementalism
	High	II: Administered SD strategies	IV: Comprehensive SD strategies as strategic processes

these attempts is, of course, another issue that varies not only from country to country, but also from challenge to challenge. While most sustainable development strategies have paid relatively close attention to the temporal and cross-sectoral aspects of integration, cross-jurisdictional efforts (both downwards to the sub-national and upwards to the European level) have played a minor role only.

Since most strategy processes are still quite young, taking stock of their overall performance can only be a very general and preliminary endeavour. Overall, a review of the first experiences suggests that most sustainable development strategy processes in Europe have followed a pattern of 'administered sustainable development strategies' (see Table 5.2).

Comprehensive sustainable development strategies seem preferable to incremental policy making but they hardly exist
The pattern of comprehensive sustainable development strategies (as described by the United Nations and OECD guidelines), resembles strategic processes that orchestrate several instruments and mechanisms and are backed by high-level political commitment and administrative ownership (Steurer and Martinuzzi 2005). Drawing mainly on the work of Mintzberg *et al.* (1998) (see also Lindblom 1979; Meadowcroft 1997; Steurer and Martinuzzi 2005; Tils 2005), such comprehensive sustainable development strategies (Type IV in Table 5.2) seem to be preferable to incremental policy making that works on an ad hoc basis, lacking a shared vision and a sense of direction (Type III in Table 5.2). While the incremental model of policy making (Lindblom 1959) 'is likely to exhaust itself in faddism, drifting from one fashionable innovation to the next, without leaving a lasting imprint' (Schick 1999: 2), sustainable development strategies can provide a sense of direction and they ought to orchestrate different policy instruments as well as governance mechanisms (Steurer and Martinuzzi 2005). Both orientation and orchestration seem to be particularly important in the context of complex issues such as sustainable development. However, since none of the existing sustainable development strategies come close to the compre-

hensive pattern (the closest one being perhaps the UK's), we have to wait for further evidence in order to verify the hypothesis that comprehensive sustainable development strategies are preferable to incremental sustainable development policy making.

Sustainable development strategies in Europe have tended to be administered strategy processes. Although existing sustainable development strategies fall short compared to the comprehensive pattern, they have triggered a number of features. They have: facilitated inter-ministerial coordination with administrative committees and Green Cabinets; supported policy learning by incorporating monitoring and/or assessment mechanisms; and fostered public participation and other forms of stakeholder involvement through NCSDs.

Nevertheless, their effectiveness seems to be limited for at least four reasons. First, as indicated above, not all strategy features are equally well accepted and employed in all countries. Although most countries have, for example, an inter-ministerial committee or an NCSD, the differences regarding their political relevance are considerable (see, for example, European Environment Agency 2005a).

Second, as Russel (2007) and Lafferty *et al.* (2007) show for the UK and Norway respectively, sustainable development strategies have triggered a broad array of supportive features such as (ministerial) action or work plans, indicator-based monitoring schemes and participation mechanisms, but sometimes fail to link and orchestrate them in a comprehensive and coherent way. In other words, sustainable development strategies not only face the four integrative governance challenges described in Table 5.1, but also the challenge of better linking and orchestrating their own features.

Third, most sustainable development strategies have suffered from a serious lack of high-level political commitment. With the exception of Germany (during the red–green government, 1998–2005) and the UK, most sustainable development strategy coordinators believe that their politicians show very little interest in long-term strategic processes (Martinuzzi and Steurer 2005: 465). An explanation is provided by Hansen and Ejersbo (2002: 738ff). They argue that politicians and administrators are dealing with the formulation and implementation of policies in distinct ways (see also Page 2003: 673). Politicians on the one hand approach particular issues case-by-case and focus on the competing interests involved. By utilizing such an 'inductive logic of action', at times they not only ignore existing strategies but also personal commitments or treaties. Administrators on the other hand prefer to deal with particular issues deductively by referring to general laws or guidelines. In the context of sustainable development strategy processes, this 'logic of disharmony' between politicians and administrators implies that while administrators regard sustainable development strategies as important guidance for policy making, politicians will probably not care much about the strategy documents as a guidance-providing instrument, but consider them a form of political communication. In this sense, the four challenges of policy integration are also about managing the 'logic of disharmony' between politicians and administrators.

Fourth, a lack of high-level political commitment seems to imply a lack of ownership among 'non' environmental administrators. As several case studies (Martinuzzi and Steurer 2005; Lafferty 2007; Russel 2007) and an exchange of experience among sustainable development strategy coordinators (Berger and Steurer 2006b) have shown, the handful of (mostly environmental) administrators who coordinate the sustainable development strategies, struggle not only with the political environment but also with a widespread indifference amongst their colleagues in other ministries.

Consequently, most sustainable development strategies in Europe seem to become 'administered strategy processes' (Type II), that is, fragmented processes driven by a few administrators who are not capable of shaping key policy decisions in line with sustainable development objectives. Thus, high-profile policy decisions such as the subsidy of alternative energies in Austria or the social policy reform programme Agenda 2010 in Germany (Tils 2005: 276 and 282; Tils 2007) are hardly discussed in the context of the strategy process, at least not in public.

Administered sustainable development strategies are more than symbolic documents . . .

At first glance, many sustainable development strategies may appear as purely symbolic, that is, politically irrelevant façades. But what is the difference between such strategies (Type Ib) and administered ones (Type II)? First, the latter try to overcome the one-off nature of many environmental plans by framing sustainable development strategies as ongoing processes. Cyclical efforts such as frequent coordination meetings, annual or biennial work plans or regular monitoring, reviewing and reporting activities, enable administrators and stakeholder groups to shape the government's political agenda a bit towards sustainable development. Second, administered sustainable development strategies are more than symbolic because those responsible for their implementation often succeed in introducing innovative governance structures and mechanisms, such as interministerial bodies and NCSDs (many of which were introduced in the context of sustainable development strategies), and in initiating small sustainable development projects that are within their scope. The fact that politicians do not care much about sustainable development strategies implies not only that key decisions are made frequently without reference to the sustainable development strategy process, but also that administrators can make use of their limited scope. By doing so, sustainable development strategies give them both legitimacy and guidance.

. . . but the mere presence of sustainable development strategy features is not sufficient

As neither a well-written sustainable development strategy document nor the presence of (often fragmented) sustainable development strategy features can ever compensate for the lack of high-level political commitment, administered sustainable development strategies can make small differences, but will fail to shape sustainable development policies and EPI significantly. In order to move towards the comprehensive pattern, they need, inter alia, to become more political, for example by better involving political actors such as cabinet offices and parliaments. As Tils (2005, 2007) emphasizes, sustainable development strategies also need to improve their strategic orientation, for example by proactively exploring feasible options and advocacy coalitions in the context of limiting actor constellations. Although the functioning of public administrations is certainly important for advancing 'strategic public management' (Steurer 2007), demanding environmental objectives like the reduction of greenhouse gas emissions can certainly not be administered or managed; they need to be actively governed.

SUMMARY DISCUSSION

This chapter has shown that the concept of sustainable development and the use of sustainable development strategies affect EPI by broadening the notion of what should be integrated. Crucially, while EPI is concerned with integrating environmental issues into other policy sectors within a particular jurisdiction, sustainable development strategies should seek to balance social, environmental and economic goals in the short and long term across jurisdictions, with a strong input from different stakeholders. In so doing, sustainable development strategies employ not one, but at least three approaches or logics of EPI (Nilsson and Persson 2003). First and foremost, sustainable development strategies both rely on and foster institutional capacities for inter-ministerial collaboration. This appears in the form of network-like arrangements and other integrative structures within governments. Second, by employing monitoring and reviewing mechanisms, sustainable development strategies seek to achieve policy change through learning processes. From the perspective of learning approaches, sustainable development strategies appear as cyclical processes that evolve constantly based on internal and external feedback loops. Third, sustainable development strategies also seek to foster participatory arrangements with the purpose of harnessing and resolving conflicts of interest. So far, however, only a few countries (such as the UK with its Sustainable Development Commission) and Finland (with its high-profile NCSD), have influential participatory bodies in place.

In general, sustainable development strategies seem to rely chiefly on the institutional approach, followed by the learning approach. In its report on EPI in Europe, the European Environment Agency (2005b, 10) concluded that 'among the developments that are most explicit, both in terms of institution building and the introduction of instruments or tools for improving coordination, the majority are in fact concerned with sustainable development rather than EPI'. This can be traced back to some of the original thinking on sustainable development. As Sneddon *et al.* (2006) emphasize, the Brundtland Report is first and foremost 'a bold call to recalibrate institutional mechanisms at global, national and local levels', paying relatively little attention 'to power relations among the local-to-global actors and institutions supporting unsustainable development'. Thus, many documents on sustainable development strategies emphasize that 'getting the process right' is the key to achieving sustainable development (see for example Williams 2002; European Commission 2004: 7; Steurer and Martinuzzi 2005: 461). This perception is perfectly in line with strategic management theory. For example, Henry Mintzberg (1994: 352), who is one of the leading scholars of strategic management, stresses that communication and coordination are not side effects of strategic management and planning, 'but the essential reasons to engage in it'. Consequently, most sustainable development strategies offer little guidance on how to solve trade-offs and conflicts of interests between the three dimensions of sustainable development (European Commission 2004). In this respect, the more conflictual nature of EPI (Lenschow 2002; Nilsson and Persson 2003) potentially fills a conceptual vacuum in the thinking on sustainable development.

How effectively do sustainable development strategies facilitate sustainable development and/or EPI? Compared to the disappointing experience with environmental plans in the 1980s and 1990s, the observed signs of transition from grand planning schemes to flexible strategy processes, and from clear-cut sectoral authorities to cross-cutting strategic coordination bodies are encouraging (Steurer and Martinuzzi 2005: 469). In theory, sustainable development strategies should provide a normative sense of direction, and facilitate and orchestrate different integrative structures and mechanisms. As such, they have the potential to contribute to the implementation of sustainable development and EPI. However, most sustainable development strategies fall some way short of the comprehensive ideal associated with Type IV (depicted in Table 5.2). One of the key shortcomings is not so much technical or managerial, but political: most sustainable development strategy coordinators in Europe feel their effectiveness is seriously limited by weak high-level political will, leadership and commitment. Consequently, many sustainable development strategies become 'administered' processes. That is to say, they create new administrative structures and mechanisms that are fragmented rather than well orchestrated, and not effectively used by policy makers (Lafferty *et al.* 2007; Russel 2007; Tils 2007).

CONCLUSIONS

In 2002, Lafferty (2002: 20) emphasized that a sustainable development strategy 'is extremely important, as its existence demonstrates a political commitment to giving EPI the crucial role in the national policy making context assigned to it by the UNCED'. At the time, he was correct, because sustainable development strategies were rare.[7] Since then, however, sustainable development strategies have spread quickly and need to be viewed more cautiously. They are now a standard instrument used in most European countries, and neither the existence nor even a high presence of strategy features (such as action plans or monitoring schemes) allow us to draw firm conclusions regarding their effectiveness.

Overall, the record of sustainable development strategies is quite mixed. Although most have fallen short of effectively reshaping policies towards EPI and sustainable development, even administered strategies can generate new points of political advantage and hence are more than just symbolic exercises. Their cyclical review mechanisms, for example, are important drivers of sustainable development policy making, and give administrators some leeway regarding both sustainable development policies and governance arrangements. Although sustainable development strategies can certainly be a step away from one-off planning schemes in predominantly hierarchical settings, towards more permanent strategic processes that try to facilitate networking and incremental learning, the road towards a more comprehensive form of 'strategic public management' is still a long and winding one (Steurer 2007).

NOTES

1. As noted by Martinuzzi and Steurer (2003) in a case study on the Austrian sustainable development strategy, some of these guidelines (such as combining a government-independent long-term vision with concrete policy objectives) are overly demanding and unrealistic. On the other hand, however, Steurer (2007) also notes that overall, they demonstrate clear progress when compared to earlier environmental planning practices.
2. While the Italian strategy can hardly be regarded as a sustainable development strategy because it covers the environmental dimension only, three old and four new Member

States cover a fourth dimension of sustainable development, namely governance and culture (European Commission 2004: 12ff).
3. For an overview of sustainable development strategy features in different countries, see the country profile section at http://www.sd-network.eu/?k=country%20profiles or Steurer and Martinuzzi (2005), Volkery *et al.* (2006) and OECD (2006).
4. Because some Member States objected to parts of the European Commission's (2001b) draft sustainable development strategy, the Gothenburg European Council 'welcomed' it but did not endorse it as the EU strategy. Instead, it included 14 modestly ambitious paragraphs on sustainable development in Europe in its Conclusions (European Council 2001) that served as a temporary EU sustainable development strategy.
5. For further details see: www.sd-network.eu.
6. For the sake of coherence, this chapter does not distinguish between the terms 'ministry' and 'department'.
7. As mentioned briefly in section 2, only Ireland (1997), Finland (1998) and the UK (1999) had an SD strategy in place before 2000. Most other European countries followed their example in preparation for the World Summit for Sustainable Development in Johannesburg in the early 2000s.

BIBLIOGRAPHY

Berger, G. and R. Steurer (2006a), *Evaluation and Review of National Sustainable Development Strategies*, http://www.sd-network.eu/?k=quarterly%20reports& report_id=2, accessed 19 March 2008.
Berger, G. and R. Steurer (2006b), *Sustainable Development Goes Mozart: Conference Proceedings of the European Sustainable Development Network/ESDN Conference 2006*, http://www.sd-network.eu/pdf/doc_salzburg/Proceedings_ ESDN%20Conference%202006.pdf, accessed 19 March 2008.
Berger, G. and R. Steurer (2006c), *The Finnish National Commission on SD and the UK's SD Commission: Two Distinct Models of Involving Stakeholders in SD Policy Making*, http://www.sd-network.eu/?k=quarterly%20reports&report_id=3, accessed 19 March 2008.
Berger, G. and R. Steurer (2008), 'The regional level in National Sustainable Development Strategy processes: experiences with vertical policy integration in Europe', in S. Baker and K. Eckerberg (eds), *In Pursuit of Sustainable Development: New Governance Practices at the Sub-National Level in Europe*, London: Routledge.
Busch, P.-O. and H. Jörgens (2005), 'International patterns of environmental policy change and convergence', *European Environment*, 15, 80–101.
Cabinet Office (2000), *Wiring It Up: Whitehall's Management of Cross-Cutting Policies and Services*, A Performance and Innovation Unit Report, London: Cabinet Office.
Dalal-Clayton, B. and S. Bass (2000), *National Strategies for Sustainable Development: The Challenge Ahead*, http://www.nssd.net/pdf/Issues2.pdf, accessed 19 March 2008.
Dyllick, T. and K. Hockerts (2002), 'Beyond the business case for corporate sustainability', *Business Strategy and the Environment*, 11, 130–141.
European Commission (2001a), *European Governance: A White Paper*, Brussels: Commission of the European Communities, http://eur-lex.europa.eu/ LexUriServ/LexUriServ.do?uri=OJ:C:2001:287:0001:01:EN:PDF, accessed 19 March 2008.
European Commission (2001b), *A Sustainable Europe for a Better World: A*

European Union Strategy for Sustainable Development, Brussels: Commission of the European Communities, http://eur-lex.europa.eu/LexUriServ/LexUriServ. do?uri=CELEX:52001DC0264:EN:HTML, accessed 19 March 2008.

European Commission (2004), *National Sustainable Development Strategies in the European Union: A First Analysis by the European Commission*, Brussels: Commission of the European Communities http://europe.eu.int/comm/ sustainable/docs/sustainable_development_strategies.pdf.

European Commission (2005), *Draft Declaration on Guiding Principles for Sustainable Development*, COM (2005) 218 final, Brussels: Commission of the European Communities.

European Council (2001), *Presidency Conclusions: Göteborg European Council*, http://www.consilium.europa.eu/ueDocs/cms_Data/docs/pressData/en/ec/ 00200-r 1.en1.pdf, accessed 19 March 2008.

European Council (2005), *Presidency Conclusions: Brussels European Council, 16 and 17 June 2005*, http://www.consilium.europa.eu/ueDocs/cms_Data/docs/ pressData/en/ec/85349.pdf, accessed 19 March 2008, accessed 19 March 2008.

European Council (2006), *Presidency Conclusions: Brussels European Council, 15 and 16 June 2006*, http://www.consilium.europa.eu/ueDocs/cms_Data/docs/ pressData/en/ec/90111.pdf, accessed 19 March 2008.

European Environment Agency (2005a), *Environmental Policy Integration in Europe: State of Play and an Evaluation Framework*, Copenhagen: European Environment Agency.

European Environment Agency (2005b), *Environmental Policy Integration in Europe: Administrative Culture and Practices*, Copenhagen: European Environment Agency.

Hansen, K.M. and N. Ejersbo (2002), 'The relationship between politicians and administrators: a logic of disharmony', *Public Administration*, 80 (4), 733–750.

IIED (2002), *Sustainable Development Strategies: A Resource Book*, http://www.nssd.net/res_book.html, accessed 19 March 2008.

IIED, UNDP and UKDFID (2002), *National Strategies for Sustainable Development: New Thinking and Time for Action*, http://www.nssd.net/pdf/ IIED13.pdf, accessed 19 March 2008.

ISO Advisory Group (2004), *Working Report on Social Responsibility*, http:// tinyurl.com/22vewu, accessed 19 March 2008.

Jacob, K. and A. Volkery (2004), 'Institutions and instruments for government self-regulation: environmental policy integration in a cross-country perspective', *Journal of Comparative Policy Analysis*, 6 (3), 291–309.

Jänicke, M. and H. Jörgens (2004), 'Neue Steuerungskonzepte in der Umweltpolitik', *Zeitschrift für Umweltpolitik und Umweltrecht*, 3, 297–348.

Jänicke, M., H. Jörgens, K. Jörgensen and R. Nordbeck (2001), *Governance for Sustainable Development in Germany: Institutions and Policy Making*, Paris: OECD. http://www.oecd.org/dataoecd/27/32/1828117.pdf, accessed 19 March 2008.

Jordan, A. (2002), 'Efficient hardware and light green software: environmental policy integration in the UK', in A. Lenschow, (ed.), *Environmental Policy Integration: Greening Sectoral Policies in Europe*, London: Earthscan.

Jordan, A. and A. Schout (2006), *The Coordination of the European Union*, Oxford: Oxford University Press.

Jordan, A., R.K.W. Wurzel and A.R. Zito (2003), 'New environmental policy instruments: an evolution or a revolution in environmental policy?' *Environmental Politics*, 12 (1), 179–200.

Lafferty, W.M. (2002), *Adapting Government Practice to the Goals of Sustainable Development*, http://www.oecd.org/dataoecd/30/54/1939762.pdf.

Lafferty, W.M., J. Knudsen and O.M. Larsen (2007), 'Pursuing sustainable development in Norway: the challenge of living up to Brundtland at home', *European Environment*, 17 (3), 177–188.

Lenschow, A. (ed.) (2002), *Environmental Policy Integration: Greening Sectoral Policies in Europe*, London: Earthscan.

Liberatore, A. (1997), 'The integration of sustainable development objectives into EU policymaking: barriers and prospects', in S. Baker, M. Kousis, D. Richardson and S. Young (eds), *The Politics of Sustainable Development*, London: Routledge.

Lindblom, C.E. (1959), 'The science of "muddling through"', *Public Administration Review*, 19, 79–99.

Lindblom, C.E. (1979), 'Still muddling, not yet through', *Public Administration Review*, 38, 517–526.

Ling, T. (2002), 'Delivering joined-up government in the UK: dimensions, issues and problems', *Public Administration*, 80 (4), 614–642.

Martinuzzi, A. and R. Steurer (2003), 'The Austrian strategy for sustainable development: process review and policy analysis', *European Environment*, 13 (4), 269–287.

Martinuzzi, A. and R. Steurer (2005), *Die Umsetzung der Österreichischen Nachhaltigkeitsstrategie: Erfahrungen und Einsichten von Beteiligten*, Diskussionspapier, Wirtschaftsuniversität, Vienna: Schriftenreihe des Forschungsschwerpunkts Nachhaltigkeit und Umweltmanagement.

Meadowcroft, J. (1997), 'Planning for sustainable development: insights from the literatures of political science', *European Journal of Political Research*, 31, 427–454.

Meadowcroft, J. (2000), 'Nationale Pläne und Strategien zur nachhaltigen Entwicklung in Industrienationen', in M. Jänicke and H. Jörgens (eds), *Umweltplanung im internationalen Vergleich: Strategien der Nachhaltigkeit*, Berlin: Springer.

Mintzberg, H. (1994), *The Rise and Fall of Strategic Planning: Re-conceiving Roles for Planning, Plans, Planners*, New York: The Free Press.

Mintzberg, H., B. Ahlstrand and J. Lampel (1998), *Strategy Safari: A Guided Tour Through the Wilds of Strategic Management*, New York: The Free Press.

Niestroy, I. (2005), *Sustaining Sustainability: A Benchmark Study on National Strategies towards Sustainable Development and the Impact of Councils in Nine EU Member States*, Utrecht: Lemma.

Nilsson, M. and A. Persson (2003), 'Framework for analysing environmental policy integration', *Journal of Environmental Policy and Planning*, 5 (4), 333–359.

OECD (2001), *Sustainable Development: Critical Issues*, Paris, OECD.

OECD (2002), *Governance for Sustainable Development: Five OECD Case Studies*, Paris: OECD.

OECD (2006), *Good Practices in the National Development Strategies of OECD Countries*, Paris: OECD.

OECD-DAC (2001), *Strategies for Sustainable Development: Practical Guidance for Development Cooperation*, Paris: OECD. http://www.nssd.net/pdf/gsuse.pdf, accessed 19 March 2008.

Page, E.C. (2003), 'The civil servant as legislator: law making in British administration', *Public Administration*, 81 (4), 651–679.

Peters, G. (1998), 'Managing horizontal government: the politics of coordination', *Public Administration*, 76, 295–311.

Rao, P.K. (2000), *Sustainable Development: Economics and Policy*, Oxford: Malden.

Reid, D. (1995), *Sustainable Development: An Introductory Guide*, London: Earthscan.

Rotmans, J., R. Kemp and M. Van Asselt (2001), 'More evolution than revolution: transition management in public policy', *Foresight*, 3 (1), 15–31.

Russel, D. (2007), 'The United Kingdom's sustainable development strategies: leading the way or flattering to deceive?' *European Environment*, 17 (3), 189–200.

Schick, A. (1999), *Opportunity, Strategy, and Tactics in Reforming Public Management*, http://www.olis.oecd.org/olis/1999doc.nsf/LinkTo/PUMA-SGF(99)4, accessed 19 March 2008.

Smith, R.J. (1996), 'Sustainability and the rationalisation of the environment', *Environmental Politics*, 5 (1), 25–47.

Sneddon, C., R.B. Howarth and R.B. Norgaard (2006), 'Sustainable development in a post-Brundtland world', *Ecological Economics*, 57 (2), 253–268.

Steurer, R. (2007), 'From government strategies to strategic public management: an exploratory outlook on the pursuit of cross-sectoral policy integration', *European Environment*, 17 (3), 201–214.

Steurer, R., M.E. Langer, A. Konrad and A. Martinuzzi (2005), 'Corporations, stakeholders and sustainable development I: a theoretical exploration of business–society relations', *Journal of Business Ethics*, 61 (3), 263–281.

Steurer, R. and A. Martinuzzi (2005), 'Towards a new pattern of strategy formation in the public sector: first experiences with national strategies for sustainable development in Europe', *Environment and Planning C*, 23 (3), 455–472.

Tils, R. (2005), *Politische Strategieanalyse: Konzeptionelle Grundlagen und Anwendung in der Umwelt- und Nachhaltigkeitspolitik*, Wiesbaden, VS: Verlag für Sozialwissenschaften.

Tils, R. (2007), 'The German sustainable development strategy: facing policy, management and political strategy assessments', *European Environment*, 17 (3), 164–176.

UNCED (1992a), *Agenda 21*, New York: United Nations. http://www.un.org/esa/sustdev/agenda21.htm, accessed 19 March 2008.

UNCED (1992b), *Rio Declaration on Environment and Development*, New York: United Nations. http://www.un.org/documents/ga/conf151/aconf15126-1annex1.htm, accessed 19 March 2008.

UNDESA (2001), *Guidance in Preparing a National Sustainable Development Strategy: Managing Sustainable Development in the New Millenium*, http://www.un.org/esa/sustdev/publications/nsds_guidance.pdf, accessed 19 March 2008.

UNGASS (1997), *Programme for the Further Implementation of Agenda 21*, http://www.un.org/documents/ga/res/spec/aress19-2.htm, accessed 19 March 2008.

Volkery, A., D. Swanson, K. Jacob, F. Bregha and L. Pintér (2006), 'Coordination challenges and innovations in 19 national sustainable development strategies', *World Development*, 34 (12), 2047–63.

WCED (1987), *Our Common Future*, Oxford: Oxford University Press.

Williams, P.M. (2002), 'Community strategies: mainstreaming sustainable development and strategic planning?' *Sustainable Development*, 10, 197–205.

World Bank (2003), *Sustainable Development in a Dynamic World: World Development Report 2003*, Washington: The World Bank, http://tinyurl.com/yvhq4x, accessed 19 March 2008.

WSSD (2002), *Johannesburg Declaration on Sustainable Development: From our Origins to the Future*, http://www.un.org/esa/sustdev/documents/WSSD_POI_PD/English/POI_PD.htm, accessed 19 March 2008.

6. Policy appraisal

Julia Hertin, Klaus Jacob and Axel Volkery

INTRODUCTION

The *ex ante* appraisal of policies has been a standard procedure in government for a long time. It has been used in many countries to improve the quality of regulation, to reduce implementation costs and to achieve cross-cutting objectives such as sustainable development, economic competitiveness or human health. While not an entirely new policy instrument, *ex ante* policy appraisal has recently attracted a remarkable level of attention. A considerable number of policy-making institutions at all levels of governance have started to revise their appraisal procedures with a view to strengthening, broadening and integrating *ex ante* policy assessment.

This new impetus for broader and more integrated forms of appraisal has often been supported by those promoting environmental policy because it appears to offer new opportunities for strengthening EPI and facilitating sustainable development. However, concerns have been voiced that this trend could lead to a sidelining of environmental issues if the appraisal process is dominated by concerns such as over-regulation and economic competitiveness (Wilkinson *et al.* 2005).

In this chapter, we analyse a number of policy appraisal systems in order to understand the contribution they make or possibly could make to EPI. We will analyse four cases of comparatively advanced appraisal procedures (in Canada, the United Kingdom, the Netherlands and the European Commission), highlighting the variety of institutional arrangements and functions of policy appraisal.

The remainder of this chapter is organized as follows: The following section (2) gives a brief overview of the history of *ex ante* policy appraisal. The third section analyses its conceptual foundations. Section 4 presents the four case studies, looking at both the institutional set-up of the four appraisal systems and their performance in practice. Section 5 compares and contrasts the different systems and analyses their strengths and weaknesses from the perspective of overall effectiveness and the consideration of environmental concerns. The final section (6) proposes a number of conclusions about the potential contribution of *ex ante* policy appraisal to EPI.

HISTORY

The Origins of Policy Appraisal

The integrated *ex-ante* assessment of impacts of regulatory proposals, programmes or policies can be traced back to three different origins: environmental project assessments, regulatory impact assessments (RIA) and sectoral assessments procedures.

From the very beginning of modern environmental policy in the late 1960s, the environmental assessment of large projects (for example construction and infrastructure schemes) was introduced as an obligatory instrument in many OECD countries, starting with the USA (see Chapter 13). Focusing on potential negative impacts, Environmental Impact Assessment (EIA) aims to provide decision makers with the information needed to minimize damage to the environment. Often, however, decisions taken at an earlier stage in the planning process limit the scope for reducing the environmental impacts of a given project. Project-level assessment may thus only have marginal environmental benefits. Hence, there have been calls to introduce mandatory assessment procedures at an earlier stage of the process, that is, covering policies, plans and programmes (see Chapter 7). This form of assessment – known as Strategic Environmental Assessment (SEA) – was originally developed in the 1980s and diffused more widely during the 1990s. From an environmental perspective, the procedures for integrated policy appraisal analysed in this chapter represent a further 'upstreaming' of assessment in the decision-making process, up to the higher or policy level.

Integrated policy appraisals can, secondly, be traced back to RIA, which first developed in the early 1970s, mainly in Anglo-Saxon countries. RIA assesses the economic costs and benefits of new regulation, aiming both to avoid unnecessary or overly costly regulation and to improve the design of policy. This is supposed to decrease the costs of regulation for both business (and other target groups) and public authorities, thereby enhancing economic competitiveness and contributing to a stabilization of public spending. Although it is difficult to obtain a complete overview of these activities because they are frequently informal or confidential, it is clear that RIA has diffused fairly rapidly throughout the OECD during the 1980s and 1990s (OECD 1997; Radaelli 2004, 2005). There is now also a strong trend towards devoting more efforts in appraisal processes to assessing and reducing administrative burdens. Many countries follow the Dutch example and adopt a standardized methodology (the so-called Standard Cost Model) to calculate and then reduce the costs for business complying with information obligations stemming from government regulation.

Alongside EIA and RIA, a number of other specific appraisal procedures have been developed to promote more joined-up thinking and working in government. They cover cross-cutting issues such as human health, the concerns of small and medium enterprises, the environment and different aspects of social welfare. Often consisting of simple forms or checklists, these 'single issue assessments' have the aim of making the policy department aware of unintended – and usually negative – consequences and of finding ways of minimizing these through better cross-sectoral policy coordination.

The Shift to Integrated Policy Appraisal

A number of administrations, most prominently the European Commission, have recently begun to develop more integrated appraisal procedures. Such a move (from a sectoral to a more integrated approach) implies multiple and sometimes conflicting objectives. In this chapter we ask whether this integration benefits sustainability in general and EPI in particular. It seems plausible that integrated policy appraisal should promote the integration of environmental concerns because sectoral departments would be obliged to consider the unintended environmental impacts of their policy proposals at a stage where decisions are not yet reached and where there may be a potential for win-win solutions (Hertin and Berkhout 2003). Environmental ministries (and perhaps agencies and NGOs) would be consulted early in the process, promoting cross-sectoral networking and, possibly, policy learning. There are, however, also critics who think that integrated assessment may sideline environmental concerns if the procedure is dominated by the deregulation agenda (Wilkinson *et al.* 2005). Some of the arguments in favour and against integrated assessment reiterate the debate about the effects of merging environmental and sectoral ministries (Weale 1992), where integration without a change in power relations within government is considered by some as ineffective or even counterproductive (see Chapter 3). One of the concerns is that integrated appraisal could make it easier for powerful sectoral ministries to challenge environmental policy on competitiveness grounds while doing little to help environmental ministries satisfy their environmental priorities. NGOs also see the risk that they could lose their capacity to advance their position through a conflict-oriented mode of action if they subscribe to an integrated appraisal procedure which is structurally biased against the environment (see for example the critique of the EU's chemicals policy produced by the European Environmental Bureau and the World Wide Fund for Nature),[1] or the critical statement by the European Environment and Sustainable Development Advisory Councils on EU Impact Assessment.[2]

CONCEPTUAL BACKGROUND

Ex Ante Appraisal and the Policy Process

Policy appraisal is based on the assumption that policy making can – at least to a certain extent – be designed according to principles of rational discourse and linear problem solving (Hertin *et al.* forthcoming; Radaelli 2005). Typically, the procedures set out a sequence of analytical steps that mirror the phases found in the more linear and/or rational models of the policy process. In these models, the process of policy making normally begins with the identification of a policy problem or objective, runs through an analysis of options and their impacts and leads to a weighing up of alternatives with a final selection of the 'best' policy choice (see, for example, OECD 1997 and CEC 2005). In this conception, policy assessment is – at least implicitly – based on a number of assumptions. It suggests: that policies are designed to address identified problems or objectives; that the impacts of planned policies can be anticipated with a certain degree of accuracy; that there is a central decision maker who selects a policy option on the basis of expected net benefits; and that, implicitly, the provision of more and better information leads to more rational policies. A careful analysis of the problem and the appraisal of available options should, it is claimed, identify mutually acceptable solutions in an efficient manner. Where competing objectives exist (as in relation to a policy goal like sustainability), trade-offs can be made explicit, compromises reached and compensatory measures implemented.

Many scholars of political science argue, however, that while the policy cycle may under certain circumstances be a useful heuristic device, this rational, linear conception of the policy process is not empirically valid (Sabatier and Jenkins-Smith 1993). Influential authors emphasize that political decision making is characterized by discontinuities, dynamic change and a loose coupling between problems and policies (Kingdon 1995; Sabatier and Jenkins-Smith 1999). It has also long been accepted that there is no unitary decision maker or central steering mechanism. Instead, policy decisions are the outcome of complex actor and interest constellations. Third, knowledge is seen to have a far more complex and varied role in the policy process than the positivist model would suggest (deLeon 1997; see also Owens *et al.* 2004). A range of influential authors with a more post-positivist orientation emphasize the important role of ideas, argumentation and discourse in shaping policy debates and ultimately decision making (Majone 1989; Fischer and Forester 1993). According to this view, knowledge is not merely constituted by factual information that is generated to help solve problems, but also includes ideas and argument. It is seen to be used by different actors – typically in a competitive fashion – to structure policy problems and solutions (see also Radaelli 1995). Policy appraisal, then, gives interest groups another opportunity to intervene early in the process of decision making and provides an additional forum for lobbying activities and political conflict. In short, it may be an additional arena for inter- and intra-sectoral politics, rather than a way to overcome them through rational argument.

Against this background, institutional design becomes important for determining the robustness of the different appraisal procedure. This concerns especially the clarity of rules for selecting proposals and coordinating the appraisal process, that is, the actors in charge, but also the definition of framework conditions, that is, regarding the transparency of the process.

DEPLOYMENT: PRACTICAL EXPERIENCES

United Kingdom

The UK is well-recognized for traditionally having both efficient inter-ministerial coordination procedures (Bulmer and Burch 1998) and extensive systems for administrative target setting and performance evaluation (Carter *et al.* 1992). Weale *et al.* (2000) have also observed that the UK has a tendency to deal with environmental policy problems by making changes to the policy process or the machinery of government (see also Chapter 12). It is therefore not surprising that the UK began to experiment with environmental and sustainability appraisal earlier and more extensively than most other OECD countries.

Over the last decade or so, a range of policy appraisal methodologies have been developed within different departments, several of which are at least partly concerned with environmental issues. A specific Environmental Policy Assessment procedure was first introduced in the 1990s by the environmental ministry as an instrument for promoting the 'greening of government' (DETR 1998), but it was not very widely used (Russel and Jordan 2007). The profile of environmental policy appraisal increased after Labour came into government in 1997, but it remained essentially a voluntary procedure that was hardly ever taken up by the sectors.

In parallel to this, the scope of mainstream regulatory appraisal (that is, RIA) has been broadened. RIA was first introduced in the mid-1980s and focused on the analysis of business compliance costs. The commitment to RIA was reinforced in 1998, when Prime Minister Blair announced that assessments would be carried out for all major policy proposals. It has also been extended to include unintended consequences, distributional effects and indirect costs. In principle, environmental impacts were covered by RIA, but in practice they did not usually play a major role in the assessments and little guidance was given on how to identify and evaluate environmental effects (Cabinet Office 2003).

To promote EPI while at the same time addressing the problem of there being too many issue-specific appraisals, the environmental and transport department developed Integrated Policy Appraisal. This was a checklist instrument that aimed to bring together the three departmental procedures to cover issues that were judged to be insufficiently addressed by RIA. In 2004, Integrated Policy Appraisal was abandoned and key elements of the checklist were integrated into the system of RIA overseen by the Cabinet Office (Russel and Jordan 2007).

The resulting system of integrated RIA is characterized by the following features:

- It is mandatory for all significant legislative initiatives (implementation has been brought up to 90 per cent in recent years).
- Coordination and quality assurance is provided by the Cabinet Office and backed by the personal commitment of the Prime Minister.
- Assessment is made of the costs and benefits of unintended impacts as well as the intended effects.
- The monetization of costs and benefits is strongly encouraged and guidance on cost–benefit analysis is provided.
- Environmental impacts are integrated in the form of a generic question to assess direct and indirect costs ('which may be economic, social and environmental') and a list of questions on specific environmental issues.

Although sustainability concerns still play a limited role in the British system of RIA (National Audit Office 2006), the formal strengthening of the environmental perspective has been considered as at least a partial success by the environment department, because it has moved the environment further into the mainstream appraisal procedure. It remains to be seen, however, whether this formal change has a significant effect on assessment practice because it is left to the responsible policy unit to decide which impacts to consider, and most RIAs only look at a small set of selected impacts in detail.

The European Commission

Similar to the UK, the policy appraisal system within the European Commission has also recently undergone a reorganization that aims to bring together different strands of appraisal previously developed in a rather disconnected manner. These include *ex ante* evaluations that are legally required under certain circumstances (for example, budgetary evaluation, business impact assessment and EIA) as well as those that are not (for example, gender assessment, trade impact assessment and small and medium-sized enterprises assessment). This reorganization of policy appraisal in the EU was partly a result of the 'better regulation' agenda, which has received increasing emphasis. This reflects a number of factors, not least Europe's disappointing economic performance in comparison with the US, China and India and its inability to meet the economic and employment targets set out in the EU's Lisbon strategy. The ultimate aim of implementing a new and more integrated form of appraisal was to improve the quality of regulation, promote greater stakeholder interaction and ensure that the costs of regulation are proportionate to the benefits (CEC 2002).

In parallel, the idea of sustainability impact assessment was referred to in the Gothenburg Presidency Conclusions as an instrument to implement the EU Sustainable Development Strategy (see Chapter 8). Environmental policy appraisal in the European Commission had had a rather difficult heritage. A 'green star' system was introduced in the mid-1990s. Under this procedure, it was planned that proposed new legislation with particular relevance to the environment (marked with a green star) would go through a process of environmental appraisal. As explained in Chapter 8, this system was never systematically implemented (Kraack *et al.* 2001) due to lack of methodologies and resources as well as opposition from sectoral directorates general who felt 'controlled' by DG Environment (Hertin and Berkhout 2003). In fact, Wilkinson (1997: 163) found 'no evidence that any such environmental appraisals had [ever] been undertaken'.

In 2002, plans for Sustainability Impact Assessment were integrated into the new Impact Assessment (IA) procedure (CEC 2002). This dual objective of IA is clearly expressed in the Commission Communication:

> The Commission intends to launch impact assessment as an instrument to improve the quality and coherence of the policy development process. It will contribute to an effective and efficient regulatory environment and, further, to a more coherent implementation of the European Strategy for Sustainable Development (CEC 2002).

The procedure was gradually introduced throughout 2003 and 2004. Currently, its main characteristics are as follows:

- IA should be carried out for 'key legislative proposals as well as the most important cross-cutting policy-defining non-legislative proposals' and replaces previously separate regulatory impact assessments.

- The assessment is carried out by the directorates-general responsible for the policy proposal during the process of decision making in consultation with other directorates-general and external stakeholders; external consultants may also be involved.
- The overall process is coordinated by the Secretariat-General in the European Commission; quality assurance shall be reached through inter-administrative consultation.
- The results of the appraisal are documented in an IA report which is published on a central web-site to ensure high transparency and better forward planning.
- Analysts are encouraged to quantify or monetize impacts where possible and to explore impacts qualitatively where quantification would be inappropriate.
- The European Commission is working to provide better training as well as qualitative and quantitative instruments for IA.

Several recent analyses of the IA system have revealed that many assessments were of modest quality (Hertin *et al.* 2004; Wilkinson *et al.* 2004; IMV 2006). For example, many only considered one policy option, were narrowly focused on direct economic impacts and explored social and environmental impacts only briefly. Moreover, their coverage was uneven (some policy areas undertook very few or no IAs), the evidence basis was sometimes weak, and few were clear about how and by whom the assessment was carried out. The procedure was also rolled out at a slower pace than initially planned. For 2003, the first year of operation, 43 proposals had been identified as requiring an Impact Assessment, but only 21 of those were completed (IMV 2006). Current IA practice also highlights the potential tension – although not outright contradiction – between the better regulation and competitiveness agenda pursued by the Lisbon Process on the one hand and the EU's sustainable development agenda on the other (see also Chapter 8). This has become particularly apparent during the process of assessing some of the more controversial policy proposals that have emerged from the Commission in recent years, such as the reform of the EU's sugar and chemical policies.

Nonetheless, our analysis of IA reports (Hertin *et al.* 2004) shows that most policies with a substantial environmental dimension have been assessed against environmental criteria. Although the treatment of – particularly unintended – environmental effects could rarely be considered as appropriate in terms of scope and rigour, it is clear that the introduction of IA has opened up the policy-making process in the European Commission and – unlike the Green Star procedure – served to improve transparency and forward planning (Jordan and Schout 2006). Anecdotal evidence from our stakeholder interviews suggests that the IA procedure may have triggered learning processes and opened the decision process to new knowledge (Hertin *et al.* 2004). Whether this has led to strong EPI in the sense of fundamentally changing the strategic direction of sectoral policies remains, however, open to question.

The Netherlands

The Netherlands has a strong tradition of policy planning and coordination. For instance, it pioneered the development of SEA in the mid-1980s. *Ex ante* policy appraisal was introduced, however, only as recently as 1994, with two central procedures: the Business Effect Test (B-Test) and the Environmental Test (E-Test). The preparations for the introduction of such assessments were initiated in the context of the revised National Environmental Policy Plan after 1992. Additional momentum for the introduction came in 1994 from the Quality of Legislation initiative, which aimed at a more stringent evaluation of proposed legislation. Here, the underlying goal was (as in the UK and the EU) to increase economic productivity and promote more effective administration.

The E-Test and B-Test procedures aimed at improving the quality of regulation, reducing negative effects on business and implementing environmental policy. A Joint Support Centre for Draft Regulation (the so-called 'help desk') was set up by the ministries of economic affairs and environment to coordinate appraisals and provide technical back-up (see Marsden 1999). A joint ministerial working group was responsible for selecting proposals. A Proposed Legislation Desk, a joint unit of the ministries of economic affairs, environment and justice, decided jointly with the lead ministry which aspects merited an extended policy appraisal. However, an internal evaluation found that the system was too cumbersome, was located too low down in the bureaucratic hierarchy and lacked transparency (see Volkery and Ehrhardt 2004). The system was restructured in 2001/2002, when it was simplified and its responsibilities were decentralized.

The current system is characterized by the following features:

- The tests are mandatory for all legislative proposals that might significantly impact on business, environment or administrative burdens.
- Four central instruments should be run separately in the early phase of the regulative formation process: Business Impact Assessment, Environmental Assessment, Practice and Enforceability Assessment and Cost–Benefit Analysis.

- The procedure is predominantly qualitative: the assessments mainly require a simple, criteria-based qualitative assessment; cost–benefit analysis is rarely used.
- The process is staged: after the first Quick Scan (preliminary assessment) by the lead ministry an extended policy appraisal has to be performed for selected proposals.
- There is no high-level coordination by a central institution (such as the Prime Minister's office). The Proposed Legislation Desk is in charge of quality control, but its powers are limited to giving advice. Quality control is also provided by the ministry of justice, which is responsible for legal approval. In cases where approval is not given, the legislative report has to be included in the submission of the proposal to the cabinet.
- There is a high degree of secrecy and little transparency. Assessment reports are not available to the public, but restricted to internal use.

Although the Dutch system explicitly aims to promote the integration of environmental and social issues into other policy domains, it does not really provide a truly integrated perspective. The instruments for business (B) and environment (E) testing and appraisal are mostly run independently and the results are rarely analysed from an integrated perspective. This might be explained by the low degree of central steering. The Dutch system places strong emphasis on technical support, but there is no central unit that could put pressure on ministries to comply with central requirements. The Proposed Legislation Desk cannot fill this gap because it largely functions as a technical advice body.

To conclude, although policy appraisal has been in place for a number of years, the rate of implementation appears to be quite low. In contrast to other jurisdictions covered in this chapter, policy appraisal in the Netherlands relies strongly on simple checklists and makes little use of quantitative analysis. Furthermore, the transparency of the system is low and stakeholders do not contribute directly.

Canada

Canada has been a pioneer and consistent leader in the area of regulatory reform for over 25 years. The agenda for regulatory reform emerged at the end of the 1970s; the government adopted a comprehensive Regulatory Reform Strategy in 1986. Its main principles are: the restriction of growth of regulation; the principle that benefits of regulation should exceed its costs; early public consultation; and the reduction of administrative burden. In 1992, the government adopted the overarching goal of 'maximizing net benefit to Canadians'. A central focus was on increasing international competitiveness and removing barriers to internal trade (see Volkery 2004).

Since that time, Canada has worked continuously to improve what is now a mature and well-functioning system of regulatory governance. Each ministry is responsible for conducting RIAs on its policies, but the Treasury Board and the Regulatory Affairs and Orders in Council Secretariat of the Privy Council Office play a strong coordination role. RIA is required by Cabinet directives that regulate the process for making federal acts and regulations. The key document with regard to RIA is the Cabinet Directive on Canada Regulatory Policy from 1999. Over the years, it has permeated the overall departmental policy-making culture. Quantitative cost–benefit analysis has been strengthened and it is now mandatory for all proposals with costs exceeding CAN$ 10 million.

The system is characterized by the following features:

- RIA is mandatory for all legislation and aims to cover the early stages of the policy process.
- There is a strong political commitment to RIA through approval and signature by responsible ministers. It is supported by a wide array of guidelines and manuals, which are constantly updated. Training has been improved through interactive, web-based instruments.
- Strong central coordination is provided by the Treasury Board, which oversees the overall process. It is supported by the Regulatory Affairs and Orders in Council Secretariat, which provides central quality control. Both institutions have the power to refuse the submission of the proposal to Cabinet if documents are missing or if the statement is seriously flawed.
- Consultation plays an important role: after approval, the proposal is 'pre-published' to collect public comments over a period of 30 days. For final submission to the Treasury Board, the department must amend the statement reflecting the received information, the action taken and the rationale behind it. After the final proposal has been approved by the minister, the Regulatory Affairs and Orders in Council Secretariat will again verify all documents.
- External auditing and quality control are mainly provided by the General Auditor and the Parliament. All departments fulfil watchdog functions with regard to their policy areas and intervene if they consider the proposal or the assessment to be seriously flawed.[3]
- Environmental impacts are treated separately under the Cabinet Directive on the Environmental Assessment of Policy, Plan and Program Proposals (a form of SEA). Environmental assessment has to be performed by the responsible departments or agencies, all of

which have appointed a coordination officer for SEA. These officers keep in contact with the Canadian Environmental Assessment Agency, which oversees and coordinates the SEA process.

Although Canada is often regarded as a pioneer in terms of the institutionalization of policy appraisal and the quality of its outcomes, its RIA process is nonetheless strongly biased towards an assessment of economic costs and benefits. It mostly focuses on business compliance costs, competitiveness concerns and overall administrative burdens. Environmental concerns have only been integrated to a limited degree. Like the Dutch approach, the Canadian RIA system does not provide a genuinely integrated assessment of possible impacts. Against this background, the Commissioner on the Environment and Sustainable Development (located in the General Auditor's Office) has strongly criticized departments and agencies for insufficient action regarding the integration of sustainability concerns into RIAs (Commissioner on the Environment and Sustainable Development 2004). NGOs have reiterated these criticisms, complaining that all major areas of governmental action, especially the budget, remain out of bounds to sustainability appraisal.[4] The Environmental Assessment Agency, however, notes that progress has been made.[5]

SUMMARY DISCUSSION

Our comparison of the IA systems in the four jurisdictions shows that there are similarities in their basic orientation. All four procedures aim to:

- improve the evidence base of policy decisions;
- improve regulatory quality and streamline regulation;
- increase stakeholder involvement in policy making; and
- promote policy integration and the consideration of cross-cutting objectives.

There are differences, however, with regard to the emphasis on particular functions and the underlying rationale for the entire system. In Canada and the UK, policy appraisal was introduced to reduce administrative costs, avoid unnecessary rules and increase accountability. Only later was the system broadened to address other objectives such as sustainability and EPI. Regulatory and environmental policy appraisals were originally carried out separately in both the UK and Canada, with rather poor implementation of the latter (Jordan and Lenschow 2000). The degree of coupling remains low in Canada, whereas in the UK, environmental appraisal has been formally integrated into RIA. RIA has traditionally been less developed in the European Commission and in the Netherlands and consequently the twin objectives of regulatory efficiency and sustainability have been on a more equal footing from the beginning. Interestingly, this does not mean that integration is necessarily a more prominent feature in these two systems. While the European Commission's IA procedure does seek to combine sustainability and regulatory assessment, the Netherlands has introduced its Business-Effect Test and Environmental Test as completely separate procedures.

The way in which the requirement for IA is formally defined appears to have little impact on the effectiveness of the procedure in practice. Although all four systems make *ex ante* appraisal mandatory for policies with large potential impacts, implementation rates vary from almost full implementation (the UK) to a very limited level of uptake (the Netherlands). The question of how much effort to put into appraising policies is answered in different – and sometimes complementary – ways in the four jurisdictions. Thus, formal monetary thresholds exist in Canada; the principle of proportionality is used in the EU and the UK; a staged assessment process occurs in the Netherlands, the EU and the UK; and differentiated methodologies are used in the Netherlands (Business Impact Assessment, Environmental Assessment, Practice and Enforceability Assessment and Cost–Benefit Analysis). Although the conditions under which policy appraisal is mandatory are relatively clearly defined, there is less stringency regarding the required scope of the assessment.

From the perspective of EPI, the question of the way policy proposals are selected for appraisal is crucially important. In all four jurisdictions, the responsible ministry is ultimately in charge of framing assessments, although in some cases (for example, the European Commission), interdepartmental steering groups have an influence on this decision. This also used to be the case in the Netherlands, but the process was seen as overly burdensome and the scoping decision has been given back to the respective sectoral ministry. In all four systems, lists of potential impact areas are supposed to broaden the perspective of the officials in charge of policy development. Everyday practice shows, however, that this is not sufficient if policy appraisal is to function as an instrument for EPI: in the two cases with integrated procedures (namely, the UK and the EU), assessment reports tend to cover only direct, short-term and economic costs and benefits, often considering unintended effects only in a cursory way.

Another important difference concerns the mechanisms for and the extent of central coordination. Probably as a result of the strong tradition of regulatory reform in the UK and Canada, both systems have a powerful coordinating body (the Cabinet Office and the Treasury Board respectively).

By contrast, there is hardly any central control in the Netherlands and the EU, where coordinating units play a quite technical role and evaluation is mainly left to the departments themselves (see also Jordan and Schout 2006). In Canada and the UK, the central coordinating body also provides a certain level of quality assurance and is entitled to block the adoption of a proposal if the appraisal is considered to be flawed or otherwise insufficient. Although this rarely happens, the presence of an external evaluator is an important driver for implementation – although not necessarily quality – in both countries. A similar role is played by the General Auditor's Office and its Commissioner for Sustainable Development in relation to environmental appraisals in Canada.

A range of approaches also exist with regard to the methodologies used to appraise potential impacts of new policies. In the UK and Canada, the assessment guidelines strongly encourage the quantification of impacts, particularly the use of cost–benefit analysis. The guidelines issued by the European Commission also promote quantitative analysis, but at the same time recommend some flexibility in fitting the analytical technique to the issue under consideration. In the Netherlands, more qualitative methods are favoured. In practice, however, the differences are less pronounced because methodological difficulties and limited resources for IA mean that extensive and detailed quantitative assessment is the exception rather than the rule in all four jurisdictions. Perhaps due to the scale of interests at stake, the European Commission tends to use formal assessment methods and instruments more often than the other three jurisdictions. From an environmental perspective, using quantitative methodologies can have the benefit of facilitating the integration of previously neglected ecological impacts into decision making. On the other hand, policy appraisal in the UK (and to some extent in the European Commission) shows that a heavy reliance on cost–benefit analysis tends to bias against the consideration of environmental factors, which are notoriously difficult to quantify, particularly in the long run.

Finally, the four appraisal systems differ with respect to their openness and transparency. The systems in Canada, the UK and the European Commission explicitly aim to increase the transparency of rule making through the publication of assessment results, disclosure of the methodologies used and stakeholder consultation. In these three jurisdictions, public scrutiny functions as an important driver for better compliance with the assessment guidelines. IA reports also provide NGOs and other actors with an opportunity to analyse and question the criteria which underlie policy decisions affecting the environment. By contrast, in the Dutch system, appraisal is seen as an administrative procedure, and there are no provisions for participation and disclosure. It is not surprising therefore,

Table 6.1   A comparison of impact assessment systems in four jurisdictions

	European Commission	The Netherlands	Canada	United Kingdom
Orientation				
Function of the IA procedure (derived from guidance documents)	better regulation policy integration use of evidence involvement	better regulation policy integration use of evidence	better regulation use of evidence involvement	better regulation use of evidence involvement
Institutionalization				
Central coordination mechanisms	weak	weak	strong	strong
Integration of environ. assessment	integrated	separate	separate	integrated
Focus on quantification	medium	weak	strong	strong
Transparency provisions	strong	weak	medium	medium
Performance				
Implementation of the procedure	fairly good	moderate	moderate	good
Scope, detail, quality of analysis	variable, but fairly good	modest	modest	modest
Timing in practice	variable	variable	variable, but often late	variable, but often late

that the Netherlands also has the lowest implementation rate amongst the four jurisdictions analysed.

CONCLUSIONS

Overall, we would argue that the *ex ante* appraisal of generic national-level policies represents a number of opportunities to pursue EPI. Our analysis of the appraisal procedures in four jurisdictions reveals a number of new entry points that could allow environmental issues to become more embedded in sectoral policy making. In particular:

- They promote the involvement of environmental administrations in cross-sectoral policy making: the provisions for interdepartmental consultation which are usually part of policy appraisal procedures create new opportunities for the environmental departments to influence decisions in other ministries. Although this does not change the power structure within government, the requirements for early consultation give them an opportunity to identify potential environmental impacts before any decisions have been taken. However, in order to exploit these opportunities, environmental departments must be sufficiently motivated and resourced. At present, this is far from being the case: many environmental departments seem to believe that the sectors should 'own' environmental problems for themselves, with little involvement from them (Jordan and Schout 2006).
- They provide the centre of government with a new steering instrument: much of the literature on EPI concludes that successful integration is ultimately a question of political will and that environmental responsibilities need to be institutionalized at the centre of government (for example the prime minister's office). In the UK and Canada, policy appraisal has the potential of being used by the Prime Ministers to oversee and potentially control other parts of government. If environmental concerns are high on the political agenda, policy appraisal is potentially a powerful instrument for EPI.
- They increase the role of environmental NGOs: increased involvement of stakeholders and the disclosure of decision criteria and anticipated impacts open up new opportunities for environmental NGOs to scrutinize the decision-making process. Under conditions of transparency, pursuing private objectives at the expense of public interests becomes more difficult.
- They create opportunities for *ex post* evaluation: the *ex ante* formulation of objectives, intended benefits and other anticipated effects

provides opportunities for a systematic and critical *ex post* evaluation of policies. This could further promote a balanced consideration of generic objectives in the decision-making process.

There is no simple answer to the question of whether an integrated appraisal system is better at promoting EPI than a purely environmentally focused one. On the one hand, separate environmental appraisal procedures have often been ignored by sectoral departments (for example, previous appraisal procedures in the UK and the European Commission, and the current E-Test in the Netherlands), particularly when coupled with a low degree of central coordination and monitoring. This is not just because sectoral ministries lack the expertise for or interest in addressing those issues, but also because they want to avoid drawing attention to environmental costs that could undermine political support for their policies. Therefore, integrating 'weak' environmental issues into a mandatory procedure which also deals with the 'hard' issues of competitiveness and public finances may involve a potential upgrading on the political agenda.

On the other hand, integrated IA procedures have in practice not usually been genuinely 'integrated' in the sense of a coherent, balanced consideration of impacts. Even in the European Commission, which explicitly emphasizes the objective of sustainability, most appraisals focus on short-term (mostly economic) costs and benefits. Unless there are mechanisms in place that ensure that unintended social and environmental effects are carefully considered (Canada and the European Commission come closest to this ideal), there is a risk that integrated policy appraisal becomes a new label for what is in practice little more than conventional RIA. Moreover, merging regulatory and environmental appraisal procedures also involves potential for conflict: regulatory reform aims to reduce the burden of regulation on business and society. This involves setting higher standards for the justification of policy intervention, which will often contradict the regulatory needs of addressing challenges such as climate change and biodiversity loss. Which of these objectives prevails is to some extent a question of political priorities, which vary between and within jurisdictions. But there is also common ground which carefully designed appraisal procedures can help to explore. To achieve this, policy appraisal has to be used to open up the political process by including a wide range of interests and values, making them explicit and considering marginal views and neglected issues. If policy appraisal is conceived as a purely internal instrument of analysis or is captured by political interests, however, it runs the risk of closing down the political process in order to identify the 'best' solution, legitimatize pre-existing decisions or justify a course of action advocated by the strongest set of interests. A carefully designed appraisal system should be able to avoid all these things.

NOTES

1. See http://www.eeb.org/activities/chemicals/20050113-EEB-WWF-KPMG-brief-final.pdf [accessed on 2 November 2006].
2. See http://www.eeac-net.org/download/EEAC%20WG%20Gov_IA%20statement_final_18-5-06.pdf [accessed on 2 November 2006].
3. Interview with Greg Wilburn, Senior Policy Officer at the Canadian Environmental Assessment Agency, 12 October 2004.
4. Interview with Stephen Hazell, National Executive Director, Canadian Parks and Wilderness Society and the Green Budget Coalition, 4 October 2004.
5. Interview with Greg Wilburn, Senior Policy Officer at the Canadian Environmental Assessment Agency, 12 October 2004.

BIBLIOGRAPHY

Bulmer, S. and M. Burch (1998), 'Organizing for Europe: Whitehall, the British state and the European Union', *Public Administration*, 76, 601–628.

Cabinet Office (2003), *Better Policy Making: A Guide to Regulatory Impact Assessment*, London: Regulatory Impact Unit.

Carter, N., R. Klein and P. Day (1992), *How Organisations Measure Success: The Use of Performance Indicators in Government*, London: Routledge.

CEC (Commission of the European Communities) (2002), *Communication from the Commission: Action Plan 'Simplifying and Improving the Regulatory Environment'*, COM (2002) 278 final, Brussels: CEC.

CEC (Commission of the European Communities) (2005), *Impact Assessment Guidelines*, SEC (2005) 791, Brussels: CEC.

Commissioner on the Environment and Sustainable Development (2004), *2004 Report of the Commissioner on the Environment and Sustainable Development*, Ontario: Office of the Auditor General of Canada.

deLeon, P. (1997), *Democracy and the Policy Sciences*, Albany, NY: State University of New York Press.

DETR (Department of Environment, Transport and the Regions) (1998), *Policy Appraisal and the Environment: Policy Guidance*, London: DETR.

Fischer, F. and J. Forester (1993), *The Argumentative Turn in Policy Analysis and Planning*, London: UCL Press.

Hertin, J. and F. Berkhout (2003), 'Analysing institutional strategies for environmental policy integration: the case of EU enterprise policy', *Journal of Environmental Policy and Planning*, 5 (1), 39–56.

Hertin, J., J. Turnpenny, A. Jordan, M. Nilsson, D. Russel and B. Nykvist (forthcoming), 'Rationalising the policy mess? *Ex ante* policy assessment and the utilisation of knowledge in the policy process', *Environment and Planning*, A (in press).

Hertin, J., D. Wilkinson, M. Bartolomeo, K. Jacob and A. Volkery (2004), *Making EU Policies More Sustainable? The New Impact Assessment Procedure in the European Commission*, Brighton: SPRU, University of Sussex.

IMV (Institute for Miljøvurdering/Environmental Assessment Institute) (2006), *Getting Proportions Right: How Far should EU Impact Assessments Go?* Copenhagen: IMV.

Jordan, A. and A. Lenschow (2000), ' "Greening" the European Union: what can be learned from the "leaders" of EU environmental policy?' *European Environment*, 10, 109–120.

Jordan, A. and A. Schout, (2006), *The Coordination of the European Union: Exploring the Capacities of Networked Governance*, Oxford: Oxford University Press.

Kingdon, J.W. (1995), *Agendas, Alternatives, and Public Policies*, New York: Longman.

Kraack, M., H. Pehle and P. Zimmermann-Steinhart (2001), *Umweltintegration in der Europäischen Union: Das Umweltpolitische Profil der EU im Politikfeldvergleich*, Baden-Baden: Nomos.

Lindblom, C.E. (1959), 'The science of muddling through', *Public Administration Review*, 19, 79–88.

Lindblom, C.E. and E.J. Woodhouse (1993), *The Policy Making Process*, New York: Prentice-Hall.

Majone, G. (1989), *Evidence, Argument, and Persuasion in the Policy Process*, New Haven and London: Yale University Press.

Marsden, S. (1999), 'Legislative EA in the Netherlands: the E-Test as a strategic and integrative instrument', *European Environment*, 9, 90–100.

National Audit Office (2006), *Regulatory Impact Assessment and Sustainable Development*, briefing for the Environmental Audit Committee, London: National Audit Office.

OECD (1997), *Regulatory Impact Analysis: Best Practices in OECD Countries*, Paris: OECD.

Owens, S., T. Rayner and O. Bina (2004), 'New agendas for appraisal: reflections on theory, practice, and research', *Environment and Planning A*, 36 (11), 1943–1959.

Radaelli, C. (1995), 'The role of knowledge in the policy process', *Journal of European Public Policy*, 2 (2), 159–183.

Radaelli, C. (2004), 'The diffusion of regulatory impact analysis: best-practice or lesson drawing?' *European Journal of Political Research*, 43 (5), 723–747.

Radaelli, C.M. (2005), 'Diffusion without convergence: how political context shapes the adoption of regulatory impact assessment', *Journal of European Public Policy*, 12 (5), 924–943.

Richardson, J. (1996), 'Actor-based models of national and EU policy-making', in H. Kassim and A. Menon (eds) *The European Union and National Industrial Policy*, London: Routledge.

Russel, D. and A. Jordan (2007), 'Gearing up government for sustainable development: environmental policy appraisal in UK central government', *Journal of Environmental Planning and Management*, 50 (1), 1–21.

Sabatier, P.A. (ed.), (1999), *Theories of the Policy Process*, Davis: Westview Press.

Sabatier, P.A. and H.C. Jenkins-Smith (1993), *Policy Change and Learning: An Advocacy-Coalition Framework*, Boulder, CO: Westview Press.

Sabatier, P.A. and H.C. Jenkins-Smith (1999), 'The advocacy-coalition framework: an assessment', in P.A. Sabatier (ed.), *Theories of the Policy Process*, Boulder, CO: Westview Press.

Sanderson, I. (2002), 'Evaluation, policy learning and evidence-based policy making', *Public Administration*, 80 (1), 1–22.

Volkery, A. (2004), *Regulatory Impact Analysis in Canada*, Berlin: Environmental Policy Research Centre.

Volkery, A. and K. Ehrhardt (2004), *Sustainability and Regulatory Impact Assessment in the Netherlands*, Berlin: Environmental Policy Research Centre.

Weale, A. (1992), *The New Politics of Pollution*, Manchester: Manchester University Press.

Weale, A., G. Pridham, M. Cini and D. Konstadakopulos (2000), *Environmental Governance in Europe*, Oxford: Oxford University Press.

Wilkinson, D. (1997), 'Towards sustainability in the European Union? Steps within the European Commission towards integrating the environment into other European Union policy sectors', *Environmental Politics*, 6 (1), 153–173.

Wilkinson, D., M. Fergusson, C. Bowyer, J. Brown, A. Ladefoged, C. Monkhouse and A. Zdanowicz (2004), *Sustainable Development in the European Commission's Integrated Impact Assessments for 2003*, London: IEEP.

Wilkinson, D., C. Monkhouse, M. Herodes and A. Farmer (2005), *For Better or For Worse? The EU's 'Better Regulation' Agenda and the Environment*, London: Institute for European Environmental Policy.

7. Strategic Environmental Assessment

Olivia Bina

INTRODUCTION

Strategic Environmental Assessment (SEA)[1] is widely considered to be a member of the large and diverse family of environmental assessment instruments (Goodland and Mercier 1999). Its most common interpretation is outlined by Volkery, Jacob and Lenschow (see Chapter 2) as follows: 'a procedural instrument for the evaluation of all stages of the decision-making cycle', from policies to plans and programmes. This chapter explores the actual and potential contribution of SEA to EPI, illuminating some of the complexities and opportunities that arise from the many and constantly evolving interpretations of this instrument. SEA is considered to have sprung from Environmental Impact Assessment (EIA), which was first institutionalized in the late 1960s. Despite the technocratic, rationalist nature of significant aspects of EIA (Ortolano and Shepherd 1995), its effectiveness was intended to be measured in terms of its contribution to changing political institutions and the worldviews and behaviour associated with them (Bartlett 1997), although implementation practice has often fallen far short of these ideals. During the last ten years, SEA has witnessed significant change intended to overcome some of the weaknesses of EIA. The aim of SEA is to move beyond the assessment of policies, plans and programmes (PPPs) towards 'sustainable outcomes' (Brown and Thérivel 2000: 184). As such, SEA is increasingly advocated as a means of implementing EPI *and* sustainable development (Sheate *et al.* 2001; Sadler 2002).

Thus, the purpose and role of SEA – and the expectations attached to it – share significant common ground with EPI. SEA can arguably be conceived as a potentially crucial mechanism in the 'continual process to ensure environmental issues are taken into account in all policy-making, demanding changes in political, organizational and procedural activities, so that environmental issues are taken on board as early as possible' in the policy process (EEA 2005b: 11).

The following sections explore the evolution of the concept and practice of SEA. First, the origins of the concept are reviewed, showing how SEA shares common ground with the objectives, mechanisms and challenges of

EPI. Second, a critical review of the history of SEA highlights its contribution both to EPI and sustainability over three broad periods starting in the late 1980s. Third, this process of evolution is compared to the SEA methods which are now being used in practice. The final section assesses the potential contribution of SEA to EPI, but also the benefits of EPI thinking to the future of SEA.

HISTORY

At first glance, the history of SEA appears simple and linear: increasingly evident shortcomings of EIA since the 1970s led scholars and practitioners to seek alternative approaches and instruments, eventually resulting in the emergence of a set of practices known as SEA. An early example of the basic concepts underlying SEA (although this term was not in use at the time) is found in O'Riordan and Hey (1976: 208), who argued that '[i]t is essential that proper procedures are devised to ensure that environmental implications of major policy areas are fully discussed prior to the preliminary decision to advance any particular proposal'. Not surprisingly, by the late 1980s the momentum behind the need to develop and apply SEA had also become closely linked to developments at international level. In 1987, the Brundtland Report (WCED 1987: 313) called for a shift away from the idea of the environment as a separate sphere of policy. In the same year, the World Bank's Development Committee stated that 'environmental issues must be addressed as part of the overall economic policy rather than project-by-project' (World Bank, quoted in Noble 2002: 4). During the 1990s, Chapters 8 and 10 (amongst others) of Agenda 21 advocated a number of improvements in decision making, information for decision makers, and assessment and planning instruments, and thus placed the theme of EPI centre stage in the SEA debate (UNCED 1992).

In Europe, 1992 proved to be a crucial year in the life of SEA. The United Nations Economic Commission for Europe (UNECE 1992) called for the environmental assessment (EA) of PPPs as a means of anticipating and highlighting potential environmental problems, preventing delays and assisting in long-term planning, as well as preventing or reducing litigation. It recommended that the results of such EAs be considered on a par with social and economic factors in the development of PPPs. This final point resonated with Brundtland's plea for sustainable development.

Against this backdrop the early life of SEA was merely a technical contribution, seeking to address the symptoms – rather than the causes – of a deeper malaise that was leading to serious, often irreversible environmental deterioration (Bina 2003). The problems with such a technical approach to SEA are shared – often unknowingly – with other assessment instruments (including technology assessment, risk assessment, cost–benefit analysis and policy appraisal) (see Chapter 6). Many are essentially political, institutional and policy-related, namely: a lack of political commitment to and capacity for EPI and sustainable development; weak environmental governance; and weak strategic planning (see for example Ayre and Callway 2005 and the EEA 2005a). They echo continuing debates about the limits of technical rational models of assessment, which focus on providing neutral information and scientific knowledge to inform decisions that, at root, concern important issues of value (RCEP 1998; EC 2002a; Owens *et al.* 2004; Connelly and Richardson 2005).

However, the application of SEA has gradually evolved from this technical focus into a more diverse and hence potentially more promising mechanism for assessing strategic initiatives. The changes are moving it significantly closer to the objectives and mechanisms discussed in EPI literature.

CONCEPTUAL BACKGROUND

The normative conception and practical application of SEA have evolved significantly since the late 1980s. In the process, ever more complex and diverse interpretations have emerged of how the purpose of SEA should be operationalized. The interaction between the conceptual and more practical developments in the field of SEA has been characterized by a certain lag effect. Hobbs (2003) claimed that 'SEA practice is ahead of theory . . . though we are not sure whether this is a good or a bad thing'.

In order to understand the nature of SEA and the different EPI logics at work within its framework, it is necessary to understand SEA's historical development. A critical review of the literature (Bina 2003) reveals that the evolution of SEA occurred in three broad stages. The remainder of this section discusses each one in turn, with the aim of exploring the links to thinking about EPI and sustainability.

Early Views: an Informational Instrument

The implicit aim of EIA and early SEA practice was essentially informational, that is, to offer a clearer prediction and evaluation of the impacts of a proposed development delivered in the shape of a report (Thérivel *et al.* 1992; Sadler and Verheem 1996). One of the most widely cited definitions of SEA throughout the 1990s was that provided by Thérivel and her co-workers (1992: 19–20):

SEA can be defined as the formalized, systematic and comprehensive process of evaluating the environmental impacts of a policy, plan or programme and its alternatives, including the preparation of a written report of the findings of that evaluation, and using the findings in publicly accountable decision-making.

This definition bears a striking resemblance to Munn's definition of EIA (Munn 1979). The initial aim of SEA was thus to ensure the respect of standards and limits, reduce (the risk of) adverse impacts on the environment, and mitigate and compensate for those impacts deemed to be unavoidable. It reflected the idea that the adverse effects of development should be avoided, minimized and contained, and assessment was conceived almost exclusively as a technique. In practice, the exercise was rarely performed sufficiently early on in the policy process to influence the framing of the problem, the development objectives or the subsequent ideas and strategic alternatives. Thus, everyday SEA practice fell short of the ideal expressed in the EPI literature (Russel 2004; EEA 2005b).

In the 1980s and early 1990s, the majority of SEA examples were coming from the USA, Canada and parts of Europe (Thérivel *et al.* 1992; UNECE 1992; Thérivel 1993; Wilkinson *et al.* 1994; Wood 1995). Fischer (2002: 87) maintains that in the late 1980s, SEA 'referred to the application of project-based environmental impact assessment [EIA] principles'. Thérivel's (1993: 165) overview of SEA systems up to 1993 found that, with the exception of the Dutch system for policy-level assessments, 'all other systems are a straightforward expansion of project EIA' to higher levels. She then argued that none of the countries reviewed 'would claim that this incremental expansion of EIA would itself lead to sustainability'. A case in point is the relatively more advanced (in quantity, if not in substance) experience in the USA. By 1989, the US federal system was already producing an average of 40 SEAs (or Programmatic Environmental Impact Statements) per year, the contents of which were essentially the same as those of most EIAs (Thérivel 1993). These initial efforts represented a reductionist interpretation of the concept of assessment proposed in the European Environment Agency's recent EPI framework (EEA 2005b: 10), that is, one which envisages a 'process for ex-ante environmental assessment' involving the '[c]onsultation of environmental authorities and stakeholders' and ensuring that 'environmental information [is] available for and used to inform policy-making'.

Shifting Focus: Process, Objectives and Early Start

As the momentum for SEA increased during the 1990s, the way in which it was conceived widened significantly (Bina 2007). An analysis of definitions arising from both academic and policy sources reveals the clear rise of two normative claims: 1) that SEA will contribute to sustainable development (for example: Thérivel and Partidario 1996; Queralt *et al.* 2001); and 2) that SEA will improve policy making (for example: Brown and Thérivel 2000; Partidario 2000; Caratti *et al.* 2004). Although these two claims often appear in this order, it seems evident that the latter is in fact a means of achieving the former – a tall order, no doubt, which in the second phase in the evolution of SEAs was addressed primarily in three ways: conceiving assessment as an process rather than an instrument; turning to objectives-led approaches; and emphasizing the need to start early in the policy process. These developments are also to be found in the literatures on EPI and sustainable development strategies (for example: OECD and UNDP 2002; see also Chapter 5).

In the SEA literature, the distinction between process and instruments has been dealt with rather superficially. Indeed, most definitions refer to SEA as a process, with sustainable development as the 'end' point. Petts (1999: 53) makes an important contribution by distinguishing between EIA and SEA on the one hand, and Technology Assessment, Life-Cycle Analysis, Risk Assessment, Environmental Auditing and Cost–Benefit Analysis on the other. She argues that only the first two 'meet the definition of a process', while the others are simply 'tools'.[2] Nonetheless, a surprising amount of recent guidance on strategic-level assessment still refers to SEA as a tool (for example, EC 2002b; ODPM 2003), revealing a persistent tension (and confusion) in the literature about the nature of SEA.

As part of this change, there has been a widespread uptake of objectives-led approaches to SEA, which – in their simplest form – would verify the consistency and coherence between (strategic) development initiatives and local, national and international goals of environmental protection and sustainable development (a good example of this is the SEA of European Structural Fund programmes – ERM 1998). This led to substantial changes in the practice of SEA, moving beyond the provision of sound information (Owens *et al.* 2004), towards the promotion and integration of objectives, and greater policy coordination and consistency. SEA thus became a mechanism with which to mainstream environmental policy and legislation (expressed through their goals) into sectoral policy making. Such logic is exemplified by the manner in which EPI is pursued in the EU (see Chapter 8).

The progressive focus on process and objectives then led to a third development: a move towards process integration, driven primarily by the much-acclaimed – but often elusive – rule whereby SEA should be applied 'as early as possible' (for example: Thérivel *et al.* 1992; Sadler and Verheem 1996; EC 2001) in order to be effective (compare policy assessment, in Chapter 6, which shares very similar assumptions). To implement this, practice had to grapple with the complexities of policy making, namely what Thérivel (1993: 164) saw as the 'frequent lack of a specific point in time when a decision regarding the PPP is made'. Finding and understanding that 'point', 'moment' (Partidario 1996), 'stage' (Thérivel *et al.* 1992) or 'decision window' (Caratti *et al.* 2004), preoccupied practitioners and scholars alike during the second half of the 1990s. A range of step-based SEA processes were developed, in an attempt to highlight key 'moments' when there would be an opportunity to integrate environmental concerns sufficiently early on in the policy process. Table 7.1 presents examples from a range of guidance documents published between 1992 and 2001.

Figure 7.1 suggests that these practices can be categorized according to four models of SEA which practitioners tend to combine on an ad hoc basis. The inheritance from EIA (Model A), which was partly responsible for SEA's early focus on the moment of impact assessment and reporting, is slowly being diluted as everyday practice adopts a range of models to strengthen the *ex ante* dimension. Models B and C represent a move towards closer integration between the planning and assessment processes. Model D is more common in developing contexts where planning itself is weak and SEA has to compensate for a lack of strategic thinking and planning (Bina 2003).

Despite these developments, by the end of the 1990s many problems still remained to be solved. Both the early start rule and the idea of process integration are based on technocratic-rationalistic interpretations of assessment and appraisal. In short, the idea of 'moments' in the policy process fails to account for the tensions between rationality and power (Flyvbjerg 1998; Richardson 2005), which technical-rational models of assessment are poorly equipped to deal with. This point was noted by O'Riordan and Hey (1976:174–5) as long ago as the 1970s:

> [T]he great political arguments [in relation to EIA] were about values, not facts, and involved all kinds of consequences that could not possibly be quantified. Politicians assess alternatives in terms of good and bad . . . [they] act in response to vision and outrage as well as reason.

Scholars have now begun to turn to the crucial issue of how assessment systems can address issues of value (RCEP 1998; EC 2002a; Connelly and Richardson 2005), trade-offs and priorities, all of which are intrinsic to the sustainability debate. Hildén has warned (2000: 68) that:

> [a]ssessments that are fully integrated into the planning process may appear as an ideal in the rational planning view of assessments, but in a world of conflict and diverse interests such assessments may be counter productive. In

Table 7.1 Examples of SEA steps taken from a variety of sources (1992–2001)

SEA of transport	SEA and structural fund plans and programmes	SEA in decision making	Phases in general structured framework for SEA
• Aim • Objectives • Options • Mix of options (production of a range of scenarios) • Assessment (identification and assessment of relative environmental impacts of different scenarios • Option selection.	• Assessment of the environmental situation • Objectives, targets and priorities • Draft development proposal • Identification of alternatives • Environmental assessment • Environmental indicators • Integration of the results of the assessment into the final decision.	• Reason for carrying out SEA • Who to involve • Description of PPP • Objectives, topics, targets and indicators • Description of baseline environment • Description of alternative PPPs • Test alternatives • Explain which alternative was selected and why • Describe how PPP has been changed as a result of the above • Monitoring.	• Phase I – Scoping the assessment issues • Phase II – Describing the alternatives • Phase III – Scoping the assessment components (for example, criteria used to evaluate) • Phase IV – Evaluating the potential impacts • Phase V – Determining impact significance • Phase VI – Comparing the alternatives • Phase VII – Identify the best practicable environmental option.

Source: Bina (2003: 82)

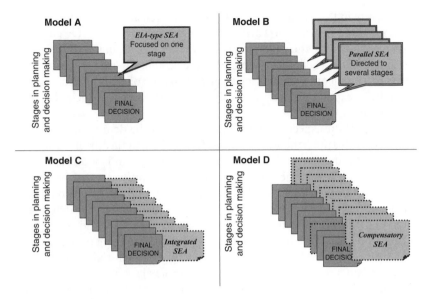

Source: Bina (2004)

Figure 7.1   The range of SEA models

controversial issues a partly independent assessment may be a precondition for a meaningful public debate.

This is an important plea, which is also relevant to the wider EPI literature.

Further Changes? SEA as a Means to Improve Governance

Based on the analysis so far, the principal claim that SEA would contribute to sustainable development remains problematic. SEA is expected to address both the weakness of sustainability conceptions and of the policy processes intended to deliver them. This translates into further challenges and profound changes to the nature and role of SEA. In this third stage in SEA's evolution, the potential contribution to EPI objectives is widened and further strengthened. Lafferty (2005) defines EPI 'as an instrument of governance for sustainable development'. The SEA community has been taking steps in similar directions. Here, we see an interesting convergence with related concepts and practice such as sustainable strategizing (Chapter 5) and policy appraisal (Chapter 6).

Although the world of SEA often remains divided on these issues, a new and much more reflexive mood has been running through the assessment community in the last ten years. Dialogical as well as technical assessment processes (and instruments) are now thought to be essential (Owens *et al.* 2004), as shown by the wide range of activities that seem to fall under the heading of SEA (Dalal-Clayton and Sadler 2005). Figure 7.2 summarizes these developments, which are changing the nature of SEA processes and – crucially – expanding the range of EPI approaches to which they can contribute.

An important aspect of this change has been the demotion of prediction and evaluation (the white oval in Figure 7.2), in favour of a range of activities. Prediction and evaluation are changing and becoming more open to participatory methods. But more significantly, they are becoming secondary to many ancillary tasks which can often better respond to the challenges of integrating the environment into policy making. Before and after the traditional impact assessment activity of EIA and SEA, additional and alternative processes and instruments are being proposed. The grey ovals in Figure 7.2 represent these changes, which range from a new emphasis on previously rare tasks, to completely new tasks under the heading of SEA. The traditional moments leading to the collection, analysis and presentation of information remain at the heart of the *ex ante* rule for many – if not most – SEAs (the black oval in Figure 7.2), but they have been expanded to include more systematic analyses of the institutional context, the decision-making process and the key actors and stakeholders who should be involved early in the process of SEA (grey oval below the black one in Figure 7.2). Furthermore, the need to anticipate and actively influence events becomes increasingly relevant also for the negotiation and debate that accompanies many key decisions and policy-making moments, such as problem definition, policy coherence and the setting of objectives (Figure 7.2). A richer understanding of the actors involved means that SEA is moving beyond discourses which emphasize the participation of 'the public' or of 'the experts', to those that stress the need for consultation and collaboration within and between all relevant actors. This can help reduce the problems of sectoral divisions (EEA 2005b) and departmentalism (Russel 2005), as well as increase the level of coordination.

Apart from this diversification of activities under the heading of SEA, a second change can be observed in the recent practice and literature: although most guidance on SEA, including very recent examples, still describes it as the assessment of PPPs, it is increasingly evident that SEAs are now being called upon to respond to a much wider set of governance-related needs than those originally expressed in the 1980s (OECD and UNDP 2002; RCEP 2002; Dalal-Clayton and Sadler 2005). As Glasson (1995: 716) argued convincingly: '[t]he problems of "ability" to carry out

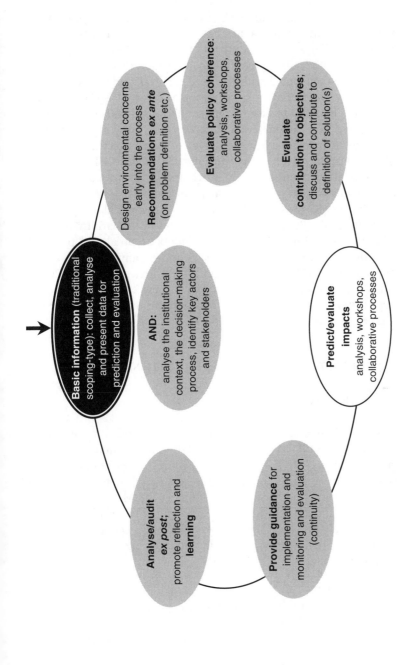

Figure 7.2 The widening range of SEA activities

SEA may in fact be of less significance than problems of "willingness"' to carry it out. Policy makers may wish to keep their policies confidential until they are well developed, instead, SEA implies power sharing between the proponent and the environmental assessor or competent authority.

In discussing policy analysis, Boothroyd (1995) also noted the need for similar 'cultural shifts'. SEA practitioners are coming to similar conclusions, as they are confronted with the need for institutional change and change of worldviews on how to do development, as well as on what such development might entail to be environmentally sound and sustainable. If designed to raise more fundamental questions about why certain choices are made, who to involve at various stages of policy making and what mechanisms are appropriate for dialogue and consultation, SEA can serve as an additional mechanism to improve transparency, coordination, effectiveness and legitimacy – all of which are crucial to good governance. Recently, scholars (Kørnøv and Nielsen 2005; Nilsson 2005) and practitioners (World Bank 2005) have been moving towards 'learning-oriented approaches' to SEA (Bina 2003: 306), finding conceptual and practical support in the literature on rational, social and organizational learning (Argyris and Schön 1974; Van der Knaap 1995; Torres and Preskill 2001), as a means to facilitate institutional change. These developments show further consistency with EPI thinking and practice, suggesting that SEA could make a significant contribution to EPI as a learning process.

DEPLOYMENT: PRACTICAL EXPERIENCES

Different Models of SEA Practice

As discussed in Chapter 2, several EU countries have applied various forms of SEA since the late 1980s and early 1990s.[3] If we accept that the purpose and practical approach to SEA can vary significantly depending on the context and on the type of initiative it is being applied to, then it can nonetheless be argued that by the late 1990s most EU Member States had developed some experience of SEA, especially in the two leading fields of application, namely transport and land-use planning. Dalal-Clayton and Sadler (2005: 46) provide the most recent and arguably complete categorization of SEA models:

- 'Formal models':
  - EIA-based (for example, US experience and the approach of Directive 42/2001/EC);
  - EIA-modified (for example, Canada and Denmark);

- 'Dual or two-track systems', combining EIA types and more strategic versions (for example, the Netherlands and Finland);
- 'Near-equivalent' models:
  - Environmental appraisal (for example, appraisal of land-use plans in the UK);
  - Regional assessments (for example, Australia and Canada); and
  - Sustainability appraisals (for example, Australia and the UK);
- 'Integrated' models:
  - Procedural integration – no separate procedure for assessment and planning (for example, New Zealand);
  - Substantive integration – no separate procedure for environmental assessment (for example, Impact Assessment in the European Commission – see Chapter 7); and
  - Integrated Assessment and Planning (for example, the UK regional planning system);
- 'Para-SEA' models:
  - Elements of SEA: procedures that have some but not all of the features or characteristics of SEA (for example, planning and assessments undertaken within sustainability-based development strategy processes).

This overview nicely illustrates the unequivocal diversity of SEA practice and further clarifies the three stages identified above. The first stage – SEA as an informational instrument – partly overlaps with the formal and near-equivalent models suggested by Dalal-Clayton and Sadler; the second – SEA as a process – is consistent with the integrated and para-SEA models; and the third – SEA as a governance mechanism and objectives-led method – may coincide with any one of these five categories, as it depends more on the purpose and cultural context than on elements of method and process alone.

This, in turn, highlights a critical aspect of practice: although the three distinct stages represent a historical evolution from the 1970s to the present, today one can find applications of SEA reflecting any combination of such stages and related models. Moreover, although SEA is applied widely throughout the world, it has not yet attained the kind of systematic application that leads to a consistent body of practice, as is now characteristic of EIA. As a result, the potential for SEA to contribute to EPI will depend on the interpretation and methods chosen in different institutional and legal contexts, as well as on the nature of the initiative being assessed (since the approach, instruments, and detail levels vary significantly between programmes and policies). Furthermore, evidence shows that a lot depends on the objectives and capacity of the individual(s) leading the planning and assessment processes.

It is therefore difficult to state precisely that a country's body of practice is at a specific stage in applying SEA, or that it has adopted a particular model of SEA. However, it is possible to classify legal requirements as representing the basic interpretation of what SEA is meant to do, and set the minimum standards for its practice. Interestingly, two examples are prominent in this sense: the USA and the EU. Both have strong legal requirements and are classified as 'formal models' by Dalal-Clayton and Sadler (2005: 46), but are at opposite ends in terms of years of experience: over 30 years in the case of the USA, and only four in the case of the EU.

SEA in the USA

The US National Environmental Policy Act (NEPA) of 1969, which established EIA, did not distinguish between projects and more strategic initiatives (Thérivel 1993; González 2001). The 1969 Act and 1978 Regulations by the Council on Environmental Quality apply to 'major federal actions', which have been interpreted to include legislation and programmes: 'actions that are related regionally, or generically by stage of technology development, or which are otherwise connected (e.g. by reference to potential cumulative effects)', especially those related to land use and integrated resource management (Dalal-Clayton and Sadler 2005: 103). The original EIA concept has therefore been applied to a range of initiatives which were strategic to a greater or lesser degree since the 1970s, making this the longest standing legally-binding mechanism for evaluating PPPs (as well as projects). These assessments produced programmatic environmental impact statements, which are generally considered to be the US equivalent of SEAs.

The procedural and content requirements for Environmental Impact Statements (EISs) laid out in the 1978 Regulations are the same for EIAs (projects) and programmatic environmental impact statements (PPPs). However, according to Bass (2005: 247)

> [I]n practice there are considerable differences in the scale of analysis, the methods of evaluation and the nature of the impacts being evaluated. A programmatic environmental impact statement is typically focused on a broad geographical area and emphasizes cumulative impacts.

The assessment of cumulative impacts is indeed a distinctive focus of SEA in the USA.

The difference in approach to the preparation of project-level EISs and programmatic environmental impact statements has increased over the last few years. A report by the NEPA Task Force suggests that the number of programmatic environmental impact statements was 'increasing at most government levels and coordination of analyses is improving' and that the approach was particularly valuable 'in addressing issues at the broad landscape, ecosystem or regional level' (quoted in Dalal-Clayton and Sadler 2005: 106). Bass (2005: 252) details further developments in programmatic environmental impact statement practice:

- Collaboration: more cooperation with stakeholders through the establishment of advisory committees, frequent meetings in local communities, task forces and so on.
- Vertical integration: Federal land management agencies are increasingly seeking cooperation with other levels of government (especially with state and local governments and tribal organizations) to ensure that federal land management plans reflect their views. Cooperation includes joint federal/state planning activities – including joint studies, joint public meetings and sharing of staff, and may lead to non-federal agencies actively participating in the preparation of programmatic environmental impact statements.
- Adaptive management and learning: increased use of continuous monitoring and evaluation, aimed to improve natural resource management policies and practices by learning from on-the ground outcomes of operational programmes.
- Policy integration: federal agencies preparing land-use plans have to comply with their own planning law and NEPA, but also with other federal and state laws. During the planning and assessment process, agencies enter into programmatic agreements with other resource management agencies setting forth how the requirements of various laws will be met during the planning process.

All these developments suggest an increasing adoption of EPI-type mechanisms, as discussed elsewhere in this book. The significant contribution of programmatic environmental impact statements in identifying and evaluating alternatives (Dalal-Clayton and Sadler 2005) is the result of effective integration between planning and assessment processes. Indeed, Bass (2005: 257) considers that '[i]ntegration between NEPA and federal land use planning [is] highly developed under the programmes of federal land management agencies – to the point that they are considered a single process'.

This review suggests that while a programmatic environmental impact statement (PEIS) is first and foremost associated with 'formal and near-equivalent' SEA models, it has expanded to include a strong process dimension (as well as the traditional product – the statement) and elements of good governance. However, despite being the oldest SEA-type mechanism, the programmatic environmental impact statement has been underutilized. Bass (2005: 242) notes that 'there is a considerable track record of SEA preparation, particularly by the federal agencies responsible for most federal land use planning and management'. He suggests that programmatic environmental impact statements prepared for such plans, and other types of strategic actions, represent more than 25 per cent of all EISs prepared under NEPA. However, Dalal-Clayton and Sadler (2005: 106) argue that 'in comparison to other types of NEPA application, the contemporary use of PEIS remains limited'.

Recent developments in the approach to programmatic environmental impact statements seem promising, and a wider application would make a welcome contribution to EPI. However, notwithstanding these developments, scholars such as Caldwell (2000) still consider that NEPA's potential is far from being reached:

> NEPA's purpose was never the writing of impact statements, but to provide an analysis and an inducement to ecological rationality. To use EIA as it was intended requires leadership committed to the objectives and subjecting budgets, strategies, programs and plans to that end . . . [I]t requires a broadened perspective, including additional scientific, technical and quality of life considerations.

These remain challenges for US practitioners, as well as for the wider community of SEA users.

SEA in the EU

In contrast to the USA, the European experience shows a great preoccupation with distinguishing between project EIA and SEA of strategic initiatives (PPPs). The task of evaluating PPPs became the shorthand for distinguishing SEA from EIA, that is, explaining both what SEA was, and why it was needed. Such differentiation was the main reason why the EU produced two Directives on environmental assessment (rather that one, as in the USA). European institutions devoted more than a decade to intensive negotiations before finally approving the text for Directive 2001/42/EC on the Assessment of the Effects of Certain Plans and Programmes on the Environment (EC 2001) – that is, SEA. Although the Directive came into force in July 2004 – making it too early to draw any conclusions on its actual contribution to the objectives of EPI – it is possible to reflect on its potential. The objective of this Directive is perfectly in line with EPI. In Article 1 it is said that the aim is to 'provide for a high level of protection of the environment and to contribute to the integration of environmental considerations into the preparation and adoption of plans and programmes with a view to promoting sustainable development' (EC 2001). The Directive emphasizes consultation with, inter alia, environmental authorities, and public participation (Article 6), and promotes transparency by stressing the need to take into account the results of these procedures during the preparation of plans and programmes and before the final decision – as well as to explain how this was done (Article 8). However, the scope is limited to plans and programmes (Article 3) despite the fact that several EU countries have already applied SEA-type instruments to their policies and legislation (for example, Denmark, Finland, UK, the Netherlands). This is likely to reduce significantly the capacity to discuss environmentally sound alternatives, as these inevitably require considerations that are within the realm of policies, not just of plans and programmes; this has direct implications for the more far-reaching and long-term objectives of EPI. Similarly, the Directive's key requirement is to produce an Environmental Report (Article 5; Annex 1 lists detailed contents): a potentially backward step compared to the evolving practice and theory of SEA (see above), which emphasize process rather than deliverables (compare the third stage discussed above).

Thus, depending on how each Member State decides to transpose the Directive into national practice, its contribution to EPI may turn out to be significant or quite minimal. This author considers that the advances in practice – albeit often ad hoc – suggest that SEA has a promising future. What remains to be explained is the choice of the EU itself, which has opted to introduce policy impact assessment in relation to its own policy proposals (see Chapter 6) instead of SEA. Given the long history of support that the EU has provided to the concept of SEA (notably in the Fifth Action Programme) (EC 1992), the significant investments made in research, pilot applications and methodological guidance (for example: ERM 1998; DHV 1999; Caratti *et al.* 2004), and applications to major policy areas such as regional development ('cohesion') and transport, it is surprising that the Commission eventually chose to shun SEA. At the very least, this choice raises questions about the long-term viability of SEA, if, as one must conclude, it has been deemed to be less appropriate than IA.

SUMMARY DISCUSSION

Shifts in Thinking

The three broad stages in the evolution of SEA analysed above reveal a shift towards a more reflexive approach during the late 1990s. The evolution from seeing SEA as an informational instrument to one emphasizing that it is a process and an objective marked a significant departure from earlier technocratic conceptions. It gave SEA a wider set of approaches to influence and change the complex processes of policy formulation, and to improve its capacity to deliver sustainable development. The third stage is more a promise and a normative construction than an observation of empirical reality. However, the potential is there. In fact, experience suggests that there is still a need to focus on improving the capacity of governance to integrate environmental issues in a range of less traditional impact assessment fora. This goes to the very conception of 'assessment', that is, one that is not centred round *the* moment of impact prediction and evaluation, but rather the key moments of development planning. This analysis shows that SEA processes and methods are increasingly consistent with the principles and practice of EPI (being capable of influencing the policy cycle, its cognitive and informative conditions, and a range of actors), despite the remarkably limited dialogue between the bodies of scholarly work that have emerged around them.

Obstacles and Challenges

This chapter has argued that over the last 20 years, the understanding of SEA's nature and role has deepened and broadened, and its practice has become more substantial and widespread. Dalal-Clayton and Sadler (2005: 299) conclude their review of practice by stressing that 'SEA is a fast-moving and still diversifying field . . . in many parts of the world, it is too early to come to a definitive view of the status and effectiveness of SEA application'. Nonetheless, they suggest that (2004: 302) 'the quality and effectiveness of much SEA practice remain questionable and increasing attention is being given to this area'. The obstacles to SEA's ability to influence and improve policy making are, of course, very similar to those holding back EPI and sustainability. These include a poor capacity to think and plan strategically (and holistically), a lack of transparency in planning and decision making and a persistent lack of political commitment and high-level leadership. While SEA can be conceived as a means to reduce some of these constraints (and not just simply adapting passively to such contextual features), there can be no doubt that the results will only be fully apparent in the medium to long term. In fact, the broadening purpose and role of SEA call for a review of the concept of effectiveness in assessment, to allow for more subtle changes in attitudes, as well as different institutional and administrative arrangements which may occur over time, as a result of the systematic application of SEA within a particular organization. This would require a departure from the more traditional view of effectiveness (as measured in terms of the provision of adequate information) to one emphasizing longer-term learning effects and, eventually, better decisions (note the similarities with impact assessment covered in Chapter 6).

CONCLUSIONS

It could be argued that in its more recent manifestations, SEA is not an assessment instrument or mechanism per se, but rather a range of governance processes and instruments. One could thus conclude (as with NSSDs – see Chapter 5) that SEA is 'neither sufficient nor necessary for EPI' (Steurer 2005). However, SEA has a potentially critical place in EPI due to the 'window of opportunity' (see Kingdon 1995) created by the broad interest in SEA, and the rapid diffusion of legal requirements throughout the developed and developing world. To ensure that SEA delivers on such promises, those responsible for designing and introducing SEA systems should pay urgent attention to the obstacles that have undermined EIA and SEA to date, adopt a broad interpretation of what assessment can entail – in terms of both *ex ante* and *ex post* activities – and make a conscious effort to build synergies with other instruments and mechanisms of EPI.

If this addresses the possible contribution of SEA to EPI, mention should also be made of how EPI can enhance the development and policy relevance of SEA in the future. As SEA is increasingly seen as a means to promote sustainable development, its *raison d'être* risks being diluted in this wider, and often ambiguous discourse. The proliferation of 'new' mechanisms that seek to integrate the three dimensions of sustainability (namely sustainability appraisal, sustainability impact assessment, impact assessment – see Chapter 6) testifies to a basic level of confusion. Recently, Wood (2003: 3–4) stated that:

> [t]he effectiveness of EIA and SEA has not, to date, been assisted by the emergence of integrated impact assessment (IIA). The integration of economic, social and environmental factors in IIA has sometimes been to the disadvantage of the environment. Some of us with long memories worry that the subordination of EIA and SEA to IIA may ignore the lessons of history. After all, EIA was originally developed to ensure that environmental costs – previously neglected – were adequately considered in decisions. It is environmentally sustainable development that EIA and SEA strive to achieve. The effectiveness of EIA and SEA (and of IIA) would be bolstered if their bottom line goal were to be 'no net environmental deterioration'.

These concerns are shared by many (Jackson and Illsley 2005; RCEP 2002). EPI may thus provide a strong reference point for those setting up new and/or bolstering existing SEA systems, so that they are better equipped to face the fundamental choices and challenges in governing the relationship between society and nature.

NOTES

1. This chapter focuses on a relatively broad interpretation of SEA, including those versions that embrace a wide scope and sometimes overlap with sustainability assessment practice. However, for reasons of space, it will not discuss in detail literature specifically aimed at sustainability assessment or 'impact assessment' (see Chapter 6 for further details).
2. Although Sheate *et al.* (2001: ix) use this terminology differently, they arrive at a similar conclusion: '[i]ncreasingly, sustainable development provides not just a purpose, but the underlying philosophy to SEA . . . so that [this] tool and technique operates much more as an approach'.
3. Note that this refers to the practical application of SEA-type methods, and not to a systematic application based on legal requirements (as discussed in Chapter 2).

BIBLIOGRAPHY

Argyris, C. and Schön, D.A. (1974), *Theory in Practice: Increasing Professional Effectiveness*, San Francisco: Jossey-Bass.

Ayre, G. and Callway, R. (eds) (2005), *Governance for Sustainable Development: A Foundation for the Future*, London: Earthscan.

Bartlett, R.V. (1997), 'The rationality and logic of NEPA revisited', in R. Clark and L. Canter (eds), *Environmental Policy and NEPA: Past, Present and Future*, Boca Raton, FL: St. Lucie Press.

Bass, R. (2005), 'United States', in C. Jones, M. Baker, J. Carter, S. Jay, M. Short and C. Wood (eds), *Strategic Environmental Assessment and Land Use Planning*, London: Earthscan.

Bina, O. (2003), *Re-conceptualising Strategic Environmental Assessment: Theoretical Overview and Case Study from Chile*, unpublished PhD Thesis, Geography Department, Cambridge: University of Cambridge.

Bina, O. (2004), 'La valutazione ambientale', in C. Cici and F. Ranghieri (eds), *La Governance locale dell'ambiente e del territorio: Percorsi di sostenibilità tra aspetti geografici e percepiti*, Milan: Edizioni Angelo Guerini e Associati SpA.

Bina, O. (2007), 'A critical review of the dominant lines of argumentation on the need for Strategic Environmental Assessment', *Environmental Impact Assessment Review*, 27 (1), 585–606.

Boothroyd, P. (1995) 'Policy assessment', in F. Vanclay and D. A. Bronstein (eds), *Environmental and Social Impact Assessment*, Chichester: John Wiley.

Brown, A. and Thérivel, R. (2000), 'Principles to guide the development of strategic environmental assessment methodology', *Impact Assessment and Project Appraisal*, 18, 183–189.

Caldwell, L.K. (2000) 'Preface', in M.P. Partidario and R. Clark (eds), *Perspectives on Strategic Environmental Assessment*, London: Lewis Publishers.

Caratti, P., Dalkmann, H. and Jiliberto, R. (eds) (2004), *Analytical Strategic Environmental Assessment: Towards Better Decision-Making*, Cheltenham: Edward Elgar.

Connelly, S. and Richardson, T. (2005), 'Value-driven SEA: time for an environmental justice perspective?' *Environmental Impact Assessment Review*, 25, 391–409.

Dalal-Clayton, B. and Sadler, B. (2005), *Strategic Environmental Assessment: A Sourcebook and Reference Guide to International Experience*, London: IIED and Earthscan.

DHV (1999), *Manual on Strategic Environmental Assessment of Transport Infrastructure Plans*, A report to the European Commission, Brussels: European Commission.

EC (1992), *Fifth Environmental Action Plan*, Brussels: Commission of the European Communities.

EC (2001), *Directive 2001/42/EC of the European Parliament and of the Council on the Assessment of the Effects of Certain Plans and Programmes on the Environment*, Luxembourg, 27 June, (PE-CONS 3619/3/01 REV 3), http://eur-lex.europa.eu/LexUriServ/LexUriServ.do?uri=CELEX:32001L0042:EN:NOT (accessed 19 March 2008).

EC (2002a), *Communication from the Commission on the Collection and Use of Expertise by the Commission: Principles and Guidelines*, 11/12/02 COM (2002) 713final, Brussels: Commission of the European Communities, http://europa.eu.int/comm/governance/docs/comm_expertise_en.pdf (accessed November 2004).

EC (2002b), *Communication from the Commissions on Impact Assessment*, COM (2002) 276 final (5.6.2002), Brussels: Commission of the European Communities.

EEA (2005a), *Environmental Policy Integration in Europe: Administrative Culture and Practices*, EEA Technical report No. 5/2005, Copenhagen: European Environment Agency, http://reports.eea.eu.int/technical_report_2005_5/ (accessed 7 June 2005).

EEA (2005b), *Environmental Policy Integration in Europe: State of Play and an Evaluation Framework*, EEA Technical report No. 2/2005, Copenhagen: European Environment Agency, http://reports.eea.eu.int/technical_report_2005_2/ (accessed 7 June 2005).

ERM (1998), *Handbook on Environmental Assessment of Regional Plans and EU Structural Funds Programmes*, a report by Environmental Resources Management, prepared for DG Environment, Brussels: European Commission.

Fischer, T. B. (2002), 'Strategic environmental assessment performance criteria: the same requirements for every assessment?' *Journal of Environmental Assessment Policy and Management*, 4, 83–99.

Flyvbjerg, B. (1998), *Rationality and Power: Democracy in Practice*, Chicago: University of Chicago Press.

Glasson, J. (1995), 'Regional planning and the environment: time for a SEA change', *Urban Studies*, 32, 713–731.

González, S. (2001) 'El Marco de la evaluación ambiental estratégica', in Fundación Casa de la Paz (ed.) *Evaluación Ambiental Estratégica: Aplicaciones y Potencialidades para Chile*, Santiago, Chile: Centro de Estudios para el Desarrollo, and Comisión Nacional del Medio Ambiente.

Goodland, R. and Mercier, J.-R. (1999), *The Evolution of Environmental Assessment in the World Bank: From 'Approval' to Results*, Environment Department Papers, No. 67, Washington DC: World Bank.

Hildén, M. (2000), 'Myths and reality in EIA and SEA: environmental assessment in the Nordic countries – experience and prospects', in H. Bjarnadóttir (ed.),

Proceedings from the 3rd Nordic EIA/SEA Conference, Karlskrona, Sweden 1999, Stockholm: Nodregio Report.

Hobbs, J. (2003) 'Intervention during workshop', in *Strategic Environmental Assessment/Sustainability Impact Assessment*, a Joint Department for International Development (DFID) and OECD-DAC Task Team Workshop, Novartis Foundation, London, 13 October 2003.

Jackson, T. and Illsley, B. (2005), 'An examination of the theoretical rationale for using strategic environmental assessment of public sector policies, plans and programmes to deliver environmental justice, drawing on the example of Scotland', paper presented at the *International Association for Impact Assessment Special Thematic Meeting*, Prague, 26–30 September.

Kingdon, J. W. (1995), *Agendas, Alternatives and Public Policies*, Second Edition, New York: Harper Collins.

Kørnøv, L. and Nielsen, E.H. (2005), 'Institutional change: a premise for IA integration', paper presented at the *International Association for Impact Assessment Special Thematic Meeting*, Prague, 26–30 September.

Lafferty, W.A. (2005), 'EPI as normative-political goal and analytic concept: taking stock', power point slides given at a *CSERGE-UEA meeting Environmental Policy Integration Mechanisms and Tools*, 21–22 March, Norwich.

Munn, R.E. (1979), *Environmental Impact Assessment: Principles and Procedures*, SCOPE Report no.5, Chichester: Wiley.

NEPA Task Force (2003), *Modernising NEPA Implementation: Report of the NEPA Task Force*, Washington DC: Council on Environmental Quality.

Nilsson, M. (2005), *Connecting Reason to Power: Assessments, Learning, and Environmental Policy Integration in Swedish Energy Policy*, Stockholm: Stockholm Environment Institute.

Noble, B. (2002), 'The Canadian experience with SEA and sustainability', *Environmental Impact Assessment Review*, 22, 3–16.

ODPM (2003), *The Strategic Environmental Assessment Directive: Guidance for Planning Authorities*, London: Office of the Deputy Prime Minister.

OECD and UNDP (2002), *Sustainable Development Strategies: A Resource Book*, London: Earthscan.

O'Riordan, T. (1976), 'Policy making and environmental management: some thoughts on processes and research issues', *Natural Resources Journal*, 16, 55–72.

O'Riordan, T. and Hey, R.D. (eds) (1976) *Environmental Impact Assessment*, Farnborough: Saxon House.

Ortolano, L. and Shepherd, A. (1995), 'Environmental Impact Assessment', in F. Vanclay and D. Bronstein (eds), *Environmental and Social Impact Assessment*, Chichester: John Wiley.

Owens, S., Rayner, T. and Bina, O. (2004), 'New agendas for appraisal: reflections on theory, practice and research, *Environment and Planning A*, 36, 1943–1959.

Partidario, M. (1996), 'Strategic environmental assessment: key issues from recent practice', *Environmental Impact Assessment Review*, 16, 31–55.

Partidario, M. (2000), 'Elements of an SEA framework: improving the added-value of SEA', *Environmental Impact Assessment Review*, 20, 647–663.

Petts, J. (1999), 'Environmental Impact Assessment versus other environmental management decision tools', in J. Petts (ed.), *Handbook of Environmental Impact Assessment*, Oxford: Blackwell Science.

Queralt, A., Sala, P. and Torres, P. (2001), *Challenges of the Implementation by the European Regions of the Directive on Strategic Environmental Assessment*, Technical Report for the Environment Conference of the Regions of Europe, Ministry of Environment, Government of Catalonia.

RCEP (Royal Commission on Environmental Pollution) (1998), *Twenty-First Report: Setting Environmental Standards*, Cm 4053, London: The Stationery Office.

RCEP (Royal Commission on Environmental Pollution) (2002), *Twenty-Third Report: Environmental Planning*, Cm 5459, London: The Stationery Office.

Richardson, T. (2005), 'Environmental assessment and planning theory: four short stories about power, multiple rationality, and ethics', *Environmental Impact Assessment Review*, 25, 341–365.

Russel, D. (2005), *Environmental Policy Appraisal in UK Central Government: A Political Analysis*, unpublished PhD Thesis, Norwich: University of East Anglia.

Sadler, B. (2002), 'The global environmental agenda: from Rio to Johannesburg', in L. Billing, C. Jones, B. Sadler, J. Walmsley and C. Wood (eds), *Environmental Assessment Yearbook*, Lincoln and Manchester: Institute of Environmental Management and Assessment/EIA Centre.

Sadler, B. and Verheem, R. (1996), *Strategic Environmental Assessment: Status, Challenges and Future Directions*, The Hague, The Netherlands: Ministry of Housing, Spatial Planning and the Environment.

Sheate, W., Dagg, S., Richardson, J., Aschermann, R., Palerm, J. and Steen, U. (2001), *SEA and Integration of the Environment into Strategic Decision-Making. Volume 1 (Main Report)*, Final Report to the European Commission, 1 May 2001, http://ec.europa.eu/environment/eia/sea-studies-and-reports/sea_integration_main.pdf (accessed 19 March 2008).

Steurer, R. (2005), 'Environmental policy integration: defining and developing the state of the art', paper presented at a *CSERGE-UEA conference, Environmental Policy Integration Mechanisms and Tools*, 21–22 March 2005, Norwich, http://www.uea.ac.uk/env/cserge/highlights/march%20conf/envpol_integration_programme.htm (accessed 22 March 2005).

Thérivel, R. (1993), 'Systems of Strategic Environmental Assessment', *Environmental Impact Assessment Review*, 13, 145–168.

Thérivel, R. and Partidario, M.R. (eds) (1996), *The Practice of Strategic Environmental Assessment*, London: Earthscan.

Thérivel, R., Wilson, E., Thompson, S., Heany, D. and Pritchard, D. (1992), *Strategic Environmental Assessment*, London: Earthscan.

Torres, R.T. and Preskill, H. (2001), 'Evaluation and organisational learning: past, present, and future', *American Journal of Evaluation*, 22, 387–395.

UNCED (1992), *Agenda 21*, New York: United Nations General Assembly, http://www.un.org/esa/sustdev/agenda21/index.htm (accessed 13 December 2002).

UNECE (United Nations Economic Commission for Europe) (1992), *Application of Environmental Impact Assessment Principles to Policies, Plans and Programmes*, Environmental Series 5, New York: United Nations General Assembly.

van der Knaap, P. (1995), 'Policy evaluation and learning', *Evaluation*, 1, 189–216.

WCED (1987), *Our Common Future*, Oxford: Oxford University Press.

Wilkinson, D., Mullard, S. and Fergusson, M. (1994), *Strategic Environmental Assessment: Implications for the English Countryside*, Final Report for the Countryside Commission, September 1994.

Wood, C. (1995), *SEA Legislation and Procedures in the Community: Volume 2*, Brussels: European Commission.

Wood, C. (2003), 'Acceptance of the Rose-Hulman Award', speech at the plenary session of the *23rd Annual Meeting of the International Association for Impact Assessment*, 14–20 June 2003, Marrakech, Morocco.

World Bank (2005), *Integrating Environmental Considerations in Policy Formulation: Lessons from Policy-Based SEA Experience*, Washington DC: World Bank, Environment Department.

PART III

National experiences and prospects

8. The European Union

Andrew Jordan, Adriaan Schout and Martin Unfried

Successful integration entails a fundamental redefinition of the role of the environment departments, and some loss of control over environmental policy. The dilemma this poses is that the focus for advancing integration . . . may therefore become less distinct (Wilkinson 1997: 165).

INTRODUCTION

There are several good reasons to expect the EU to be relatively good at integrating environmental thinking into the work of all its policy sectors. After all, it has a very extensive and innovative system of environmental policy dating back over thirty years (Jordan 2005). It has also done a great deal to popularize the idea of EPI within international environmental discourse (Lenschow 2002). EPI is a longstanding aim of EU policy – even older in formal terms than that of sustainable development. The EU's political commitment to EPI is relatively strong and precisely expressed in the heading of the 1997 Amsterdam Treaty. Article 6 states that 'environmental protection requirements *must* be integrated into the definition and implementation of . . . Community policies . . . *in particular with a view to promoting sustainable development*' (emphasis added). Lawyers believe that Article 6 represents 'the only constitutional document' in the world where EPI has been given 'explicit expression in law' (Macrory 1999: 173).

However, this quasi-constitutional commitment to EPI has proven to be much harder to implement than many people had originally expected (EEA 2005a). The European Commission has openly conceded that many of the EU's most important sectoral policies (for example, transport, agriculture and energy) fundamentally undermine EPI (COM (2004) 394 final: 5–8). From the environmental side, the verdicts have been similarly critical. One eminent EU environmental lawyer has concluded that Article 6 remains 'an empty shell which has not had much substantive content' (Kraemer 2005: 555) and Weale and Williams (1992: 49) have described the EU's implementation of EPI as a 'faltering and haphazard affair'. The head of the

European Environment Bureau of environmental pressure groups, John Hontelez (2005: 397), believes that 'actual EPI' in the EU is 'still in its infancy'. And having completed a more comprehensive assessment of environmental trends in the EU, the European Environment Agency (2003: 7) suggested that the 'implementation of more integrated approaches . . . needs to be accelerated if Europe is . . . to meet its aspirations of sectoral integration and sustainable development'.

This chapter seeks to describe what the EU has – and has not – done to implement EPI over the last thirty years, and searches for underlying causes for the overall pattern of (in)activity. Although the relationship between national and EU-level initiatives is one of deep interdependence, we primarily focus on what the EU has done to nurture EPI at EU level.[1] However, even this restricted focus covers such a wide tableau of different actors and sectors that sometimes we have to refer readers to other chapters in Part III of this book.

The rest of our argument unfolds as follows. Section 2 describes the political and institutional situation in the EU, and then charts the changing ways in which it has thought about and sought to apply the EPI principle. We show that the EU's response can be broken down into five phases. In Section 3, we describe the various instruments that the EU has deployed, and in Section 4 we assess how effectively this has been done. In Section 5, we summarize the most noteworthy features of EU involvement with the EPI principle and draw together some concluding thoughts.

HISTORY

The EU: a Unique Institutional and Political Setting?

The EU does not find it at all difficult to make an ambitious political and legal commitment to EPI. But when it comes to implementing it, there are a number of reasons why it has struggled more than some of the other political systems discussed in Part III of this book. According to two experts in administrative and policy coordination (Peters and Wright 2001: 158), 'managing the problems of fragmentation, sectoralization and policy interdependence is not peculiar to Brussels, but the extent and nature of these problems in Brussels is of a different order from that prevailing in the member states'. One cannot possibly begin to understand why this is the case without first understanding the history and institutional make-up of the EU.

First and foremost, one needs to be aware of the very complex way in which legal competences are shared across different sectors and levels of governance in the EU, the relatively weak capacity for central leadership, and the presence of deeply 'pillarised' (Peterson 1997: 5) policy-making structures (Peters and Wright 2001: 161). Whether one regards the EU as a political system (Hix 2005), a proto-federal nation state (Moravcsik 2005: 1) or a deeply integrated international organization, one thing is now almost universally accepted – it is not 'a state' and hence is not directly comparable with the other jurisdictions covered in Part III. It is very telling that the term 'multi-level governance' was originally coined to describe the *sui generis* nature of the EU (Jordan 2001a). The EU does not, for example, have a coherent 'core executive' or coordinating centre like most sovereign states. The European Commission may be the formal font of most policy initiatives and it may also administer many important aspects of the EU's day-to-day activities (for example, policy implementation), but it operates 'without the government – the prime minister, cabinet – which gives meaning to the core executive in a traditional governmental structure with a public administration as traditionally understood' (Sbragia 2002: 3). If the EU has a 'cabinet', it is the European Council. But this body meets too infrequently to get a firm grip on the detail of policy making (Bomberg 2004: 70). Political leadership (a *sine qua non* of effective coordination – Peters 1998), is therefore fragmented across a number of different locations – the Commission, the Presidency and of course the European Council itself. In theory, there is one Council of Ministers, but in practice most of its activities are strongly divided into different sectoral formations and this 'has tended to work against the effective integration of environmental considerations across the EU's main policy sectors' (Haigh 2005: 3.11–17). Therefore, the basic institutional impediments to EPI at national level are not simply reproduced at EU level, but appear there in an even more accentuated form. In the absence of a core executive, 'turf battles' are 'frequent' and the sectoral 'firewalls' are 'high and often impermeable' (Peterson 1997: 5).

Second, the EU is undeniably a very strong force for higher environmental standards at national (Jordan and Liefferink 2004) and international levels (Sbragia 2005), but at heart it remains a system of 'economic governance' (Bomberg 2004: 62). Although the quest for a single integrated market in Europe has forced policy makers to develop common environmental rules (Weale *et al.* 2000; Lenschow 2005), the core principles – what Sbragia (2000: 223) terms its 'constitutional order' – are those of international economic competitiveness, market liberalization and, ultimately, economic growth. Bomberg's (2004: 89) argument that these 'render any dramatic shift' to sustainability 'unlikely' is equally applicable to the (intimately interlinked) principle of EPI.

Finally, the EU's legal capacity (or competence) to develop environmental rules has gradually evolved over the last thirty years to the extent

that most if not all national policy is developed by or in close collaboration with EU actors. By contrast, many of the so-called 'driving force'
sectors of environmental damage such as transport or energy production
are not nearly as deeply communitized – that is, controlled by the EU institutions (Jordan and Lenschow 2000). Consequently, the EU's competence
to intervene in the social, economic and environmental spheres of sustainability is asymmetrically distributed (Wurzel 2001: 14). So, when the EEA
reports that 'much more needs to be done to achieve an effective integration of environmental actions into the "driving forces" of economic
sectors' (EEA 1998: 285), there is only so much that the EU can do to
respond. Crucially, therefore, the EU is handicapped by its fragmented
institutional structure when it comes to implementing (as distinct
from committing itself to) EPI (OECD 2001: 47; European Commission
2004: 15).

Responding to EPI

1970–1987: from awareness raising to legal codification
The history of the EU's engagement with the EPI principle dates back at
least as far as the First Environmental Action Programme (EAP) in 1973
(Lenschow 2002: 3). Of all the EU institutions, the Commission stands
out as having been the most consistently forceful advocate of EPI. At first,
however, what is now known as its Directorate General (DG)
Environment struggled to sell even the principle of better integration to
other parts of the Commission, let alone to the rest of the EU. EPI was,
for instance, mentioned in the Fourth EAP. This formally committed the
Commission to developing internal procedures to institutionalize EPI,
but these were not actually announced until the next EAP (the Fifth) in
1992 (Wilkinson 1997: 157). Undaunted, DG Environment drew fresh
political support from the publication of the Brundtland Report in 1987
(WCED 1987). An important step had, however, already been taken in
1985, when EPI was incorporated[2] into the draft text of the 1987 Single
European Act (Article 130r).

1987–1996: deeper institutionalization of the EPI principle
As several Member States began to explore different ways of incorporating
EPI into their own national policy systems (see Jordan and Schout 2006),
DG Environment was able to muster political support to get the EU's
quasi-constitutional commitment to EPI tightened up. This was eventually
achieved via a new Treaty (the Maastricht Treaty), which stipulated that
'environmental protection *must* be integrated into the definition and
implementation of other Community policies' (Article 130r (2)) (emphasis

added). EPI's transformation into a fully-fledged political objective of European political integration was completed in 1999 when this form of wording was inserted into Article 6 of the Amsterdam Treaty.

Lawyers regarded the adoption of Article 6 as a very significant legal and policy development (Macrory 1999: 173), elevating EPI from being just a narrow, 'environmental' concept, into an overarching legal principle of European integration. Well before this, however, DG Environment had tried to develop procedures to implement EPI internally. The Fifth EAP outlined a number of internal reforms, including a new integration unit and a policy appraisal system ('green star') covering all new legislative proposals. However, for reasons that are more fully elaborated below, the outcome of these reforms was rather disappointing (Wilkinson 1997). Moreover, other than issue declarations in the European Council stressing the political importance of EPI, the Member States did very little to ensure that their national EPI systems were adequately coordinated with the EU's (Schout and Jordan 2005).

1996–1998: integration programmes and strategies
In the mid-1990s, the entry into the EU of three new advocates of EPI (namely the post-1995 Member States of Sweden, Austria and Finland), gave the debate about how to implement EPI a strong fillip. With their assistance, DG Environment was able to produce a very ambitious Communication in 1998, entitled *A Partnership for Integration* (COM (98) 333: 3). This marked a new and much more purposeful phase in the life of EPI in the EU. Henceforth, many new actors, most notably the Heads of State, the European Parliament and the Council of Ministers, were drawn into a common process of sectoral reporting, reviewing and target setting known as the 'Cardiff Process'.[3] Initially, it was a partnership involving just three sectors, but it was later expanded to include another six.

1998–2001: a proliferation of coordination strategies?
At first, hopes were high that the self-imposed discipline of writing and sharing integration strategies would generate new information, intra-sectoral learning and, eventually, a new and pervasive sense of commitment in the sectors to own environmental problems; one that had previously been very weak (Wilkinson *et al.* 2002: 5). Crucially, DG Environment found itself playing the somewhat redefined role that Wilkinson predicted in the quote at the start of this chapter. That is to say, rather than prescribe standards from the outside, the Cardiff Process aimed to initiate a self-sustaining process of inter-sectoral and inter-institutional learning and acting. But as is now widely known, the resulting strategies eventually failed to live up to these high expectations (see below).

2001–2006: retrenchment and regulatory reform

In response to these problems as well as a growing political appetite for 'better' (that is less environmental) EU regulation (see below), DG Environment began to channel its energies away from Cardiff (which was perceived to be failing), to the EU's emerging Sustainable Development Strategy (SDS), its Sixth EAP and various processes of regulatory streamlining. Published by the Commission in the run-up to the 2002 Johannesburg summit, the SDS was not produced in a particularly coordinated manner. Hinterberger and Zacherl (2003: 15) argue that key inconsistencies – such as the ecologically harmful subsidies paid by the EU to the energy, fisheries and agricultural sectors – were glossed over, and the promise to include ambitious targets and timetables dropped (Wurzel 2001: 14). Moreover, insufficient thought was given to how it would eventually dovetail with the other main strands of the EU's wider sustainability programme, namely the Sixth EAP, the Lisbon and, of course, the Cardiff Processes. The relationship was clarified somewhat during a review of the SDS in 2005, but there have been few attempts to assess the extent to which it – or its successor (published in 2006) – contribute to – or even undermine – EPI (Pallemaerts *et al.* 2007: 6).

Summary

The next section describes some of these instruments in much greater detail. However, a number of underlying themes should already be obvious in relation to the overall pattern of responses. First, while the principle of EPI has achieved greater legal force and clarity over the last thirty years, it is by no means obvious who or what is primarily responsible for implementing it. Jans (2000: 22), for example, argues that Article 6 has no direct legal consequences for Member States, because it refers only to '*Community* policies and activities' (emphasis added). But later, he concedes that there may be important indirect consequences for Member States in relation to the implementation of EU legislation. By contrast, Kraemer (2001: 44) argued that states must de facto accept some responsibility for Article 6, because they implement the policies decided centrally in the EU. It is also unclear whether Article 6 could ever be used to mount a legal challenge against environmentally damaging activities pursued by the sectoral formations of the Council or a particular Member State (Grimeaud 2000). The pronounced lack of legal clarity has undoubtedly made it easier for different parts of the EU to reinterpret EPI selectively to suit their purposes.

Second, strong conceptual links between EPI and sustainable development have been made in various EAPs as well as the founding Treaties of the EU (most specifically in Article 6 – see above). In one recent review of the implementation of the EPI principle, Wilkinson (1998: 113) concluded that it was a 'fundamental prerequisite for sustainable development'. Bomberg (2004: 72) similarly concluded that EPI is 'the' key substantive principle of sustainability in the EU. In practice, the EU has (as we shall explain more fully below) tended to treat EPI and sustainability as somewhat separate policy challenges. Thus, EPI is addressed by the Cardiff Process and its various reports, strategies and stocktakes on the one hand, whereas sustainability is chiefly a matter for the SDS. According to Pallemaerts *et al.* (2007: 34) the most positive thing that can be said about the relationship between EPI and the SDS is that it is 'ambivalent'.

Third, very few EU-level actors are anywhere near as committed to EPI as DG Environment. In fact, many parts of the Commission regard it at best as essentially unimportant and at worst as something to be neutered. Crucially, the dominant axis of political and administrative support continues to run from the (environmental parts of the) Commission through to the (Environment) Council. It is especially strange that the European Parliament has only been very partially engaged in the Cardiff and Lisbon Processes, despite being one of the most consistent and forceful champions of higher environmental standards in the EU (Burns 2005), and the main architect of its green budgeting system (see Chapter 4). It has, for example, never initiated an internal review of the steps it could take to facilitate greater EPI (Jordan and Schout 2006). A similar pattern of (dis)engagement is apparent across the various policy sectors in the EU. Agriculture, energy, industry and transport were the initial targets of the Cardiff Process. These sectors were also identified by the Fifth EAP. By contrast, the financial, fisheries, social, tourism and employment sectors were either not initially identified or have never been formally targeted by either initiative.

EPI IN PRACTICE

Administrative Instruments

Only a relatively small number of the administrative instruments mentioned in Chapter 3 have been deployed at EU level. There is, for example, no high-level environmental cabinet committee in the EU. There is, of course, the European Council, but other than issuing political declarations that either stress the continuing political importance of EPI or requesting other EU-level actors to respond, it has not played a direct role. There is also no high-level committee or department in the EU overseeing the implementation of EPI. The General Affairs Council was given a loose coordinating role in relation to Cardiff, but 'this has consisted of little more than the development of a road map setting out the relevant policy issues where the environment is relevant' (EEA 2005b: 29). As enthusiasm for the Cardiff Process waned in the sectors, environmentalists called for new administrative capacities to be created at the apex of the EU. These included an 'Article 6 Committee' to coordinate and inform the Council of Ministers (Kraemer *et al.* 2001: 45–6; Kraemer *et al.* 2002: 5). At the time of writing, none of these suggestions of ways of greening the EU's 'core executive' has been formally adopted.

Consequently, the closest that the EU has come to a high-level environment cabinet committee is probably the Environment Council. However, this is primarily sectoral in nature (it comprises national environment ministers) and, as such, is not really in an ideal position to pursue EPI. In fact, Sbragia (2000: 300) argues that its sectoral isolation has allowed environment ministers to adopt much more ambitious environmental legislation at EU level than they could have in their respective cabinets back home.[4] There is a tradition of two or more councils meeting informally (for example, transport and environment), but as this normally depends on support from a particular Presidency, it is not an especially robust or enduring means of pursuing EPI (Wurzel 2001).

The EU-level actor which has done the most to utilize administrative and bureaucratic instruments in pursuit of EPI is, perhaps not surprisingly, its main administrative body – the European Commission. These measures have included the creation of a sustainable development and environmental integration unit in DG Environment and a network of environmental correspondents spanning the various DGs (Wilkinson 1997: 162). How effective have these been? The integration unit has never been that well resourced or politically supported by the apex of DG Environment. The upper echelons of DG Environment do not appear to have ever favoured a 'policing' role, perceiving their primary role to be that of producing new environment policy. Moreover, EPI implies frequent intervention in the work of other DGs, but this goes against the tradition of respecting 'turf' boundaries in the Commission. The unit has not even enjoyed consistent leadership – there have been frequent changes of head of unit. Meanwhile, the correspondents were supposed to make the organization more transparent and reduce coordination costs, but they found it hard to promote EPI in battles between different DGs.

It is fair to say that neither initiative has ever commanded sufficient support from the apex of the Commission. They were part of a package of internal measures listed in the Fifth EAP that were allegedly adopted after 'very little discussion' amongst the various DGs. Consequently, 'most Commissioners seem not to have properly absorbed their full implications' (Wilkinson 1997: 160). And even if they had worked perfectly, they would not have been sufficient because EPI at EU level is a multi-actor challenge. The Commission can try all that it likes to produce perfectly coordinated proposals for new legislation, but EPI will fail to take root in the EU if other actors continue to have ample opportunities to unpick them later on in the policy process (Jordan and Schout 2006).

Green Budgeting

Because around 80 per cent of the EU's annual budget is spent on agriculture and regional development, the opportunities for employing this particular instrument are potentially quite good. In 1975, the European Parliament (or more correctly, its budgetary committee) was given a number of powers, including the right to approve or not to approve the way in which the Commission spends this money (Judge and Earnshaw 2004: 37).[5] Following an environmental pressure group campaign in the 1980s, DG Environment and the European Parliament started to work together to turn this 'power of the purse' (Wilkinson 1997: 166) to environmental ends. One of the most obvious effects has been to ensure that all projects and programmes funded by the cohesion and structural funds now require an environmental appraisal. If the Parliament feels that these are not satisfactory, it has the power to block spending (see Lenschow 1999).

In a more recent development, EU financial support for regional and agricultural projects was tied to adequate compliance with the Habitat, Nitrates and Birds Directives (this conditionality is known as 'cross-compliance'). From 2000, approval of structural funding was made contingent upon adequate implementation of the Habitats and Birds Directives (Haigh 2005: 3.11–14). This was subsequently extended to agricultural spending under the Rural Development Regulation (Haigh 2005: 3.11–14). For a more detailed summary of green budgeting activities in the EU, see Chapter 4.

Strategies and/or Strategy Developing Processes

Four strategic EU-level initiatives fall under this sub-heading: the Fifth EAP; the Cardiff Process; the Lisbon Process; and the Sixth EAP. The Fifth EAP was adopted just three months before the Rio conference (Wilkinson 1997: 158) and was subsequently re-badged as the EU's response to the sustainability agenda. It laid out some medium- and long-term targets for reducing key pollutants, and recommended some appropriate instruments, including some new environmental policy instruments such as eco-taxes. However, its targets were not binding. In fact, it was not even completely clear to whom the entire programme was formally addressed.[6] The UK environment ministry produced an implementation report (DoE 1994) and a number of other Member States initiated national sustainable development strategies, but they were in the minority and the Commission lacked the power to improve the situation. A 1994 review concluded gloomily that 'sustainable development essentially continues to be seen as the business of those who deal with the environment' (COM (94) 453). In 1996, the Commission approved a progress report (COM (95) 624, final), which revealed how little had been achieved across the EU. A range of other stakeholders arrived at much more critical assessments during a wide-ranging review process organized by DG Environment, dubbed 'the Global Assessment'. In his assessment, Wilkinson (1997: 164) concluded that any integration generated during this period was 'as much the consequence of exogenous factors [for example the global competitiveness pressures on the Common Agricultural Policy] as of [DG Environment's] measures'.

The adoption of the Cardiff Process is symptomatic of a wider change in the EU towards 'soft' or networked forms of coordination (Stubb *et al.* 2003: 152; see also Jordan and Schout 2006). These typically involve states mimicking one another's best practices via peer review, benchmarking and policy learning activities in a way that induces voluntary policy coordination (Scott and Trubek 2002: 5–6). They seek to build upon the EU's existing coordinating capacity not by legislating (as in the Community Method), but via more 'networked' forms of multi-level governance (Stubb *et al.* 2003: 148). When it was launched, the Cardiff Process was vaunted as 'one of the EU's "big ideas" on environment' (*ENDS Europe Daily*, No. 1679, 3 June 2004). But the initial strategies produced by the sectors were very poorly received (Fergusson *et al.* 2001; Jordan and Schout 2006). The sectors presented their policies as 'given' and hence not open to any substantial change (that is, integration) to achieve EPI. By late 2002, the production of new strategies and/or the updating of existing ones had all but ceased, as the entire process began to fall into the long shadow cast by the newly emerging Lisbon Process on social and economic reform. The EEA (2003: 272) subsequently concluded that 'the [Cardiff] process . . . lacked urgency and has yet to have a significant impact on sectoral policy making, let alone on improvements on the ground'. A stocktake undertaken by DG Environment in 2003–4 concluded that that EPI was 'still largely to be translated into further concrete results for the environment . . . [and] . . . has failed to deliver fully on expectations' (COM (2004) 394, final: 31).

With hindsight, failure was the most likely outcome because a number of hugely important issues had not been properly clarified at the start. For example, the Cardiff Process failed fully to engage several key actors, namely the European Parliament and the Member States. It also relied heavily upon the different sectors of the Council producing and evaluating their own strategies. DG Environment was an obvious candidate to fill the role of network manager (that is a *primus inter pares*, capable of leading from the front, resolving conflicts and maintaining momentum), but neither it nor the Environment Council were asked to take on this job by the European Council. Worse still, no one was really sure if the process had an end point or how (or by whom) its performance would eventually be assessed. Formally, the Cardiff Process is still alive, but politically speaking it is dead in the water.

Established in 2000, the Lisbon Process aims to make the EU 'the most competitive and dynamic knowledge-based economy in the world, capable of sustainable economic growth with more and better jobs and greater social cohesion' (European Commission 2000). Its appearance reflected a growing concern among some of the larger Member States that what the EU needed most was 'old-fashioned' economic growth to provide more jobs, not EPI or, for that matter, sustainable development. To the very great disappointment of many environmentalists, at first the Lisbon Process made only very passing references to environmental protection. In 2003, DG Environment complained that 'to many actors the environment still appears as an "add on" to the annual synthesis reports that are submitted to the European Council each spring (COM (2003) 745, final). The 2001 Swedish Presidency eventually succeeded in retrofitting Lisbon with an environmental dimension (Hinterberger and Zacherl 2003). So, rather late in the day, DG Environment started (in 2003) to produce the first of what has become an annual Environmental Policy Review (EPR) to feed into the production of the Lisbon synthesis reports. Nonetheless, the Lisbon process continues to be skewed heavily in the direction of economy and growth. The current list of fourteen indicators of progress includes only one direct environmental indicator (greenhouse gas emissions) and two indirect ones (energy intensity and transport volume).

Finally, the EU's EAPs have taken the form of 'lists of proposed legislation often selected in response to events' (Wilkinson 1997: 158). Traditionally, they had no legal force; instead they sought to identify new strategic directions for EU environmental policy to follow. By contrast, the Sixth EAP, which covers the period 2002–2012, was shorter and had legal force, but contained no new targets and timetables. The Commission said that they would be elaborated in a series of thematic strategies drawn up after extensive negotiation with different stakeholders, and covering broad, thematic topics such as marine areas, soil and air quality. These thematic strategies could be seen as another step in the direction of more inclusive and networked forms of EPI, that is, they seek to build better linkages between different policies by bringing together all the relevant DGs to support their design and implementation. DG Environment hoped they would provide a 'test bed for [more] innovative approaches' to EPI (COM

(2004) 394 final: 35). However, their publication was repeatedly delayed during 2005, as DG Environment came under intense pressure from other DGs to water them down (Wilkinson *et al.* 2005). At the time of writing, it is still too early to reach a definitive judgement on their overall quality, but the early indications are that the participation of many stakeholders and sectors has 'contributed to a reduction in the level of ambition of the EU's environment policy' (Wilkinson 2007: 23).

In the mid-2000s, the Commission tried to dovetail these and several other strategy processes into the Lisbon Process, which in 2005 was relaunched as the EU's Partnership for Growth and Jobs (COM (2005) 24) – a title which appeared to downplay still further the environmental dimension(s) of sustainability. In June 2005, the Director General of environmental protection in DG Environment openly admitted that while 'the idea of integration is very much alive . . . the Cardiff process is not going anywhere' (ENDS Ltd, No. 365: 24). The 2004 EPR conspicuously avoided any mention of it, and instead emphasized the importance of much older and better established instruments of EPI such as 'new' environmental policy instruments (NEPIs), policy appraisal, and EIA and SEA at Member State level (COM (2005) 17 final (Annex): 38).

Policy Appraisal Systems

Formal policy appraisal did not take root in EU environmental policy making as early as it did at the national level (Pearce 1998). However, as part of the package of measures adopted in the early 1990s (see above), the Commission pledged to appraise all new proposals for environmental impacts (COM (97) 1844/1 and 2). In a wide-ranging assessment, Wilkinson (1997: 163) struggled to find a single DG that had produced an environmental appraisal of one of its proposals. The lead DGs in the sectors evidently saw no reason to produce them, and in any case DG Environment had not put in place the relevant methodologies and support systems for their use.

In the early 2000s, the Commission sought to learn from these problems by moving on to what has become known as impact assessment (IA) (see Chapter 6 and also below). The Gothenburg European Council in June 2001 had originally called upon the Commission to subject all major new policy processes to a Sustainability Impact Assessment (SIA). A few months later, the Commission issued a Communication (COM (2001) 726) setting out the basic approach it intended to follow. It pointedly referred to 'impact analysis' as well as SIA. But when the Commission finally issued a set of formal proposals (COM (2002) 276), it was simply referred to as 'impact assessment', the 'S' having been quietly ditched during internal, inter-DG negotiations.

Despite some critical early reports on its performance (Wilkinson *et al.* 2004), the new IA system does have a much higher political profile outside DG Environment than its predecessor, Green Star. According to the Commission's own assessment, it successfully contributes to a culture of greater transparency and more formalized policy planning and evaluation (COM SEC (2004) 1377: 4). But whether it leads to greater EPI at the level of individual sectoral policy proposals is still far from clear. In 2004, the regime was 'refocused to give greater attention to factors that are widely considered to be important to productivity and hence to the competitiveness of the EU' (COM SEC (2004) 1377: 5). Even more importantly, it remains primarily an EU-level instrument. There are, for example, no structured arrangements for involving Member State authorities in the production of IAs, even though they may possess far more detailed information on the likely impact of proposals than Commission officials working centrally in Brussels (Wilkinson *et al.* 2004: 33). And even if policy appraisal in the Commission was perfect (the early indications are that it is not – Wilkinson *et al.* 2004: 5), it will never be a panacea when EPI at EU level is a multi-actor and multi-level problem.

Strategic Environmental Assessment

The EU does have a formal system of Strategic Environmental Assessment, but it applies to Member State not EU-level activities (and even then, primarily to projects rather than policies and programmes). Meanwhile, the EU does not formally subject all its policies to SEA. Nonetheless, many EU-level activities have been identified as needing SEAs. Trans-European Transport Networks (TEN-T, a key element of the European transport policy) were seen as good candidates for SEA. However, despite significant debate in the European Parliament, the Commission and at Member State level, an SEA of the TEN-T has yet to be carried out. Some DGs have chosen to undertake sustainability impact assessments on their policy activities (for example, on international trade agreements – see Lee and Kirkpatrick 2001), but generally the EU seems to have turned its back on SEA in favour of IA, presumably because it provides a better coverage of the politically important social and economic dimensions of sustainability (see below).

SUMMARY DISCUSSION

There are a number of points that emerge from our analysis of the various ways in which the EU has sought to implement EPI. The first is that the main drivers of EPI have mostly been environmental in nature, namely environmental pressure groups, environmental agencies and environmental ministries at national level. Chief amongst these has been the Commission's DG Environment, whose crowning achievement was probably the adoption of Article 6. But as the sectors have gradually become more aware of the potential long-term implications of Article 6, so they have made ever-stronger attempts to neutralize it. In many ways, the political debate in the EU has moved in their favour, now that many influential actors see increasing global economic competition as the most significant threat to Europe's continuing prosperity and way of life. *ENDS Europe Daily* (No. 1679, 3 June 2004) concluded that 'the debate [is now] . . . less of integrating environment into sectoral policies, and more of reverse integrating competitiveness into EU environmental policies'. In this sense, the debate in the 1990s (which was essentially about integrating the environment into the sectors) has turned around: now, DG Environment finds itself under growing pressure to fight its corner in a three-way battle with those representing the economic and social pillars of sustainability. In some cases, it has had its work cut out simply to defend the existing environmental *acquis communautaire* against those arguing that it threatened employment prospects and economic growth (COM SEC (2005) 1530; COM (2006) 70). Many of these arguments have been marshalled under the banner of 'Better Regulation' – which in practical terms has meant the streamlining, simplification and possible repeal of existing environmental laws (Wilkinson *et al.* 2005; COM (2005) 535; COM (2005) 462). The 2000s witnessed the decline of the Cardiff Process, the refocusing of the Lisbon Process on to jobs and growth, and DG Environment searching ever harder for less intrusive ways to implement EPI. Cardiff tried to push the sectors into 'owning' their environmental problems, but failed to make much headway. The Sustainable Development Strategy (SDS) has since emerged to take its place, but 'seems rather remote to sectoral policy makers' (Pallemaerts *et al.* 2007: 34). Whichever way you look at it, the environmental sector has largely failed to get the sectors to 'own' (let alone implement) EPI.

External political pressure – particularly that generated by the environmental pressure groups – have played a successful part in raising the political and legal profile of EPI, but there are clear limits to what it can achieve when EU policy making is so spatially and temporally expansive. There is simply too much going on in the EU for the environmental groups to campaign on everything: they have to be selective. This brings us to our second point, which is that, apart from DG Environment (which is a relatively small and politically weak part of the Commission), there is still no clear and consistent political leadership on EPI coming from the EU's 'core executive' (EEA 2005a: 34): DG Environment is essentially being left to fight its own corner in battles with the other sectors. It is certainly hard to think of a Commission President or head of state in the last decade who has powerfully and consistently championed the twin causes of EPI and sustainability. Far from it: many parts of the EU expect Commission officials to act as the legal and political guardians of EPI, because they often lack the time or the incentives to do this for themselves. The Commission – and principally DG Environment – has sought to develop this guardianship role, for example, through the EAPs and Article 6. However, DG Environment has discovered (to its cost) that if it does the running on EPI, the other actors tend not to feel so compelled to pay attention to it. In practice, the only significant source of political leadership has had to come from the Member State holding the EU Presidency. The problem here is that some Presidencies (for example, Sweden and the UK) have been much more proactive on environmental and EPI-related matters than others (Wurzel 2001). Consequently, important initiatives like Cardiff and the SDS have tended to proceed in fits and starts, depending on the political ambitions and energy of the state holding the Presidency.

One way to address this might be to embed EPI more deeply in the institutions and administrations of policy making (OECD 2002: Chapter 2) to ensure that it is consistently applied. However, our third point is that the EU's administrative structures are relatively weaker than those at national level (Kassim 2003). Therefore, the EU finds itself having to rely heavily on a relatively small number of fairly weak coordination instruments. Administrative instruments are particularly weakly applied at EU level (see above). Regulation, meanwhile, is no longer regarded as an effective or legitimate means of compelling the sectors to integrate the environment into their thinking (Knill and Lenschow 2000). The Commission believes that the use of market-based NEPIs such as eco-taxes offer 'one of the fastest', most flexible and cost-effective routes for environmental integration (COM (2004) 394 final: 35). However, markets do not yet constitute a viable means of facilitating EPI at EU level because of, inter alia, political opposition from polluters and some Member States' principled objection to vesting the EU with (environmental) tax raising or harmonizing powers (Jordan *et al.* 2003). The environment is one of a small number of EU policy areas in which the adoption of 'new' modes such as voluntary agreements and eco-management standards has been the most conspicuous (Héritier 2001), but the total number remains very small (Jordan *et al.* 2005). Consequently, the EU continues to rely very heavily on its mostly untried and untested impact assessment system and the gamut of high-level strategic approaches described above – all things considered, a rather fragile basis.

This leads to our fourth point, which is that there is now a '*piling up* of strategies . . . that are insufficiently harmonized with one another' (Hinterberger and Zacherl 2003: 32, emphasis added). For instance, the EU now has not one, but two long-term environmental strategies (the SDS and the Sixth EAP), and two integration processes – Lisbon and Cardiff. There are also other important strategic activities with a strong sustainability dimension which could be mentioned (the Commission is, for example, reforming key instruments such as the CAP and the Structural Funds). Some have argued that these activities 'need to be brought together in an overarching EU environmental strategy or road map' (Wilkinson *et al.* 2002: 17). The idea of a super-coordinated 'strategy of strategies' certainly sounds appealing, but unless it is adequately supported by coordination capacities (that is, instruments to exchange information, consult and arbitrate and so on), it will 'be superficial and vulnerable to the disruption of unresolved conflicts and the emergence of unforeseen problems' in daily policy making at lower levels (Metcalfe 2000: 832).

DG Environment appeared to have accepted this point when it conceded that 'the institutional and top down approach of [the Cardiff] process, [now] needs to be complemented by more practical steps at both Community and national levels' (COM (2004) 394, final: 34). Our final point, therefore, is that despite widespread agreement that EPI has both a horizontal and a vertical dimension (OECD 2001: 47), the EU does not actually conceptualize (or tackle) it in this holistic way (EEA 2005a: 35). For instance, the Cardiff integration strategies pay very little attention to vertical relationships, including the issue of capacities for coordination at EU and national levels (Schout and Jordan 2005). National and EU policy appraisal systems are similarly weakly connected. Finally, national-level administrative capacities could, in theory, be pooled or in some way better coordinated to compensate for the 'management deficit' (Metcalfe 2000) at EU level. However, there appears to be precious little appetite for this either within the Commission or amongst the Member States.

CONCLUSIONS

The EU presents a rather puzzling case in that it is both a leading advocate of EPI, but also (via its sectoral funding and policy decisions) a significant cause of unsustainable development in Western Europe. As with sustainability more generally, the EU's willingness to advocate EPI both within and outside its borders continues to outstrip its capacity to translate its political promises and legal principles into practice (Bomberg 2004: 61). A significant causal factor here is the EU's basic institutional structure, particularly the divisions between the EU institutions at EU level and the 27 Member States. These are simultaneously a source of strength and weakness. The weak horizontal coordinating links between these actors in the past has paradoxically made it easier for DG Environment and other pro-environment actors in the EU to achieve an ambitious legal and political commitment to EPI at EU level. However, they have made the implementation of this ambitious commitment extremely difficult to achieve, not least because DG Environment has been forced to rely heavily on 'persuasion rather than power' (Wilkinson 1998: 113) (manifest in the widespread reliance on new modes of governing) in its dealings with cognate sectors.

These difficulties have been compounded by the fact that the Commission and the European Parliament – the two most environmentally focused institutions in the EU and hence natural allies in the pursuit of sustainability – have often not seen eye to eye on EPI. Thus, the Commission now has a functioning policy appraisal system, but the Parliament does not; the Commission has reviewed and upgraded its internal coordination capacities, but the Parliament has not; the Commission developed an innovative implementing mechanism in the 1990s (the Cardiff Process), but the Parliament never felt the need to join; and the Commission has tried to develop more internally integrated ways of working (Jordan and Schout 2006: Chapter 9), but the Parliament's committees are still structured in a very vertical fashion, with no 'sustainable development' or 'EPI'-type committee (as an example, see Chapter 12 on the UK). Meanwhile, the links between EU-level and national-level EPI activities are still not formally coordinated, although the Commission has started to show an interest in indirectly coordinating (via benchmarking-type activities) national sustainability strategies (see Chapter 5).

Another equally important underlying issue is the political unwillingness of states to subject policy making in 'driving force' sectors to more EU involvement (hence the significant reliance on non-hierarchical or 'new' modes of governance such as Cardiff and the thematic strategies), or to grant the Commission a stronger role in pursuing EPI in a holistic manner for example, linking green budgeting with greener revenue-raising measures such as environmental taxes. In the past, DG Environment has arguably tried to overcome this structural weakness by pursuing EPI 'by stealth' (Weale *et al.* 2000), that is, developing strong environmental policies within the environmental parts of the EU and then 'imposing' them on the sectors. This has led to significant implementation deficits and in any case did not tackle the root causes of unsustainable development (Jordan 2002). In the last ten years, there has been a discernible shift away from this approach towards new, less hierarchical modes, starting with the Fifth EAP and the Cardiff Process, through to the Sixth EAP and impact assessment. In so doing, DG Environment has seen, as Wilkinson predicted in the 1990s (see epigraph to this chapter), the focus of environmental policy dissipate as the sectors have taken on a stronger policy-defining and development role in relation to environmental and sustainability matters. The problem is that DG Environment has still not fully worked out what to do when – as now appears to be the case – the sectors are slow to accept ownership of environmental problems, or when they develop practical interpretations of EPI and sustainability that are wholly inconsistent with its preferred interpretation of Article 6.

NOTES

1. But see Jordan *et al.* (2007) and Jordan and Schout (2006) for an analysis of the Member State–EU links.
2. Largely, it has to be said, at DG Environment's insistence.
3. A reference to the location of the June 1998 European Council.
4. That is, by behaving in precisely the poorly coordinated manner that they accuse other Councils of (see also Jordan 2001b).
5. But note that the Parliament has relatively little influence over 'obligatory spending items', most notably all 'market guarantee' elements of the CAP. These happen to be the most environmentally (as well as economically and socially) unsustainable parts.
6. See, for example, the ambiguous wording of the Council's Resolution on the Fifth EAP (*Official Journal* C138/1 17-5-93).

BIBLIOGRAPHY

Bomberg, E. (2004), 'Adapting form to function? From economic to sustainable development governance in the EU', in W. Lafferty (ed.), *Governance for Sustainable Development*, Cheltenham: Edward Elgar.

Burns, C. (2005), 'The European Parliament: environmental champion or political opportunist?' in A. Jordan (ed.), *Environmental Policy in the European Union*, 2nd edn, London: Earthscan.

DoE (Department of the Environment) (1994), *Towards Sustainability: Government Action in the UK*, London: DoE.

EEA (European Environment Agency) (1998), *Europe's Environment: The Second Assessment*, Copenhagen: EEA.

EEA (European Environment Agency) (2003), *Europe's Environment: The Third Assessment (Full report)*, Copenhagen: EEA.

EEA (European Environment Agency) (2005a), *Environmental Policy Integration in Europe: State of Play and an Evaluation Framework*, EEA technical report, No 2/2005, Copenhagen: EEA.

EEA (European Environment Agency) (2005b), *Environmental Policy Integration in Europe: Administrative Culture and Practices*, EEA technical report, No 5/2005, Copenhagen: EEA.

ENDS (Environmental Data Services) Ltd. (various years), *Environmental Data Services Report*. London: ENDS.

ENDS Europe Daily (various years), *ENDS Europe Daily*, London: ENDS.

European Commission (2000), *The Lisbon European Council – An Agenda of Economic and Social Renewal for Europe: Contribution of the European Commission to the Special European Council in Lisbon, 23–24 March 2000*, Brussels: European Commission.

European Commission (2004), *National Sustainable Development Strategies in the EU: A First Analysis by the European Commission*, Commission Staff Working Document, April, Brussels: European Commission.

Fergusson, M., C. Coffey, D. Wilkinson and D. Baldock (2001), *The Effectiveness of EU Council Integration Strategies and Options for Carrying Forward the 'Cardiff' Process*, London: IEEP.

Grimeaud, D. (2000), 'The integration of environmental concerns into EC policies', *European Environmental Law Review*, 9 (7), 207–218.

Haigh, N. (ed.) (2005), *Manual of Environmental Policy: The EU and Britain*, Institute for European Environmental Policy, Leeds: Maney Publishing.

Héritier, A. (2001), *New Modes of Governance in Europe: Policy Making Without Legislating?* Max Planck Project Group, Preprints, 2001/14, http://papers.ssrn.com/sol3/papers.cfm?abstract_id=299431, accessed 19 March 2008.

Hinterberger, F. and R. Zacherl (2003), *Ways Towards Sustainability in the European Union*, Vienna: SERI Institute.

Hix, S. (2005), *The Political System of the European Union*, 2nd edn, Basingstoke: Palgrave.

Hontelez, J. (2005), 'The impact of European NGOs on EU environmental regulation', in F. Wijen, K. Zoetoman and J. Pieters (eds), *A Handbook of Globalization and Environmental Policy*, Cheltenham: Edward Elgar.

Jans, J. (2000), *European Environmental Law*, 2nd edn, Groningen: Europa Law Publishers.

Jordan, A.J. (2001a), 'The European Union: an evolving system of multi-level governance . . . or government?' *Policy and Politics*, 29 (2), 193–208.

Jordan, A.J. (2001b), 'National environmental ministries: managers or ciphers of European environmental policy?' *Public Administration*, 79 (3), 643–663.

Jordan, A.J. (2002), 'The implementation of EU environmental policy', in A. Jordan (ed.) *Environmental Policy in the EU*, London: Earthscan.

Jordan, A.J. (ed.) (2005), *Environmental Policy in the EU*, 2nd edn, London: Earthscan.

Jordan, A. and A. Lenschow (2000), 'Greening the European Union: what can be learned from the leaders of EU environmental policy?' *European Environment*, 10 (3), 109–120.

Jordan, A. and D. Liefferink (eds) (2004), *Environment Policy in Europe: The Europeanization of National Environmental Policy*, London: Routledge.

Jordan, A. and A. Schout (2006), *The Coordination of the European Union: Exploring the Capacities for Networked Governance*, Oxford: Oxford University Press.

Jordan, A., A. Schout, M. Unfried and A. Zito (2007), 'Environmental policy: shifting from passive to active coordination?' in H. Kassim, A. Menon and B.G. Peters (eds), *Coordinating the European Union*, Lanham, USA: Rowman and Littlefield.

Jordan, A., R. Wurzel and A. Zito (2005), 'The rise of "new" policy instruments in comparative perspective', *Political Studies*, 53 (3), 477–496.

Jordan, A., R. Wurzel, A. Zito and L. Brueckner (2003), 'European governance and the transfer of "new" environmental policy instruments', *Public Administration*, 81 (3), 555–574.

Judge, D. and D. Earnshaw (2004), *The European Parliament*, Basingstoke: Palgrave.
Kassim, H. (2003), 'The European administration', in J. Hayward and A. Menon (eds), *Governing Europe*, Oxford: Oxford University Press.
Knill, C. and A. Lenschow (eds) (2000), *Implementing EU Environmental Policy*, Manchester: Manchester University Press.
Kraemer, A. (ed.) (2001), *Results of the Cardiff Process*, report to the Federal German Environmental Agency and the Federal Environment Ministry, Berlin: Ecologic.
Kraemer, L. (2005) 'The dispersion of authority in the European Union and its impact of environmental legislation', in F. Wijen, K. Zoeteman and J. Pieters (eds), *A Handbook of Globalization and Environmental Policy*, Cheltenham: Edward Elgar.
Kraemer, R., A. Klassing, D. Wilkinson and I. von Homeyer (2002), *EU Environmental Governance: Final Report*, Berlin/London: Ecologic/IEEP.
Lee, N. and C. Kirkpatrick (2001), 'Methodologies for sustainability impact assessments of proposals for new trade agreements', *Journal of Environmental Assessment Policy and Management*, 3, 395–412.
Lenschow, A. (1999), 'The greening of the EU: the Common Agricultural Policy and the structural funds', *Environment and Planning C*, 17, 91–108.
Lenschow, A. (ed.) (2002), *Environmental Policy Integration*, London: Earthscan.
Lenschow, A. (2005), 'Environmental policy', in H. Wallace, W. Wallace and M. Pollack (eds), *Policy Making in the EU*, 5th edn, Oxford: Oxford University Press.
Macrory, R. (1999), 'The Amsterdam treaty: an environmental perspective', in D. O'Keefe and P. Twomey (eds), *Legal Issues of the Amsterdam Treaty*, Oxford: Hart Publishing.
Metcalfe, L. (2000), 'Reforming the Commission: will organizational efficiency produce effective governance?' *Journal of Common Market Studies*, 38 (5), 817–841.
Moravcsik, A. (2005), 'The European constitutional compromise', *EUSA Review*, 18 (2), 1–7.
OECD (2001), *Sustainable Development: Critical Issues*, Paris: OECD.
OECD (2002), *Governance for Sustainable Development: Five OECD Case Studies*, Paris: OECD.
Pallemaerts, M., M. Herodes and C. Adelle (2007), *Does the EU Sustainable Development Strategy Contribute to EPI?* Berlin: Ecologic.
Pearce, D. (1998), 'Environmental appraisal and environmental policy in the EU', *Environmental and Resource Economics*, 11 (3–4), 489–501.
Peters, G.B. (1998), 'Managing horizontal government', *Public Administration*, 76, 295–311.
Peters, G.B. and V. Wright (2001), 'The national coordination of European policy-making', in J. Richardson (ed.), *European Union: Power and Policy-Making*, London: Routledge.
Peterson, J. (1997), 'States, societies and the EU', *West European Politics*, 20 (4), 1–23.
Sbragia, A. (2000), 'The EU as coxswain', in J. Pierre (ed.), *Debating Governance*, Oxford: Oxford University Press.
Sbragia, A. (2002), *The Dilemma of Governance with Government*, Jean Monnet Working Paper 3/02, New York: NYU School of Law.
Sbragia, A. (2005), 'Institution-building from below and above', in A. Jordan (ed.), *Environmental Policy in the European Union*, 2nd edn, London: Earthscan.

Schout, A. and A.J. Jordan (2005), 'Coordinating European governance: self organising or centrally steered?' *Public Administration*, 83 (1), 201–220.

Scott, J. and D. Trubek (2002), 'Mind the gap: law and new approaches to governance in the European Union', *European Law Journal*, 8 (1), 1–18.

Stubb, A., H. Wallace and J. Peterson (2003), 'The policy making process', in E. Bomberg and A. Stubb (eds), *The European Union: How Does it Work?*, Oxford: Oxford University Press.

WCED (World Commission on Environment and Development) (1987), *Our Common Future*, Oxford University Press.

Weale, A., G. Pridham, M. Cini, D. Konstadakopulos, M. Porter and B. Flynn (2000), *Environmental Governance in Europe*, Oxford: Oxford University Press.

Weale, A. and A. Williams (1992), 'Between economy and ecology? The single market and the integration of environmental policy', *Environmental Politics*, 1 (4), 45–64.

Wilkinson, D. (1997), 'Towards sustainability in the European Union?' *Environmental Politics*, 6 (1), 153–173.

Wilkinson, D. (1998), 'Steps towards integrating the environment into other EU policy sectors', in T. O'Riordan and H. Voisey (eds), *The Transition to Sustainability*, London: Earthscan.

Wilkinson, D. (2007), *EPI at EU level*, EPIGOV state of the art report, Berlin: Ecologic.

Wilkinson, D., M. Fergusson, C. Bowyer, J. Brown, A. Ladefoged, C. Monkhouse and A. Zdanowicz (2004), *Sustainable Development in the European Commission's Integrated Impact Assessments for 2003: Final Report*, London: IEEP.

Wilkinson, D., J. Skinner and M. Ferguson (2002), *The Future of the Cardiff Process*, London: IEEP.

Wilkinson, D., C. Monkhouse, M. Herodes and A. Farmer (2005), *For Better or Worse? The EU's 'Better Regulation' Agenda and the Environment*, London: IEEP.

Wurzel, R. (2001), 'The EU presidency and the integration principle', *European Environmental Law Review*, 10, 7–15.

9. Germany

Rüdiger K. Wurzel

INTRODUCTION

Germany is often portrayed as an environmental lead state because it adopted a relatively progressive domestic environmental policy in the early 1970s. Post-unification, Germany[1] has actually lost some of its environmental credentials, but is still widely regarded as one of the EU's environmental pioneers (Andersen and Liefferink 1997). However, with the exception of a brief period in the early 1970s, Germany has not acted as a pioneer in relation to EPI. EPI and also the related concept of sustainable development were, for a long time, seen as distracting from the need to develop a stringent environmental policy. It is only since the late 1990s that Germany has started to re-engage with the concept of EPI and take the concept of sustainability more seriously. The main drivers for the renewed interest in EPI are new environmental challenges (notably climate change), legally binding EU commitments (for example, the directives on environmental impact assessment and strategic environmental assessment – EIA and SEA), the belated acceptance of the concept of sustainable development and various domestic political factors (for example, changes in government).

This chapter summarizes Germany's engagement with the concept of EPI. Section 2 provides a brief history of EPI in Germany. It explains when, why and how Germany became an EPI pioneer in the 1970s, then slipped back in the 1980s, only to be 'reconverted' to the idea of EPI in the 1990s. Section 3 focuses on EPI in practice, describing Germany's implementation experience. Section 4 offers an assessment of the main findings, while Section 5 draws together a number of conclusions.

HISTORY

Broadly speaking, three phases in Germany's engagement with EPI can be identified: 1) 1969–74, when pioneering attempts to integrate the environment in policy making were made; 2) 1974 to the late 1990s, when the commitment to EPI fell; and 3) the period since the late 1990s, when Germany 'reconverted', somewhat reluctantly, to EPI. In order to understand this pattern, it is necessary to analyse domestic and international policy developments, as well as the prevailing political context.

1969–74: Germany as a Pioneer

The election of a reform-minded Social Democratic Party (SPD) – Free Democratic Party (FDP) (Social–Liberal) coalition government in 1969, marked the beginning of modern-day environmental policy in Germany (Hartkopf and Bohne 1983; Jänicke *et al.* 2002; Müller 1986). The Centre-Left coalition adopted ambitious environmental programmes, created environmental administrative capacities, approved relatively stringent environmental laws, introduced some 'new' environmental policy instruments (NEPIs) and, most relevant for our purposes, experimented with different ways of implementing EPI.

Environmental policy formed part of a wider reform agenda which the Social–Liberal coalition initially pursued at great pace (Baring 1984). The early 1970s were characterized by a general reform and 'planning euphoria' (Jänicke 2007) which Chancellor Brandt (SPD) tried to exploit to bring about 'the modern Germany' (Brandt 2003: 271). Brandt pushed for internal and external reforms which included the adoption of a modern-day environmental policy and a new *Ostpolitik*. He had already campaigned 'for blue skies over the Ruhr' during the 1961 elections (Brandt 2003: 274) and emphasized the importance of environmental policy while promising to 'dare more democracy' in his 1969 government declaration.

The small FDP supported Brandt's reform agenda while trying to develop its own political profile, especially in those policy areas (notably the environment) for which it had ministerial responsibility. Hans-Dietrich Genscher (FDP), who acted as Interior Minister and FDP deputy party leader from 1969–74, exhibited a strong personal commitment to environmental issues. He supported the allocation of environmental policy competences to the Interior Ministry (BMI) because 'this big and influential ministry knew how to succeed against other Ministries during the legislation making process' (Genscher 1995: 131). Similar arguments were later advanced by critics of an independent Environmental Ministry, who argued that it would lack sufficient political clout (Müller 1986) and be 'isolated instead of integrated' (Pehle 1998).

The conceptual foundations of modern-day German environmental policy were sketched out in the 1969 Immediate Environmental Programme and, later, the more comprehensive 1971 Environmental Programme (updated in 1976) (Bundesregierung 1971, 1976). In 1974, the Advisory

Council on the Environment (*Sachverständigenrat für Umweltfragen* – SRU), which was set up in 1972, stated that the 1971 Environmental Programme 'in principle assumes equal ranking of environmental policy objectives with other state objectives such as social security, educational objectives or objectives related to internal and external security' (SRU 1974: 7). More than fifteen years before the 1987 Brundtland Report, the SRU in effect claimed that the 1971 Environmental Programme was a sustainable development strategy, although it pointedly did not use that term. The seeds for what was later termed ecological modernization (a philosophy which assumes that stringent environmental protection measures are compatible with economic growth) were therefore sown in the early 1970s.

The 1971 Environmental Programme emphasized the following three core principles: 1) the polluter pays principle; 2) the precautionary principle; and, 3) the cooperation principle. The last two principles in particular encouraged the adoption of EPI measures. The precautionary principle aims to prevent pollution from occurring. It requires the integration of environmental considerations into those policy sectors which are the (potential) causes of pollution; Genscher even described it as an instrument for 'anticipatory planning' (Weale *et al.* 1991: 115). The cooperation principle should have encouraged horizontal coordination between different government departments and improved vertical coordination between different levels of government (for example, within the federal system and between the government and the main societal groups). However, important structural barriers have made its implementation difficult.

The 1971 Environmental Programme was followed up by major implementation legislation such as the revision of the 1974 Water Management Act (*Wasserhaushaltsgesetz* – WHG) and the 1974 Federal Air Quality Protection Act (*Bundesimmissionsschutzgesetz* – BImSchG). Importantly, these two statutes introduced the best available technology (BAT) principle for controlling pollution discharges to different environmental media. The BAT principle was a very successful approach for reducing mass pollutants (for example, sulphur dioxide) from point sources (for example, power stations). However, it did little to control pollution from diffuse sources such as agriculture. Even more importantly, the BAT-derived approach complicated the implementation of EPI because it relied on tightening 'the emission values in all three media of air, water and soil, in the expectation that this will eventually solve any cross-media problems' (Weale *et al.* 1991: 133). In other words, it focused largely on ('end of pipe') environmental pollution control, rather than pollution prevention. Furthermore, it soon became clear that environmental policy suffered the same implementation deficits that plagued other public policies (Mayntz 1980, 1983; Weidner and Knoepfel 1983), and this hindered the pursuit of greater EPI (Müller 2002).

Table 9.1   EPI-related policy measures in Germany in the 1970s

---

Conceptualizing EPI:
1969   Immediate Environmental Programme
1971   Environmental Programme
1976   Updated Environmental Programme

Reorganizing administrative capacity:
1969   Interior Ministry is allocated core environmental policy competences
1972   Cabinet Committee for Environment and Health ('Green Cabinet')
1972   Permanent Committee for Director Generals for Environmental
             Questions
1974   Environmental Agency (UBA–Umweltbundesamt)
1975   EIA for federal government measures

Creating advisory capacity:
1972   Advisory Council on the Environment (SRU)

Creating societal awareness:
1970   Working Group for Environmental Questions
Since the   Financial support for environmental groups
  1970s

Source: Hartkopf and Bohne (1983); Jänicke *et al.* (2002); Müller (2002)

With the benefit of hindsight, Brandt (2003: 272) conceded that 'not every-thing had been planned well enough' and 'perhaps we [that is, the Social–Liberal coalition] simply tried to achieve too much' too soon.

One of the obstacles to EPI was Germany's federal structure, which grants the states (*Länder*) far reaching environmental policy competences and guarantees local government the constitutional right of self-gover-nance. In 1972, the Social–Liberal coalition government revised the consti-tution to gain competences for air pollution control, waste management and noise pollution control. However, the *Länder* resisted further constitutional changes which would have granted the federal government similar powers for water management and nature conservation. Constitutional constraints have so far been the main obstacle preventing the adoption of a unified federal Environmental Act (*Umweltgesetzbuch* – UGB), which would have brought together the environmental laws focusing on single environmental media, while enshrining EPI as an overarching principle (Kloepfer 2004).

Horizontal and vertical coordination instruments between the *Länder* and the federal government as well as amongst the *Länder* (for example, the Environmental Ministers Conference – have developed over the years. In the early 1970s, Germany emerged as a pioneer in relation to EPI despite these constitutional constraints (see Table 9.1). In 1972, Germany was one of the first states to set up a 'green cabinet' in the form of a Cabinet Committee for Environment and Health. In 1976, it adopted EIA for all domestic federal government measures. Moreover, environmental policy was formally declared a cross-sectoral policy objective in the revised 1976 Environmental Programme (Jänicke 2007; Jänicke *et al.* 2002).

The former East Germany (German Democratic Republic – GDR) did not rely on a media-centred approach to pollution control. It emphasized the need to control pollution in the round and enshrined the protection of the environment in its constitution in the 1960s. However in practice, economic development was given priority over environmental protection, and the GDR acted mainly as an example of how not to protect the environment (Rehbinder 1992).

1974 to about 1998: EPI Back in the Doldrums

Although conceptual thinking about EPI developed in Germany in the early 1970s, in practice it faced increasingly higher implementation hurdles. The 1973 oil crisis pushed the advocates of higher environmental standards on to the defensive. The subsequent economic recession allowed economic actors to resist the implementation of the EPI instruments noted above (Müller 1986, 2002). In 1974, the Economics Ministry (*Bundesministerium für Wirtschaft* – BMWi) set up its own environmental unit to track the environmental policy activities of the BMI. During the next few years, other ministries also set up their own 'mirror units'. The appearance of these environmental mirror units seemed to suggest that EPI was finally making inroads into the sectors. However, it soon became clear that their main purpose was to keep the BMI's environmental activities in check rather than to further integration (Müller 2002; Pehle 1998). EPI's importance as a guiding principle was further downgraded by Helmut Schmidt, (SPD), who succeeded Willy Brandt as German Chancellor in 1974. Schmidt, who belonged to the economic right within the SPD, downplayed the importance of environmental issues. He reinstated corporatist interest intermediation patterns in which the government consulted closely with employers and unions at the expense of other societal actors. Jänicke and colleagues (2002: 118) have pointed out that from the mid-1970s onwards 'the initial strategic planning approach and the attempt to treat environmental protection in an integrated manner lost much of its impetus and gave way to a medium-term, command-and-control approach based mainly on permits and standard setting'. In other words, due to economic pressures, environmental policy settled back into a regulatory pattern which matched Germany's traditions.

From the late 1970s, German environmental policy entered a period of recovery despite the second oil crisis in 1979 and Chancellor Schmidt's lack of interest in environmental issues (Müller 1986). However, EPI remained stuck in the doldrums well into the 1990s for three interrelated reasons. First, the German Chancellor, who has the prerogative to issue policy guidelines (*Richtlinienkompetenz*), was constrained by the relatively high independence of the sectoral ministries, particularly those headed by a minister from the coalition partner, over which the Chancellor had limited influence. Environmental policy remained an important political issue for the FDP, which fielded the BMI's ministers until 1982. While Chancellor Schmidt downplayed the importance of environmental issues, the BMI carried on pressing for ambitious environmental measures. Relatively strong ministerial independence may therefore work both ways – in favour of and as a constraint to EPI, depending on the Chancellor's views about the importance of environmental policy in general and EPI in particular. Second, there were constitutional and institutional barriers (see above), together with the dominant national environmental regulatory style which hindered the implementation of EPI. Finally, on a conceptual level, many German environmental policy makers perceived EPI as a distraction from the main task of developing a progressive environmental policy. Because the media-centred BAT-derived approach to pollution control was highly successful in tackling mass pollutants from point sources during the 1980s and 1990s, policy makers were reluctant to adopt a more EPI approach which was perceived to have failed in the 1970s (Jänicke *et al.* 2002).

Although EPI was placed on the back burner, Germany continued to make important environmental policy developments. During the 1980s, advocates of ecological modernization gained cross-party support at a time when Germany emerged as a leading exporter in pollution reduction technology. The ecological modernization doctrine challenged the conventional (neo-liberal and socialist) paradigm which claimed that there is always a zero sum relationship between stringent environmental regulation and economic growth. It suggested instead that the relationship could be positive sum (Weale 1992a, 1992b). For a while it looked as if the 'social market economy' doctrine, which had been the dominant political paradigm in post-World War II Germany, might give way to a 'social and ecological market economy' doctrine. However, the cost of unification, the recession of the early 1990s and the *Standort Deutschland* debate (which concerns Germany's future as a production and investment location) weakened support for ecological modernization and environmental regulation (Wurzel 2002). The then Christian Democratic Union/Christian Social Union (CDU/CSU) – FDP (Centre-Right) coalition government began to give preference to voluntary agreements over environmental regulation in its coalition agreement although, in practice, regulation remained the dominant environmental policy instrument (Wurzel *et al.* 2003). It was within this changed political context that Germany began to take more seriously the concept of sustainable development, with its emphasis on stakeholder participation as well as environmental, economic *and* social concerns.

1998–2007: a Reluctant Conversion to EPI

In the late 1990s, Germany began, albeit reluctantly, to accept once more the need to think about environmental policy more holistically, with EPI serving as an important guiding principle. One of the critical drivers of this change was political. In 1998, the Green Party entered a coalition government with the SPD (Red–Green coalition) for the first time in German history. The Red–Green coalition government adopted some NEPIs (for example, ecological tax reform) and a national sustainable development strategy (Jänicke 2007; Jänicke *et al.* 2002; Statz 2007). In 2001, it set up a Committee for State Secretaries for Sustainable Development, which acted as a Green Cabinet, and an Advisory Council for Sustainable Development (*Rat für Nachhaltige Entwicklung*).

However, despite the introduction of innovative environmental and sustainable development measures, the Red–Green coalition government did not achieve a break from the dominant environmental regulatory style in Germany. Instead, incremental policy change took place which emphasized a notion of EPI that relied heavily on sectoral strategies. In other words, environmental policy considerations were integrated into different sectoral policies, including not only agricultural and transport policy, but also foreign policy. One of the Red–Green coalition's most successful sectoral EPI strategies concerned agriculture, where Germany was perceived to be a leader in 'ecological farming'. However, sectoral EPI has not solved all environmental problems resulting from agriculture. For example, nitrate pollution of water has remained a serious problem.

Many German environmental policy makers remained sceptical about a form of sustainable development which aims to give equal weight to environmental, economic and social concerns across all sectoral policies. Together with the EU's emphasis on procedural measures (such as EIA and SEA) in the 1990s, BMU (*Bundesministerium für Umwelt, Naturschutz und Reaktorsicherheit*) officials often perceived the national and EU sustainable development strategies as a potential threat to hard-won domestic environmental policy achievements. Statements such as the following from a Ministry for Transport (*Bundesministerium für Verkehr*) official make understandable some of their initial unease: '[w]e [in the Transport Ministry] support the principle of sustainable development because it is high time that the BMU starts to take more seriously competitiveness considerations instead of focusing purely on environmental issues' (interview

2002). This response amply confirms Andrea Lenschow's belief (2002: 7) that 'the fact that EPI is widely perceived as tied to sustainable development is not unproblematic'.

The government which was formed by the CDU/CSU – SPD (Grand Coalition) after the 2005 election, endorsed sustainable development, without however discrediting traditional environmental regulation. It stated in its coalition agreement that it would be 'guided by the principle of sustainable development . . . [and that] ambitious national environmental policy can contribute decisively to the modernization of our society' (CDU/CSU and SPD 2005, 49). Importantly, the coalition agreement also stated that Germany's 'current environmental law . . . is highly fragmented both with regard to subject matter and between the federal government and the *Länder*. It does not meet the requirements of an integrated environmental policy' (CDU/CSU and SPD 2005: 51).

The Grand Coalition therefore promised that it would 'create the prerequisites for . . . a reorganization of German environmental law in the context of the reform of the German constitution' (CDU/CSU and SPD 2005: 52). However, the Grand Coalition's initial attempt to reform the federal system resulted in failure. In 2006, the SRU (2006) warned that decentralizing environmental policy powers (from the federal government to the *Länder* level) could trigger a 'race to the bottom' in which 'cooperative federalism' increasingly gives way to 'competitive federalism'.

EPI IN PRACTICE

Administrative Instruments

There were four major opportunities for establishing EPI organizationally within the lead ministry responsible for environmental policy. The first was when the BMI was allocated the core environmental policy competences in 1969. However, it had to share responsibility for nature protection with the federal agriculture ministry (*Bundesministerium für Landwirtschaft* – BML) and chemicals policy with the BMWi and the Ministry for Youth, Family and Health (*Bundesministerium für Jugend, Familie und Gesundheit*), which was responsible for chemical regulations relating to food (Pehle 1998: 29). According to Genscher (1995: 115–116), the split in competences for nature protection between the BMI and the BML was due to two factors. First, Genscher did not want to endanger his friendship with the BML's Minister, Josef Ertl (FDP), who had informed Chancellor Brandt that he wanted the core nature protection competences within the BML. Second, Genscher (1995: 115) did not want 'a social democratic Chancellor to act as a referee between two FDP Ministers'. Genscher's anecdotal recollection illustrates that coalition government can have significant implications for the internal organization of ministries. It also shows that EPI considerations were not the driving factor for the internal organization of the BMI. Importantly, Müller (1986: 312) later came to the conclusion that the drafting of the federal nature protection act (*Bundesnaturschutzgesetz*) between the BMI and BML in the 1970s constituted a classic example of 'negative coordination' (Scharpf 1972). In other words, rather than adopting a problem-solving strategy (that is, 'positive coordination'), these two ministries mainly went about defending their existing ministerial interests.

In 1972, the Social–Liberal coalition government set up a Cabinet Committee for Environment and Health, which functioned as a Green Cabinet. It was chaired by the Chancellor. However, the Green Cabinet rarely met and had little practical influence on government policy (Jänicke *et al.* 2002; Müller 2002; Pehle 1998). In 1972, a permanent Committee for the Director Generals for Environmental Questions was set up, chaired by the Interior Minister. Inter-ministerial working groups were also set up and the common rules of procedure for federal government ministries were changed to allow for better horizontal coordination. Moreover, Chancellor Brandt and Interior Minister Genscher provided high-level political leadership on environmental policy matters.

Despite the favourable political context for EPI, Müller (2002: 67) has argued that neither the Green Cabinet nor the Committee for the Director Generals for Environmental Questions fulfilled its function of integrating environmental concerns within other policies. On the contrary, they effectively served as a watchdog, controlling the actions of the Interior Ministry and later the Environment Ministry, preventing them from intruding into sectoral policies with ambitious environmental measures. According to Müller (2002: 70) (who was a former BMI/BMU official), coordination turned out to be a one-way street; the sectors simply used it as an excuse to try to minimize the annoying political 'noise' emanating from the environmental sector. However, more detached observers have confirmed that the innovations of the early 1970s were poorly implemented (Jänicke *et al.* 2002; Pehle 1998; Weale *et al.* 1991).

The second missed opportunity came in 1986, when an independent Environmental Ministry – (BMU) was founded. Its creation followed severe public criticism of the BMI and in particular, its Minister, Fritz Zimmermann (CSU), for the poor information policy following the 1986 Chernobyl disaster. The decision to set up the BMU was an 'overly rushed one . . . which ruled out detailed prior considerations of [its] internal organization' (Pehle 1998: 46). Nine days before an important *Land* election and four months before federal elections, Chancellor Kohl (CDU) pressed ahead with setting up the BMU because he was hopeful that it would increase his re-election chances (Pehle 1998; Weale *et al.* 1991).

In addition to the Interior Ministry's environmental policy competences, the BMU was given the competences for nature conservation (from the Agricultural Ministry) as well as radiation and chemicals in food (from the Ministry for Youth, Family and Health). However, the BMU's internal organization still largely mirrored the media-centred environmental regulatory style, which severely constrained its efforts to implement environmental policy considerations into other policy sectors for two main reasons. First, the media-centred organizational structure of the BMU, which was reinforced by the implementation of the BAT principle on a media-by-media basis, made it difficult to take a holistic approach. Second, the other ministries argued that the BMU's attempt to integrate the environment was an unwarranted interference in their constitutionally guaranteed ministerial affairs. For Albert Weale and colleagues (1991: 133) 'the most striking feature . . . [was therefore] the extent to which new policy thinking was expressed within a traditional style of administration'.

A third missed opportunity occurred in 1999, when the seat of government was moved from Bonn to Berlin. The BMU's core political management competences and the central section (*Zentralabteilung*), which deals with cross-cutting issues such as sustainable development, were transferred to Berlin, whereas the media-focused units remained in Bonn.

In 2007, the BMU was made up of the following five major administrative units in addition to the above mentioned *Zentralabteilung*: 1) climate change and renewable energy, and international cooperation; 2) nuclear safety; 3) water management, waste management and soil protection; 4) environment and health, air quality, safety of industrial sites and transport, and safety of chemicals; and, 5) nature protection. Hence, it largely followed a media-centred arrangement which has remained virtually unchanged since it was set up in 1986. The BMU did not follow the lead given by the Federal Environmental Agency (*Umweltbundesamt* – UBA), which reformed its internal organization from a media-centred structure into a sector-oriented administrative structure in the mid-1990s. However, the BMU has experimented with new cross-media working groups. Green housekeeping rules have been implemented by the BMU and UBA, as well as the *Länder* administrations. Some *Länder* have set up ministries in which environmental ministries are amalgamated with other ministries (such as Health).

The section for climate change policy is (in addition to the *Zentralabteilung*) an exception to the BMU's media-centred organizational set up. Since the late 1980s, climate change has received a high political priority from German Chancellors. There was considerable horizontal cooperation between different ministries and vertical cooperation between different levels of government once the German government had committed itself to a voluntary 25 per cent carbon dioxide (CO_2) emission reduction target by 2010 (compared to 1990 levels) and a legally binding 21 per cent Kyoto protocol target for the same date and baseline. An interministerial working group on CO_2 reduction was set up to draft and implement the ambitious climate change programme which was adopted in 1995. It was revised in 2000 and 2005. The BMU's climate change policy competences and coordination role were further strengthened when the Red–Green coalition moved the renewable energy unit from the Economics Ministry to the BMU after its re-election in 2002. Most observers have argued that climate change policy constitutes a successful example of the implementation of EPI in Germany (Jänicke *et al.* 2002; Müller 2002; OECD 2001), although others are more critical (Pehle 1998: 96).

The last two government changes – one installing a Red–Green coalition, which was expected to give new environmental impulses, and the other a Grand Coalition of CDU-CSU and SPD, which could secure large majorities in both houses of the German legislature – created the most recent opportunities to strengthen sustainable development and EPI. In fact, under the Red–Green and the Grand Coalition governments, sustainable development became the 'chief business' (*Chefsache*) for both Chancellor Schröder and Chancellor Merkel. As mentioned above, the Committee of State Secretaries for Sustainable Development was set up by the Red–Green coalition government in 2001, functioning as a Green Cabinet composed of members of 10 ministries. The Green Cabinet is chaired by the Chief of the Chancellery, which shows that sustainable development has – albeit belatedly – gained high political priority in Germany. Also in 2001, a Working Group of Deputy Director Generals for Sustainable Development was set up alongside the Council for Sustainable Development. Moreover, significant government funding has been made available for sustainable development activities (Statz 2007). Under the Grand Coalition, the Chancellery tried to increase the importance of the Green Cabinet by inviting all ministries, including the Defence Ministry and Justice Ministry, which had not previously taken part in meetings, although they were kept informed (interview 2007). Importantly, while the Chancellery remains in charge of the national sustainable development strategy, it is the BMU which is the lead department for the EU's sustainable development strategy.

However, despite the government's increasing commitment, the public's knowledge about sustainable development issues remains poor (Jänicke *et al.* 2002). More importantly, critical political decisions, such as Chancellor Schröder's (SPD) so-called Agenda 2010, which reformed the labour market, were decided outside the sustainable development decision-making framework (Statz 2008).

Sustainable development was reconfirmed as a guiding principle by the Grand Coalition within its coalition agreement in 2005. Chancellor Merkel's endorsement of sustainable development was seen as important by BMU officials because it strengthened the Environmental Ministry's efforts to adopt an ambitious national strategy (interview 2007). However, the sustainable development strategy cannot remove barriers to the implementation of EPI, as can be seen, for example, from the continuing failure by the German government to adopt a unified Environmental Act (UGB), which would have given EPI an overarching guiding principle function (Kloepfer 2004).

In sum, we have identified four occasions when Germany had the opportunity to adapt its federal environmental administrative set-up in order to facilitate EPI. But structural and ideational factors – ranging from independent ministries to a media-focused and technology-oriented environmental policy – mutually reinforced each other in ways that made it difficult to break with national path-dependence.

Green Budgeting

There are no formal green budgeting procedures in Germany, although a greening of the budget has occurred over the years. The most important development in this context was the Red–Green coalition government's ecological tax reform in 1999 (OECD 2001; Wurzel *et al.* 2003). The principal idea behind the revenue-neutral ecological tax reform was to increase the cost for non-renewable resources while reducing non-wage labour costs. In essence, the ecological tax reform tried to bring about a more sustainable development path by implementing fiscal EPI measures.

Germany was amongst Europe's eco-tax pioneers when it adopted a waste water levy in 1976; it was, however, only implemented in 1981. It was only moderately effective, the level of charging having been reduced in the face of industry opposition (Genscher 1995; Müller 2002: 59). Moreover, the introduction of the BAT principle in the Water Management Act (WHG) diminished the steering capacity of the levy. Since the 1980s, the federal government has made wide use of tax incentives for consumers to speed up the market uptake of less polluting technologies. Moreover, the federal government has made available significant subsidies for the development of renewable energy and less polluting technologies (OECD 2001: 118–21). Significant sums of public money have been invested from federal and *Länder* budgets to subsidize public transport. The Red–Green coalition reduced subsidies for polluting activities while increasing subsidies for less polluting technologies. Nevertheless, the OECD (2001: 120) concluded that '35 per cent of federal subsidies are estimated to be potentially environmentally counterproductive'. And despite the introduction of market-based instruments, traditional (command-and-control) regulations have remained the dominant policy instrument (Wurzel *et al.* 2003).

Strategies and/or Strategy Development Processes

The 1971 Environmental Programme came close to what one could call a national strategy for the implementation of EPI. In the 1990s, central strategic EPI measures were revived when preparations for a national sustainable development strategy started slowly under a Centre-Right coalition government with a 'step process' in 1996 (see Table 9.2). But only when the Red–Green coalition gave a higher priority to sustainable development, was the national sustainable development strategy, entitled *Perspectives for Germany*, adopted in 2002. It contained four key elements: international equity, quality of life, social cohesion and international responsibility (Bundesregierung 2002; Statz 2008). It has since been supplemented by a progress report which added four 'action fields', which require cross-sectoral cooperation. An updated draft programme entitled *Landmarks for Sustainability* (Bundesregierung 2005) was not formally adopted by the cabinet under the Red–Green coalition due to early elections in 2005. The Grand Coalition focused its efforts on producing an indicator report for 2007 and a progress report on the national sustainable development strategy for 2008.

Neither the 1971 Environmental Programme nor the 2002 sustainable development strategy dealt exclusively with EPI, although 'the concept . . . is embedded in the sustainability paradigm' (Müller 2002: 65). Jänicke and colleagues comment that while German '[e]nvironmental policy . . . has . . . at a relatively early stage been connected to social and economic aspects such as employment, technology and competitiveness' (Jänicke *et al.* 2002: 145), a 'comprehensive reorientation of environmental policy towards a national strategy for sustainable development did not occur' (ibid.: 118). Since the late 1990s, sustainable development has caught the attention of German chancellors and become administratively anchored within the Chancellery. However, thus far Germany has largely pursued a sector-focused EPI strategy which relies heavily on the integration of environmental policy requirements into selected sectoral policies, including foreign policy (BMU 2006).

Although Germany failed (with the exception of the early 1970s) to pursue vigorously a national EPI strategy, German governments were already advocating EPI at EU level in the 1980s. For example, Germany lobbied successfully for the insertion of an EPI provision into the 1986

Table 9.2   EPI-related sustainable development measures

Conceptualizing EPI within the sustainable development strategy:	
1991–94	BMU-led participation in UNCED process
1998	Cabinet failed to adopt draft programme 'Sustainable Development in Germany' prior to elections
1998–2001	Red–Green coalition government took sustainable development more seriously
2002	National sustainable development strategy
2004	National sustainable development strategy progress report
2005	Cabinet failed to adopt progress report due to early elections
2005	Grand coalition agreement: commitment to EPI and sustainable development

Reorganizing the core administrative capacity:

2001	Committee of State Secretaries for Sustainable Development ('Green Cabinet') chaired by Chancellery
2001	Working Group of Deputy Director Generals for Sustainable Development
c.2002	Renewable energy unit transferred from Economics Ministry to BMU

Parliamentary activities:

1986	Environmental Committee
1992–94	Inquiry Commission 'Protection of Humankind and Sustainable Development'
2004	Parliamentary Advisory Council on Sustainable Development

Creating advisory capacity:

2001	Council for Sustainable Development

Creating societal sustainability awareness:

1991	National Sustainable Development Committee set up by Chancellor. Renamed in 1994. Dissolved in 1998.
1996–98	BMU-led step process
late 1990s	Increased government funding for sustainable development activities

Source: Interviews and Jänicke (2007); Jänicke *et al.* (2002); Müller (2002) and Statz (2008)

Single European Act. Germany even advocated the use of EPI processes during its 1998 EU Presidency, when it formally pushed forward the so-called Cardiff strategy (see Chapter 8). However, Germany's commitment to the Cardiff Process faltered when its Presidency ended (Jänicke *et al.* 2002: 146; Wurzel 2001). And significantly, no attempt was made to develop a national-level Cardiff Process in Germany.

Policy Appraisal Systems

The implementation of EPI depends on the monitoring of policy sectors and activities which cause pollution and/or threaten sustainable development. The Federal Statistical Office (*Statistisches Bundesamt*) has published an environmental-economic account since 1989 (Jänicke *et al.* 2002: 118). It provides information on 'all three forms of interaction between the economy and the environment – environmental pressures, the state of the environment and environmental protection measures' (Statistisches Umweltant 2008). Similarly, the UBA has produced the German Environment Index or DUX (*Deutscher Umwelt Index*).[2] It is based on an Environmental Barometer for Germany, which the UBA produced for the national sustainable development strategy. However, it is not widely known, although 'indicator charts from the Environmental Barometer were included in the Federal Government's annual economic report since 1999' (OECD 2001: 111). The UBA has produced periodically updated comprehensive environmental data since 1984 (UBA 1984).

Environmental policy appraisal

The German administrative system is often seen as being relatively immune to the adoption of Anglo-Saxon style policy appraisal systems, new public management practices and what Chapter 3 refers to as 'management by objectives' (EEA 2005: 19). A recent OECD (2004: 4) report concluded that '[t]here is no serious challenge to the Rechtsstaat and the basic functioning of the rule-making system: administrative action is based on elaborate legislation and codes, and public sector reforms remain firmly based on the Weberian administrative model of steep hierarchies with narrowly defined responsibilities'.

Significantly, in Germany there are still no comprehensive environmental appraisal systems for draft laws or a system of SIA, although there is a system of RIA (see Chapter 6). Moreover, EIA for federal government activities was introduced in 1975. When adopting these appraisal systems, German policy makers often looked to America for guidance (Genscher 1995; Müller 1986). On the other hand, strict economic cost–benefit analysis as adopted in America has been rejected as too narrow by German environmental policy makers.

Regulatory impact assessment

It is perhaps surprising then that Germany has become a pioneer in the use of RIA, which was adopted by cabinet in 1984 (De Francesco 2006). The so-called blue checklist required a general impact assessment of all legislative proposals rather than merely an impact assessment of draft environmental laws (Jänicke *et al.* 2002: 129). It was drawn up by a Centre-Right coalition government which wanted to bring about a leaner state (OECD 2001: 9). It could therefore be seen as an 'ideological" reaction to the "new social regulation"' (De Francesco 2006). This interpretation fits the fact that the Centre-Right coalition adopted three 'acceleration acts' (*Beschleunigungsgesetze*), which 'rendered licensing, disclosure and reporting obligations easier' (OECD 2001: 135). However, the Red–Green coalition government also pressed for an 'enabling state' with its Modern State–Modern Administration programme (OECD 2001: 9). Some observers have argued that attempts to modernize the administration could potentially have a beneficial impact on the implementation of EPI because lean management is likely to encourage cooperation between different ministerial units (Pehle 1998: 307). However, in practice environmental policy makers worry that general appraisal systems will make it easier for influential ministries (for example, the Economics Ministry) to veto draft environmental laws on competitiveness grounds (see also Chapter 6).

Strategic Environmental Assessment

Strategic Environmental Assessments in Germany were initially limited to EIA. According to Müller (2002: 59) 'preparations . . . began in 1971'. But they were 'obstructed at the early planning stage'. The EIA act would have entitled the BMI to:

> [a]ssess the programmes of other departments and prevent those programmes with negative environmental impacts. Hence, the environment would have gained horizontal influence in a similar manner to finance and constitutional law (Müller 2002: 59).

In 1975, the cabinet instead adopted non-binding 'general principles for the environmental impact assessment of federal government measures'. However, in practice this type of EIA remained ineffective (Hartkopf and Bohne 1983; Müller 1986). Federal ministries and agencies were left to their own devices in carrying out the EIA and did not have to publish the results. Moreover, the general principles stated explicitly that specific environmental laws would override EIA obligations (Pehle 1998: 73). German environmental law therefore 'had to wait until 1990', when the EU EIA Directive – restricted to certain projects, not to public programmes – 'was transposed into German legislation' (Müller 2002: 59). Reluctance to introduce far-reaching environmental assessment procedures was evident both in EU decision making and during the implementation of the Directive. Once again, Germany perceived them to be a threat to its BAT-centred domestic environmental (Knill and Lenschow 2000). In fact, even with external EU pressure, Germany was late in implementing the Directive. Moreover, Germany interpreted the EIA Directive so narrowly that its implementation hardly had any practical impact (Kloepfer 2004: 324).

The EIA Directive forms part of procedural EU policy measures which Germany opposed on principle, fearing that they might threaten its preferred environmental regulatory style. However, Germany supported the SEA Directive, which is aimed at general programmes and projects (see Chapter 7), although the BMU's enthusiasm for this measure is not shared by all ministries. In particular, the then Environmental Minister, Jürgen Trittin (Greens), pushed for SEA during the German EU Presidency (interview 2002). SEA is in line with sustainability assessments and other environmental assessments which emphasize the need for increased transparency, coordination, effectiveness and legitimacy in public policy making. Germany's support for SEA and its belated adoption of a national sustainable development strategy demonstrates that its political system is perhaps more adaptable to new challenges than some of its critics have claimed (Kitschelt and Streeck 2004).

SUMMARY DISCUSSION

Support for EPI has waxed and waned in Germany, largely as a result of shifts in the political cycle. Thus it waxed strongly in the early 1970s, driven by a newly elected Social–Liberal coalition government which had a reformist agenda. During the planning euphoria of the early 1970s, particular emphasis was put on innovative administrative measures (such as a Green Cabinet). Moreover, EIA for federal government activities was adopted well ahead of EPI pioneers such as Britain, although a more far-reaching draft EIA law, which would have included all government policies, was vetoed by influential actors such as the Economics Ministry (Müller 2002). A greening of budget-related measures also took place, although formal green budgeting procedures were not introduced. The 1971 Environmental Programme (and its 1976 update) acted both as overall plans (or strategies) as well as programmatic statements which conceptualized EPI. However, despite the existence of a strong planning division within the Chancellery (Jänicke *et al.* 2002), there were few high-level policy appraisals which took into account EPI. Thereafter, political support waned.

Support waxed again from the late 1990s, although this time at a much slower pace. To a large degree it was the Red–Green coalition's decision to take more seriously the national sustainable development strategy which pushed EPI up the domestic political agenda. Administrative EPI measures were given a higher priority, as can be seen from the decision to create a

Green Cabinet and the Working Group of Deputy Director Generals for Sustainable Development in 2001. Moreover, interdepartmental cooperation was strengthened with the setting up of inter-ministerial working groups (for example, on CO_2 reductions). Germany's climate change policy, which preceded its national sustainable development strategy, has turned out to be a reasonably successful example of EPI. However, formal green budgeting procedures have still not been introduced in Germany.

The belated appearance of a national sustainability strategy triggered important innovations in policy appraisal and SEA, which should facilitate the implementation of EPI. The UBA's Environmental Barometer and DUX, as well as the Federal Statistical Office's environmental-economic account, have made the achievements and failures of the sustainable development strategy more transparent (Statz 2007).

CONCLUSIONS

Germany was an early pioneer with respect to EPI in the early 1970s. However, EPI considerations were mainly confined to the agenda setting and programme formulation stages of the policy-making cycle. However, although the EPI concept figured prominently in the Social–Liberal coalition government's 1971 environmental programme, its implementation remained poor. Between the mid-1970s and late 1990s, support for EPI sank into the doldrums. Crucially, even amongst German environmental policy actors, support for EPI remained low – the media-centred, BAT-driven environmental regulatory style seemed to offer a more successful means of dealing with problems. It is only since the late 1990s that Germany has started to take EPI more seriously, this time within the context of the need to develop a credible national strategy on sustainable development.

All along, important constitutional, structural and ideational constraints have militated against the implementation of EPI in Germany. Coalition government, relatively strong ministerial independence, the federal system and the media-centred BAT-driven environmental regulatory style all make it difficult for the federal government to impose EPI on the policy actors. Moreover, German governments have to take seriously powerful 'parapolitical institutions' (Katzenstein 1987) such as the Constitutional Court. For example, a well-advanced draft of the Environmental Act, which would have unified the media-centred environmental laws while stipulating EPI as an overarching guiding principle, was not adopted for fear that this court might strike it down as an unconstitutional violation of the *Länder's* environmental competences.

However, the appearance of the climate change policy issue shows that, in some circumstances, EPI can work. The German climate change policy implemented EPI without major formal administrative rearrangements (apart from the setting up of an inter-ministerial working group on CO_2 reduction and the transfer of the renewable energy unit from the Economics Ministry to the BMU). Rather, it adopted a mixture of NEPIs, including ecological tax reform, voluntary agreements and some subsidies. Kenneth Dyson and Stephen Padgett (2005: 123) have identified within German economic policy making a 'paradox of institutional continuity and behavioural change', which they explain 'by the absence of a critical juncture or crisis' in economic reform. A similar conclusion could be drawn from the issue of climate change, in the sense that innovative initiatives crossed traditional policy boundaries, yet largely within the existing institutional framework. When assessing EPI in Germany, it is therefore important to look beyond the named EPI instruments, strategies and programmes, and take into account changes within particular policy sectors and/or with regard to particular policy problems.

Jänicke and colleagues' assessment (2002: 144–5) that '[t]here is a clear contradiction in Germany between the late, slow – and probably weak – process of implementing the concept of sustainable development and a much stronger – path-dependent – environmental and climate policy' needs modification. The media-focused, BAT-driven environmental regulatory style of old has brought about important environmental policy achievements, which have made Germany an environmental lead state. However, there is an increasing recognition amongst policy makers that the more diffuse and interconnected challenges posed by unsustainable development cannot be solved in the same old ways. A recent OECD report (2001: 112) on Germany's environmental performance therefore concludes that '[w]hile the initial focus of environmental law was on individual media . . ., cross-media focus has gained importance'. This message is beginning to be accepted by policy elites, so perhaps the best way to characterize the implementation of EPI in Germany is work which is still very much 'in progress'.

ACKNOWLEDGEMENTS

The author would like to thank German officials for granting interviews and to the editors for extremely helpful comments on earlier drafts. Klaus Jacob, Martin Jänicke, Edward Page and Albert Statz also provided very useful information. The research for this chapter has benefited from a British Academy grant (SG-46048). The usual disclaimers apply.

NOTES

1. The term 'Germany' refers to the Federal Republic of Germany both before and after unification. References to the former Democratic Republic of Germany (that is, East Germany) are made explicit.
2. The abbreviation DUX is a play on words as DAX is the abbreviation of the German Equity Index (*Deutscher Aktienindex*).

BIBLIOGRAPHY

Andersen, Mikael and Duncan Liefferink (eds) (1997), *European Environmental Policy: The Pioneers*, Manchester: Manchester University Press.

Baring, Arnulf (1984), *Machtwechsel: Die Ära Brandt-Scheel*, Munich: Deutscher Taschenbuch Verlag.

BMU (2006), *BMU-Pressedienst Nr. 242/06*, 25 September 2006, Berlin: Bundesministerium für Umwelt, Naturschutz und Reaktorsicherheit.

Brandt, Willy (2003), *Erinnerungen*, Munich: Ullstein.

Bundesregierung (1971), *Umweltprogramm der Bundesregierung*, Bonn: Deutscher Bundestag.

Bundesregierung (1976): *Umweltbericht '76: Fortschreibung des Umweltprogramms*, Stuttgart: Kohlhammer.

Bundesregierung (2002), *Perspektiven für Deutschland*, Berlin: Bundesregierung.

Bundesregierung (2005), *Wegweiser Nachhaltigkeit 2005*, Berlin: Bundesregierung.

CDU/CSU and SPD (2005), *Working Together for Germany: With Courage and Compassion*, Berlin: CDU/CSU and SPD.

De Francesco, Fabrizio (2006), 'Towards an "Impact Assessment State" in Europe?' Paper given at the *56th PSA annual conference*, Reading: University of Reading.

Dyson, Kenneth and Stephen Padgett (2005), 'Introduction: global, Rhineland or hybrid Capitalism?' *German Politics*, 14 (2),115–123.

EEA (2005), *Environmental Policy Integration in Europe*, Copenhagen: European Environment Agency.

Genscher, Hans-Dietrich (1995), *Erinnnerungen*, Berlin: Siedler Verlag.

Hartkopf, Günter and Eberhard Bohne (1983), *Umweltpolitik 1*, Opladen: Westdeutscher Verlag.

Jänicke, Martin (2007), '"Umweltstaat": eine Basisfunktion des Regierens. Umweltpolitikintegration in Deutschland', *Politische Vierteljahresschrift*, 39, special issue, 342–59.

Jänicke, Martin, Helge Jörgens, Kirsten Jörgensen and Ralf Nordbeck (2002), 'Germany', in OECD (ed.), *Governance for Sustainable Development*, Paris: Organisation for Economic Development, pp. 112–153.

Katzenstein, Peter (1987), *Policy and Politics in West Germany*, Ithaca: Cornell University.

Kitschelt, Herbert and Wolfgang Streeck (eds) (2004), *Germany: Beyond the Stable State*, London: Frank Cass.

Kloepfer, Michael (2004), *Umweltrecht*, third edition, Munich: Beck.

Knill, Christoph and Andrea Lenschow (eds) (2000), *Implementing EU Environmental Policy*, Manchester: Manchester University Press.

Lenschow, Andrea (2002), 'Greening the European Union: an introduction', in Andrea Lenschow (ed.), *Environmental Policy Integration*, London: Earthscan, pp. 3–21.

Mayntz, Renate (ed.) (1980), *Implementation Politischer Programme: empirische Forschungsberichte*, Königstein: Athenäum.

Mayntz, Renate (ed.) (1983), *Implementation Politischer Programme: Ansätze zur Theoriebildung*, Opladen: Westdeutscher Verlag.

Müller, Edda (1986), *Innenpolitik der Umweltpolitik: Sozial-Liberale Umweltpolitik – (Ohn) Macht durch Organisation?* Opladen: Westdeutscher Verlag.

Müller, Edda (2002), 'Environmental policy integration as a political principle: the German case and the implications for European policy', in Andrea Lenschow (ed.), *Environmental Policy Integration*, London: Earthscan, pp. 57–77.

OECD (2001), *Environmental Performance Review: Germany*, Paris: Organisation for Economic Cooperation and Development.

OECD (2004), *OECD Reviews of Regulatory Reform: Regulatory Reform in Germany*, Paris: Organisation for Economic Cooperation and Development.

Pehle, Heinrich (1998), *Das Bundesministerium für Umwelt, Naturschutz und Reaktorsicherheit: ausgegrenzt statt integriert?* Wiesbaden: Deutscher Universitätsverlag.

Rehbinder, Eberhard (1992), 'Rethinking environmental policy', in G. Smith, W. Paterson, P. Merkl and S. Padgett (eds), *Developments in German Politics*, Basingstoke: Macmillan, pp. 227–243.

Scharpf, Fritz W. (1972), 'Komplexität als Schranke der politischen Planung', *Politische Vierteljahresschrift*, 13 (4), 168–192.

SRU (1974), *Umweltgutachten 1974, Bundestags-Drucksache 7/2802*, Bonn: Sachverständigenrat für Umweltfragen.

SRU (2006), *Föderalismusreform, Pressemitteilung 18.5.2006*, Berlin: Sachverständigenrat für Umweltfragen.

Statistisches Umweltant (2008), http://www.destatis.de/jetspeed/portal/cms/Sites/destatis/Internet/EN/Content/Statistics/Environment/EnvironmentalEconomic Accounting/Content75/InfoUER.psm, accessed 12 June 2008.

Statz, Albert (2008), 'Die deutsche Nachhaltigkeitsstrategie: Bilanz und Perspektiven', in Nina Amelung, B. Mayer-Scholl, M. Schàfer and J. Weber (eds), *Einstieg in die Nachhaltige Entwicklung*, Frankfurt: Lang.

UBA (1984), *Daten zur Umwelt '84*, Berlin: Umweltbundesamt.

Weale, Albert (1992a), *The New Politics of Pollution*, Manchester: Manchester University Press.

Weale, Albert (1992b), 'Vorsprung durch Technik? The politics of German environmental regulation', in Kenneth Dyson (ed.), *The Politics of German Regulation*, Aldershot Dartmouth, pp. 159–183.

Weale, Albert, Timothy O'Riordan and Louise Kramme (1991), *Controlling Pollution in the Round*, London: Anglo-German Foundation.

Weidner, Helmut and Peter Knoepfel (1983), 'Innovation durch international vergleichende Politikanalyse dargestellt am Beispiel der Luftreinhaltepolitik', in R. Mayntz (ed.), *Implementation politischer Programme*, Königstein: Athenäum, pp. 221–255.

Wurzel, Rüdiger K.W. (2001), 'The EU Presidency and the integration principle', *European Environmental Law Review*, 10, 7–15.

Wurzel, Rüdiger K.W. (2002), *Environmental Policy-Making in Britain, Germany and the European Union*, Manchester: Manchester University Press.

Wurzel, Rüdiger K.W., Andrew Jordan, Anthony Zito and Lars Brückner (2003), 'From high regulatory state to social and ecological market economy? "New" environmental policy instruments in Germany', *Environmental Politics*, 12 (1), 115–136.

10. Norway

William M. Lafferty, Olav Mosvold Larsen and Audun Ruud

INTRODUCTION

Norwegian environmental policy implementation is based on the principle of sectoral responsibility. This states that specific ministries and directorates have the responsibility to implement and enforce political decisions made by the Norwegian Parliament. The goal of achieving greater EPI has been sporadically pursued in Norway, including attempts to create comprehensive institutional and procedural systems for implementing and monitoring EPI processes. The chapter outlines three 'waves' of EPI-related initiatives during the period 1989–2006. These waves have come with differing intensities and time spans, and have left different impressions on the Norwegian political shore. Overall, we argue that attempts to improve EPI in Norway have shown great promise – but little fulfilment. Ambitious attempts to establish institutional provisions for EPI in all policy sectors were introduced in 1989. These were initiated by the government with support from high-ranking officials and strategists in the ministry of environment. The political will behind the effort did not, however, penetrate through to the upper echelons of the ministerial bureaucracy, and gradually the increasingly dominant interests of a petroleum-driven economy deflected and undermined the EPI initiatives.

HISTORY

Engagement with Environmental Policy Issues

With a population of only 4.5 million people in a country blessed with generous amounts of natural resources (oil, gas, hydropower, forests, fish and so on), Norway emerged in the second half of the 20th Century as one of the wealthiest and most socially secure countries in the world (Lafferty 1990; Heidar 2000). The citizens of Norway have declined EU membership twice, but the country is nonetheless strongly integrated into the EU internal market, and is an active participant in the EU through the European Economic Area agreement.

Environmental politics became a key concern in Norway as early as 1972, with the establishment of the Norwegian Ministry of Environment (MoE), one of the world's first ministries for environmental protection. Important subsequent developments included the establishment of the Norwegian Pollution Control Authority (SFT) in 1974 and the enactment of the Pollution Control Act in 1981. Prior to the founding of the MoE, environmental matters were handled in Parliament by the Standing Committee on Local Government. With the arrival of the MoE, this body was renamed the Committee on Local Government and the Environment. In 1993, it was again reorganized as the Standing Committee on Energy and the Environment (Jansen and Osland 1996). The fact that environmental concerns have often been coupled with local and regional development in Parliament has clearly played a role in shaping Norway's overall response to the challenge of sustainable development.

The environmental policy process – its choice of instruments and mode of interest representation – was rooted in technical and judicial expertise in the early years of the MoE. Toward the end of the 1980s, however, new signals began to appear. Strongly influenced by the role of Gro Harlem Brundtland as both Chairperson of the World Commission on Environment and Development (1983–87) and a major promoter of the Rio Earth Summit in 1992, Norway moved strongly towards 'ecological modernization'.[1] The traditional focus on nature conservation through administrative and judicial instruments was transcended by White Paper 58 (MoE 1997), and a suite of new policy instruments, particularly economic instruments, was introduced. Cost-effectiveness became a guiding principle in environmental politics. The attempt to introduce a green tax system is a key example of the transition to ecological modernization in this period (Ruud 2002). White Paper 58 also signalled a shift to a more cross-sector approach. Sustainable development issues were henceforth to be integrated into all aspects of societal planning and sectoral policy (Langhelle 2000; Hovden and Torjussen 2002).

Three 'Waves' of EPI Initiatives

Looking more closely at EPI in practice, the Norwegian system has gradually evolved through three identifiable phases or 'waves'. Each wave is associated with a specific White Paper.

The start of the first wave can be traced to White Paper 46, *Environment and Development*, presented by the second Brundtland Government in

1989. This document marked the immediate follow-up to the Brundtland Report (WCED 1987) and initiated the first EPI-related reform in Norway. It clearly states that: 'the Government places decisive emphasis on the inclusion of sustainable development considerations into all societal planning and sectoral policy' (MoE 1989: 71) [Authors' translation]. A form of 'green budgeting' (designated as the 'Environmental Profile of the State Budget' – EPSB) emerged as a crucial instrument for highlighting interdepartmental EPI. During this initial period, several coordinating committees were established, and procedures promoting EIA, environmental policy appraisal and SEA were introduced.

The second wave was initiated by White Paper 58 in 1997. The document outlined a clear and relatively forceful environmental policy for sustainable development with strong EPI ambitions:

> An environmental problem is seldom caused by only a single sector . . . An efficient environmental policy must ensure that environmental considerations are integrated into the policy frameworks and concerns for all sectors in society. Integration of environmental concerns early in the decision-making process will prevent environmental problems from arising, which in most cases is less costly than having to 'repair' them (MoE 1997: 25) [Authors' translation].

Whereas the green budgeting procedures of the first wave focused primarily on a documentation of monetary input, the EPI-related initiatives of the second wave were designed to chart a broader spectrum of policy output. The so-called 'National Environmental Monitoring System' (NEMS),[2] introduced in this period, can be characterized as an ambitious and comprehensive procedural instrument to organize national environmental policies and to integrate environmental concerns into other policy areas.

The beginning of the third (and current) wave of EPI in Norway can be traced back to a change of government in 2001, but it is manifested by White Paper 21 (MoE 2005a), which established that most of the initiatives related to NEMS would be discontinued. The election was won by a coalition of the Conservative Party, the Liberal Party and the Christian Democratic Party, and they initiated (under the leadership of Børge Brende, a dynamic young Conservative Minister of the Environment) a process both for following up the NEMS and EPSB, as well as launching a new 'National Strategy' and 'National Action Plan for Sustainable Development'. Responsibility for the National Action Plan was placed directly within the Ministry of Finance so as (in theory) to guarantee a tighter integration between the pursuit of sustainable development and the preparation of the National Budget.

EPI IN PRACTICE

As evident from Chapter 2, several of the key instruments and procedures for EPI are in place in Norway. In fact, Norway has been an 'early mover' in many cases. While some of the instruments and provisions are explicitly designed to promote EPI as such, others are directed towards a stronger consideration of environmental issues in planning processes, or more generally towards sustainable development in a broad sense. Although the boundaries between the different initiatives are often blurred, the provisions and instruments clearly heighten awareness as to the nature of environmental concerns in non-environmental policy areas. The initiatives and provisions established during the first two waves will be elaborated upon in this section, and the third wave – which in many ways sums up the experiences from the two first waves – will be discussed in the final sections of this chapter.

Administrative Instruments

Constitutional commitments

Since the launching of the Brundtland Report, Norwegian governments of both the 'right' and 'left' have presented White Papers, Long-term Plans, a National Strategy and a National Action Plan, all proclaiming 'sustainable development' as an overarching goal for Norwegian society. Even more importantly, however, strong environmental prescriptions (and implied 'rights') were included as Article 110b of the Norwegian Constitution in 1992:

> Every person has a right to an environment that is conducive to health and to natural surroundings whose productivity and diversity are preserved. . . . [T]his right will be safeguarded for future generations as well. . . . [C]itizens are entitled to be informed of the state of the natural environment and of the effects of any encroachments on nature that are planned or commenced (Stortinget 2007).

Although this constitutional provision is not as strong and direct a commitment as, for example, the EU's Article 6, the White Paper 8 (MoE 1999: 9) clearly states that the intention is 'to emphasize the ecological perspective as a foundation for policy formulation in all areas of society'. There can be little doubt that these constitutional provisions imply a status of 'principled priority' for the ecological/environmental aspect,[3] and that a strong potential 'mandate' for applying EPI is thus in place in Norway.

Green ministers and amalgamated ministries

The Minister of the Environment has held a permanent position in cabinet since 1972. At its inception, the MoE took over issues related to emission control from the Ministry of Industry, as well as all other environmental issues from the Ministry of Local Administration. In contrast to the situation for many other ministries, amalgamation of the MoE with other ministries has never been a political issue in Norway. Environmental issues are, however, treated in a Standing Committee on Energy and the Environment in Parliament. The Ministry of Foreign Affairs – which includes a separate Minister of International Development – has also been strongly involved in sustainability issues. The Ministry of Foreign Affairs was, for example, given responsibility for the National Strategy on Sustainable Development issued in 2002. It was the Ministry of Finance, however, which was given responsibility for following up the strategy through a separate National Action Plan for Sustainable Development (NAPSD), adopted in 2003. Formally, therefore, it is now the Ministry of Finance which, through its influence on the national budget, is principally responsible for Norwegian sustainable development policy and sectoral integration.

Interdepartmental and cabinet committees
Throughout the 1990s, as part of the first wave, Norwegian authorities established a number of interdepartmental committees and groups to address sustainable development issues. Some of the groups were ad hoc, reporting on single issues such as environmental taxes, climate policy, environmental policy instruments, biodiversity and sustainable consumption (Hovden and Torjussen 2002). An official Norwegian Report (MoE 1995) concluded that these initiatives had succeeded in laying a better general foundation for inter-ministerial cooperation, but that specific manifestations of EPI were lacking. To our knowledge, no EPI-related guidelines or initiatives have been introduced for standing committees of either the Parliament or State Administration.

In the wake of the 1992 Rio Earth Summit, the Government set up two coordinating bodies: a National Committee for Sustainable Development (NCSD), with representatives from five key ministries, local and regional authorities, business, labour and Friends of the Earth Norway; and a Committee for International Environmental Issues (NIM),[4] chaired by the Minister of the Environment with representatives from the Office of the Prime Minister, six sectoral ministries and major business, labour, environmental and research groups. In Norway's initial reports to the UN Commission for Sustainable Development, these two committees were portrayed as key national coordinating instruments for the 'Norwegian Agenda 21' (despite the fact that the Norwegian Agenda 21 – the NAPSD – was not actually in place until 2003). As for the NCSD and the NIM, the former was convened periodically at the start and then quietly phased out in 1995, and the latter has served only to coordinate Norwegian positions on environment and development issues for international fora. As nearly as we can determine, these bodies have made no significant contributions to promoting EPI in Norwegian domestic politics.

Independent evaluation bodies and parliamentary committees
There is no independent evaluation body or parliamentary committee specifically related to the evaluation of the effectiveness of EPI instruments. Both the Office of the National Auditor (*Riksrevisjonen*) and the Standing Committee on Scrutiny and Constitutional Affairs in the Parliament could focus on EPI issues, but thus far have only done so to a limited degree. The Office of the National Auditor conducted an analysis of the green budgeting procedures in 1999 (see below), but the Standing Committee in Parliament on Scrutiny and Constitutional Affairs has no record of hearings or other initiatives related to environmental policy.

Green Budgeting

Chapter 2 indicates that Norway is one of the few European countries to establish 'green budgeting' procedures. This system has been in place since 1989, when White Paper 46 (MoE 1989) introduced the Environmental Profile of the State Budget (EPSB) (see above):

> In the State Budget for 1989 the ministries presented environmental initiatives within their sectoral domains in their respective budgetary bills to Parliament. The most important challenges, goals and strategies are described in a separate chapter in the overall State Budget . . . The Government aims to develop this practice into an important incentive for promoting sustainable development. The goal is to provide an overview of public initiatives within each sector related to environmental challenges. . . . The overview will be further developed so as to be comparable from year to year (MoE 1989: 72) [Authors' translation].

Over the ensuing years, several changes have been made with respect to reporting environmental efforts in the State Budget. Until 1992, the EPSB was only presented in the main publication of the budget under the heading: 'Follow-up on the World Commission for Sustainable Development'. From 1992 onwards, however, it was taken out of the State Budget and a summary of each ministry's EPSB was published as part of the MoE's annual Budget Bill. In addition, a full-text version was published in the respective Budget Bills for each ministry. In 1992 the MoE also asked the ministries to classify their environmental allocations into three categories according to 'the degree of environmental motivation' (see Box 10.1).

In 1994, the presentation of the EPSB was again changed (MoE 1994), with the ministries now instructed to drop the Category 2 and Category 3 assessments, and report only on Category 1 initiatives. The reporting now,

---

**BOX 10.1   GUIDELINES BY THE NORWEGIAN
MINISTRY OF THE ENVIRONMENT
FOR CLASSIFYING ENVIRONMENTAL
EFFORTS ACCORDING TO 'DEGREE
OF ENVIRONMENTAL MOTIVATION'***

Category 1:   Solely environmental initiatives* (at least two-thirds
environmentally motivated).

Category 2:   Environmental initiatives with considerable environmental motivation* (at least one-third environmentally motivated).

Category 3:   Environmental initiatives with partial environmental
motivation* (at least one-tenth environmentally
motivated).

* As estimated by the respective ministries

Source: MoE (1996) (cited in: Riksrevisjonen 1999)

---

however, was to be estimated for 19 designated policy areas, with targets
and indicators as a basis for organizing the environmental information
from the ministries. Through these changes the Government aimed to
emphasize strategic management – 'governance by objectives' (that is,
specification of output – see Chapter 3) – and the documentation of
achieved and expected results.

In 1997, the list of 19 policy areas was reduced to 11, consisting of eight
priority areas applicable for all ministries (Box 10.2), plus three areas to be
mainly addressed by the MoE: regional planning; maps and geodata; and
cross-sectoral policy instruments and municipal tasks. The eight priority
areas constitute the current (2007) thematic baseline for Norwegian environmental reporting and documentation and designate explicit terms of
references for both the EPSB and the NEMS, which we will return to
shortly.

The EPSB has clearly developed and improved over time. The criteria for
the 'degree of environmental motivation' (see Box 10.1) were, for example,
very diffuse at the outset of the system. This led to some amusing results. For
example, the Ministry of Defence argued that virtually the entire ministry's
spending was 'environmentally motivated', since most of its activities could
be related to the prevention of nuclear destruction! Another ministry claimed
that expenses related to the renovation of bathrooms in the ministry's buildings were 'solely environmentally motivated' (Nøttestad 1999: 133).

```
BOX 10.2   THE EIGHT PRIORITY AREAS FOR
           OFFICIAL ENVIRONMENTAL
           REPORTING IN NORWAY

1.  Conservation and sustainable use of biological diversity
2.  Outdoor recreation
3.  Cultural heritage
4.  Eutrophication and oil pollution
5.  Hazardous substances
6.  Waste and recycling
7.  Climate change, air pollution and noise
8.  International cooperation and environmental protection in the
    polar areas

Source:   MoE (1997)
```

Strategies and/or Strategy Developing Processes

A national strategy for sustainable development was hastily prepared for the World Summit in Johannesburg in 2002. One year later (October 2003), a National Action Plan for Sustainable Development (also referred to as 'National Agenda 21') was published as a separate chapter of the annual National Budget (MoF 2003). The plan was authored by a committee of ministerial state secretaries headed by the Ministry of Finance.

While the commitment to EPI in the NAPSD was (once again) made very clear (MoF 2003: 184), with a broad range of relatively specific goals, the NAPSD has subsequently been criticized for being even less concrete than already published policy documents (ProSus 2003). The only initiative related to a follow-up of the plan is a set of 16 key 'Indicators for Sustainable Development' (MoF 2005). The indicators cover the following themes: greenhouse gas emissions; ozone and trans-border air pollution; biodiversity; cultural heritage; hazardous chemicals; natural resources; sustainable economy (national accounts); and social indicators with (posited) direct relevance for sustainability. Oddly enough, however, only the indicator for greenhouse gas emissions corresponds with the eight 'priority areas' for national reporting used in NEMS (Box 10.2). Progress reports on the indicators have thus far been very superficial. However, in 2006 the current Government launched a major revision of both the 2002 NSSD and the 2003 NAPSD (along with an external peer review of the strategy coordinated by the Swedish Ministry of Finance).

Policy Appraisal Systems and Strategic Environmental Assessment

There have been provisions for EIA in Norway since 1990, when the instrument was incorporated into the Planning Act, the Building Act and the Pollution Control Acts. The regulations conform to corresponding legislation in the relevant EU Directive (85/337/EEC) (Hovden and Torjussen 2002). Measures for Environmental Policy Appraisal (EPA) and SEA were introduced at a strategic level in 1995 by an administrative order. The order stipulated that environmental assessments and appraisals were to be carried out in connection with white papers, ministerial proposals, new acts, budgets and reports prepared by Government to be discussed in Parliament (Husby 1997; Tesli 2002). With the adoption of the EU SEA Directive (2001/42/EC), plans and programmes derived from acts and formal regulations become subject to assessment. More politically initiated processes are subject to appraisal in accordance with the Administrative Order, which was updated in 2004. When white papers, proposals and so on are completed, the responsible ministry or directorate can, if it is considered necessary, initiate a hearing process. In such cases, all relevant public authorities and private institutions and organizations are invited to present their views. As all hearing processes in Norway are public, the views of private persons or companies are also accepted, but not formally invited.

Experiences of more than ten years of formal EIA legislation and practice have been 'relatively good' (Tesli 2002: 7). Assessments of EPA and SEA are, however, more limited. Husby (1997), for example, has surveyed all white papers, proposals to the Parliament and Official Norwegian Reports (NOU) for the years 1995–97 and concluded that only 10 per cent would qualify as environmental assessment. Of the 66 cases evaluated, 62 contained references to the environment, but the qualitative analyses of the documents revealed that the focus was on the environmental consequences of the general policy area and not on the presumed consequences of the changes in question (*ibid*). According to MoE officials, the threshold for pursuing assessments in accordance with the Administrative Order is currently so high that they are undertaken only in cases with obvious environmental policy impacts.

The National Environmental Monitoring System (NEMS)

NEMS can be characterized as a multi-faceted procedural instrument to organize the reporting and assessment of national environmental policies, and to coordinate environmental goals within and across sectors. The system was introduced in White Paper 58 (MoE 1997) as follows:

> As part of a comprehensive cross-sectoral environmental policy, the Ministry [MoE] will improve control, reporting and the follow-up of targets and policy

instruments. . . . The national environmental monitoring system will constitute a basis for assessing whether the overall effort is satisfactory with regard to existing targets and obligations, and whether the distribution between sectors and resources is cost-effective. The environmental monitoring system will be an instrument for adjusting the targets and instruments in environmental policy. An important part of the task of the environmental authorities will be to coordinate the Government's efforts on these matters (MoE 1997: 27) [Authors' translation].

Two years after the launch of the system, it was further developed in White Paper 8, which emphasized a more substantive integration of 'ecological' concerns in 'policy formation in all areas of society' (MoE 1999: 9). NEMS is the most ambitious attempt to ensure EPI in Norwegian politics and policies to date and an assessment of the NEMS provisions goes, therefore, to the very core of EPI initiatives in Norway. NEMS aims to provide continuous reporting and updates on the outcomes and impacts of both national and sectoral environmental policies. It was originally presented as a five-stage 'circular' effort (Figure 10.1) with the following interrelated procedures:

1. The single most important element of NEMS is the series of biennial[5] White Papers: *The Government's Environmental Policy* and *State of the Environment Reports*. The series constitutes the principal publication and cornerstone of NEMS. A total of four *State of the Environment Reports* (SERs) have been published thus far. The main body of the report focuses on the environmental policies and state of the environment pertaining to the eight priority areas referred to in Box 10.2. Following the core idea of New Public Management, namely management by objectives (that is, specification of output – see Chapter 3), it presents the goals and targets for the specific area; the state of the environment; goals achieved; and the policy instruments and initiatives in use. The goals are divided into two levels: 'strategic objectives' and 'operational national targets'. The targets are intended to reflect the main environmental problems and challenges within each priority area and should, given a sound scientific basis for assessment, be verifiable and related to specified time limits. The operational targets are, in addition, to be used as a basis for drawing up sectoral working targets, thereby enabling the formulation of Sectoral Environmental Action Plans for each Ministry.

2. The Sectoral Environmental Action Plans (SEAPs) stipulate sectoral targets and objectives. Each ministry is responsible for presenting a SEAP in terms of the eight policy priority areas; it should cover the administrative domain of the ministry and sectoral areas of responsibility, delineating the instruments and initiatives to be used to deal with

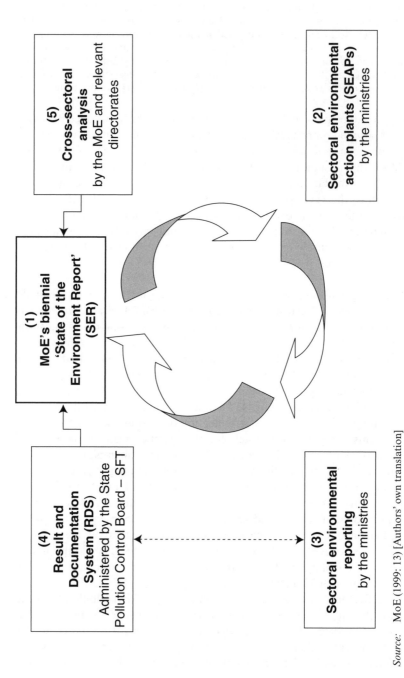

Source: MoE (1999: 13) [Authors' own translation]

Figure 10.1 Elements of the National Environmental Monitoring System (NEMS) in Norway

the identified challenges. Furthermore, the action plans should show how each ministry can contribute to fulfilling the government's overall policy on sustainable development. The Parliament had originally decided, in accordance with White Paper 8 (MoE 1999), that the SEAPs should be updated every four years. To date, however, only one generation of SEAPs has been prepared.

3. Sectoral reporting on the implementation of the SEAPs was supposed to be executed annually. It was meant to facilitate the internal follow-up of ministerial activities; to enable the functioning of the other elements of NEMS in accordance with the established routines, formats and standards; and to contribute to the reporting section in the SERs. As nearly as we can discover, however, no ministry has actually initiated this task.

4. NEMS is dependent on a well-functioning system for reporting and documentation of environmental policy implementation in each sector. To this end, the SFT was asked by the MoE to develop a system of key indicators. SFT responded with the Results and Documentation System (RDS), a prototype for a web-based system, bringing together the results from sectoral reporting with statistics and information from the SFT, Statistics Norway (SSB) and other environmental public policy agencies. But the response from the MoE was ambivalent and work on the RDS is currently reported by the SFT to be 'on ice'.[6]

5. With reference to information derived from the RDS, cross-sectoral analyses[7] were highlighted as a potential source of integrated assessment within the NEMS. Such analyses were intended to form the basis for cross-sectoral applications and assessments of policy instruments. Reference to this aspect in the NEMS procedure has been dropped in the SERs following White Paper 8 (MoE 1999). We have not been able to document why this part of the system simply vanished.

SUMMARY DISCUSSION

We have looked at the status of EPI in Norway in terms of three successive 'waves' (see Figure 10.2). The very focused rhetoric of the 'first wave' of EPI initiatives – particularly in the transition period between the Brundtland Report in 1987 and the Rio Summit in 1992 – was strongly formulated in terms of institutions and procedures, but only half-heartedly executed in practice. The second wave started in 1997 with the introduction of the first elements of the ambitious NEMS system. This was followed up in 2002 by the long-awaited National Strategy for Sustainable Development. And then (in 2003) came the National Action Plan for Sustainable Development. The

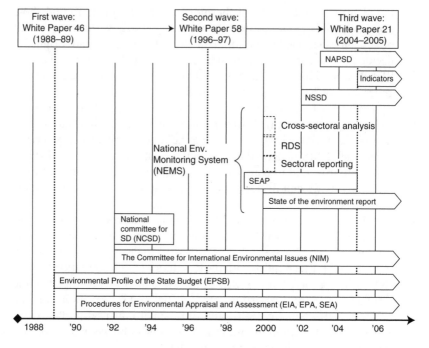

Figure 10.2   The three 'waves' of environmental policy integration in Norway

final initiative of this cycle was the adoption of provisional indicators for sustainable development in 2005. Even this most marginal of EPI-related efforts came after the start of the third wave; however, due to the failure to implement NEMS, this now appears to be a regressive step.

By way of a summary evaluation, we can say that Norway – at the height of the second wave – warranted a 'front-runner' label in terms of selective EPI procedures. The effect of the procedures in achieving 'integrated' or 'balanced' policy making was, however, much more unclear. Except for the EPSB and SEAPs, committees and instruments were not subjected to EPI-relevant assessments. The coordinating committees, at both the interdepartmental and national levels, were gradually phased out, with few traces of their activity (Hovden and Torjussen 2002). The EPSB was evaluated by the Office of the General Auditor in 1999 (Riksrevisjonen 1999), and judged to suffer from a number of significant weaknesses. Most importantly, the criteria for classifying the environmental impacts of budgetary allocations were seen as unclear, leading to different classifications by different ministries. These weaknesses virtually invalidated meaningful monitoring and inter-ministerial comparison. More generally, the evaluation report criticized the coordinating role of the MoE, stating that it should take a stronger lead in the entire EPSB process, particularly with respect to training and the provision of more general follow-up of the specific ministerial EPSBs.

A quote from the 1993 OECD environmental performance review of Norway sums up the status of the committees and the EPSB as follows: 'integration does not operate in practice as satisfactorily as it should' (OECD 1993: 80). The lack of inter-ministerial cooperation was also confirmed by the longest-serving Minister of the Environment for the period, Thorbjørn Berntsen, who identified difficulties in trying to establish common interests and targets for sustainable development within the central administration (Sverdrup 1997: 67). Sverdrup also claims that diminishing political support from Prime Minister Brundtland for the sustainable development agenda was an important factor (see below).

As for the SEAPs more specifically, all ministries have prepared the required action plans. They were evaluated twice (in 2001 and 2003) by the quasi-public assessment agency Statskonsult. The evaluations were not positive. The degree of political involvement in the process was judged to vary strongly from ministry to ministry, and work on the plans was in general given low priority. Few effects from the SEAPs could be documented. The most positive effect was that the process had given the ministries a better overview of their environmental challenges. However, efforts to meet the challenges were diffuse with respect to both targets and deadlines, thus weakening the possibility for either adequate reporting or effectiveness evaluation. According to Statskonsult, the SEAPs could not be said to function either as sectoral steering documents or as a basis for cross-sectoral analysis. The plans had not improved cooperation between ministries related to cross-sectoral horizontal challenges, since none of the ministries had reported inter-ministerial collaboration on environmental initiatives. Finally, the plans did not appear to have any effect on policy development or the distribution of resources. The SEAPs had, in short, failed to function as an appropriate policy instrument for integrating environmental considerations into the ministerial decision-making processes. Based on these conclusions, Statskonsult recommended that efforts related to sectoral integration should be continued by coupling it more strongly to the EPSB or the SERs.

This opinion appears to have sealed the fate of the SEAPs. As the following statement from the most recent SER indicates, they have vanished by default:

Sector-encompassing policy instruments are important for viewing environmental initiatives for the sectors coherently. . . . An important foundation for sectoral responsibility in environmental policy was laid with the work by the ministries on Sectoral Environmental Action Plans (SEAPs) 1998 – 2000. . . . Based on an evaluation of the SEAPs, it was concluded in 2004 that the principle of sectoral responsibility should be continued through the ordinary budgetary processes and the work on the 'State of the Environment Reports' (MoE 2005a, 13–14) [Authors' translation].

As for the overall NEMS process, this has been specifically recognized by the SFT as an innovative effort to enable policy coordination and integration across different sectoral interests and responsibilities.[8] The original depiction of the NEMS in *all* written material relating to the system leaves no doubt as to its intended integrative character. The SEAPs and NEMS were specifically welcomed by the Standing Committee on Energy and Environment in Parliament in 2000. However, the evisceration of cross-sectoral analyses, sectoral reporting, the RDS and finally the SEAPs, has been carried through in silence. In the most recent committee discussions, the system itself is no longer even mentioned (see for example: Innst. S. nr. 228, 2004–2005). It thus seems clear that the initial hype around NEMS has faded, and that no systematic evaluation of the system has been carried out, despite (or perhaps because of) the strong criticism of its component parts.

Only the biennial SER can be considered a partially successful element of NEMS. The SERs have been relatively detailed and easily accessible, but most targets are nonetheless diffuse and without timelines. It must also be pointed out that the latest reports are clearly biased towards only environmental reporting. The section on governmental environmental policy has become smaller over the years, and detailed information on the institutional provisions for EPI has almost disappeared.

With only the SER left as the key element of the NEMS, the design and follow-up of the 'new' EPSB will be crucial. It might be upgraded to include both more issues and a more effective follow-up with respect to sectoral targets. Sectoral reporting would then be completed every year in a 'formal' policy document subject to budgetary assessment. The downside of connecting it to the budgetary process is, however, that environmental issues have a tendency to vanish in the backwash of the budgetary process (indicating a clear lack of mechanisms for resolving EPI trade-offs) (Lafferty 2004). Furthermore, negative connotations have already emerged related to the EPSB in the ministries. The 2006 proposal for the National Budget (MoE 2005b) includes no new guidelines for the EPSB, and the separate budgetary bills for the ministries reveal a diverse picture. Some ministries report clearly and thoroughly in accordance with the priority areas (Box 10.2); others hardly report on environmental issues at all. Ministerial reporting thus continues within the general idea of the EPSB, but in a highly variable fashion and with no compensation for the weakening of the NEMS.

Finally, by way of emphasizing the lack of integration of environmental policies into other policy fields and the lack of coordination and coherence of the policy documents that aim to promote policy integration, we can briefly mention the NAPSD. As indicated above, the plan was first published as part of the annual National Budget in the autumn of 2003. As such it falls into the Norwegian tradition of incorporating major policy integration plans into the budgetary process. The document contains a clear commitment to promoting policy integration, but nothing of significance has actually been either stated or done to integrate the NAPSD with either the EPSB or the NEMS. At the launch of the NAPSD it was specifically maintained that the allocation of responsibility for the plan to the Ministry of Finance would guarantee an active and consequential implementation. This has not, however, been the case. At the time of writing, the only initiative to materialize under the leadership of the Ministry of Finance has been the above-mentioned list of Indicators of Sustainable Development (MoF 2005). Given that even this limited effort was, in general, poorly received by leading NGOs and academic institutions in the field,[9] there is indeed very little to indicate that the action plan has led to any new actions, or contributed significantly to environmental policy integration. The outcome of the process of revising the national strategy on sustainable development (see above) remains to be seen.

CONCLUSIONS

As pointed out by numerous scholars (Liberatore 1997; Jordan 2002; Lenschow 2002; Lafferty and Hovden 2003; Nilsson and Persson 2003; Lafferty 2004), and as confirmed and codified by the OECD (2001, 2002) and the EEA (2005), a general lack of political will covers a multitude of EPI-related sins. In the current analysis, it is clear that it was the political will of Gro Harlem Brundtland that triggered the first wave of EPI initiatives in Norway. It is equally clear, however, that neither Brundtland's personal political will nor that of her successors has been fully carried through in practice. A second wave of initiatives was grafted on to the first wave after Brundtland's withdrawal from the leadership of the Labour Party in 1996. But these efforts were neither adequately coordinated with the first generation of instruments nor followed through in their own right. More recently, the instruments from the second wave have been replaced and/or undermined by a third wave of changes, so that the situation for EPI in Norway throughout the period can be succinctly characterized as 'long on promise – short on fulfilment'.

What accounts for the obvious decline in the 'seriousness' of pursuing sustainable development through EPI initiatives in Norway? There are a number of possible ways to answer this question. The most simple, of course, is that all policy programmes suffer from the endemic weakness of converting rhetoric to reality. There are, however, several features of the Norwegian case which may provide more specific insights into the problems of implementation.

First, there is Brundtland herself. The level of enthusiasm and leadership exhibited by Brundtland in her initial 'international period' – that is, when she prepared the WCED Report (1983–1987) and then 'fronted' it in the run up to Rio (1988–1992) – dwindled considerably when it came to the domestic task of 'realizing Rio in Norway' (Lafferty *et al.* 1997, 2002). The reason for this would seem to be that: (1) she was disappointed with the results from Rio, feeling that it should have gone much farther towards institutionalizing mechanisms to realize the goals of *Our Common Future*; and (2), lacking more radical initiatives at the international level, Brundtland and her ministers felt that Norway had already established itself as a 'beacon' of sustainable development values and activities. The latter meant that she could – after nearly ten years of working at the international level – rest on her laurels domestically, and wait for the world to catch up with Norway. This explanation has, at any rate, been documented for Norway's strange reticence and lack of performance on 'Local Agenda 21' (Lafferty 2001; Bjørnæs and Norland 2002; Lafferty *et al.* 2006), and would seem to cover the general lack of implementation pressure that characterized the Brundtland government up to 1996 (Lafferty *et al.* 1997).

This dynamic also corresponds to another feature of Norway's post-Brundtland leadership on sustainable development issues, namely a clear tendency to perform better 'away' (that is, in international fora) than at home. This characteristic applies to virtually every Norwegian Prime Minister and Minister of the Environment since Brundtland. Ministers of the Environment such as Siri Bjerke (Labour) and Børge Brende (Conservative), for example, have played strong roles in (respectively) the negotiations on the Kyoto Protocol and the running of the UN Commission on Sustainable Development (UNCSD) (where Brende was Chairperson for the 2003–2005 session). Neither, however, used their periods in power either to front the concept of sustainable development in general or to make any significant contribution to strengthening EPI in Norway.

Such leadership characteristics (by such accomplished politicians) usually reflect deeper underlying causes, however. We can mention only three rather obvious factors that play a role in Norway: the dependence on oil; political coalitions; and 'administrative recalcitrance'. The impact of the petroleum-export economy in Norway has been so massive as to defy any simplistic analysis. Marx may be dead, but the influences of materialism and the means of production and consumption are definitely *not* dead in Norway. With respect to the EPI problematic, this has most crucially meant: (1) a significant shift in values away from the collective ethos of the 'social-democratic state'; (2) a significant shift in intra-governmental power from the ministries dealing with issues of allocation and welfare to those dealing with energy and business; (3) an enormous increase in government revenues, with a corresponding increase in the potential largesse of government vis-à-vis special interests.

All of these factors have directly contributed to: (1) a strengthening of the demands of private enterprises within the economic 'pillar' of sustainable development; (2) a strengthening of lobbying and special-interest politics within the social pillar; and (3) a weakening of the normative global values which characterize the environmental pillar – particularly values associated with the Rio agenda. Given the fact that the major negative consequences of the petroleum economy are off-shore and global (principally greenhouse emissions), the cumulative result is a political culture of values and priorities which undermines by default the political 'weight' of environmental concerns in EPI-related trade-offs in Norway.

A second important factor is a reflection of the petroleum economy and politics of largesse in the political system itself. The rise of the populist Progressive Party throughout the period of the three 'waves' (and, at the time of writing, a party equal in popularity to the long-dominant Labour Party), has resulted in a situation where coalition, and even minority governments have become the rule rather than the exception. Every government between 1997 and 2005 was in a minority in Parliament, and three of the four cabinets have been multi-party constellations. There can be no doubt that this fragmentation and general weakening of the steering potential of national politics has undermined the practical potential of EPI instruments. The need to accomplish party-political trade-offs within government has further weakened the general status of environmental concerns in relation to the economic and social-welfare concerns of intra-sectoral politics.

Finally there is the issue of administrative recalcitrance. As a direct consequence of the first two factors, there has evolved a general unwillingness within the public-administration hierarchy to take on a leadership role on any cross-sectoral issues. The Norwegian situation is a reflection of the general trend towards a hollowing out and abrogation of national governing willpower, but it clearly enlightens the Norwegian profile of strong EPI promise – poor EPI performance. Our analyses indicate, moreover, that the effects of this factor are particularly pronounced within the one ministry that can be expected to stand up for EPI – the MoE. As we have shown, the

MoE has been very reluctant to either defend or implement the EPI potential of the NEMS system, and shows numerous signs of retreating to the more legalistic and technical focus of the pre-Brundtland environmental agenda.

A final word of caution is, however, in order. The election of 2005 resulted in a so-called 'Red–Green Coalition'. For the first time in its history (with the exception of a five-month 'Unity Government' at the end of the Second World War), the Norwegian Labour Party is sharing Cabinet power with the Centre Party (regional and primary-sector interests) and the Socialist Left Party (a more radical breakaway party from Labour in 1961, which has never had ministerial responsibility). The Socialist Left Party has been considered a major exponent of sustainable development in Norwegian politics. Its common governmental declaration (The Soria Moria Declaration) includes a number of strong signals on environmental policy. More importantly, the Head of the Socialist Left Party, Kristin Halvorsen, has been appointed Minister of Finance, and another Socialist-Left woman, Helen Bjørnøy, has taken over the Ministry of the Environment. Given the fact that it is these two ministries which have the strongest responsibility and potential for strengthening EPI as a governing mechanism, it remains to be seen whether the 'promise' this time round can reach fulfilment.

In sum, Norwegian attempts to institutionalize EPI have been relatively high-profile, thorough and ambitious. Since most of the EPI instruments were decoupled from political influence and left largely to the bureaucracy to handle, their set-up and design were expected to be fairly robust. However, and in direct contrast to Norway's neighbour Sweden (see Chapter 11), political interest in sustainable development issues has strongly declined since the mid-1990s. In Norway, this lack of political interest combined with administrative recalcitrance seems to have weakened an already sceptical administrative interest in EPI. This downward spiral has made the concept of EPI and the EPI instruments even more unattractive to both Norwegian politicians and civil servants. Thus, the results have not corresponded with either intentions or possibilities. A large part of the explanation must be sought in the effects of a transformation to a petroleum economy. Without an overarching commitment to sustainable development goals, EPI has little chance of success – an interdependency clearly illustrated by the Norwegian case.

NOTES

1. Gro Harlem Brundtland was Norway's fourth Minister of the Environment (1974–79) and three times Prime Minister (1981, 1986–89 and 1990–96).

2. 'National Environmental Monitoring System' (NEMS) is a term coined by the authors. It is a loose translation of the Norwegian word *resultatoppfølgingssystemet*. No official translation into English has been proposed by the authorities.
3. On the issue of 'principled priority' in an EPI context, see Lafferty (2004).
4. Nasjonal komité for internasjonale miljøspørsmål.
5. The original intention was to publish annual reports, but the Parliament only asked the MoE to prepare biennial reports.
6. Telephone interview with an official from the Norwegian Pollution Control Authority (SFT), 10 May 2005.
7. The Norwegian term is *tverrsektorielle tiltaksanalyser.*
8. Stated by an SFT official during a ProSus seminar 6 November 2003.
9. Stated in several reference group meetings, conferences and hearings in the process leading up to NOU 5, 2005 (MoF 2005).

BIBLIOGRAPHY

Bjørnæs, T. and I.T. Norland (2002), 'Local Agenda 21: pursuing sustainable development at the local level', in W.M. Lafferty, M. Nordskag and H.A. Aakre (eds), *Realizing Rio in Norway: Evaluative Studies of Sustainable Development*, Oslo: ProSus.
EEA (2005), *Environmental Policy Integration in Europe: State of Play and Evaluation Framework*, EEA technical report No 2/2005, Copenhagen: EEA.
Heidar, K. (2000), *Norway: Center and Periphery*, Boulder CO: Westview Press.
Hovden, E. and S. Torjussen (2002), 'Environmental policy integration in Norway', in W.M. Lafferty, M. Nordskag and H.A. Aakre (eds), *Realizing Rio in Norway: Evaluative Studies of Sustainable Development*, Oslo: ProSus.
Husby, S.R. (1997), *Miljøvurderinger: Hvor Ofte og Hvordan Omtales Miljøhensyn i Offentlige Utredninger?* NIBR Prosjektrapport, no. 31, Oslo: NIBR.
Innst. S. nr. 228 (2004–2005), *Innstilling til Stortinget fra Energi- og Miljøkomiteen*, Oslo: Stortinget.
Jansen, A.I. and O. Osland (1996), 'Norway', in P.M. Christiansen (ed.), *Governing the Environment: Politics, Policy and Organization in the Nordic Countries*, Copenhagen: Nordic Council of Ministers.
Jordan, A. (2002), 'Efficient hardware and light green software: environmental policy integration in the UK', in A. Lenschow (ed.), *Environmental Policy Integration: Greening Sectoral Policies in Europe*, London: Earthscan.
Lafferty, W.M. (1990), 'Political change in Norway: the transformation of a social democratic state', *West European Politics*, 13 (1), 79–100.
Lafferty, W.M. (ed.) (2001), *Sustainable Communities in Europe*, London: Earthscan.
Lafferty, W.M. (2004), 'From environmental protection to sustainable development: the challenge of decoupling through sectoral integration', in W.M. Lafferty (ed.), *Governance for Sustainable Development: The Challenge of Adapting Form to Function*, Cheltenham, UK and Northampton, MA, US: Edward Elgar.
Lafferty, W.M., C. Aall, G. Lindseth and I.T. Norland (eds) (2006), *Lokal Agenda 21 i Norge: Så Mye Hadde Vi – Så Mye Ga Vi Bort – Så Mye Har Vi Igjen* [Local Agenda 21 in Norway. We Had This Much – We Gave Away This Much – We Have This Much Left], Oslo: Unipub.
Lafferty, W.M. and E. Hovden (2003), 'Environmental policy integration: towards an analytical framework', *Environmental Politics*, 12 (3), 1–22.

Lafferty, W.M., O. Langhelle, P. Mugaas and M. Holmboe Ruge (eds) (1997), *Rio +5. Norges Oppfølging av FN-Konferansen om Miljø og Utvikling* [Rio +5: Norway's Follow-up of the UN Conference on Environment and Development], Oslo: Tano Aschehoug.

Lafferty, W.M., M. Nordskag and H.A. Aakre (eds) (2002), *Realizing Rio in Norway: Evaluative Studies of Sustainable Development*, Oslo: ProSus.

Langhelle, O. (2000), 'Norway: reluctantly carrying the torch', in W.M. Lafferty and J. Meadowcraft (eds), *Implementing Sustainable Development: Strategies and Initiatives in High Consumption Societies*, Oxford: Oxford University Press.

Lenschow, A. (ed.) (2002), *Environmental Policy Integration: Greening Sectoral Policies in Europe*, London: Earthscan.

Liberatore, A. (1997), 'The integration of sustainable development objectives into EU policy-making: barriers and prospects', in S. Baker, M. Kousis, D. Richardson and S. Young (eds), *The Politics of Sustainable Development*, London: Routledge.

MoE (Ministry of the Environment, Norway) (1989), *Miljø og Utvikling: Norges Oppfølging av Verdenskommisjonens Rapport*, White Paper 46 (1988–89), Oslo: Ministry of the Environment.

MoE (Ministry of the Environment, Norway) (1994), *For Budsjetterminen 1994: Miljøverndepartementet*, St.prp. nr. 1 (1994–95), Oslo: Ministry of the Environment.

MoE (Ministry of the Environment, Norway) (1995), *Virkemidler i Miljøvernpolitikken*, Nov. 4, Oslo: Ministry of the Environment.

MoE (Ministry of the Environment, Norway) (1996), *For Budsjetterminen 1996: Miljøverndepartementet*, St. prp. nr. 1 (1996–97), Oslo: Ministry of the Environment.

MoE (Ministry of the Environment, Norway) (1997), *Miljøvernpolitikk for en Bærekraftig Utvikling: Dugnad for Framtida*, White Paper 58 (1996–1997), Oslo: Ministry of the Environment.

MoE (Ministry of the Environment, Norway) (1999), *Regjeringens Miljøvernpolitikk og Rikets Miljøtilstand*, White Paper 8 (1999–2000), Oslo: Ministry of the Environment.

MoE (Ministry of the Environment, Norway) (2005a), *Regjeringens Miljøvernpolitikk og Rikets Miljøtilstand*, White Paper 21 (2004–2005), Oslo: Ministry of the Environment.

MoE (Ministry of the Environment, Norway) (2005b), *For Budsjetterminen 1996: Miljøverndepartementet*, St.prp. nr. 1 (2005–2006), Oslo: Ministry of the Environment.

MoF (Ministry of Finance) (2003), *Nasjonalbudsjettet 2004*, White Paper 1 (2003–2004), Oslo: Ministry of Finance.

MoF (Ministry of Finance) (2005), *Enkle Signaler i en Kompleks Verden: Forslag til et Nasjonalt Indikatorsett for Bærekraftig Utvikling*, NOU 5, Oslo: Ministry of Finance.

Nilsson, M. and Å. Persson (2003), 'Framework for analysing environmental policy integration', *Journal of Environmental Policy and Planning*, 5 (4), 333–359.

Nøttestad, Ø. (1999), *Miljøvernforvaltningen i Tidsperspektiv, del III, (1982–1992)*, Oslo: Ministry of the Environment.

OECD (1993), *Environmental Performance Reviews: Norway*, Paris: OECD.

OECD (2001), *Sustainable Development: Critical Issues*, Paris: OECD.

OECD (2002), *Improving Policy Coherence and Integration for Sustainable Development: a Checklist*, OECD Policy Brief, PUMA, October, Paris: OECD.

ProSus (2003), *Skisse til Nasjonal Agenda 21: Kommentarer og Anbefalinger fra Program for Forskning og Utredning for et Bærekraftig Samfunn (ProSus)*, Arbeidsnotat nr 1/03, Oslo: ProSus, University of Oslo.

Riksrevisjonen (1999), *Riksrevisjonens Undersøkelse Vedrørende Regjeringens Miljørapportering til Stortinget*, Riksrevisjonens administrative rapporter no. 1, Oslo: Riksrevisjonen.

Ruud, A. (2002) 'Industry and environmental responsibility: from proactive to reactive public policies', in W.M. Lafferty M. Nordskag, and H.A Aakre (eds), *Realizing Rio in Norway: Evaluative Studies of Sustainable Development*, Oslo: ProSus, University of Oslo.

Stortinget (2007), *The Constitution of the Kingdom of Norway*, http://www.stortinget.no/english/constitution.html, accessed 25 February 2007.

Sverdrup L.A. (1997), 'Norway's institutional response to sustainable development', *Environmental Politics*, 6 (1), 54–82.

Tesli, A. (2002), *The Use of EIA and SEA Relative to the Objective of Sustainable Development*, Background paper for the 2003 World Development Report 2003, Washington: World Bank.

WCED (World Commission on Environment and Development) (1987), *Our Common Future*, Oxford: Oxford University Press.

11. Sweden

Måns Nilsson and Åsa Persson

INTRODUCTION

Both internationally and domestically, Sweden is usually perceived as being a front-runner in environmental policy. It has adopted a very similar stance in relation to EPI. For instance, Sweden was an important force behind the launch of the Cardiff Process in 1998 (see Chapter 8). Since the late 1980s, Sweden has also pursued EPI in domestic policy making, with a range of concrete EPI instruments implemented throughout the 1990s and early 2000s. This chapter reviews the evolution in EPI at the national government level in Sweden, and describes some of the key implementing instruments that have been introduced. It then discusses the conditions for the effectiveness of the instruments undertaken, in terms of the performance of different sectoral policies. Finally, we discuss some generic lessons for EPI policy and practice.

Sectoral responsibility is the key policy principle underpinning the Swedish approach to EPI. It implies that sectoral government agencies should be responsible for considering the environment in their strategies and operations. Today, the most important framework for EPI is the system of National Environmental Quality Objectives (NEQO) introduced in 1999. This system provides an explicit vision of what EPI efforts should ultimately aim towards: namely, 'to hand over to the next generation a society in which the main environmental problems have been solved' (Government Bill 1997/98/145: 2), as well as broad objectives, interim targets and follow-up indicators.

Overall, existing institutions, procedures and traditions of policy making in Sweden appear to resonate relatively well with the principle of EPI. Furthermore, the environmental front-runner image and the strong political commitment to environmental protection in Swedish society give rise to an expectation that the implementation of EPI should be relatively unproblematic, that is, that the 'non' environmental sectors should be prepared to deploy and be capable of implementing the various EPI instruments that have been put in place over the last two decades. This chapter will explore whether this has indeed been the case.

HISTORY

Before going through the most important EPI-related milestones in Sweden, some reflections on the policy-making context and the general characteristics of its political and administrative system are necessary. In particular, it is worth mentioning the management-by-objectives approach (an example of 'specification of output' – see Chapter 3), the relative independence and size of the governmental agencies and the general aspiration to decentralize responsibility and enhance efficiency in government wherever possible. Most efforts to implement EPI have addressed the work of governmental agencies. Being much larger than the ministries, they carry out much of the policy preparatory work as well as implementing policy. In day-to-day activities, they are (according to the national constitution) independent from the ministries with regard to policy implementation. They are, therefore, governed through standing instructions as well as a set of annually updated directions. In this system, key levers for change have been to alter agency mandates, objectives and procedural requirements towards EPI, which they have been relatively free to shape into modified sector strategies and operations. The agencies are accountable for and obliged to report on their new environmental mandates. However, there have been few incentives and usually no extra resources allocated to the agencies to deliver on this new mandate.

At the ministerial level (that is, the Government Offices), the normal administrative procedure (known as joint drafting) is an important instrument for policy coordination. This procedure stipulates that when a policy issue impinges on another ministry's area of responsibility, it should be dealt with in consultation with that ministry. This bureaucratic rule (see Chapter 3) is supported by the principle of collective responsibility amongst Swedish government ministers. If a policy coordination issue cannot be resolved by civil servants in their respective ministries, it is moved up to the ministerial level. This administrative coordination function offers some potential for EPI. However, the realization of this potential is dependent on: how policy issues are defined and given institutional homes; how environmental implications are initially identified; and the relative bargaining powers of the environmental and sectoral ministries (Nilsson and Persson 2003).

Moving on to the evolution of EPI, it is clear that concern for nature and the environment has traditionally enjoyed strong public support in Sweden. By the late 19th Century, art, literature and political and intellectual debates fuelled a strong romantic interest in the whole issue of 'nature'. Indeed, this underlying interest in the environment has been shown to be stronger in Sweden than in most comparable countries (Lundgren 1995).

For example, the Swedish Society for Nature Conservation, the largest environmental NGO in Sweden, was created as early as 1909. Despite this early start, until the 1960s environmental protection remained a relatively marginal policy concern in mainstream politics, developing in two largely isolated streams (Vedung 1991; Lundgren 1995). The green stream had to do with the conservation of nature. In the early days, its aim was to conserve species, habitats and environments for scientific inquiry and analysis. Over the years, concern for cultural and social values and preservation of landscapes became steadily more important. The very first nature protection law was adopted in 1909. By contrast, the blue stream dealt with controlling pollution and degradation. This line of policy emerged out of a concern for deteriorating living conditions in urban areas, linked to the rapid industrialization of the 19th Century and associated public health problems. In order to abate epidemics, sewage treatment facilities and drinking water pipes were constructed.

In the 1960s, public and political awareness grew rapidly and the number of environmental bills doubled from 1965 to 1968 (Löfstedt 2003). The main concern at the time was to ensure that the environment was given a legitimate role in a policy-making landscape already dominated by economic and social issues (Lundqvist 1998). The Environmental Protection Act of 1967 provided, for the first time, a holistic perspective that sought to integrate the green and blue streams. From the late 1960s to the late 1980s, environmental policy was a legitimate and prominent but rather detached policy area, characterized by a regulatory end-of-pipe approach.

The idea of EPI was first introduced in the late 1980s in the policy bill *Environmental Policy for the 1990s* (Government Bill 1987/88/85). This could be termed the initial phase in the history of EPI, establishing a general governmental commitment to the principle of EPI. This bill proposed a new perspective on environmental protection, abandoning the view of the environment as a separate sector and instead emphasizing its cross-cutting nature. The inspiration for this came from the Brundtland Report, which highlighted the need for a source-based and preventive approach to environmental policy (WCED 1987; Kronsell 1997).

Over the next 10–15 years, this perspective became an important departure point for a range of EPI instruments (see Box 11.1). A few initiatives were taken in the early 1990s, such as the introduction of national environmental accounts and a government communication that all policy proposals should be subject to an environmental assessment. However, it was not until 1996 that the political momentum for EPI was significantly strengthened. In his first statement of government policy, the new Social Democratic Prime Minister, Göran Persson, set out a vision to build the

---

BOX 11.1   MILESTONES IN ENVIRONMENTAL POLICY INTEGRATION: SWEDEN

1988 Ministry for the Environment is created
1988 The Environment Bill establishes the 'sector responsibility' principle
1992 National environmental accounts launched
1994 Government Communication: all policy proposals subject to environmental assessment
1995 Generic sector responsibility legally established for all agencies
1996 Prime Minister presents vision of 'green people's home'
1997 Interdepartmental ministerial delegation proposes EPI measures
1997 Environmental Management Systems (EMSs) to be adopted in all agencies
1998 Local Investment Programmes for environment and employment
1998 Special sector responsibility established for 24 government agencies
1999 New Environmental Code enters into force
1999 15 National Environmental Quality Objectives (NEQOs) introduced
2001 EMS to be adopted for Government Offices (Ministries)
2002 First version of a National Sustainable Development Strategy, revised in 2004
2004 Sustainable development coordination unit established in Government Offices
2005 Ministry of Sustainable Development created
2007 Ministry for the Environment again

'green people's home'.[1] This second phase of EPI was thus characterized by strengthening high-level political commitment and a more comprehensive strategy. The new challenge for the Social Democrats was how best to create an ecologically sustainable welfare state and an eco-cycle society (*kretsloppssamhället*) (Lundqvist 2001). This greener orientation partly resulted from their cooperation with the Green Party, upon which the Social Democrats had to depend for a parliamentary majority since 1998.[2] In 1997, an interdepartmental delegation of ministers was established to propose concrete instruments for ecologically sustainable development (Delegationen for Ekologiskt Hållbar Utveckling 1997). Furthermore, the Environmental Advisory Council (an advisory body reporting to the Environment Minister) developed proposals for ways in which environmental considerations could be integrated across the administration (SOU 1996: 112; Environmental Advisory Council 1997).

This momentum was used to introduce several instruments to green the machinery of central government in the late 1990s. Government agencies were, for example, instructed to develop Environmental Management Systems (EMS), modelled on their use in the private sector. Twenty-four agencies were assigned special sector responsibility. Generic sector responsibility, stated as a guiding principle already in 1988, was given a legal basis in the ordinance governing the working procedures of agencies. In 1999, the Parliament adopted the NEQOs. Today, these constitute the overarching framework for environmental policy – and also EPI – in Sweden (Government Bill 2000/01/130).

In the early 2000s, a third phase of EPI can be discerned, as the government started taking initiatives that addressed sustainable development as a broader concept. In 2002, the first national sustainable development strategy (NSDS) was adopted (revised in 2004 and 2006) (Government Communication 2001/02/172; Government Communication 2003/04/129; Government Communication 2005/06/126). In 2004, a coordination unit for sustainable development was established in the Prime Minister's Office. In 2005, a Ministry of Sustainable Development was created, expanding both the political clout and mandate of the Ministry for the Environment to take over housing and energy issues from the Ministry of Industry, Employment and Communications. Aside from the focus on sustainable development more broadly, in this phase there was also an emphasis on implementing and consolidating all the instruments introduced in the previous phase. In 2006, the elections led to a change of government to a centre-right coalition, for the first time since 1994. Whether this shift will entail a new phase of EPI remains to be seen.

EPI IN PRACTICE

In this section we describe the mechanisms and instruments put in place to enhance the implementation of EPI. It should be noted that drawing the boundary between what is an instrument for EPI and what is an instrument for environmental policy (or even sustainable development more broadly) is often difficult.

Administrative Instruments

Legal provisions
The Environmental Code established in 1998 is the main legal provision for environmental protection generally in Sweden (SFS 1998/ 808). Its stated intentions adhere to EPI concerns, such as 'to build a platform for decentralized and preventive environmental measures' (Lundqvist 2004: 127). Apart from this, legal provisions work through directives. According to one such directive adopted in 1995, all government agencies are legally required to consider the implications of their work for sustainable development (SFS 1995/1322: §7). This general sector responsibility requires policy makers to address environmental implications in all major sector policy bills such as transport, forestry, energy, agriculture and cultural heritage. On top of this, a special sector responsibility for 24 central government agencies was established in 1998 (Government Bill 1997/98/145) (see above). Agencies with this special sector responsibility should:

- integrate environmental issues into their activities and act as driving forces for environmentally sustainable development in their respective sectors;
- conduct a dialogue with the agencies responsible for relevant NEQOs (see discussion below) about specific measures and data supply;
- report to the Environmental Objectives Council on their work on sector responsibility every fourth year, giving, for example, trends analyses of the sector's environmental impact; reports on actions and measures; proposals for instruments and measures that are needed but are beyond the mandate of the authority; and a summary of goal conflicts and synergies between environmental and other objectives, within the sector and in relation to other sectors.

Cabinet committees
A committee of ministers presented proposals for EPI in 1997, after which it was dismantled. Over the next ten years, there was no network of ministers or senior officials to drive EPI forwards and no council or round-table for sustainable development at the national level. In 2007, however, the new government appointed a Commission for Sustainable Development, chaired by the Prime Minister, with the task of promoting cooperation across sectors and between industry and government, and with a focus on innovation and climate change. At the administrative level, a small coordination unit for sustainable development was established in 2004 in the Prime Minister's Office, responsible for further development of

the NSDS and interaction with all ministries as well as international sustainable development processes. The unit was staffed with people from right across government to encourage coordination. However, after a short period, the unit was moved to the Ministry of Sustainable Development, which could be interpreted as a demotion, although its mandate remained the same.

Independent evaluation bodies

There is no specific evaluation body or audit committee dedicated to environmental and/or EPI issues in government or parliament. The official independent auditing body – Riksrevisionen (National Audit Office) – covers all policy areas. Official evaluation activities also take place in various governmental agencies and institutes such as the Statskontoret (Swedish Agency for Public Management) and ITPS (Swedish Institute for Growth Policy Studies). To date, however, these general bodies have paid little attention to environmental and/or EPI-related concerns. The Environmental Objectives Council is responsible for follow-up (annually) and evaluation (every fourth year) of the NEQOs and the progress made in the sectors, but it is not an independent body.

The amalgamation of ministries

Before 1988, the two ministries for agriculture and housing were responsible for environmental issues. Paradoxically, when the new perspective on environmental issues as a cross-cutting sectoral responsibility was introduced in 1988, the environmental policy function at ministerial level became more – not less – sectoral: environmental functions were concentrated in a separate ministry. The founding environment minister, Ms Birgitta Dahl, informed the Prime Minister that she wanted to play a cross-cutting role (Dahl, personal communication, January 2004). In 2004, the Ministry for the Environment expanded its scope when it became a Ministry of Sustainable Development,[3] encompassing energy and housing issues formerly governed by the Ministry of Industry, Employment and Communications. This reshuffle was officially made to restate the political importance of the green welfare state, a vision that had been receiving decreasing political attention since 1996. In 2007, the new government moved energy issues back into the Ministry for Industry, and the Ministry of Sustainable Development reverted back to being a traditional ministry for the environment.

Environmental management systems

Most major governmental agencies have implemented EMSs since 1997. The agencies report annually to their ministries on progress. However, it has been suggested that the effectiveness of EMS as an instrument to implement EPI has been limited to date, primarily because the environmental issues dealt with have for the most part been related to housekeeping activities (Naturvårdsverket 2005a). There have been limited efforts to address each ministry's core strategic activities, such as the distribution of agricultural subsidies, transport infrastructure decisions and energy programmes (that is, indirect impacts, in EMS terminology). If EMS addressed these types of core activities, it could become a more strategic and hence powerful administrative instrument for EPI. Indeed, there is a movement in this direction, as the government decided in 2001 that EMS will be implemented and:

> concern for the environment and health shall be natural parts of the government office's activities. The government offices shall pay attention to and examine possible consequences for the environment in the development of proposals for government decisions (Miljödepartementet 2004: 3–4).

However, a recent self-assessment suggests that these aspirations are not achieved to a satisfactory extent across the various government offices (Miljödepartementet 2003).

Green Budgeting

There is no systematic environmental assessment or green profiling of the budget. Since the 1990s (and after political demands from the Green Party), the Finance Ministry's budget bills report on a set of green headline indicators, to illustrate trends and developments of environmental pressure factors (SOU 1998/170). However, no linkage is made between these indicators and interventions in the macro economy or government expenditures. Therefore, they have only a limited policy function.

Spending and taxation

Two government initiatives should be mentioned here. First, the spending power of the government was used in the Local Investment Programmes in 1998–2003. This policy programme set aside 6.2 billion SEK (about 0.9 billion US dollars) from the state budget for local projects to stimulate employment and environmental improvement jointly. Municipalities, in collaboration with the private sector and NGOs, were invited to apply for grants on a competitive basis. Second, the Social Democrat government (under heavy political pressure from the Green Party) committed to a significant green tax shift, worth 30 billion SEK (about 4.2 billion US dollars) over 10 years.[4] This was partly implemented but was discontinued when the new central-right government presented its first budget bill in 2006.

Green procurement

Another way for the government to use its spending power to foster EPI is to ensure that public procurement gives preference to eco-labelled products and services. A committee was organized in 1998–2001 to propose how public bodies could increase this kind of procurement. This led to the launch of an internet-based instrument in 2001. In parallel with these efforts, there are public eco-labelling schemes and schemes targeted at private firms (for example, Environmental Product Declarations). A survey of the effectiveness of the procurement instrument showed that 60 per cent of governmental and public bodies set environmental criteria in tendering procedures, but only 23 per cent thought they were doing this well in practice (Naturvårdsverket 2005b).

Strategies and/or Strategy Developing Processes

Sustainable development indicators

There are several overlapping indicator sets in Swedish government today. In the early 1990s, the government instructed Statistics Sweden and the National Economic Research Institute to create a system of environmental accounting, following a UN commitment. In the late 1990s there followed a set of green headline indicators designed to communicate better the relationship between economic and environmental development (SOU 1998/170). These are still reported in the annual budget bills. Rather awkwardly, a set of sustainability indicators was then developed before the NSDS was issued (Statistiska centralbyrån (SCB) and Naturvårdsverket 2001). Prior to the strategy and indicators, each ministry had reported annually (until 2001) on its efforts to promote sustainable development under the title *Sustainable Sweden*. These reports increased the transparency of the decisions made at ministerial level (Government Communication 2001/02/50). Finally, environmental indicators to follow up the NEQOs were defined in the early 2000s (see below). These soon became the most important ones.

National sustainable development strategy

The relationship between the environment and sustainable development in Swedish policy remains ambiguous. In the mid-1990s, the Swedish government chose to view sustainable development as being mainly an environment-related concept, by pointedly referring to *ecologically sustainable development*. The role of the Swedish Environmental Protection Agency was somewhat vaguely formulated 'to promote sustainable development starting from the ecological dimension' (§1 of its Appropriation Direction). In 2002, there was a shift towards a broader view incorporating economic and social dimensions in the first NSDS.[5] A basic premise of the strategy is that 'sustainable development policies, measures and concerns must be mainstreamed, that is integrated into all existing policy areas' (Government Communication 2003/04/129: 4). However, there is little to suggest that this strategy has a significant political role. First, it contains few original proposals, as it mostly reiterates policy objectives adopted in other bills. This offers little guidance on how to manage sector goal conflicts. Second, it has not been given a particularly strong political status or a strong legal basis as in some other European countries. Overall therefore, it seems to suffer from many of the same problems as the other NSDSs, namely a lack of clear ownership, clear paths to achieve stated objectives, clear objectives and resources allocated to implementation (European Environment Agency 2005: 16) (see also Chapter 5).

It is still unclear whether the more comprehensive view of the NSDS will broaden the scope of EPI (that is, into something like 'sustainable development policy integration'), and to what extent this would represent an effective approach to EPI. Indeed, some agencies have argued that the sector responsibility should be extended to sustainable development issues, rather than just environmental ones (Government Bill 2004/05/150: 365).

National environmental quality objectives and action strategies

The NEQO system, adopted by Parliament in 1999, was an attempt to rationalize a messy policy situation in which the Ministry for the Environment had to account for no less than 167 different policy objectives in different bills. It was not always clear who owned these and how they should be followed up. NEQO has been given significantly more political weight and organizational and financial resources than the NSDS. In fact, it has become *the* overarching framework for EPI. In brief, the system currently consists of 16 objectives (Box 11.2). Around 70 interim targets have been adopted, along with three major action strategies. Indicators to monitor the objectives and targets have also been developed (Government Bill 2000/01/130; Government Bill 2004/05/150).[6]

The NEQO system is inextricably linked to the sector responsibility principle. Although the Swedish EPA is responsible for most of the 16 NEQOs, several have been allocated to other agencies such as the Swedish Board of Agriculture and the National Board of Housing, Building and Planning. The Environmental Objectives Council, consisting mainly of representatives from governmental agencies, county administrations and local authorities, is responsible for coordinating the work of the agencies and reporting to the government annually, with an extended evaluation every four years. The NEQOs have also acted as a framework for the development of regional and local environmental objectives. At an early stage in

---

BOX 11.2 NATIONAL ENVIRONMENTAL QUALITY OBJECTIVES IN SWEDEN

1   Reduced climate impact
2   Clean air
3   Natural acidification only
4   A non-toxic environment
5   A protective ozone layer
6   A safe radiation environment
7   Zero eutrophication
8   Flourishing lakes and streams
9   Good-quality groundwater
10   A balanced marine environment, flourishing coastal areas and archipelagos
11   Thriving wetlands
12   Sustainable forests
13   A varied agricultural landscape
14   A magnificent mountain landscape
15   A good built environment
16   A rich plant and animal life

Source: Government Bill (2004/04/150)

---

the NEQO process, the intention was that they should also be used as a basis for developing sectoral environmental objectives. However, such a hierarchical and sector-based system of objectives (that is, specification of output in its true form – see Chapter 3) has not yet appeared. Instead, sectoral environmental objectives not formally linked to the NEQO have been adopted in conjunction with formulating general policy objectives for relevant sectors, including the transport, energy, consumer and forestry sectors.

Policy Appraisal Systems

In Swedish policy making, a committee of inquiry is often appointed to make an initial analysis of a new policy issue and propose suitable policy responses. Often, government agencies contribute their own analyses and proposals. The government then builds on these recommendations to varying degrees, as ministries prepare bills that they submit to Parliament for adoption. After parliamentary decisions, implementation and preparation of secondary legislation is the responsibility of the government agencies. This means that appraisal systems can be used at three levels of policy preparation. As will be seen below, the systems appear quite ineffective at all three levels.

Impact assessment in committees of inquiry
Although there are formal provisions for appraisal in the generic committee instructions, evaluations have shown that resulting proposals have usually been poorly assessed for both environmental and other impacts (Forss and Uhrwing 2003; Riksrevisionen 2004a). The opportunities for such early appraisals are further constrained by the fact that environmental impacts have not been one of the seven mainstreaming themes (for example, impacts on gender equity and small businesses) that all inquiries are required to consider. The government intends to review the regulations governing committee work to see how this situation can be improved (Government Bill 2004/05/150: 22).

Impact assessment in the ministries
The intention of assessing policy proposals prepared by the ministries for environmental impacts has been stated in several bills and communications since 1994 (Government Bill 1993/94: III; Government Bill 1997/98/145: 288–299). The commitment was recently restated in the revised environmental policy for the Government Offices (Miljödepartementet 2004). However, an evaluation showed that implementation has been limited. In particular, the budget bills have lacked impact assessments (Miljödepartementet 2003). Furthermore, implementation processes have been weak, mainly consisting of ticking off items on a one-page checklist of NEQOs. Other guidance has not been developed. The evaluation also revealed that officials tend to spend less than an hour (and at the very most half a working day) on an assessment. A further problem is that the assessments that are produced remain internal government documents and hence are not publicly available. Consequently, their quality and scope cannot be scrutinized in the same way as those in other countries (see Chapter 6). However, the latest NSDS, which was issued in 2006, promised to develop better instruments for impact assessment in the Government Offices.

Impact assessment in government agencies
When preparing secondary legislation, government agencies are legally required to undertake an RIA (SFS 1995/1322: §27–29). Importantly, other kinds of proposals or policy activities are not subjected to this requirement, which is very brief, as is the guidance provided. As in many other jurisdictions (see Chapter 6), it only lists environmental impacts as one kind of impact that should be considered. Evaluations have shown that the rules

are either not followed in a satisfactory way or are completely ignored. In many cases, assessments are too limited to be useful as a basis for decision making (Naturvårdsverket 2004a).

Strategic Environmental Assessment

EIA requirements were introduced into Swedish law in the late 1980s and since then have gradually become stricter (SFS 1998/808/6: §7). The EU Directive on SEA (see Chapter 7) was incorporated into the Environmental Code in 2004 (Government Bill 2003/04/116). This directive calls for an environmental assessment of all plans and programmes that are set up by a public authority, are legally required, and are assumed to have significant environmental impact. However, in the current planning system in Sweden, very few strategically important plans fall into this category; most are to be found at local or regional levels (for example, municipal land-use planning, municipal energy planning, waste plans and regional transport infrastructure plans). Implementation of this legislation has been quite slow and it is still too early to say whether it significantly changed national planning practices.

EPI in Three Key Sectors

The responsibility for implementing EPI is supposed to fall on all sectors. However, a brief look at the actual processes, policies and outcomes in three sectors reveals that it has been taken up more enthusiastically by some sectors than others. In this overview, the decisions and policies are not explicitly linked to the implementation of specific EPI measures. Therefore we cannot say much about their relative effectiveness. However, we can give a rough indication of how far the general commitment to EPI has affected sectoral policy making.

Transport

In several ways, transport has been a problem sector when it comes to EPI. At the level of strategy and aspirations, EPI in transport policy has progressed, and the implementing instruments described above have had some impact. First, recent bills have included environmental objectives and emphasized the status of the NEQOs in this policy area (Government Bill 2001/02/20). Second, the National Road Administration has developed its own environmental objectives and routines for environmental consideration in planning (Vägverket 2001). However, goal conflicts remain severe. In particular, increasing accessibility to support rural areas has proven difficult to reconcile with the goal of stabilizing road traffic. Apart from taxation of fuels (traditionally a fiscal tax rather than a green tax), to date there have been few policies in place to safeguard an environmentally sound transport sector. However, more recently policies have moved towards increased differentiation in vehicle taxation, based on carbon dioxide emissions and on promoting the use of alternative fuels. Congestion charges were introduced in Stockholm in January 2006, and have since been continued by the subsequent centre-liberal government. This government also intends to launch subsidies for more environmentally friendly cars. Looking at environmental outcomes, there have been negative trends in relation to emissions, traffic volumes and congestion (Naturvårdsverket and Energimyndigheten 2004; Vägverket 2005). Studies have shown that traditional planning practices, such as the use of cost–benefit analysis, stand in the way of environmental integration requirements (Falkemark 1999). Furthermore, powerful lobbies have worked against a greening of the sector (Bogelund 2003).

Energy
EPI has been an important aspect of the energy sector over the last 15 years, in particular regarding the issue of climate change. In 1997, the government launched a programme for the ecological transition of the energy system, involving a move away from nuclear and fossil fuels to renewables (Government Bill 1996/97/84). Policy instruments have been put in place to achieve this shift, including green electricity certificates, tradeable permits and a carbon tax (Naturvårdsverket and Energimyndigheten 2004). Indeed, these policies – introduced since the early 1990s – have led to a conversion of thermal heat and electricity production to renewables and energy-from-waste technologies. The relative success of EPI in relation to climate change can, however, be attributed to a combination of factors: international policy such as the Kyoto commitments and the EU's Emissions Trading System (which forced political action); changing actor interests (such as the powerful energy companies realizing that they stand to benefit from a general price increase as a result of emissions trading); and also institutional factors which have led the sectors to accept responsibility for climate issues (Nilsson 2005).

However, it appears that the political attention devoted to climate policies has crowded out other relevant environmental issues such as biodiversity, landscape and air pollution. Furthermore, the overall effect on the environmental burden of the sector as a whole has been limited for two reasons. First, the thermal plants that are affected constitute only a minor fraction of the Swedish electricity production system, which is dominated by hydro (40–50 per cent) and nuclear power (40–50 per cent). Second, the Swedish electricity sector is integrated into a Nordic market. This means that national policies often have instant spillover effects that shift production abroad. Because the marginal power source in the Nordic system is normally coal-fired power (from Denmark), emissions of both CO_2 and local and regional air pollutants have increased as a result of Swedish policies related to carbon taxation and the phasing out of nuclear power.

Agriculture
In the agricultural sector, environmental concerns have been central for some time, with the NEQOs playing a relatively strong role (Jordbruksverket 2005). Policies to control emissions to air, soil and water have been in place since the 1980s, for example, taxes on fertilizers and pesticides. Agricultural policy is also different from the other two sectors because of the overriding influence exerted by the EU's Common Agricultural Policy. Sweden has advocated a reform of European policies from direct production support towards more environmentally-based support (Government Bill 1997/98/142). Support measures under the Common Agricultural Policy are implemented in Sweden within the Environmental and Rural Development Plan 2000–2006 (Jordbruksdepartementet 2000). This programme has a significant environmental focus. In 2006, a proposal for a new Rural Development Plan for 2007–2013 was submitted to the European Commission. Environmental issues were somewhat downplayed in this compared to the earlier plan. Nonetheless, they remain at least on a par with employment, housing and growth issues (SOU 2005/36). Among the environmental issues, the main emphasis is put on landscape issues, both in terms of cultural and natural values. However, the potential for the agricultural sector to contribute to climate change mitigation through bio-energy production, which could also carry many co-benefits in terms of, for example, reduced nutrient leakage, has not been developed (Söderberg 2005).

SUMMARY DISCUSSION

Overall, Sweden performs fairly well against many of the evaluation criteria used in international benchmarking exercises (European Environment Agency 2005). For example, there is high-level political commitment to EPI and a strategic political vision, expressed through the NSDS and the NEQOs. Lundqvist (2004) therefore rightly concludes that policy intentions and aspirations have been clearly set out in Sweden. Moreover, administrative reforms have been made to implement them, which include expanding mandates, pushing the sectors to accept responsibility, and instituting organizational changes at the ministry level. Requirements for policy appraisal have also been introduced. Finally, several indicator schemes have been established to follow up on environmental pressures, impacts and policy responses.

However, having a comparatively strong array of EPI instruments does not, of course, automatically translate into substantive policy change within the sectors. An assessment of the effectiveness of EPI instruments depends on whether we are interested in changes in policy processes, policy outputs or, ultimately, environmental outcomes in the sectors (see Chapter 1). Our brief analysis of three major policy sectors in Sweden suggests that EPI is proceeding in the energy and agriculture sectors. However, this progress is actually rather weakly linked to the introduction of different EPI instruments. The EPI instruments have played a role, but this has often not been a very instrumental one. When it comes to making hard decisions about environmental priorities, other factors such as policy styles, planning traditions and actors' interests and beliefs have been more important than newly imposed EPI instruments. However, because the potentially more potent EPI instruments (for example, the NEQOs) have been in place for a relatively short time, it is still too early to reach a full judgement.

Despite the difficulties associated with evaluating EPI, the Swedish experience does offer a number of important lessons. The sector responsibility principle strongly supports EPI. Changing and expanding the mandates of established specialized bureaucracies has been a baseline prerequisite to enable EPI to occur. However, changing mandates and ensuring coordination between agencies is administratively burdensome. The NEQO system has usefully clarified the division of responsibility and established effective collaboration instruments. These issues remain tricky to resolve due to, for instance, weak administrative capacities (see Chapter 3). Expanded mandates have not been followed by expanded budgets and competences. We have witnessed a range of instruments being imposed on agencies with no extra administrative and financial capacities.

Furthermore, environmental concerns are only one of a number of cross-cutting aspects (for example, gender, regional development, employment and ethnic minorities) that sectors need to take into account. Combining all these represents a complex 'multi-integration' puzzle in practical decision-making situations. Furthermore, EPI requires the environment ministry and agency to share their responsibility for achieving environmental goals with sector ministries and agencies. Interestingly, less attention has been paid to the possible unwillingness of specialist environmental organizations to share their mandate with the sectors. Indeed, despite the coordination mandate of ministries, specialist agencies appear to be better at cooperating than ministries, which have more political prestige to maintain. In Sweden, there has been a strong emphasis on putting pressure on governmental agencies to implement EPI. However, one must also enhance EPI practices at ministry and committee levels, where the broader policy directions, agendas and courses of action are often considered.

It is clear from the Swedish experience that political will and high-level leadership are key ingredients for successful EPI. Since the mid-1990s, political leadership has remained relatively strong (at least in broad terms), even though environmental issues have continued to move down the domestic political agenda since the 1990s (Holmberg and Weibull 2001). Despite earlier commitments, a systematic approach to EPI in government procedures and organizations did not emerge until the Prime Minister made the 'green people's home' a high-profile issue in 1996. At that time, it was said that Sweden should be an international driving force for ecologically sustainable development. This arguably gave efforts to implement EPI greater legitimacy and prestige. Also, the Green Party was (after 1998) a collaborating partner with the Social Democrats in a minority government, and this helped to push sectoral policies in a greener direction. When interviewed, policy makers say that without this political pressure, sector administrations were usually inclined to ignore or downplay the environmental responsibilities they were given. However, there is still plenty of room to strengthen political leadership: politicians have tended to shy away from striking delicate trade-offs between environmental and sectoral objectives, preferring instead to focus on synergies and complementarities.

EPI has also progressed further in some sectors than others, suggesting that factors internal to particular sectors may matter. An evaluation found that in agencies whose sector is well defined and where the environmental implications are clearly expressed in legislation, such as energy and agriculture, the main problems were a lack of resources, goal conflicts and lack of competence. For agencies whose environmental implications were more diffuse or indirect, such as education or health, the main problems had more to do with a lack of knowledge and expertise (Naturvårdsverket 2004b). Indeed, the evaluation identified a need to prioritize and focus the whole effort. This led to the number of agencies charged with achieving EPI through the 'special sector responsibility' being reduced from 24 to 18.

Today, the NEQO system is the central and most effective instrument in the Swedish EPI toolbox. It provides both a vision and concrete and measurable targets. Crucially, it adds a substantive dimension to Sweden's EPI effort, which otherwise has often tended to focus on the procedural dimension. In this way, the ultimate purpose of EPI has become clearer and less easy for policy makers to evade. Crucially, the NEQOs can be used as handy reference points in daily policy making and implementation decisions, since they are simpler than some of the more aggregated sustainable development objectives. The fact that they were passed through a Parliament with a broad political majority has also given them added political weight and stability over time, which has undoubtedly facilitated implementation.

Quality control, follow-up and accountability mechanisms are essential elements of any management-by-objectives system such as the NEQOs. However, follow-up systems and accountability have been relatively poor in Sweden. The problems of steering and poor reporting in relation to the NEQOs, constraining their effectiveness, have been noted in official evaluations (Riksrevisionen 2004b). Also, policy appraisal procedures have been ineffective EPI instruments (see Chapter 6). First, there is little guidance on how to identify and assess environmental impacts from sector policy proposals. Second, with no mechanisms for quality control of the policy appraisal reports there are few incentives for policy makers to improve appraisal practices. This is particularly troublesome in the Government Offices, as their working files are not publicly accessible. More recently, there has been an increasing focus on follow-up and evaluation, which suggests an increasing interest in learning systems in relation to the management-by-objectives approach.

A final and much more general lesson to emerge from the Swedish case is that after the relatively rapid expansion of so many, often overlapping, EPI initiatives and instruments, agencies have recently emphasized the need for greater harmonization. The current situation is a cause of frustration among civil servants. It is, for example, still unclear how the sector responsibility (general and specific), the NEQOs and the EMS are related to each other, and how they can be better coordinated. This is particularly important considering that the environment is only one of several themes that demand the attention – and resources – of the agencies.

CONCLUSIONS

Overall, Sweden has been very active in pushing EPI domestically and internationally. To implement EPI, it has issued principal commitments, implemented directives (dating back to the late 1980s) and issued legal provisions (in the late 1990s). It has also introduced an increasingly complex mix of instruments to achieve this purpose. When examining the quite broad portfolio of instruments created, it is difficult to discern a clear conceptual approach to or plan for EPI. Rather, there has been a rather ad hoc accumulation of different instruments. The approach has been consistent with the dominant working style of the governmental machinery, which is to delegate policy preparation and implementation tasks to central government agencies through new instructions and adjusted mandates. Some of Sweden's traditional institutional features have been conducive to policy coordination in general. As such, they also enhance the potential for EPI, notably the committee-of-inquiry system, the joint-drafting procedure, the management-by-objectives approach to governmental steering and a tradition of cooperative and consensus-based decision making.

EPI instruments have been translated into sectoral processes. However, the overall effect has primarily been in terms of reporting requirements, or sometimes changing aspirations, rhetoric and strategies; many day-to-day policy decisions in the sectors are still governed by internal (that is, sectoral) logics, underpinned by strong sectoral planning traditions and belief systems. The expectations concerning sectoral EPI performance noted at the beginning of this chapter have therefore not been met fully, although there is variation between sectors.

In the 2000s, some important steps towards EPI were taken with the NEQOs and the environmental management systems for governmental decision making. The intention was to govern by specifying objectives and leaving the sectors to respond accordingly. For this to facilitate EPI, political will and leadership remain essential. With signals from the central political level about the importance of environmental sustainability, those concerned with environmental issues in the sectors have had strategic ammunition in policy deliberations and negotiations. However, the notion of political will needs to be further unpacked (see Chapter 3): while there might be signals that EPI is important at the highest political level, the sectoral agency heads and their counterparts in the ministries have often played down environmental issues in daily policy making. Furthermore, political will is, by definition, not robust and enduring; Sweden needs to institutionalize stronger procedures firmly in its public administrative systems, including appraisal systems (with rigorous quality controls) and independent auditing functions, to withstand changes of government and party-political dynamics.

To summarize, the Swedish experience offers the following main lessons. First, establishing a political commitment to EPI in the form of a principle that sectors should take greater responsibility for the environment is necessary to anchor an EPI effort. Second, one must match procedural requirements with substance, in the form of environmental objectives, targets and time frames. Third, a broad political agreement must be established to stabilize and support the overall EPI effort. Finally, it is also necessary to institutionalize procedures firmly in the administrative system to make it less vulnerable to political shifts.

NOTES

1. Det gröna folkhemmet. 'The people's home' is a popular metaphor for the Swedish welfare state.
2. Between 1998 and 2006, the Social Democrats formed minority governments that depended on the Green and Left Parties for a parliamentary majority.
3. However, the grand English title can be somewhat misleading: the Swedish name can be translated as *Ministry for Environment and Societal Planning*.
4. This shift contributes to 'greening' government revenues, but it is arguable whether the use of economic instruments to achieve environmental policy objective is an EPI instrument per se.
5. New versions were issued in 2004 and 2006.
6. For more details on the NEQO system, see the official website www.miljomal.nu.

BIBLIOGRAPHY

Bogelund, Pia (2003), *Greening the area of car taxation? A comparative study of environmental policy integration in Sweden and Denmark*, PhD Thesis, Aalborg: Department of Development and Planning at Aalborg University.

Delegationen for Ekologiskt Hållbar Utveckling (1997), *Ett hållbart Sverige [A sustainable Sweden]*, Stockholm: Regeringskansliet.

Environmental Advisory Council (1997), *Eco-management for governmental authorities: A guide to the integration of environmental considerations*, Stockholm: Regeringskansliet.

European Environment Agency (2005), *Environmental policy integration in Europe: State of play and an evaluation framework*, Copenhagen: EEA.

Falkemark, Gunnar (1999), *Politik, lobbyism och manipulation [Politics, lobbyism and manipulation]*, Nora: Nya Doxa.

Forss, Kim and Marie Uhrwing (2003), *Kvalitet i utredningsväsendet [Quality in the committee system]*, Stockholm: Regeringskansliet.

Government Bill (1987/88/85), *Om miljöpolitiken inför 1990-talet [Environmental-policy for the 1990s]*, Stockholm: Regeringskansliet.

Government Bill (1993/94: III), *Med sikte på hållbar utveckling – genomförande av besluten vid FN:s konferens om miljö och utveckling UNCED [Aiming at sustainable development – implementation of the decisions from the UN conference on environment and development UNCED]*, Stockholm: Regeringskansliet.

Government Bill (1996/97/84), *En uthållig energiförsörjning [A sustainable energy supply]*, Stockholm: Regeringskansliet.

Government Bill (1997/98/142), *Riktlinjer för Sveriges arbete med jordbruks – och livsmedelspolitiken inom Europeiska Unionen [Guidelines for Sweden's work on agricultural and food policy in the European Union]*, Stockholm: Regeringskansliet.

Government Bill (1997/98/145), *Svenska miljömål: Miljöpolitik för ett hållbart Sverige [Swedish Environmental Objectives: Environmental Policy for a Sustainable Sweden]*, Stockholm: Regeringskansliet.

Government Bill (2000/01/130), *Svenska miljömål: delmål och åtgärdsstrategier [Swedish environmental objectives: targets and strategies]*, Stockholm: Regeringskansliet.

Government Bill (2001/02/20), *Infrastruktur för ett långsiktigt hållbart transport-system [Infrastructure for a long-term sustainable transport system]*, Stockholm: Regeringskansliet.

Government Bill (2003/04/116), *Miljöbedömningar av planer och program [Environmental assessments of plans and programmes]*, Stockholm: Regeringskansliet.

Government Bill (2004/05/150), *Svenska miljömål: ett gemensamt uppdrag [Swedish environmental objectives: a joint mission]*, Stockholm: Regeringskansliet.

Government Communication (2001/02/50), *Hållbara Sverige: uppföljning av åtgärder för en ekologiskt hållbar utveckling [Sustainable Sweden: follow-up of measures for an ecologically sustainable development]*, Stockholm: Regeringskansliet.

Government Communication (2001/02/172), *Nationell strategi för hållbar utveckling [National strategy for sustainable development]*, Stockholm: Regeringskansliet.

Government Communication (2003/04/129), *A Swedish strategy for sustainable development: English summary*, Stockholm: Regeringskansliet.

Government Communication (2005/06/126), *Strategiska utmaningar: En vidareutveckling av svensk strategi för hållbar utveckling [Strategic challenges: a further elaboration of Swedish strategy for sustainable development]*, Stockholm: Regeringskansliet.

Holmberg, Sören and Lennart Weibull (eds) (2001), *Det våras för politiken: SOM-undersökningen 2001 [Springtime for politics: the SOM poll 2001]*, Göteborg: SOM-institutet.

Jordbruksdepartementet (2000), *Miljö och landsbygdsutvecklingsprogrammet 2000–2006 [Environmental and Rural Development Plan for Sweden 2000–2006]*. Förordning 2000: 577, Stockholm: Regeringskansliet.

Jordbruksverket (2005), *Tekniskt underlag för nytt landsbygdsprogram [Technical basis for new rural development programme]*, Jönköping: Jordbruksverket.

Kronsell, Annica (1997), 'Sweden: setting a good example', in Mikael Skou Andersen and Duncan Liefferink (eds), *European environmental policy: The pioneers*, Manchester: Manchester University Press.

Löfstedt, Ragnar (2003), 'Swedish chemical regulation: an overview and analysis', *Risk Analysis*, 23 (2), 411–421.

Lundgren, Lars J. (1995), 'Sveriges gröna historia [Sweden's green history]', in H. Strandberg (ed.), *Människa och miljö: Om ekologi, ekonomi och politik [Man and environment: on ecology, economics, and politics]*, Stockholm: Tidens Förlag.

Lundqvist, L. (1998), 'Sweden: from environmental restoration to ecological modernisation', in K. Hanf and A. Jansen (eds), *Governance and Environment in Western Europe: Politics, Policy and Administration*, Harlow: Longman.

Lundqvist, Lennart (2001), 'Implementation from above: the ecology of power in Sweden's environmental governance', *Governance*, 14 (3), 319–337.

Lundqvist, Lennart (2004), *Sweden and ecological governance: Straddling the fence*, Manchester: Manchester University Press.

Miljödepartementet (2003), *Promemoria: Utvärdering av Regeringskansliets miljöledningsarbete i beslutsprocesser mm [Evaluation of the Government Offices' environmental management work in decision processes etc]*, Stockholm: Regeringskansliet.

Miljödepartementet (2004), *Regeringskansliet och miljön: Bilaga till protokoll från regeringssammanträde 2004-05-06. [Government offices and the environment]*, M2003/4023/Hm. Stockholm: Regeringskansliet.

Naturvårdsverket (2004a), *Ekonomiska konsekvensanalyser av myndigheternas miljöarbete [Economic impact assessment of authorities' environmental activities]*, Stockholm: Naturvårdsverket.

Naturvårdsverket (2004b), *Myndigheternas miljöansvar: Vidareutveckling av det särskilda sektorsansvaret [The agencies' environmental responsibility: Further development of the special sector responsibility]*, Stockholm: Naturvårdsverket.

Naturvårdsverket (2005a), *Environmental Management Systems (EMSs) in Swedish governmental agencies*, Stockholm: Naturvårdsverket.

Naturvårdsverket (2005b), *Miljöanpassad offentlig upphandling: En enkätstudie 2004 [Environmental public procurement: a survey 2004]*. Stockholm: Naturvårdsverket.

Naturvårdsverket and Energimyndigheten (2004), *Sveriges klimatstrategi: Ett underlag till utvärderingen av det svenska klimatarbetet [Sweden's climate strategy: a basis for the evaluation of the Swedish climate efforts]*, Stockholm: Naturvårdsverket and Energimyndigheten.

Nilsson, Måns (2005), 'Learning, frames and environmental policy integration: the case of Swedish energy policy', *Environment and Planning C: Government and Policy*, 23, 207–226.

Nilsson, Måns and Åsa Persson (2003), 'Framework for analysing environmental policy integration', *Journal of Environmental Policy and Planning*, 5 (3), 333–359.

Riksrevisionen (2004a), *Förändringar inom kommittéväsendet [Changes in the committee system]*, Stockholm: Riksrevisionen.

Riksrevisionen (2004b), *Miljömålsrapporteringen – för mycket och för lite [Environmental objectives reporting – too much and too little]*, Stockholm: Riksrevisionen.

SFS (1995/1322), *Verksförordningen [Government decree on agency structure]*, Stockholm: Riksdagen.

SFS (1998/808), *Miljöbalken [Environmental code]*, Stockholm: Riksdagen.

Söderberg, C. (2005), Much ado about nothing? Energy forest cultivation in Sweden: on policy coordination and EP in a multi- sectoral issue, paper presented at the ISA RC 24 Conference *Double Standards and Simulation: Symbolism, Rhetoric and Irony in Eco-Politics*, University of Bath, 1–4 September.

SOU (1996/112), *Integrering av miljöhänsyn inom den statliga förvaltningen [Integration of environmental concerns in the governmental administration]*, Stockholm: Regeringskansliet.

SOU (1998/170), *Gröna nyckeltal för en ekologiskt hållbar utveckling [Green indicators for ecologically sustainable development]*, Stockholm: Regeringskansliet.

SOU (2005/36), *På väg mot en hållbar landsbygdsutveckling [Towards a sustainable rural development]*, Stockholm: Regeringskansliet.

Statistiska centralbyrån (SCB) and Naturvårdsverket (2001), *Sustainable Development Indicators for Sweden: a First Set*, Stockholm: Statistiska centralbyrån (SCB) and Naturvårdsverket.

WCED (1987), *Our common future: Report by the World Commission on Environment and Development*, Oxford: Oxford University Press.

Vägverket (2001), *Vägverkets nationella miljöprogram 2002-2005 [Road agency's national environmental programme]*, Borlänge: Vägverket.

Vägverket (2005), *Klimatstrategi för vägtransportsektorn [Climate strategy for the road transport sector]*, Borlänge: Vägverket.

Vedung, Evert (1991), 'The formation of green parties: environmentalism, state response and political entrepreneurship', in Jens A. Hansen (ed.), *Environmental concerns: an inter-disciplinary exercise*, London: Elsevier.

12. The United Kingdom

Duncan Russel and Andrew Jordan

INTRODUCTION

The United Kingdom (UK) is widely regarded as having a very coordinated system of government, especially in relation to the management of foreign policy (Metcalfe 1994: 285; Bulmer and Burch 1998; Jordan 2002a: 37). Its widely admired 'Rolls-Royce' coordination system was created to ensure that all the constituent parts of the UK government 'speak with one voice' in European and international negotiations (Bulmer and Burch 1998; Jordan 2002a: 37). Under Tony Blair (1997–2007), the UK made a concerted political effort to pursue more joined-up government across a range of other cross-cutting issues, including sustainable development, social exclusion, race and gender (Cabinet Office 1999; Pollitt 2003). The UK also has a long history of trying to achieve greater environmental coordination; it was one of the very first EU Member States to develop a national EPI system (Jordan and Schout 2006). What is more, it has been a strong advocate of EPI at EU level (Jordan 2002a: 41). Additionally, the UK has led in the development and deployment of particular EPI instruments (for example, environmental cabinets, interdepartmental committees, policy appraisal and national sustainable development strategies) (see Chapters 3 and 6 respectively).

Given this apparently supportive context, it is not entirely surprising that the OECD (2001, 2002) decided to praise the UK for its handling of EPI. In this chapter, we try to weigh all the available evidence and seek to arrive at a more detailed and balanced assessment of the UK's performance. Overall, we find that the UK has an impressive array of EPI instruments, but that their implementation has been far from perfect (see also Jordan 2002a and Ross 2005). Indeed, there seems to be a puzzling disparity between the UK's ability to act in an internally coordinated manner on general matters like foreign policy and on a more narrowly focused policy coordination challenge with a distinctly sectoral bias such as EPI.

The remainder of this chapter unfolds as follows. First, we provide a historical overview, including a summary of the key factors that led to the adoption of EPI as a formal policy goal in the late 1980s. Then we describe the main instruments deployed as part of the UK's EPI system and explore how well they have performed. The main theme of this section is that performance has failed to match initial expectations. Next, we discuss where the UK's EPI system might be breaking down and some of the potential reasons for this. Finally, we conclude by drawing some transferable lessons for other jurisdictions seeking to pursue EPI.

HISTORY

The evolution of the UK's EPI system can be broken down into three distinct periods. The first of these (1970–1990), covers the time when the environment was first recognized as an urgent policy problem meriting a separate department. Crucially, beyond the setting up of the Department of the Environment – then the world's first integrated environment ministry – there were very few concerted attempts to engineer EPI across all sectors. The second period (1990–1997) was marked by the Conservatives' first attempt to establish a national EPI system within central government. Significantly, EPI was not established as a formal constitutional principle but largely as a policy goal supported by an administrative process and administrative guidance (for example, DoE 1991), overseen by the environment department. The final period (1997–2007) saw the election of a Labour government and the strengthening of the UK's EPI instruments, as well as the introduction of several new ones. Notably, a transition from EPI to something more akin to sustainability policy integration occurred during this period.

1970–1990: National Environmental Policy in the Doldrums?

The UK government first gave the environment a stronger political focus in the late 1960s. This was a period of heightened public concern (Osborn 1997: 4) and one of the main responses was the creation of the Department of the Environment. Created in 1970, it arguably represented the UK's first attempt to pursue (administrative) environmental coordination. It was a 'super ministry' (see Chapter 3) which housed the functions of the former Ministries of Housing, Local Government, Transport, Public Buildings and Works (Painter 1980) under one roof. In the same year, the ruling Labour government produced the UK's first national environmental plan in the form of a White Paper (Her Majesty's Government 1970). Crucially, this made no mention of cross-governmental responsibility for the environment or to EPI, and generally generated very little attention within or outside government. The Labour party was swept from power by the Conservatives later that year. In 1974, a significant piece of environmental legislation, the Control of Pollution Act, was produced (Osborn 1997: 4). However, it was also much more concerned with old-style environmental regulation than integration, and in any case was never fully implemented (Jordan 2002b).

In the late 1970s and early 1980s, the UK's progress on environmental policy issues fell away (Rose 1990; Jordan 2002a: 43). By the 1980s, its record had slipped so badly that it was derided as '*the* Dirty Man of Europe' by national and European environmental pressure groups (Rose 1990, emphasis added). During the 1980s, pressure from the EU's environmental policies and high-profile environmental degradation, such as the destruction of the ozone layer and acid rain, once again led to increased public concern over the environment (Jordan 2002a: 42). Against this background, and following the publication, in 1987, of the Brundtland Report on sustainable development, the Conservative government (since 1979, under the leadership of Margaret Thatcher) hurriedly produced a response entitled *Sustaining Our Common Future* (DoE 1989). This report sought to claim that the UK was already implementing sustainable development through its extensive body of environmental legislation. It summarily dismissed the need for changes to the machinery of government, arguing that 'the concept of collective responsibility inherent in the British system of government' would suffice (DoE 1989: 13).[1]

1990–1997: Environmental Policy under the Conservatives

Following her speech on environmental matters to the Royal Society in September 1988 and the unprecedented success of the domestic Green Party in the 1989 European elections (Osborn 1997: 5), Thatcher sought to improve the UK's environmental relations with other Member States. She appointed the young, Europhilic politician Chris Patten to be a more media-friendly environment minister (Jordan 2002a: 44), and gave him the task of producing a new and far more comprehensive national environmental plan (Her Majesty's Government 1990). In contrast to the government's previous stance on sustainable development and the environment, this White Paper outlined a comprehensive cross-governmental approach which was publicly endorsed by all government departments. Crucially, it sought to reorientate the machinery of government to 'integrate environmental concerns more effectively into all policy areas' and as early in the decision-making process as possible (ibid: 230). So was born the UK's – and, arguably, also the world's – first comprehensive national EPI system.

Crucially, the UK system was primarily, although not exclusively, administratively orientated and led not by the Prime Minister or her core executive, but by the Department of the Environment. Specifically, it harnessed existing coordination instruments to establish: an Environment Cabinet Committee (which was, in fact, an extension of the committee that had originally drawn up the 1990 White Paper) to pursue cross-departmental environmental coordination; an inter-ministerial network of Green Ministers to oversee the delivery of the White Paper within their respective departments; and a process through which the White Paper would be regularly reviewed and its targets revised. In addition, it announced a cross-sectoral procedure for conducting *ex ante* environmental policy appraisal (see also Chapter 6) to assess the potential impacts of new policy proposals. Environmental policy appraisal was supported by guidance published by the environment ministry (DoE 1991). Furthermore, the White Paper also contained a whole annex on one particular aspect of what is now known as green budgeting: namely the raising of environmental revenues through environmental taxes. Subsequently, on top of the existing differential on unleaded petrol (established in 1987, this set the duty on leaded petrol at a higher rate), the Conservatives introduced three revenue-raising, market-based instruments aimed at better internalizing environmental costs: a landfill tax (in 1996); automatic annual tax increases on vehicle fuel (from 1993); and indirect tax on domestic fuel (from 1993) (Helm 1998: 11; Jordan *et al.* 2003: 187). In 1994, the Conservative government also produced a national sustainable development strategy (Her Majesty's Government 1994), making the UK one of the first countries to follow up on international agreements made at the 1992 Earth Summit (Sustainable Development Commission 2004: 9) (see also Chapter 5).

The commitment to EPI in the 1990s was not, however, particularly forceful. There was, for example, a very clear preference for non-justiciable guidelines rather than rigid rules to be followed in all cases (Her Majesty's Government 1990: 231), which reflected the absence of a formal national constitution in the UK. Why did it choose to adopt this particular approach to EPI? There are arguably several reasons. First, the UK has a well-known tendency to deal with environmental policy problems by changing its machinery of government rather than adopting binding laws governing emissions (Weale *et al.* 2000: 176). Second, as mentioned above, the UK central government already had strong coordination instruments for policies connected to international and EU affairs (Bulmer and Burch 1998: 48). The 1990 White Paper tried to work with the grain of these pre-existing structures by building in a slightly more explicit environmental dimension. The approach was therefore very incremental rather than revolutionary in nature. Third, the policy style of pollution control in the UK had traditionally evolved around the principle of cooperation and discretion in the setting and application of standards. The informal manner in which policy has traditionally been made in the UK was a good example of 'club government' (Weale *et al.* 2000: 181). For EPI, this meant tweaking the machinery of government rather than imposing tighter environmental standards and targets on the sectors and their associated constituencies in the business world. Crucially, it also did not disturb the policy status quo or the working practices of the various sector departments. Finally, the content of the 1990 White Paper also reflected the strong input made by Patten's external advisors, such as David Pearce, who was a strong advocate of cost-benefit analysis and market-based environmental instruments.

1997–2007: Environmental Policy under Labour

Shortly after being elected in 1997, Tony Blair attended the Rio plus 5 international conference and pledged to 'make the process of government green'. He added that: '[t]he environment must be integrated into all our decisions, regardless of sector. [It] must be in at the start, not bolted on later' (Blair 1997). This commitment was very much in line with his government's pursuit of more 'joined-up' and 'evidence-based' policy making (Cabinet Office 1999; Pollitt 2003). It can also be seen as a continuation of efforts that he had made to court the green vote when in opposition. Under Blair's leadership, the new Labour administration sought to inject fresh impetus into the UK's EPI system, first by significantly strengthening existing instruments and second, by adding some entirely new ones (Jordan 2002a). With respect to the existing instruments, Labour raised the political profile of the Environment Cabinet Committee by placing it under the chairmanship of the then Deputy Prime Minister, John Prescott (Jordan 2002a: 47). In 2005, it was given even more political clout by adding energy to its brief. Even more importantly, at the same time, the chair was taken over by no less than the Prime Minister, a move which seemed to suggest that henceforth, the national EPI system would enjoy the very highest level of political support in government (EAC HC 698, session 2005–2006, para 17). Moreover, the status of the Green Ministers' network was raised by making it a sub-committee of the Environment Cabinet Committee (Ross 2005: 29). It was also given a new responsibility to produce an annual report on the progress made by government departments in meeting EPI and sustainable development targets.

One of Labour's more revolutionary initiatives was the decision to (re)combine the environment and transport departments into one large 'super-ministry', called the Department for the Environment, Transport and Regions (DETR). In 2001, this was changed once again, when transport was hived off into a separate department, and agriculture, fisheries and food were added in its place. This new department was named the Department of the Environment, Food and Rural Affairs (DEFRA), and, like its predecessors, was primarily responsible for leading the UK's EPI system. In addition, a special cross-departmental integration unit, the Sustainable Development Unit (SDU), was established within DETR to support the Green Ministers, promote best practice and report on progress made by other departments (Jordan 2002a: 46; Ross 2005: 29).

Procedures for policy appraisal were also strengthened by Labour, through the issuing of new guidance on environmental policy appraisal (Russel and Jordan 2007). Eventually, however, it was dropped in favour of a more integrated form of appraisal known as Regulatory Impact Assessment (RIA) (Russel and Jordan 2007; see also Chapter 6). This is akin to sustainability appraisal and, unlike the rest of the UK EPI system, is managed by the Cabinet Office.[2] In addition, strategic environmental assessment is also in the process of being rolled out for regional and local-level programmes and plans in line with the 2001 EU Directive.

One of the other eye-catching elements of Labour's more purposeful and integrated approach to pursuing EPI was the publication of a new sustainable development strategy (Her Majesty's Government 1999). This strategy identified new and much more detailed priorities for pursuing sustainability, including reducing social exclusion and improving energy efficiency. It was supported by the publication of 15 headline indicators to measure progress on sustainability. This strategy was subsequently updated in 2005 and promised a more robust departmental reporting system, a more explicit focus on sustainable consumption issues and climate change and so on (Her Majesty's Government 2005). The UK's sustainable development indicators were also expanded to cover 68 areas.

The Labour government also created two independent bodies to audit EPI and sustainability in a more transparent and detailed manner, namely: a parliamentary Environmental Audit Committee; and a Sustainable Development Commission (SDC) to act as an independent advisory body to the government. The parliamentary Environmental Audit Committee was established in the House of Commons towards the end of 1997 (ENDS No. 271: 3–4). Its principal task is to scrutinize and report on how EPI and sustainable development are implemented across government (Jordan 2002a: 46; Ross 2005: 38). Over time, the parliamentary Environmental Audit Committee has increasingly received assistance from the much larger and better resourced National Audit Office (NAO).[3] The SDC was established in 2000 and currently comprises 14 commissioners. In the 2005 Sustainable Development Strategy (Her Majesty's Government 2005: 154), the Commission was given a stronger watchdog role, which involves monitoring the government's progress on sustainable development. Moreover, in 2005, responsibility for producing the annual reports on the progress made by government departments on EPI and sustainable development was removed from the Green Ministers and handed to the Commission (ENDS No. 372: 8).

Finally, Labour also made a number of important changes to embed EPI in the national budgeting system. First, on the revenue-raising side it expanded the range of market-based environmental policy instruments introduced by the Conservatives. Labour added a vehicle excise escalator in 1999, with lower rates for smaller cars and lorries, and a tax on aggregates (freshly mined rock) in 2002 (Jordan *et al.* 2003: 187–189). In 2001, the unleaded petrol differential was replaced with a ban on leaded petrol. Second, to improve the strategic planning of expenditure priorities (an earlier and more strategic element of the green budgeting cycle discussed in Chapter 4), a two-yearly cross-departmental process of reviewing spending was introduced in which all departments had to bid to the Treasury for their upcoming spending allocations (Russel 2005). Essentially, it aimed to align future spending programmes with the government's core priorities (EAC HC 92, session 1998–1999, para. 2). As part of the process, the Treasury agreed Public Service Agreements with each department, which stipulate specific policy targets (Russel 2005).[4]

While the spending review is not specifically an EPI instrument, it has been partially used to foster integration (see Chapter 4). For instance, in the 1998 and 2000 reviews, the Deputy Prime Minister and the Treasury asked departments to consider sustainable development in their spending plans (EAC HC 92, session 1998–1999, para. 11; HC 70, session 2000–2001, appendix). In the 2002 and 2004 reviews, a more systematic sustainable development reporting process was introduced to support each department's bid for funding (Russel 2005: Chapter 6). Moreover, Public Service Agreements are mentioned in the latest Sustainable Development Strategy (Her Majesty's Government 2005: 165) as a means to enforce the government's sustainability commitments.

Overall, under Labour, the political status and comprehensiveness of the UK's EPI system grew significantly. But at the same time, it also gradually evolved into something which was more holistic than simply EPI – something more akin to 'sustainable development policy integration' than environmental policy integration. For instance, in 2002 the government claimed that the changes it had instituted 'signal[ed its] commitment to practice what [it] preach[es] by considering the full range of economic, environmental and social impacts of the government estate and [the] policy making process' (Green Ministers Committee 2002: 5). This reorientation was very much reflected in the creation of the Sustainable Development Unit, the production of the 1999 sustainable development strategy and the establishment of a set of sustainable development indicators. In 2002, the government refocused its EPI reporting process still further when it rebranded the Green Ministers as Sustainable Development Ministers (EAC HC 698, session 2005–2006: para. 17).

EPI IN PRACTICE

This short historical overview suggests that, at least on paper, the UK's EPI system was and remains innovative. The UK certainly possesses many more EPI instruments than other comparable Member States (that is, 11 in total, compared to Germany (7), Sweden (6–7) and France (5) – see Chapter 2 for details). But how well have these instruments actually performed, either individually or collectively?

Administrative Instruments

As indicated above, the UK's earliest attempt to pursue EPI involved combining three existing departments to create one large super-ministry – the Department of the Environment – in 1970. More recently, under Blair, Labour demonstrated a similar if not stronger appetite for administrative reform. However, the original Department of the Environment was downsized in 1976 after only six years, when transport was hived off. One senior official remembers it being far too unwieldy to be effective (Osborn 1997: 4). More recently, Labour's Department of the Environment, Transport and the Regions was reformed after just four years (see above). The reasons for its dismemberment arguably had more to do with the political need to get to grips with the 2001 foot and mouth crisis than pursuing EPI or sustainability. According to the parliamentary Environmental Audit Committee, however, this reorganization had a negative impact on the UK's pursuit of sustainable development. It absorbed huge amounts of administrative time, undid a great deal of work that had been done at the interface of environment and transport, and distracted ministers and senior officials from strategic initiatives like EPI (EAC HC 624-I, session 2003–2004, para. 84). Both the parliamentary Environmental Audit Committee and the SDC voiced their concern about the loss of transport and local planning responsibilities, as these are two crucial aspects of the sustainable development *problematique* (EAC HC 624-I, session 2003–2004, para. 84; Sustainable Development Commission 2004: 20).

The performance of the Environment Cabinet Committee under both the Conservatives (1990–1997) and Labour (1997–2005) has also been strongly criticized, although examining its work is hindered by the cloak of secrecy which tightly envelops all its work (EAC HC 426-I, session 1998–1999: para. 10; Ross, 2005: 36). Under the Conservatives, it was criticized for not showing enough political leadership: it met infrequently and only ever in secret (Jordan 2002a: 44). The majority of its time was devoted to resolving major policy clashes or failures, that is, negative coordination (ENDS No. 200: 15–17). Under Labour, it continued to display very little leadership. Critics suggest that it met too infrequently to drive the government's pursuit of sustainable development. It was simply not proactive or powerful enough to resolve inter-sectoral conflicts (EAC HC 426-I, session 1998–1999: para. 10; Jordan 2002a: 48).

It is widely reported that the political profile of the Green Ministers in Whitehall under the Conservatives was very low (Jordan 2002a: 44): they only ever met seven times. When they did, many Green Ministers failed to attend or sent their deputies instead (CPRE 1996). Furthermore, the meetings of the Green Ministers tended to focus on green housekeeping issues like office paper recycling rather than more substantive policy concerns (ENDS No. 246: 26–27; CPRE 1996: 1; Jordan 2002a: 44). Under Labour, though, the Green Ministers have taken a more proactive role. For example, they have produced annual reports on EPI and, more lately, sustainable development. In a sense, they have started to grow into the focal role that the Conservative administration had first envisaged for them. The turnout, focus and frequency of the first meetings under the Labour administration appeared much better than under the Conservatives. For instance, in their first meeting, 15 out of 19 members attended and the agenda was deliberately focused on substantive policy issues rather than housekeeping matters (ENDS No. 274: 33). Moreover, their improved status as a sub-committee of the Environment Cabinet Committee gave them a 'clear remit to tackle key cross-government sustainable development issues from both a policy and operations perspective and deliver greater progress' (Green Ministers' Committee 2001: para. 7.7). However, assessing their performance became harder as their operations were then governed by the doctrine of cabinet secrecy (EAC HC 961, session 2002–2003: para. 72).

The SDU has been criticized by the parliamentary Environmental Audit Committee and some academics with regard to its role, status and position in Whitehall (EAC HC 426-I, session 1998–1999; Jordan 2002a: 48; Ross 2005: 39). Concerns have been expressed about its location (relatively low down in the environmental part of DEFRA), which is too peripheral to make a difference (ENDS No. 294: 33–34; Jordan 2002a: 48; Ross 2005: 39). Instead, a more appropriate home might have been found in the Cabinet Office, where Labour originally promised to put it when in opposition (Labour Party 1994). The Cabinet Office has much more central authority and a remit covering strategic coordination issues (Jordan 2002a: 48; Ross 2005: 39). The SDU's work has also been overshadowed by the more high-profile Social Exclusion and Performance and Innovation Units in the

Cabinet Office, both of which deal with sustainability-related issues (Ross 2005: 40).

Since their creation, both the parliamentary Environmental Audit Committee and the SDC have actively reported on the UK's progress. According to Ross (2005: 38), many of the parliamentary Environmental Audit Committee's recommendations have been accepted by the government. A recent report on the SDC argues that 'it is evolving into a more effective organization after a slowish start and now has a significant impact at many levels' (Plowman 2004: para. 28). Be that as it may, both bodies have undoubtedly helped to open up the working of government to greater scrutiny and external evaluation by politicians and environmental NGOs.

Green Budgeting

On the revenue-raising side of green budgeting, the Conservatives' attempts to use environmentally-orientated market instruments were very fitful. Problems arose when the level of indirect tax on domestic fuel was doubled to 17.5 per cent. This sparked fears about rising fuel poverty and the government was forced into an embarrassing climb-down (Jordan *et al.* 2003: 187). Questions have also been asked about the environmental credentials of the fuel duty escalator, with critics claiming that its primary purpose was to raise the maximum amount of revenue possible rather than tackle environmental problems (Helm 1998: 11).

As discussed above, the Labour administration under Blair also sought to increase the revenues derived from the environmentally-targeted taxes established by the Conservatives. However, in an attempt to placate fuel tax protesters, the fuel duty escalator was spectacularly suspended in 2001 (Jordan *et al.* 2003: 187). Since then, Labour has been much more wary about introducing new environmental taxes, and the percentage share of total taxation revenues raised by environmental measures has gradually fallen. Crucially, the parliamentary Environmental Audit Committee has frequently noted that very few of the UK's budgetary measures are independently appraised *ex ante* or evaluated *ex post*, making it difficult to establish whether they have been environmentally successful or not (for example, EAC HC 547, session 1997–1998; HC 71-I, session 2001–2002; HC 216, session 2004–2005). Overall, the SDC (Sustainable Development Commission 2004: 21) claimed that the use of environmental taxation is one area where 'the government has clearly failed "to put the environment into the heart of government"'.

In relation to spending, Labour has been more innovative in its attempts to integrate the environment and sustainable development considerations into strategic planning. That said, the actual performance of its spending review process does not appear to have been an overwhelming success. The

Environmental Audit Committee's reports indicate that the 1998 and 2000 spending reviews showed no evidence that the environment or sustainable development had been integrated into departmental spending plans (EAC HC 92, session 1998–1999: para. 28; Russel 2005). Even when departments were required to produce a sustainable development report (as in the 2002 review), their quality was poor (many seemed to have been written long after the main spending priorities had been decided) (Russel 2005: Chapter 6). And thereafter, the requirement to conduct separate reports for the 2004 review was downgraded to a voluntary activity; the Treasury argued that sustainable development considerations should be integrated into individual departments' submissions. The parliamentary environmental audit committee has drawn attention to the paucity of environment targets in the Public Service Agreements produced as part of the 2002 and 2004 reviews (EAC HC 261, session 2004–2005: 33–36). For instance, in the 2004 review, only ten out of 124 departmental targets were environmental, of which six were DEFRA's responsibility (ibid.)! Although Public Service Agreements are supposed to explain who is responsible for the delivery of individual targets (that is, specification of output – see Chapter 3; see also James 2004), they are typically framed in such imprecise and hence unenforceable terms that they are effectively little more than weak mission statements (see Chapter 3).

Strategies and/or Strategy Developing Processes

While the profile of the Conservatives' sustainable development strategy seems to have been relatively low, it did provide 'a framework for shaping some of the first moves towards sustainability up to 1997' (Sustainable Development Commission 2004: 9). Labour's 1999 strategy (Her Majesty's Government 1999) was supposed to be more wide-ranging than its predecessor (Sustainable Development Commission 2004: 9). However, while acknowledging that the strategy had positive elements, the parliamentary Environmental Audit Committee (EAC HC 624-I, session 2002–2003) argued that it 'had not driven environmental progress [as was] originally envisaged' (ibid. para. 44); 'traditional socio-economic concerns still largely dominate policy making' (ibid. para. 40). Both the parliamentary Environmental Audit Committee and the SDC have acknowledged that the production of sustainable development indicators has been a significant step forward. However, the parliamentary Environmental Audit Committee claimed that they failed to provide a sufficiently broad measure of the UK's performance (EAC HC 624-I, session 2003–2004: para. 69). It is still too early to pass judgement on the 2005 Sustainable Development Strategy and its greatly expanded set of indicators. However, the SDC felt that they were an improvement on what had gone before (Sustainable Development Commission 2005: 1).

Policy Appraisal Systems

Overall, it appears that the use of appraisal (and particularly environmental policy appraisal) has been rather limited and generally of poor quality. Under the Conservatives, an analysis of parliamentary questions to ministers revealed that no department could provide tangible evidence that it had followed the environment department's guidance on environmental policy appraisal when producing new policies (Young 2000: 252). In 1997, a report commissioned by the Department of the Environment into the use of environmental policy appraisal was published, which concluded that there was plenty of room for a much 'more comprehensive and systematic consideration of the environmental impacts of policy' (DETR 1997: 32).

Labour's performance on environmental policy appraisal has also fallen short of what it promised (DETR 1998), with even the Green Ministers (2001: para. 3.7) admitting that the overall performance was 'somewhat disappointing'. Russel and Jordan (2007: 9) were only able to uncover 65 published environmental policy appraisals for the period 1997–2003, 47 of which had been conducted by DEFRA or the Department for Transport. Not only did the output of environmental policy appraisals appear to be limited, but questions were raised about their quality. For instance, the parliamentary Environmental Audit Committee has noted that they 'varied greatly in their coverage of environmental issues' (EAC HC 426-I, session 1998–1999: para. 47–48), while Russel and Jordan (2007: 10) found that very few fulfilled all nine of the best-practice criteria set by the environment ministry (DETR 1998). The vast majority were little more than simple *ex post* assessments that sought to 'green proof' unsustainable policies that had effectively already been decided (Russel and Jordan 2007: 10–11). Therefore, the overall pattern was not nearly as strategic or comprehensive as one would expect of an EPI instrument.

Given this apparent failure, it is hardly surprising that stand-alone environmental policy appraisals were recently discontinued in favour of more integrated RIAs (see Chapter 6). However, far from improving the situation, this move might well marginalize environmental issues further, as RIA has traditionally concentrated on reducing regulatory burdens on business. Indeed, the parliamentary Environmental Audit Committee has been sufficiently concerned about this to recommend that the government 'considers restructuring the present RIA procedures by inserting a new higher tier . . . [to] separately identify economic, environmental and social impacts' (EAC HC 261, session 2004–2005: para. 55). In response, the government promised that the National Audit Office would examine RIAs for their coverage of sustainable development issues (Her Majesty's Government 2005: 155). In their first report on this issue, the National Audit Office (2006) found that the coverage of sustainability issues in RIAs was limited, adding weight to the claim that the more integrated form of RIA would fail to prioritize environmental issues.

Strategic Environmental Assessment

The UK's opposition to SEA at a wider policy level is long-standing. It opposed the European Commission's initial attempts to extend the original EIA Directive to policies (Jordan 2002b: 185). As a result of the UK's lobbying efforts, the 2001 SEA Directive is aimed only at plans and programmes. Moreover, the UK does not advocate the use of SEA in its own policy appraisal guidance (for example, DETR 1998). Nonetheless, the UK has conducted at least one SEA at policy level – the Ministry of Defence's Strategic Defence Review – which was one of the most comprehensive environmental policy appraisals conducted under the Labour administration (Russel 2005: 163).

SUMMARY DISCUSSION

Overall, the UK has innovated, it has been a pathfinder and it has an extensive and growing repertoire of instruments in place. Despite this, however, the evidence presented in this chapter does suggest that these efforts have not been uniformly effective. Indeed, some of the individual elements have been very weakly implemented and some (like policy appraisal) have been spectacularly ineffective. Moreover, even though it has been in existence for more than fifteen years, the UK's EPI system appears not to have significantly improved the state of the UK's environment. For instance, in a recent environmental performance review of the UK, the OECD (2002: 19) remarked that:

> there is considerable *margin for further environmental progress*, as the UK . . . has not yet achieved a number of its environmental objectives and still presents a deficit of environmental infrastructure (e.g. waste and waste water treatment infrastructure) (emphasis added).

Having said that, some recent developments could restore the UK's reputation. For instance, there appears to be more central leadership, manifest by the Prime Minister's decision to chair the Environment Cabinet Committee and the Cabinet Office's supervision of integrated RIA. There have been other positive developments such as the 2005 Sustainable Development Strategy (see above) and the 2003 Energy White Paper (DTI 2003), both of which had a strong environmental component. But aside from these, the UK government has failed 'to grasp the over-arching nature of sustainable development' (EAC HC 517-I, Session 1997–1998: para. 1). As the SDC comments, the EPI 'machinery and . . . instruments, although desirable in themselves, have not yet been used consistently across [central departments] and not vigorously enough to deliver rapid enough change [for sustainable development]'. This section goes on to explore some of the possible underlying reasons for this state of affairs.

The UK's EPI system appears to command political support at the highest political levels. So where might it be breaking down? According to Schout and Jordan (2005: 215), a good flow of information between departments within the course of daily policy making is an essential precondition for EPI. One reason why the administrative and bureaucratic elements of the UK's EPI system may be struggling to make an impact is that they do not appear to have enough information on potential environmental spillovers to chew on. One might argue that this lack of supply has a lot to do with the poor implementation of policy appraisal.

One way in which to elaborate this point is to use Metcalfe's coordination scale (Box 12.1). Essentially, this is 'a flight of steps in which qualitatively different components of coordination are added from the bottom-up' (Metcalfe 1994: 281), that is, it conceptualizes coordination as a cumulative process. Consequently, the mechanisms for higher levels of coordination require the existence and proper functioning of the lower ones. With regard to the UK's EPI system, Level One could be represented by a situation in which all departments accept some responsibility for the environment (see above), which evidently they do not. Levels Two to Three relate to a situation in which the production of policy appraisals, or sustainable development reports in the spending reviews, provide data on policy spillovers that can be shared between cognate and central departments. However, given the poor implementation of environmental policy appraisal and the sustainable development reports in the spending review process, coordination appears to be breaking down at these levels. Consequently, the higher-level coordination bodies such as the Sustainable Development Unit (Levels Three to Four), the Green Ministers' Committee (Levels Five to Six), the Environment Cabinet Committee (Levels Six to Seven) and, in the case of the spending reviews, the Treasury (Levels Four to Seven) have little information on poorly coordinated (that is, integrated) policies to work with. Indeed, the Environment Cabinet Committee's main task is to resolve interdepartmental conflicts, but with no information on policy spillovers it has been starved of work. Overall, therefore, the UK's use of grand,

BOX 12.1 THE METCALFE SCALE OF COORDINATION

Level 1
Independence: each department retains autonomy within its own policy area but accepts some responsibility for cross-sectoral issues.

Level 2
Communication: departments inform one another of activities in their areas via accepted channels of communication.

Level 3
Consultation: departments consult one another in the process of formulating their own policies to avoid overlaps and inconsistencies.

Level 4
Avoiding divergence in policy: departments actively seek to ensure that their policies converge.

Level 5
Seeking consensus: departments move beyond simply hiding differences and avoiding overlaps and spillovers to work together constructively through joint committees and teams.

Level 6
Conciliation: neutral (possibly central) bodies are brought in or are imposed upon conflicting departments to act as a mediatory body. The onus, though, is still on the ministries to reach agreement between themselves.

Level 7
Arbitration: sometimes disagreement and conflict are too strong for voluntary approaches to overcome; therefore, a central or neutral actor plays a stronger role.

Level 8
Setting common parameters: parameters are predefined which demarcate what departments can and cannot do in their own policy-making arenas.

Level 9
Joint strategy and priorities: the core executive (Cabinet/Prime Minister/Cabinet Committee) sets down, and through co-ordinated action secures, the main lines of policy at the early stage of the decision cycle.

Source: Adapted from: Jordan (2002a: Box 3.1) and Metcalfe (1994: 280–284)

sustainable development strategies or the publication of sustainable development-related Public Service Agreements (Levels Eight to Nine) was not being sufficiently supported by the lower-level mechanisms. Moreover, the higher-level committees do not appear to have put political pressure on the lower levels to bring inter-sectoral conflicts to their attention. Consequently, cross-sectoral coordination never really gets going.

Of course the problem is more complex than simply a failure to communicate information on environmentally-related spillovers. For instance, why has the demand for such information at the top of the UK government failed to trickle down and stimulate greater cross-sectoral communication? Aside from some prime ministerial speeches, the parliamentary Environmental Audit Committee (EAC HC 517-I, Session 1997–1998; HC 363-I, session 2001–2002), Jordan (2002a: 40), and Russel and Jordan (2007: 12–14) have identified a lack of sustained high-level leadership as a contributory factor. This issue is particularly pertinent with regard to DEFRA, which supervises the main elements of the UK's EPI system. It has a relatively lowly political status in Whitehall (ENDS No. 356: 33–34). It cannot, for example, compel the sectors to implement EPI in the same way that the Prime Minister or the Treasury could. In the absence of determined central leadership, the other departments have found it all too easy to ignore EPI (Jordan 2002a: 53).

This lack of high-level political support is reflected in the distribution of resources devoted to the various implementing instruments. The parliamentary Environmental Audit Committee has suggested that 'little in the way of staff resources' was devoted 'to the sustainable development agenda' in Whitehall. Crucially, relatively few senior staff routinely addressed these issues (EAC HC 961, session 2002–2003: 3). And while there were allegedly 137 civil servants dealing with sustainable development issues out of a total of around five hundred thousand across Whitehall, 93 of them worked in just three departments (EAC HC 961, session 2002–2003: 13–14), namely international development, foreign affairs and DEFRA. In some departments, only one or two officials were responsible for sustainable development and there was little by way of training or incentives for the rest (Russel and Jordan 2007: 12 and 14), thus helping to exacerbate the low levels of political attention and leadership (see also Chapter 3).

Finally, while UK non-governmental organizations have provided strong political support for environmental progress, very few audit the government's pursuit of EPI regularly or closely enough (Jordan 2002a: 42). This is not to say that non-governmental organizations have not engaged with the UK's implementation of EPI. For instance, a small pressure group, the Green Alliance, has attempted to track the UK's implementation of EPI regularly since the mid-1990s, and larger groups such as Friends of the

Earth have frequently given oral and written evidence to parliamentary investigations. However, the Green Alliance is a very small organization with a tiny office in London (Jordan 2002a: 42); by contrast, the larger groups have tended to give it only passing attention, finding it easier to campaign on higher-profile issues like climate change and genetically modified organisms than dry and sometimes very complex 'machinery of government' concerns like EPI. Therefore, there is relatively limited external pressure on the UK to internalize environmental protection by developing and implementing a comprehensive EPI system. Finally, the UK has a relatively powerful and independent Sustainable Development Commission, but there has never been an equivalent body responsible for EPI.

CONCLUSIONS

At the start of this chapter, we identified two apparently conflicting descriptions of the UK's EPI system: one from the OECD applauding its advanced machinery of governance, and the other expressing doubts about the UK's EPI performance in practice. In this chapter we have sided with the second view and have sought to demonstrate that the UK's system is not nearly as effective or well coordinated on environmental matters as is sometimes claimed. The implementation of EPI is actually quite sectorized, with its individual elements not working as well as envisaged. The mismatch between the OECD's positive review of the UK's EPI system and our much more negative account is partly a function of the level of analysis adopted. For instance, the OECD's (2001, 2002) assessments tend to rely upon self-reporting by the government. They also involve a largely superficial description of the component parts, rather than a more detailed assessment of how each element functions individually and in combination. By contrast, this chapter has analysed the latest developments in the UK's EPI system; covered a much broader number of EPI instruments and explored the relationship between them; and examined the important role that information flows play in promoting and/or retarding environmental coordination.

Overall, our analysis adds weight to the claims made by other authors (for example, Richardson and Jordan 1979: 26–28; Richards and Smith 2002: 9 and 22) that decision making in the UK is routinely departmentalized; that is, unless coordination is of direct interest to the departments concerned (for example, on EU and foreign policy issues) or there are strong central controls (for example, on economic matters where the Treasury has a strong guiding hand). 'Departmentalism' describes a situation when policy makers operate in vertically-configured departments, thinking and acting in terms of 'their' department's interests instead of more horizontal objectives, such as EPI (Richards and Smith 2002: 22). It is associated with so-called 'turf wars', which typically arise when departments compete over policy competences. For example, Richards and Smith (2002: 9) argue that the 2001 foot and mouth crisis led departments to 'automatically slip . . . into the role of defending [their] own sector's interests, rather than considering the larger picture'. This situation is more than apparent in relation to a cross-cutting issue like EPI and can arguably lead to sub-optimal policy making (Richards and Smith 2002: 9 and 22).

There are, however, areas in which departments have successfully worked together. For example, joint planning programmes for rural affairs were created between the Ministry of Agriculture, Fisheries and Food and the DETR (Perri 6 *et al.* 2002: 25). Accounts of departmentalism, however, imply that effective cooperation is the exception not the rule, with critics arguing that UK central government is 'more suited to coordination and integration in theory than in practice' (Bogdanor 2005: 3).

What, then, does the UK need to do to overcome these difficulties? And what lessons can be drawn from the UK's experience with EPI? First, as the OECD implies (2001, 2002), having a variety of EPI elements to pursue coordination at different levels is a necessary but not a sufficient condition for greater EPI. The various component parts have to work well individually but also in combination. In this chapter, we have shown that policy appraisal and some of the administrative innovations have not supported one another as strongly as the OECD claimed. Second, an effective supply of information on potential policy spillovers is very important to the success of an administratively-based EPI system such as the UK's. In particular, the reliability of lower-level coordination mechanisms to produce information on policy spillovers is vital for the effective functioning of the institutional and bureaucratic instruments which appear higher up Metcalfe's scale. Moreover, the various coordination instruments need to link into one another; simply creating administrative instruments (such as committees, rules and adjudication devices – see Chapter 3 for a more comprehensive typology) without adequate foundations at lower levels, can easily leave them rootless and, eventually, under-utilized.

The practical implication of this point is hugely important: 'the more basic but less glamorous aspects of the policy coordination process' are vital (Metcalfe 1994: 288) but all too often overlooked. It implies that the underlying coordination capacities (the instruments to exchange information, consult and arbitrate and so on – see Chapter 3) need to be in place before political energies are invested in setting strategic objectives, creating high-level committees and writing grand strategies. This is a point which does not come easily to politicians looking for a media-grabbing headline or a quick institutional fix to an EPI-related problem.

Third, only focusing on whether sufficiently configured coordination instruments are in place ignores the fact that the political processes encapsulated in the term 'departmentalism' can all too easily derail EPI initiatives. It is vital, therefore, that departmental officials are adequately incentivized to engage with environmental coordination initiatives in order to think beyond their department's core sectoral interests. This could be done, for example, by integrating EPI goals into job descriptions and making involvement in environmental coordination initiatives an everyday aspect of everyone's career development. Moreover, in contrast to the Metcalfe scale, which suggests that coordination builds from the bottom up, sustained active central leadership (by the Prime Minister and Ministers of State and so on) is also crucial to create a demand for EPI within the sectors to prevent the lower level mechanisms from breaking down, especially when the environment ministry is politically weak. So, rather than the bottom-up and cumulative model suggested by Metcalfe (1994), coordination should be seen as a system of mutual interdependence between the bottom and the top. As Peters (1997: 52) observes, leadership is a vital way to override departmental sectoral interests in the pursuit of cross-cutting goals. However, central leadership has a tendency to ebb and flow (Ross 2005: 47) depending on the level of pressure and scrutiny from environmental non-governmental organizations, public bodies and the wider public. This is why we are driven to conclude that the implementation of EPI is still 'founder[ing] on the rocks of interdepartmental wrangling . . . as a succession of governments have seen no political reason to promote it' (Jordan 2002a: 36).

NOTES

1. Namely, the convention that all members of government should jointly accept responsibility for decisions made in cabinet regardless of their personal views.
2. Initially, RIA was promoted as a way to assess the impact of a policy on business, charities and the voluntary sector.
3. The National Audit Office is responsible for reporting to Parliament on the efficiency and effectiveness of public spending.
4. For example, one of the targets in the Department of Trade and Industry's Public Service Agreements was simply 'to reduce greenhouse gas emissions to 12.5 per cent below 1990 levels in line with [the UK's] Kyoto commitment' (Her Majesty's Treasury 2004: 31).

BIBLIOGRAPHY

Blair, A. (1997), Speech by the Prime Minister Tony Blair to the UN General Assembly on the Environment and Sustainable Development, 23rd June 1977, http://www.number-10.gov.uk/output/Page1045.asp, accessed 12 June 2008.

Bogdanor, V. (2005), 'Introduction', in V. Bogdanor (ed.), *Joined-Up Government*, Oxford: Oxford University Press.

Bulmer, S. and M. Burch (1998), 'Organizing for Europe: Whitehall, the British state and the European Union', *Public Administration*, 76 (4), 601–628.

Cabinet Office (1999), *Modernising Government*, London: HMSO.

CPRE (Council for the Protection of Rural England) (1996), *From Rhetoric to Reality*, London: CPRE.

DoE (Department of the Environment) (1991), *Policy Appraisal and the Environment*, London: HMSO.

DoE (Department of the Environment) (1989), *Sustaining Our Common Future*, London: HMSO.

DETR (Department of the Environment, Transport and Regions) (1997), *Experience with the 'Policy Appraisal and the Environment' Initiative*, London: HMSO.

DETR (Department of the Environment, Transport and Regions) (1998), *Policy Appraisal and the Environment: Policy Guidance*, London: HMSO.

DTI (Department of Trade and Industry) (2003), *Our Energy Future: Creating a Low Carbon Economy*, London: HMSO.

ENDS (Environmental Data Services) (various years), *ENDS Report*, various issues.

Green Ministers' Committee (2001), *Greening Government: Third Annual Report*, London: HMSO.

Green Ministers' Committee (2002), *Sustainable Development in Government: First Report*, London: HMSO.

Helm, D. (1998), 'The assessment: environmental policy objectives, instruments, and institutions', *Oxford Review of Economic Policy*, 14 (4), 1–19.

Her Majesty's Government (1970), *The Protection of the Environment*, London: HMSO.

Her Majesty's Government (1990), *This Common Inheritance*, London: HMSO.

Her Majesty's Government (1994), *Sustainable Development: The UK Strategy*, Cmnd 2426, London: HMSO.

Her Majesty's Government (1999), *A Better Quality of Life: A Strategy for Sustainable Development for the United Kingdom*, London: HMSO.

Her Majesty's Government (2005), *The UK Government Sustainable Development Strategy*, London: HMSO.

Her Majesty's Treasury (2004), *Spending Review: Public Service Agreements White Paper*, London: HMSO.

James, O. (2004), 'The UK core executive's use of Public Service Agreements as a tool of governance', *Public Administration*, 82 (2), 397–420.

Jordan, A. (2002a), 'Efficient hardware and light green software: environmental policy integration in the UK', in A. Lenschow (ed.), *Environmental Policy Integration: Greening Sectoral Policies in Europe*, London: Earthscan.

Jordan, A. (2002b), *The Europeanization of British Environmental Policy*, Basingstoke: Palgrave.

Jordan, A. and A. Schout (2006), *The Coordination of the European Union: Exploring the Capacities of Networked Governance*, Oxford: Oxford University Press.

Jordan, A., R. Wurzel, A. Zito and L. Bruckner (2003), 'Policy innovation or "muddling through"? "New" environmental policy instruments in the United Kingdom', *Environmental Politics*, 12 (1), 179–200.

Labour Party (1994), *In Trust for Tomorrow*, London: The Labour Party.

Metcalfe, L.M. (1994), 'International policy coordination and public management reform', *International Review of Administration Sciences*, 60, 271–290.

National Audit Office (2006), *Regulatory Impact Assessments and Sustainable Development: A Briefing for the Environmental Audit Committee*, London: NAO.

OECD (Organisation for Economic Cooperation and Development) (2001), *Sustainable Development: Critical Issues*, Paris: OECD.

OECD (Organisation for Economic Cooperation and Development) (2002), *Environmental Performance Reviews: the UK*, Paris: OECD.

Osborn, D. (1997), 'Some reflections on UK environmental policy, 1970–1995', *Journal of Environmental Law*, 9 (1), 3–22.

Painter, M.J. (1980), 'Policy co-ordination in the DoE, 1970–1976', *Public Administration*, 58, 135–154.

Perri 6, D. Leat, K. Seltzer and G. Stoker (2002), *Towards Holistic Government*, Basingstoke: Palgrave.

Peters, B.G. (1997), *Managing Horizontal Government: The Politics of Coordination*, Ottawa: Canadian Centre for Management Development.

Plowman, J. (2004), *Review of the Roles and Responsibilities of the Sustainable Development Commission and the Sustainable Development Unit*, unpublished report prepared for the UK Sustainable Development Commission.

Pollitt, C. (2003), 'Joined-up government: a survey', *Political Studies Review*, 1 (1), 34–49.

Richards, D. and M.J. Smith (2002), *Governance and Public Policy in the UK*, Oxford: Oxford University Press.

Richardson, J. and G. Jordan (1979), *Governing Under Pressure*, Oxford: Martin Robinson.

Rose, C. (1990), *The Dirty Man of Europe: The Great British Pollution Scandal*, London: Simon and Schuster.

Ross, A. (2005),'The UK approach to delivering sustainable development in government: a case study in joined-up working', *Journal of Environmental Law*, 17 (1), 27–49.

Russel, D. (2005), *Environmental Policy Appraisal in UK Central Government: A Political Analysis*, PhD Thesis, Norwich: University of East Anglia.

Russel, D. and A. Jordan (2007), 'Gearing up government for sustainable development: environmental policy appraisal in UK central government', *Journal of Environmental Planning and Management*, 50 (1), 1–21.

Schout, A. and A. Jordan (2005), 'Coordinated European governance: self-organizing or centrally steered?' *Public Administration*, 83 (1), 201–220.

Sustainable Development Commission (2004), *Shows Promise – But Must Try Harder*, London: SDC.

Sustainable Development Commission (2005), *Stepping up the Pace*, London: SDC.

Weale, A., G. Pridham, M. Cini, D. Konstadakopulos, M. Porter and B. Flynn (2000), *Environmental Governance in Europe*, Oxford: Oxford University Press.

Young, S.C. (2000), 'The United Kingdom: from political containment to integrated thinking', in W.M. Lafferty and J. Meadowcroft (eds), *Implementing Sustainable Development Strategies and Initiatives in High Consumption Societies*, Oxford: Oxford University Press.

13. The United States of America
John Hoornbeek

INTRODUCTION

Observers have criticized American environmental policy for its failure to confront global climate change, address high rates of energy consumption and restrain a culture of high consumer-oriented consumption. It is not surprising in this context that the phrase 'environmental policy integration' is rarely heard in American political discourse. On a practical level, however, the United States of America (USA) has taken steps to integrate environmental considerations into other policy sectors, to the point where they now constitute a substantial component of US environmental policy. This chapter explores these efforts, and suggests that the US has been backing toward EPI and sustainability in a slow and piecemeal fashion. The slow rate of progress is attributable at least in part to the US's fragmented policy structures and processes (compare the European Union – Chapter 8).

This chapter begins with a brief history of EPI efforts in the USA. It then overviews EPI practices at the national and sub-national levels, and provides an initial assessment of progress in the federal agriculture, energy and transportation sectors. It suggests that state and local governments make greater use of the full range of EPI instruments than does the federal government, but that practices vary among states and across policy sectors. It concludes that there is no shared vision of a 'sustainable America' to guide these EPI efforts, and that greater commitment is needed if the USA is to address the environmental challenges that confront it. The analysis is based on existing literature and interviews with American policy practitioners. However, because existing American literature in this area is relatively sparse, this chapter represents an initial effort to overview EPI practices in the USA rather than a comprehensive assessment of their effectiveness.

HISTORY

The challenge of EPI 'consists of integrating one type of concern (environmental) into already existing sets of sector concerns and related policy processes, organizational arrangements, and power structures' (Persson 2004: 20–21). While this challenge has not been the subject of extensive scholarly inquiry in the US (but see Mazmanian and Kraft 1999 and Portney 2003), it has been addressed in the formation and implementation of American environmental policy.

The Early Years: Relying on the States

Prior to the (mid-to-late) 1960s, environmental issues were considered to be the responsibility of state and local governments. Early clean air and water legislation at national level focused on providing funding and technical assistance to build state and local capacities. These federal policies envisioned state and local governments as being primarily responsible for environmental protection and EPI. In general, state policies aimed to set ambient air and water quality standards, and then work backwards to establish appropriate strategies to reduce harmful pollution from whichever sectors it emerged. On a practical level, EPI-related concepts were implicit in early American environmental policy, even if they received relatively little direct attention and emphasis.

The National Onslaught: Integration by Federal Regulation

In 1969, Congress passed the National Environmental Policy Act (NEPA), a landmark piece of federal legislation which sought to establish a comprehensive and coordinated federal environmental policy. This law is probably still the most explicit and official statement of (that is, commitment to) EPI-related principles in the US. NEPA pioneered the use of SEA (see also Chapter 7), and was motivated in part by Senator Henry Jackson's observation that federal agencies were not doing a good job of coordinating environmentally-related activities (Oldham 2003). NEPA envisioned ongoing coordination across federal agencies through a Council on Environmental Quality (CEQ), which was established in the White House. NEPA also envisioned integration of environmental concerns with other policies through Environmental Impact Statements, which were required for major federal actions.

These Environmental Impact Statement processes created by NEPA, and the major changes to media-based laws enacted in the 1970s (Clean Water Act and so on), fostered regulatory approaches to protecting the environment. They were also accompanied by continuing investments of federal funds to build sufficient state and local capacities to implement and comply with them. These regulatory and public investment strategies set the US apart as an international environmental pioneer, and have also been fundamental building blocks for significant environmental progress. However, they have not been particularly effective at enabling a holistic consideration of environmental concerns in other policy sectors.

In the late 1970s, increasing public concern focused on energy and the economy. In turn, these concerns gave rise to new kinds of EPI efforts. The Carter administration's approach was to create centralized responsibility for energy policy in a new cabinet-level Department of Energy, while investing in renewable energy sources and encouraging conservation. These approaches effectively sought to integrate environmental concerns into the nation's energy policies, even though EPI was not explicitly cited as the motivating focus for these efforts.

Targeting Federal Policies: Cost-Consciousness and EPI

The election of Ronald Reagan to the Presidency in 1980 heralded a reversal of the Carter administration's approaches, and led to a new era of environmental policy – one that sought to limit the cost of environmental programs and encourage more targeted approaches. For example, the Reagan administration discontinued the renewable energy investments made in the Carter era (Smith 2000), cut the budget of the Environmental Protection Agency (EPA), executed policy reversals in both the EPA and the Department of the Interior, and instituted Regulatory Impact Assessment (RIA) processes (see also Chapter 6) to ensure that all new regulations were cost-effective. These changes engendered much controversy, led to the resignation of an EPA administrator accused of contempt of Congress, and effectively politicized the Reagan administration's environmental policies (Collins 2006).

In an effort to repair this damage, Reagan appointed William Ruckelshaus to lead the EPA, and he and his successors – Lee Thomas and William Reilly – sought to re-energize and refocus American environmental policies based on comparative risk analyses and a search for new, less expensive and more targeted instruments. These efforts culminated in major reports that highlighted disconnections between EPA budgetary priorities and expert evaluations of environmental and public health risks (USEPA 1987, 1990). These reports forced a reconceptualization of existing policies, and focused attention on problems that had not been addressed adequately by the policies of the 1970s – 'unfinished business', to borrow the phrase used in the first report (USEPA 1987). A number of these sources of risk grew from particular industry sectors (for example, agriculture and transportation), and helped trigger a search for new ways to integrate environmental considerations into these policy areas.

The Congress acted on these concerns and integrated environmental considerations into major agriculture, transportation and energy laws between the mid-1980s and mid-1990s. The 1985 Food Security Act encouraged farmers working on highly erodible land to use protective farming practices, and also authorized significant funds for a new conservation reserve program and expanded environmental technical assistance. These environmental efforts were expanded in subsequent legislation in 1996. The Inter-modal Surface Transportation Efficiency Act (ISTEA) of 1991 funded mass transit, required transportation planning that recognized the value of the environment, and provided monies for projects that sought to alleviate the polluting effects of automobile congestion. And the Comprehensive National Energy Policy Act of 1992 sought – among other things – to encourage energy conservation and efficiency, while also promoting renewable energy. None of these laws was enacted primarily to protect the environment or implement EPI, but all included new programs and provisions that sought to integrate environmental concerns into the practices of key industry sectors.

A New Era: Backing toward Sustainability?

In 1993, the Clinton administration went a step further and acted upon the sustainable development ideas associated with the Brundtland Report and the Rio Earth Summit by establishing a President's Council on Sustainable Development. The Council's efforts helped foster further thinking about 'smart' growth and other related concepts that sought to guide economic behaviour in ways that were consistent with environmental protection. They even led some scholars to suggest that the US had entered the formative stages of a new environmental epoch that focused on sustainable communities (Mazmanian and Kraft 1999: 30). However, while the concept of sustainable development caught on in a number of states and communities, it failed to have significant influence in many others.

When viewed from a national perspective, the changes flowing from the President's Council on Sustainable Development appear modest. The EPA's strategic focus began to turn toward sustainable communities around the turn of the century, but the effectiveness of the Agency's efforts have been limited by budgetary factors and the policy instruments available to it. In the USA, spending on traditional environmental programs has been stagnant or diminishing (Brown and Kiefer 2003; USEPA 2006a), and federal policy instruments continue to have limited reach with respect to state and local land-use practices. These factors have limited the extent to which EPA's programs can effectively foster sustainability at the state and local levels.

Arguably, however, Congress expanded EPI efforts in some (limited) respects by passing the 2002 Farm Security and Rural Investment Act, the Farm Bill, and major energy and highway bills in the summer of 2005.

While these actions fell well short of adherence to the concepts of sustainability and EPI, they do – in combination with legislation enacted in the last decade and a half of the twentieth century – signal an evolution in American environmental policy toward greater reliance on sector-based environmental policies.

EPI IN PRACTICE

Across the landscape of American government, one can find instances in which the EPI-related policy instruments discussed in Part II of this book have been used, alongside mandatory requirements that have been a mainstay of American environmental policy since the 1970s. It is, however, important to recognize that the concept of EPI is grounded primarily in practices that have accumulated over time, and not in any explicit recognition of it as a broad principle to be applied routinely in the policy process in pursuit of sustainable development – as has been the case, for example, in Europe (see Chapters 1 and 8). The following discussion reveals considerable usage of EPI policy instruments in the US, along with significant variation in specific practices across federal agencies, between federal and state levels of government, and among the states.

The variable pattern of usage can be related back to the structure of American government. National competencies for environmental policy are based largely on the commerce clause of the US Constitution,[1] and this has had the effect of limiting federal policies to those that can be legally justified under this clause (Hoornbeek 2004). And, while the commerce clause has often been interpreted broadly by the American courts (although this pattern has changed somewhat in recent years), national policy instruments still do not extend deeply into some issues that are central to sustainable development and EPI, such as local land-use decision making.

Administrative Instruments

Administrative instruments are commonly used to foster EPI in the USA. A number of the instruments outlined in Chapter 3 have been used at both the national and sub-national levels, with varying degrees of success.

Hierarchical instruments
Hierarchical instruments have been commonly used to pursue EPI in the USA, but their influence has varied with the interests of leaders overseeing their implementation. In the USA, they can be traced back to the Council on Environmental Quality, a council established in 1969 in the Office of the

President to help foster improved coordination among federal agencies on environmental matters (see above) and develop annual reports on environmental quality. As one looks back over the decades that have passed since that time, variable levels of executive commitment are evident. Even the size and impressiveness of the annual reports themselves appear to be a rough surrogate for political commitment. During the late 1970s, the CEQ annual reports were large and impressive documents; during the early Reagan years in the 1980s, they diminished in size as the CEQ's budget was cut (Vig 2003); by the late 1990s, the CEQ's annual environmental reports were even less apparent.

Even as the CEQ's influence appeared to diminish during the 1990s, the Clinton administration took steps to foster EPI through other hierarchical means. For example, it ordered the EPA and the US Department of Agriculture to develop a unified, government-wide Clean Water Action Plan in cooperation with other federal agencies. The plan identified 111 water quality-related actions to be taken through 2008 (US Federal Government 1999: 18). During the final years of the 20th century, the Clean Water Action Plan enjoyed strong support and appeared to foster improved coordination of federal water quality protection efforts. Watershed assessments and indicators were established, conservation buffers were created, and expanded funding was made available for efforts to combat polluted run-off through the US Department of Agriculture's Conservation Reserve Enhancement Program and the EPA's Shared Revolving Fund Program (US Federal Government 1999). With clear support from the White House, the Clean Water Action Plan appeared to give added focus to water quality improvement efforts.

Because hierarchical approaches require support from chief executives and senior officials, some have viewed this type of administrative reform with scepticism, particularly since the election of George W. Bush in 2000. While the Bush administration has used these approaches, some would argue that recent efforts of this type reflect the Bush administration's scepticism of the need for any environmental advocacy. Vice-President Dick Cheney undertook an administrative effort to establish a coordinated energy policy in 2001 that became mired in criticism because of a perceived bias toward energy producers. The 2005 highway bill signed by President Bush created a senior-level task force to streamline NEPA reviews of transportation projects. While this effort sought to force actors to resolve environmental conflicts earlier on in the policy process, it did so in the context of diminished opportunities for environmental challenges at later stages in the development of transportation projects.

Top-down hierarchical approaches are also evident at sub-national levels. Massachusetts, for example, has linked the state's transportation, environmental and housing agencies together within a new Office for Commonwealth Development (Greenblatt 2005). Under Governor Arne Carlson, Minnesota's Environmental Quality Board created a public–private Round Table to guide the state toward more sustainable forms of development.

Horizontal instruments

More horizontal instruments to encourage EPI have also been commonly deployed. In recent years, this kind of approach has been used extensively in the agri-environmental sector and in other sectors as well. With respect to agri-environmental issues, officials from EPA and the US Department of Agriculture now meet regularly to coordinate cross-cutting issues. One official whom I interviewed reported that the EPA Administrator now has a full-time adviser on agriculture issues, and that EPA and US Department of Agriculture officials are asked to comment and provide input on key policies emanating from one another's agencies. Instances of joint policy pronouncements have also become more evident. In October 2006, for example, the EPA and the Department of Agriculture signed a partnership agreement to promote the establishment of 'viable water quality trading markets' (USEPA 2006b). And state-specific technical assistance committees, which include both agricultural and environmental representatives, now broker distribution of agri-environmental grant funds at the state level, thus providing an instrument for incorporating environmental concerns into agricultural decision making.

At the sub-national level, state and regional planning authorities have sought to enable horizontal coordination across government jurisdictions. Some states – Oregon and New Jersey, for example – have issued statewide planning frameworks that can foster cross-sector consideration of environmental concerns at a statewide level (Siy *et al.* 2001). And in a number of states, regional Councils of Government have coordinated programs and services that draw federal funds from sector-based agencies and seek to provide horizontally coordinated support and services at local levels. These state and sub-state efforts have been complemented by a range of multi-state regional efforts that seek to foster EPI at multiple levels of government in an effort to protect valuable water resources such as the Chesapeake Bay and the Great Lakes, and estuarine environments such as Narragansett Bay and the Puget Sound.

Federal agencies have also been tasked with EPI-related responsibilities as they develop and revise their mission statements and strategic plans. Since the passage of the Government Performance and Results Act in the mid-1990s, federal agencies have become increasingly consistent in their preparation of publicly available strategic plans, which typically include mission statements and strategic objectives; recent iterations of these plans in the Departments of Agriculture (USDA 2002), Energy (USDOE 2003) and Transportation (USDOT 2003) all include clear references to environmental concerns. While there can be arguments about the impact of mission statements and strategies on agency behaviours (see Chapter 3), official documents and statements recognizing the importance of environmental concerns can serve as a legitimate source of guidance to support judgments made by lower-level officials (Hoornbeek 2000).

Green Budgeting

The federal government has also made substantial use of green budgets – interpreted here to mean monetary subsidies and incentives to foster environmentally friendly behaviour (see also Chapter 4). Unlike some countries (see Chapter 2), the USA does not have a broad and systematic instrument for reviewing the environmental implications of government expenditure decisions (outside of the project-based instruments provided for in NEPA), so this working definition seems more appropriate to the American context.

For many years, the US federal government has developed and administered grant programs to further environmental objectives. Since the passage of the Federal Clean Water Act in 1972, for example, the federal government has contributed over $70 billion for wastewater treatment plant construction (ASIWPCA 2004: 18). And in 2003 alone, state environmental and natural resource programs received $5 billion in federal funds – approximately one-third of $15 billion in total state expenditures in these areas (Brown and Kiefer 2003).

Increasingly, these traditional federal environmental and natural resource grant programs are being supplemented by subsidies in other policy sectors. In the agriculture sector, these subsidy programs come in three main forms. The first encourages agricultural producers to retire land that had previously been used for farming, and therefore seeks to reduce the polluting impacts of farming practices. One of the most important of these programs is the Conservation Reserve Program for croplands. Similar programs exist for wetlands and environmentally sensitive agricultural lands. The second involves the US Department of Agriculture supporting technical assistance to improve awareness of environmental concerns and efforts to address them through state soil and water conservation programs. And the third seeks to foster environmentally friendly farming practices. The Environmental Quality Incentives Program enacted in the 1996 Farm Bill is one of the largest of these programs, and it – along with other programs of this kind – provides incentives and cost sharing to foster environmentally friendly land management practices (Bernstein *et al.* 2004: 69).

These budgeting programs are central to EPI efforts in the agriculture sector, and they have been increasing in size. In 1999, funding made available to support them through the US Department of Agriculture totalled approximately $2.5 billion, an increase of approximately $1.5 billion over the funding levels provided in the mid-1980s (Bernstein *et al.* 2004: 70). A recent Congressional Research Service analysis of US Department of Agriculture funding identified over $5 billion in total conservation expenditures in 2004. This broader measure also showed a substantial funding increase over previous years, as it had almost doubled since 1990 (Womach 2005).

In the energy sector, there has been a long history of applying federal subsidies. A number of these come in the form of tax incentives to entice energy production, efficiency and conservation measures. Tax incentive policies in the energy sector were initiated during World War II and were applied to oil (Smith 2000: 140), but tax-based efforts to foster EPI through greater use of renewable fuels have developed – albeit sporadically – over the last several decades. Federal energy legislation enacted in the summer of 2005 supplemented existing subsidies to foster EPI. This legislation included incentives to produce energy from wind and other renewable sources, tax breaks for energy conservation improvements in homes and office buildings, and tax credits for the purchase of fuel-conserving hybrid vehicles (Babbington and Blum 2005: A-8; Kiely 2005: 1).

However, of the $14.5 billion in tax incentives contained in the 2005 energy bill, 58 per cent of the benefit over a ten-year period is estimated to accrue to traditional energy industries, including oil, natural gas, electric utilities and nuclear power. About 36 per cent of the total would go for renewable sources of energy, energy efficiency and cleaner burning vehicles (Blum 2005: A-4). The nuclear power industry was also a winner, as it received 'billions of dollars in subsidies and tax breaks covering almost every facet of its operations' (Babbington and Blum 2005: A-8).

The US Department of Transportation also administers green budgeting subsidy programs. The law creating the Congestion Mitigation Air Quality Program, for example, authorizes over $1.6 billion annually for Metropolitan Planning Organizations and others to support transportation-related projects that yield air quality benefits (Beardon 2004: 6). It is supplemented by other subsidies, including environmental expenditures from a 10 per cent set-aside in the Department of Transportation's Surface Transportation Program for 'enhancements' relating to multi-modal, cultural, historic, and environmental aspects of the nation's surface transportation (Beardon 2004: 14).

The federal highway bill enacted during the summer of 2005 authorized additional subsidies to support EPI efforts in the transportation sector. It devoted approximately 18 per cent of its $286 billion in costs (over ten years) toward addressing mass transit needs (Blum 2005: A8), and increased authorizations for Congestion Mitigation Air Quality funding by 27 per cent (EDF 2006). It also provided additional funds for pedestrian and bicycle programs, with the authorized funding exceeding $600 million for a five-year period.

The sector-specific subsidies described above total well into the billions of dollars each year, and rival or exceed existing grants to state environmental and natural resource agencies. Few, if any, of these sector-specific subsidies existed (in their current form) even a quarter of a century ago. Furthermore, these subsidies are often passed through for actual expenditure at the state and local levels, where they can be supplemented by additional state and local expenditures. Massachusetts, for example, has devoted a $5 billion capital budget and $500 million in annual grants to support projects that follow 'smart' growth principles such as fostering more compact development around transit lines and downtown commercial centres (Greenblatt 2005). In the USA, budgets for sector-based programs at the federal, state and local levels do appear to be taking on a greener shade than they have in the past – even as budgets for traditional environmental programs are stagnant or diminishing.

Strategies and/or Strategy Developing Processes

Sustainable development strategy efforts have been undertaken at all levels of government in the USA: federal, state and local. In general, state and local governments have been more active in this area than has the US federal government, although even these state and local efforts – while quite noteworthy in some cases – have been somewhat episodic when viewed from a national perspective. Still, the efforts that have been undertaken do reflect a perceived need to factor environmental concerns into sector-based policy making and implementation, and they appear to have been influential in some states and communities (Portney 2003).

As noted above, the Clinton administration established the President's Council on Sustainable Development in the 1990s. The Council was comprised of both private and public sector representatives and developed strategic reports that were released in the late 1990s. Despite significant rhetoric and fanfare surrounding this effort, the strategic reports it developed have had little influence (Baker and McCormick 2004).

The strategy-development processes undertaken at the state and local levels have been more numerous and probably more effective in fostering EPI related activities. At least three states – Oregon, New Jersey and Minnesota – have created strategies to help them implement sustainability directives within their jurisdictions (Siy *et al.* 2001). Consistent with the spirit of its Environmental Stewardship Plan, the State of Oregon developed a Transportation and Growth Management Program to integrate 'transportation planning with the state wide land use planning program to achieve benchmarks for mobility, air quality, and community design' (Siy *et al.* 2001: 36). A component of New Jersey's Sustainable State effort has been the development of a transatlantic relationship with the Netherlands to share information and ideas regarding sustainable development (ibid: 37–40). And the Minnesota State Legislature required all of its government agencies, departments and boards to assess how well their activities implemented principles established by Minnesota's Round Table for Sustainable Development (ibid.: 41) – a process that appears to bear some similarity to the Cardiff Process in the EU (see Chapter 8). However, these three states remain the exception rather than the norm; only about a dozen states have the kind of statewide planning authorities that would even enable implementation of state sustainable development strategies if they were developed (Siy *et al.* 2001).

There are also efforts to develop strategic approaches to sustainability at the local level. Portney's (2003) study identifies a number of American cities that have taken significant steps toward sustainability. Some of these have developed specific strategies to guide their efforts. Chattanooga in Tennessee, for example, developed a sustainability plan to help guide a range of its activities, including those relating to clean water, land and forest conservation, and energy and transportation (*ibid.*: 36). Seattle, Washington and Portland, Oregon have taken another approach, one that involves introducing sustainability goals into broad comprehensive strategic plans (ibid.: 36). In both cases, however, the focus is on developing broad strategic frameworks to guide a range of activities that incorporate environmental considerations into other policy sectors.

Policy Appraisal Systems

While the USA was an early innovator with respect to RIA (see Chapters 2 and 6), standardized national policy-appraisal processes in the USA remain focused primarily on economics rather than the environment. At the same time, the research conducted to support the writing of this chapter did not uncover widespread and systematic efforts to assess new policy proposals according to environmental criteria among state and local governments.

Even *ex post* federal appraisal processes (that is, occurring after the adoption of legislative or administrative programs) appear to be limited with respect to environmental assessment. The Program Assessment Rating

Tool process used by the current Bush administration to evaluate existing federal programs does not appear to focus extensively on environmental concerns, except in cases where environmental improvement is a central objective of the program being rated (as is the case with programs at the EPA). And even efforts to develop state of the environment reports have been limited at the federal level, in spite of the fact that over thirty states have now developed such reports at the state level (Siy *et al.* 2001: 26).

Strategic Environmental Assessment

Here, the USA has been an international innovator since the 1960s (see Chapters 2 and 7). In fact, NEPA's Environmental Impact Statement requirements have been applied to hundreds of major federal actions over the past 35 years. Notably, however, NEPA's requirements are process-based; they do not give the environment 'principled priority' (see Chapter 1) and hence do not require achievement of environmentally favourable outcomes. Because of this they have been criticized by some as relatively weak (see Chapter 7). In fact, the trend in the USA in recent years has been toward loosening them still further through various streamlining efforts. Still, NEPA has had substantive impacts. For example, environmental groups and others have used the court system to delay environmentally questionable projects. It has also spawned a generation of state-level 'mini-NEPAs', which are intended to help assure that environmental considerations are taken into account in the implementation of state-level projects. To date, at least 25 states have enacted this kind of legislation (CEQ 1997).

While NEPA applies to many federal actions, it is arguably of greater importance in the transportation sector than in any other. The federal Department of Transportation has tended to file more Environmental Impact Statements than other federal agencies and it is also named frequently as a defendant in NEPA-related litigation (Horan *et al.* 1999: 222). The importance of NEPA has not been lost on either transportation authorities or environmental groups. The Congressional Research Service reports that planning and construction of major highway projects typically takes between 9 and 19 years, and that preliminary design and environmental review processes can account for up to one-fourth of this time (Beardon 2004: 17). This has led to calls for a 'streamlining' of NEPA review processes for transportation projects, which have been heeded by Congress both in the 1998 reauthorization of the 1991 ISTEA legislation and then again in the 2005 highway bill. Environmental groups have been sceptical of this kind of process. There has, for example, been a marked increase in NEPA-related litigation since the turn of the millennium (Austin *et al.* 2005).

Other Instruments – Mandatory Requirements

It is appropriate to recognize that this increasing flow of litigation is based on the fact that NEPA is a regulatory statute which imposes requirements in cross-cutting fashion on sector-based federal agencies. In this respect, one might argue that SEA in the USA is not an instrument of EPI but rather belongs among the traditional command and control policy instruments referred to in Chapters 1 and 2. However, this argument would overlook the multiple forms of mandatory requirements used in the USA, and the fact that mandatory requirements are an important means through which EPI is built into American sector-based policy making and implementation. Indeed, as I spoke with environmental professionals while conducting this research, they often emphasized the importance of mandatory requirements as a means of ensuring that sector-based agencies address environmental concerns. Thus, while EPI is often thought of as an alternative to regulation, it is also a supplement to it.

Mandatory requirements come in at least four major forms, all of which can have impacts on EPI efforts. First, they may come as cross-cutting requirements which apply across multiple executive agencies, as in the case of NEPA. Second, they may come in the form of sector-specific requirements authorized by Congress in statutes that apply to specific industry sectors, such as energy efficiency standards written into energy legislation. Unlike more traditional command and control regulations, these requirements are implemented by sector-based agencies rather than environmental and natural resource agencies such as the EPA and the Interior Department. Mandatory requirements may also come in a third form, which associates specific environmental requirements with the receipt of federal subsidies. The 1985 Farm Security Act's requirement that farmers use conservation systems on previously cropped and highly erodible land, or risk the loss of support through other federal programs that provide farm price and income support (Bernstein *et al.* 2004: 69) is one example of this kind of requirement. The Clean Air Act's requirement that states and Metropolitan Planning Organizations 'demonstrate that their transportation plans "conform" to their air quality plans' (Beardon 2004: 4) or face the loss of federal highway funds is another important example.

And finally, mandatory environmental requirements may be applied by environmental agencies such as the EPA or the Department of the Interior based on powers delegated by Congress. Such activities include emissions of pollutants into the air through stationary or mobile sources, waste-water discharges to surface waters, management practices in large concentrated animal feeding operations, and required protections for endangered species. This fourth form of mandatory requirement defines the core of traditional command and control American regulatory policies, and is perhaps most separable of the four forms of mandatory requirements from EPI, analytically. However, even it has important influences on EPI, as is suggested by the growing interest in agri-environmental issues that took place in the Department of Agriculture after the EPA took an increasing regulatory interest in concentrated animal feeding operations over a decade ago.

America's system of separated powers may make mandatory requirements relevant to EPI in ways that are not typical in Europe. The separation of powers between the legislative and executive branches of government in the USA – as well as among Congressional Committees – means that policy influences over federal agencies are commonly divided among multiple and relatively independent political principals rather than one ruling party or coalition (Aberbach and Rockman 1988). Mandatory requirements in this context become a means through which differing societal actors (for example, environmental interests) can insert their concerns in policy forums where they may not have had access or significant influence in the past. These mandatory requirements may also have important and direct effects on organizational arrangements, bureaucratic politics and learning processes that affect EPI in sector-based agencies. In other words, they may become – in some cases – a surrogate for (or even equivalent to) the administrative rules and procedures referred to in Chapter 3. As a result, it may be difficult for practitioners in the USA (and even scholars) to conceive of mandatory requirements as distinct and separable from EPI in the USA in the same way as may be the case in Europe.

EPI AT THE SECTORAL LEVEL

Much work remains to be done before one can argue that EPI is occurring in a comprehensive fashion in the USA. There are, however, signs suggesting that EPI progress is occurring in particular sectors. The following subsections discuss signs of progress at procedural and substantive levels in the agriculture, energy and transport sectors.

Agriculture Policy

There has been progress in expanding EPI in the agriculture sector over the past twenty years. A growing number of environmentally oriented programs are administered by the US Department of Agriculture, alongside the farming assistance and forest management activities that have long defined its mission and primary constituencies. Environmental concerns are also playing at least some role in processes for coordinating policies across agencies.

But how does one assess this situation when substantive criteria relating to intended outcomes for EPI are considered? In general, agri-environmental policies appear to have had beneficial effects on the environment and natural resources. Since the mid-1980s, about thirty-five million acres have been taken out of agricultural use (Bernstein *et al.* 2004: 68), and the Conservation Reserve Enhancement Program enacted in 1996 has targeted some of those land retirement efforts toward highly sensitive lands. At the same time, a recent US Department of Agriculture analysis found that soil erosion has been reduced in the USA in recent years, and at least 25 per cent of the reduction is attributed to the cross-cutting compliance programs required to maintain eligibility for federal subsidies (Claassen *et al.* 2004).

Conversely, however, a relatively recent OECD study reports that pesticide use in the USA increased slightly between the early 1990s and the turn of the century (OECD 2004), and there appears to be little evidence at this point to suggest that agriculture is declining as a source of water pollution. Interviews conducted by this author also suggested that the US Department of Agriculture's conservation programs were not always targeted effectively to achieve environmental results.

Energy Policy

The picture of EPI progress that emerges in the energy sector is mixed. From a procedural viewpoint, there are certainly instances in which the Department of Energy attempts to coordinate with the EPA and/or other federal agencies on environmental matters. However, these interactions appear to be sporadic and/or of limited scope. And when high-level coordination efforts are undertaken, they often appear to succumb to fragmentation, controversy and distributive politics.

One can also arrive at both positive and negative assessments of progress with respect to outcomes. It is clear that the USA has made major gains in energy efficiency over the last several decades through the production of more fuel-efficient vehicles and energy-efficient building practices (Smith 2000: 149–166). At the same time, however, fossil fuels continue to account for over 80 per cent of American energy consumption (USDOE 2004: Table 1.1, 5), and reliance on imported oil has also increased (USDOE 2003: 15). In addition, Americans continue to increase their use of automobiles (USDOE 2004: Table 2.8). Thus, while the technology improvement strategies underlying existing policies are helping in energy efficiency, they do not (yet) appear to be ensuring a reliable and environmentally friendly energy future.

Transport Policy

A mixed picture also emerges in the transportation sector. On a procedural level, inter-agency coordination efforts are evident, but they appear to be developed ad hoc, and they are often limited in scope. At the same time, communities have benefited from funding for environmental programs associated with the transportation sector, and environmental interests continue to exercise influence through both Clean Air Act conformity requirements and Environmental Impact Statement reviews.

However, even with these points of procedural leverage for environmental interests, the evidence remains mixed when substantive criteria are applied. One federal official with many years of Environmental Impact Statement review experience commented positively about the improvements that s/he had seen in the environmental sensitivity of state transportation projects over the last several decades. Still, a 2002 National Academy of Sciences review encountered difficulty demonstrating substantial air quality improvements after ten years of Congestion Mitigation Air Quality Program implementation, and this result may raise questions about the cost-effectiveness of the strategy used in the current Congestion Mitigation Air Quality Program (TRB 2002). While the National Academy of Sciences panel expressed clear support for the Program, it also indicated that the weight of the (limited) evidence available suggested that the Congestion Mitigation Air Quality subsidies are not as cost-effective as emissions controls in reducing air emissions (TRB 2002). Mobile sources of air pollution continue to be important factors contributing to localized air pollution problems and greenhouse gas emissions, and the number of vehicle miles travelled in the USA has continued to increase (USDOE 2004: Table 2.8). Indeed, even total fuel efficiency (all vehicles) – which has increased substantially since the middle of the 20th century – has recently levelled off somewhat, as it has not increased significantly over the last 12 or 13 years (USDOE 2004: Table 2.8). This situation now appears to be undergoing some change as debate about the need for increased fuel efficiency has intensified recently on the back of rising gasoline prices.

SUMMARY DISCUSSION

While the language of sustainability has become apparent in American discourse, there is still no clear, explicit and continuing nationwide commitment to sustainable development. Even the formal national commitment to EPI is not explicit or comprehensive; some would argue that it is effectively limited to major federal actions as outlined in the NEPA. Nonetheless EPI policy instruments have been used widely in the USA. At the federal level, there has been a growing focus on green budgeting and a continuing use of administrative instruments, both of which have become increasingly intertwined with mandatory requirements in ways that help foster EPI. At the sub-national level, one can discern a growing interest in and use of EPI instruments, often accompanied by more extensive use of sustainable development strategies and state of the environment reports to appraise overall progress. Indeed, EPI efforts in some states and communities have been and remain substantial. SEA is also of continuing importance, although it is undergoing a period of revision at federal level.

The American case, therefore, presents an interesting contrast to the EU (see Chapter 8), where the rhetoric of sustainability and EPI appears to be much stronger and more committed than its actual implementation. Still, at the federal level, the USA appears to favour policy instruments that add to existing policies, as opposed to more comprehensive and strategic policy instruments that help foster altered frames of reference.

How does one explain these patterns of instrument use? The lack of a strong and explicit national commitment to sustainable development, and the minimal use of comprehensive federal EPI strategies, appear to be at least partially traceable to the widely recognized fragmentation in American policy-making structures. National policies affecting EPI have developed in piecemeal fashion and remain incomplete, often without a clear rudder. Clearly, America's system of separated powers at the national level and divided powers between national and state governments, when combined with its large size and individualistically oriented culture, are not conducive to building a nationwide consensus on any issue, let alone EPI. However, these same structural characteristics have enabled significant levels of EPI activism in some states and localities, and are allowing various targeted EPI efforts in the federal agriculture, energy and transportation sectors. At sub-national levels, there are signs of direction and focus, as well as more comprehensive approaches, but these signs are concentrated in a limited number of active jurisdictions.

What do these findings suggest for future research? America's apparently growing reliance on subsidy programs to foster EPI highlights the value of future efforts to assess the target efficiency and effectiveness of its current mix of policy instruments. Further research into the relationships among all of the key variables mentioned above – levels of fragmentation in the policy-making process, the mix of EPI-related policy instruments used, and target efficiency and policy effectiveness – would therefore be beneficial for understanding how best to structure future EPI efforts.

CONCLUSIONS

The USA has, it seems, been backing toward sustainability in an incremental fashion. This process has now reached the point where it represents a significant change in American environmental policy. Budgets are being cut at the EPA, while environmental budgets are growing in other federal agencies. This situation gives added incentive to the EPA and state environmental agencies to work productively with sector-based agencies. At the same time, however, the environmental challenges facing the USA and the world seem daunting. Global climate change threatens coastlines, habitats and human beings, and recent events have highlighted the risks associated with America's continuing reliance on fossil fuels. Water pollution remains a problem throughout the USA, and shortages of clean water are looming in the future. These and other challenges emphasize the importance of EPI for a healthy and sustained future.

Against this backdrop, the progress flowing from current EPI efforts appears insufficient. At the end of the last century, scholars and practitioners declared that the USA had moved into a new era of sustainable development (Mazmanian and Kraft 1999). While this was at least partially true in some states and communities, it has not yet proven to be true for the nation as a whole. Crucially, there remains no shared vision of a 'sustainable America' to guide federal EPI efforts and inspire the wider public. State and local EPI efforts – while substantial in a number of cases – remain partial and inconsistent across the many jurisdictions. At the same time, widely accepted institutions for reviewing and measuring the effectiveness of EPI and sustainable development measures (for example, national sustainable development councils – see Chapter 2) are not yet apparent. If America is to maintain a leadership role in addressing environmental concerns as it did in the 1960s and 1970s, it must begin to assess and accelerate actively its EPI efforts to address the challenges confronting the USA and the rest of the world.

NOTE

1. The interstate commerce clause in the US Constitution provides the national government with the power to regulate commerce across states. The national government has used this clause to support national environmental laws that affect commercial actors and can help level the playing field in the inter-state market.

BIBLIOGRAPHY

Aberbach, J. and Rockman, B. (1988), 'Mandates or mandarins? Control and discretion in the modern administrative state', *Public Administration Review*, March/April, 606–612.

ASIWPCA (Association of State Water Pollution Control Administrators) (2001), *Historical Municipal Wastewater Treatment Infrastructure Funding*, http://www.asiwpca.org/, accessed 29 June 2007.

ASIWPCA (Association of State Water Pollution Control Administrators) (2003), *Historical Municipal Wastewater Treatment Infrastructure Funding*, http://www.asiwpca.org/, accessed 4 January 2007.

ASIWPCA (Association of State Water Pollution Control Administrators) (2004), *Clean Water Act Thirty Year Retrospective: History and Documents Related to the Federal Statute*, ed. Brian Van Wye), Washington DC: ASIWPCA.

Austin, J., Carter, J, Klein, B. and Schang, S. (2005), *Judging NEPA: A 'Hard Look' at Judicial Decision Making Under the National Environmental Policy Act*, Washington DC: Environmental Law Institute.

Babbington, C. and Blum, J. (2005), 'On capitol hill, a flurry of GOP victories', *Washington Post*, 30 July, A-1.

Baker, S. and McCormick, J. (2004), 'Sustainable development: comparative understandings and responses', in Norman Vig and Michael Faure (eds) *Green Giants? Environmental Policies of the United States and the European Union*, Cambridge, MA: MIT Press.

Beardon, D. (2004), *Highway and Transit Program Reauthorization: An Analysis of Environmental Protection Issues*, Congressional Research Service, 21 June, Washington DC: Library of Congress.

Bernstein, J., Cooper, J. and Claassen, R. (2004), 'Agriculture and the environment in the United States and EU', in M.A. Normile and S.E. Leetmaa (eds) *US–EU Food and Agriculture Comparisons*,WRS-04-04, www.ers.usda.gov/publications/WRS0404/WRS0404g.pdf accessed 6 August 2005.

Blum, J. (2005), 'Energy tax breaks total $14.5 billion', *Washington Post*, 28 July, A-4.

Brown, S. and Kiefer, M. (2003), 'ECOS Budget Survey: Budgets are Bruised, but Still Strong', *ECO-States*, Summer, pages 10–15 www.ecos.org/files/892_file_2003BudgetsArticle.pdf, accessed 17 March 2008.

Claassen, R., Breneman, V., Bucholtz, S. Cattaneo, A., Johansson, R. and Morehart, M. (2004), *Environmental Compliance in US Agriculture Policy: Past Performance and Future Potential: A Report from the Economic Research Service*, www.ers.usda.gov/publications/AER832/, accessed 6 August 2005.

CEQ (Council on Environmental Quality) (1997), *National Environmental Policy Act, 25th Anniversary Report: Council on Environmental Quality – 1994–1995*, Washington DC: US Government Printing Office.

Collins, R. (2006), *The Environmental Protection Agency: Clean Up America's Act*, Westport, CT: Greenwood Press.

EDF (US Environmental Defense Fund) (2006), SAFETEA-LU *Transportation Reauthorization: Environmental Scorecard*, 21 February, Updated Edition, www.environmentaldefense.org/documents/4726_TransScorecard.pdf, accessed 1 April 2007.

Greenblatt, A. (2005), 'Observer – getting smarter: the smart-growth movement isn't making much noise these days, but it's learning how to win', *Governing*, August, 15–16.

Hoornbeek, J. (2000), 'Information and environmental policy: a tale of two agencies', *Journal of Comparative Policy Analysis*, 2 (2), 145–187.

Hoornbeek, J. (2004), 'Policy-making institutions and water policy outputs in the European Union and the United States', *Journal of European Public Policy*, 11 (3), 461–496.

Horan, T., Dittmar, H. and Jordan D. (1999),'ISTEA and the new era in transportation policy: sustainable communities from a federal initiative', in D. Mazmanian and M. Kraft (eds), *Toward Sustainable Communities: Transition and Transformations in Environmental Policy*, Cambridge, MA: MIT Press.

Kiely, K. (2005), 'Energy policy overhaul on way', *USA Today*, 29–31 July, 1.

Mazmanian, D. and Kraft, M. (eds) (1999), *Toward Sustainable Communities: Transition and Transformations in Environmental Policy*, Cambridge, MA: MIT Press.

OECD (Organisation for Economic Cooperation and Development) (2004), *Agriculture and the Environment: Lessons Learned from a Decade of OECD Work*, www.oecd.org/dataoecd/15/28/33913449.pdf, accessed 20 August 2005.

Oldham, K. (2003), *President Richard Nixon Signs Senator Henry Jackson's National Environmental Policy Act into Law on January 1 1970*, www.historylink.org/essays/output.cfm?file_id=5615, accessed 7 August 2005.

Persson, A. (2004), *Environmental Policy Integration: An Introduction*, Policy Integration for Sustainability (PINTS) background paper, Stockholm: Stockholm Environment Institute.

Portney, K. (2003), *Taking Sustainable Cities Seriously: Economic Development, the Environment, and Quality of Life in American Cities*, Cambridge, MA: MIT Press.

Siy E., Koziol, L. and Rollins D. (2001), *The State of the States*, San Francisco, CA: Renewable Resource Institute.

Smith, Z. (2000), *The Environmental Policy Paradox*, 3rd edn, Upper Saddle River, NJ: Prentice Hall.

TRB (US Transportation Research Board) (2002), *TRB Report Summary: The Congestion Mitigation and Air Quality Improvement Program – Assessing 10 Years of Experience*, TRB Special Report 264, Washington DC: Transportation Research Board.

US Federal Government (1999), *Clean Water Action Plan: The First Year*, Washington DC: US Federal Government.

USDA (US Department of Agriculture) (2002), *Strategic Plan for 2002–2007*, Washington DC: US Department of Agriculture.

USDOE (US Department of Energy) (2003), *The Department of Energy Strategic Plan*, Washington DC: Office of Program Analysis and Evaluation, US Department of Energy.

USDOE (US Department of Energy) (2004), Energy overview in *Energy Information Administration Annual Energy Review 2004*, Washington DC: US Department of Energy, http://tonto.eia.doe.gov/FTPROOT/multifuel/=038404.pdf, accessed 5 September 2005.

USDOT (US Department of Transportation) (2003), *Department of Transportation Strategic Plan: 2003–2008*, Washington DC: US Department of Transportation.

USEPA (US Environmental Protection Agency) (1987), *Unfinished Business: A Comparative Assessment of Environmental Problems – Overview Report*, Washington DC: Office of Policy, Planning, and Evaluation, US Environmental Protection Agency.

USEPA (US Environmental Protection Agency) (1990), *Reducing Risk*, Washington DC: EPA Science Advisory Board.

USEPA (US Environmental Protection Agency) (2006a), *History: EPA's Budget and Workforce, 1970–2003*, www.epa.gov/history/org/resources/budget.htm, accessed 9 October 2006.

USEPA (US Environmental Protection Agency) (2006b), *USDA and EPA Sign Water Quality Credit Trading Agreement, Agreement Offers Farmers and Ranchers Market-based Incentives to Improve Water Quality*, Press Release from EPA News Room, www.epa.gov/water/waternews/2006/061027.html, accessed 24 October 2006.

Vig, N. (2003), 'Presidential leadership and the environment', in N. Vig and M. Kraft (eds) *Environmental Policy: New Directions for the Twenty First Century*, 5th edn, Washington DC: Congressional Quarterly Press.

Womach, J. (2005), *Previewing the 2007 Farm Bill*, Report for Congress, Washington DC: Congressional Research Service, The Library of Congress, 18 August.

14. Australia

Andrew Ross

INTRODUCTION

Australia can be characterized as being cautiously supportive of sustainable development (Lafferty and Meadowcroft 2000: 412). Although it has not led the world on EPI, it has adopted some distinctive institutions and instruments in areas where environmental protection has been seen as a core policy concern, for example, natural resource management. In other areas such as industry, transport and health, sustainability objectives are not considered explicitly in the development of policies or programs (Productivity Commission 1999: xx).

In Australia, primary responsibility for land use and conservation matters rest with the eight state and territory governments. The Australian government provides leadership and coordination, plus some funding. Natural resource management policies are a partnership between the Australian, state and territory governments. Australia has adopted a light-touch style of EPI, preferring market-based approaches and voluntary government–industry agreements to hierarchical approaches (Papadakis and Grant 2002: 32). The national government has pursued a policy of cooperative federalism (Toyne 1994: 9). In recent years, it has limited intervention to urgent national problems, policies that affect several states and obligations under international agreements. In these areas it has been increasingly involved as the initiator and coordinator of national environmental strategies (OECD 2001: 124).

This chapter proceeds with a brief history of Australian environmental policy. The main part provides an analysis of Australia's experience in implementing EPI, drawing on a review of the main instruments used to promote EPI in six of the Australian states and territories.[1] It does so because of the important role that the states and territories play in managing the environment. This analysis reveals that Australian governments have used a wide range of centralized and decentralized instruments to promote EPI. This chapter concludes with a discussion of the main success factors, barriers and gaps affecting EPI in Australia, and examines what lessons can be drawn from the Australian experience for other jurisdictions.

HISTORY

The history of environmental policy and EPI in Australia has been shaped by its geographical, socioeconomic and institutional features. Firstly, Australia is a very large, lightly populated and resource-rich nation. It has a very large landmass (7.68 million km²). The population density averages 2.3 inhabitants per square kilometre, but most of the population is concentrated around the coasts and is highly urbanized. Air quality is generally good; Australia does not normally suffer from the acute air pollution problems that afflict other industrialized countries (OECD 1998: 25). Australia's economic output is relatively dependent on the environment and natural resources.[2] Land and water resources are being degraded in many parts of the continent (OECD 1998: 23).

Secondly, Australia's federal intergovernmental system involves relatively weak central control of environmental policy and substantial devolution of responsibilities. Australia is a federal parliamentary state, divided into six states and two territories. The environment is omitted from the national constitution, that is, it is a residual power. Most environmental policy and legislative responsibilities rest with state and territory governments, and many day-to-day government decisions affecting the environment are taken by local government. National government has constitutional powers such as trade and commerce, taxation and external affairs that enable national control of most large-scale development. But it rarely exercises those powers, despite the fact that it receives most of the revenue from taxation. National governments have been reluctant to interfere in areas of states' responsibility (Toyne 1994: 178). It has been argued that a stronger national approach to the environment is needed because of the size and scale of many environmental problems (Knockenberger *et al.* 2000: 18).

Although the Australian government sets the framework for EPI, the appropriate balance between its roles and responsibilities (vis à vis public and private, national, state and local) is a central question for policy makers in Australia, as in many other comparable federations. The history of EPI in Australia can be divided into three phases: the initial development of environmental policies and institutions (prior to 1989); the development of an integrated national sustainability strategy and associated policies (from 1989 to 1996); and consolidation and re-prioritization (post-1996).

Developments Prior to 1989

In the 1950s and 1960s, Australian state governments took responsibility for the environment, which was perceived as a resource to be exploited. At first, the adverse consequences appeared to be relatively minor and therefore state and local government policy-making responses to the ensuing damage appeared rather later than in most other OECD countries (OECD 1998: 28). By the mid-1960s, partly prompted by overseas developments, state governments started to develop some environmental regulation, for example to tackle air pollution. An interstate ministerial council for the environment was established in 1972.

The Whitlam Labour Government established a government agency with responsibility for the environment, known as the Australian National Parks and Wildlife Service. The 1974 Environment Protection (Impact of Proposals) Act included a legislative provision to undertake Environmental Impact Assessment (EIA). As the political salience of environmental issues grew in the 1970s and 1980s, so too did the environmental policy constituency. In 1983, following national political protests, the Commonwealth government acted under its foreign relations power to halt the construction of a dam in a world heritage area on Tasmania's Franklin River. In 1984, the government adopted Australia's first major environmental strategy, the National Conservation Strategy. By the late 1980s, a national debate had emerged which questioned the long-term sustainability of Australia's resource-based economy; for example, the green independents party attracted nearly 20 per cent of the vote in Tasmania (Grant and Papadakis 2004: 284–285).

1989–1996: the Development of an Integrated Sustainability Strategy

In the 1990s, the emphasis of national and international environmental policy shifted from pollution to the management of global environmental systems and global and national environmental resources. Australia has faced both growing domestic policy challenges owing to natural resource depletion and environmental degradation, and growing international pressures for action on matters such as climate change, biodiversity conservation and the management of transboundary resources and pollution. Following the development of community-based land care groups in the early 1980s, in 1989 the Australian government committed $360 million to a national Decade of Landcare Program (Curtis 2003: 442). Landcare mobilized a large cross-section of the rural population and increased community awareness of the costs of land degradation. Community groups developed some low-cost integrated and adaptive approaches. However, an unclear definition of the roles and responsibilities of regional organizations, a lack of strategic approaches to biodiversity conservation and funding shortfalls have all reduced the effectiveness of this program.

The Hawke Labour government adopted a proactive and consensual style of EPI. In 1989, the Australian Prime Minister released a comprehensive environmental statement entitled *Our Country Our Future*. This statement foreshadowed increased national government action to conserve land, water and biodiversity, and to tackle climate change as well as address air pollution and waste issues (Australian Government 1989). Following extensive stakeholder and community consultations led by a set of working groups, in 1992 the Australian Government released a National Strategy for Ecologically Sustainable Development (NSESD) (Australian Government 1992). This strategy defined core objective and guiding principles for sustainable development and set out new policies and institutions to implement them in eight economic sectors and across 22 inter-sectoral issues. The strategy was gradually superseded by subsequent policy developments, but when it was published it represented the first comprehensive national initiative on EPI.

After 1992, EPI under Keating's Labour government reflected the devolved and deregulated approach set in train with microeconomic reform. The government delayed implementation of most recommendations of the ecologically sustainable development working groups, but endorsed the 1992 Intergovernmental Agreement on the Environment (Economou 1999: 71). This agreement defined and delimited national, state and local government responsibilities and interests in relation to the environment, and set out agreed principles and schedules in relation to environmental policy. In 1997, the *Council of Australian Governments: Heads of Agreement on Commonwealth/States Roles and Responsibilities for the Environment* (essentially a revised Intergovernmental Agreement on the Environment) gave a clear statutory basis for national government responsibility for environmental issues of national significance. These are limited to: world heritage properties; Ramsar wetlands of international importance; threatened species and communities; migratory species protected under international agreements; nuclear activities; and the offshore marine environment. This Agreement also represented a further step towards the implementation of EPI. National environmental legislation, which was consolidated in the Environmental Protection and Biodiversity Conservation Act 1999, gave effect to national government responsibilities for matters of national environmental significance.

1996 to 2006: Consolidation and Re-prioritization

In 1996, the election of a Conservative coalition government led to a consolidation and re-prioritization of EPI activities. Coalition governments have tended to define the national interest in economic terms. Not surprisingly, it made no effort to update the NSESD. Sustainable development and EPI have been pursued through initiatives to address major cross-sectoral environmental issues such as natural resource management and climate change. Although there is still conflict between departments responsible for industry and the environment, this has become less severe. In the 2000s, the traditional regulatory-based instruments of environmental policy were supplemented with economic instruments and voluntary measures, highlighting the preference for decentralized and deregulatory approaches. However, the success of these 'new' environmental policy instruments (Jordan *et al.* 2003) depends on continuing government involvement to set incentives and penalties. For example, the establishment of water markets is complex and costly (Connell *et al.* 2005: 94–95), and requires a good deal of central steering.

The centrepiece of the coalition's environmental policy was the AUS $1.25 billion Natural Heritage Trust, aimed at improving natural resources management in rural and regional areas, building on the community-based Landcare movement. The Trust included a number of institutional innovations to encourage EPI: it was jointly managed by the ministers responsible for agriculture and the environment; and a special joint implementation team including staff from the agriculture and environment departments administers the program (while the departments have retained their separate entities). The Trust's programs were developed on a decentralized (regional) basis (that is, based on integrated regional development plans, sometimes including detailed programs of action) and implemented through catchment-based organizations that cut across state and local administrative boundaries (Australian Government 2005).

During this period, the national government also brought forward a number of strategies and policies that addressed key sustainable development issues (Yencken and Wilkinson 2000: 310–314). Important national strategies in addition to the National Strategy for Ecologically Sustainable Development include Australia's Oceans Policy, the National Forest Policy, the National Greenhouse Strategy, the National Strategy for the Conservation of Australia's Biological Diversity, the National Action Plan for Salinity and Water Quality and the National Water Initiative. These have generally specified policy objectives, principles and some program elements, but their impact on EPI has been lessened by the relative absence of quantitative targets, timetables or responsibilities for implementation.

EPI IN PRACTICE

Administrative Instruments

Constitutional instruments and legislation
Australia's Constitution does not give the national government specific powers to legislate in relation to the environment, but it has nonetheless

intervened in a limited number of cases by using its broader constitutional powers. For example, international world heritage obligations provided the rationale for national action to prevent the construction of a dam on Tasmania's Franklin river (see above). The intergovernmental agreement on the environment also provided the national government with authority to intervene in relation to matters of national environmental significance.

Incorporating environmental integration and sustainability principles into legislation can be an important instrument for embedding EPI in government policy and practice. But although principles of ecologically sustainable development have been expressed in over 120 Australian statutes, thus far, the manner of their inclusion has not been linked to specific actions. Consequently, they have failed to instruct decision makers or aid legal interpretation. This has left decision makers heavily reliant on political commitment in order to uphold the law in the face of objections from adversely affected parties. However, in Australia, political commitment and implementation capacity have been relatively weak in some sectors. For example, Australia's major environmental law – the Environmental Protection and Biodiversity Conservation Act 1999 – requires details of any action impacting on matters of national environmental significance to be referred to the national environmental minister. But before 2005, only a quarter of referred actions were deemed to require assessment under the Act, and only 2 (0.2 per cent) were refused. There were very few referrals by the agriculture, fisheries and forestry sector. Moreover, the national government did not have all the necessary administrative systems and infrastructure in place to monitor compliance and enforce conditions (Macintosh and Wilkinson 2005: 148).

Central coordination instruments
The key bodies for intergovernmental environmental policy coordination and integration in Australia are the intergovernmental ministerial councils. These councils include ministers from the federal government and each of the eight states and territories. They cover cross-cutting matters such as such as: environmental protection and heritage; natural resource management; primary industries; minerals and petroleum resources; energy; and transport. These councils are an important forum for discussion of interjurisdictional issues and preparing common national approaches to them. It has been argued that while there has been some improvement in communication and coordination between the councils responsible for environment, agriculture and natural resource management, communications between the minerals (and petroleum), energy and health councils and their environmental counterpart have been less productive (Productivity Commission 1999: 98–101 and 107).

Both the federal and state governments have specific cabinet committees that deal with environmental and sustainable development issues. For example, the Australian Government's Sustainable Environment Committee takes a particular interest in natural resources management and greenhouse policy. These committees have the potential to play a powerful role in facilitating EPI, but their proceedings are generally confidential and there has been little evaluation of their impact. According to officials, their purpose seems to be more about managing cabinet business in an efficient and cost-effective manner, than embedding and implementing EPI across government. The Sustainable Environment Committee certainly does not exercise the degree of coordination and political leadership provided by some European cabinet-level coordination committees such as those in Germany and the UK (see Chapters 9 and 12 respectively).

State governments have, however, shown some commitment to EPI through high-level inter-agency coordination instruments. In South Australia, the Office of the Executive Committee of Cabinet coordinates the implementation of the State Plan and ensures that targets in the Plan are integrated into agency plans. It also undertakes dialogues with agency chief executive officers (CEOs) to link plan targets and budgets. In New South Wales, CEO consultation and coordination groups have been established to promote 'whole of government' collaboration. These arrangements have been effective in ensuring smoother communication between CEOs, better problem solving and better program integration. The 2006 New South Wales State Plan establishes further high-level coordination arrangements, namely: a new Cabinet Standing Committee on State Plan Performance; a Program Management Office to monitor all agency progress against the State Plan; and a new budget process where agency results, service plans and business plans will need to align with the State Plan.

Bureaucratic instruments
A very wide range of bureaucratic coordination instruments at all levels of government in Australia are relevant to EPI. These include coordinators, working groups, task forces and teams which develop or implement specific policy initiatives and carry out particular tasks. While many of these instruments do not have EPI as their primary goal, those which are primarily concerned with taxes and subsidies, agriculture, energy and transport, may have important environmental policy implications. Most coordination instruments are temporary, ad hoc, and neither transparent nor accountable, other than to bureaucratic executives. These instruments are continually evolving, and the choice of what and how to coordinate and

aggregate reflects the preferences of the government of the day as well as administrative priorities.

The political commitment to EPI expressed through these instruments has been highly variable. Individually, their contribution to EPI depends on their mandate and authority, the capacity of their members to consider environmental issues, whether their leaders emphasize the importance of EPI, and the relative seniority and resources available to environmental policy representatives. Successful 'whole of government' EPI has been assisted by the formation of high level 'adhocracies' able to design complex policy initiatives drawing on the expertise of not only their own agencies, but also the wider bureaucracy and external stakeholders (Lindquist 2004: 21). In the area of natural resource management, the experiment of national, state, regional and local governments working together to address sustainable agriculture in a sustainable environment and a sustainable social setting has introduced a totally new way of working across (and between) governments and stakeholders (Beale 2004: 25). However, stronger coordination can result in a weakening of environmental consideration as well as strengthening, and in aggregate it is very difficult to assess the overall impact of administrative instruments.

Lead agencies
Australian jurisdictions have used a wide range of agency models to promote EPI. Broadly these can be divided into three categories: those led by the environment minister; those led by the first minister (prime minister or premier); and hybrids involving mergers between environment and other agencies. At the national level, EPI has been led by the Department of Environment and Heritage (since early 2007, the Department of Environment and Water), which has provided a strong skills base and enthusiastic support. There has been less support from most other agencies, exacerbated by an emphasis on economic objectives and a lack of strong political and administrative backing.

The Australian government has also experimented with some innovative structures to promote EPI. In 1998 the Australian Greenhouse Office was established to provide national coordination for greenhouse policy. Since December 2002, the ministers responsible for the environment and industry have been jointly responsible for climate change matters, with the Australian Greenhouse Office reporting to both. Two high-level officials' groups have been set up to ensure a 'whole of government' approach to climate change (Australian Greenhouse Office 2004). However, these coordination arrangements have not been able to reconcile national differences of views on greenhouse strategy. In 2004, the greenhouse office was absorbed into the environment department.

The sustainability offices in South Australia, Western Australia and the Australian Capital Territory provide examples of policy coordination led by the first minister. These examples show that leadership by the first minister gives additional legitimacy and authority to environmental policy coordination and helps ensure that other ministers and their agencies support environmental and sustainable development strategies and policies. At the same time, this experience coincides with overseas findings that there can be some narrowing or dilution of environmental objectives, and a risk of severe loss of momentum if the political agenda changes.

The location of environmental responsibilities in a multifunctional ministry has the advantage that it is easier for environmental issues to be put on the agenda in that particular area (for example, urban planning or agricultural policy). Informal and formal communication and coordination can be increased and appreciation of environmental issues improved. But gains in some aspects of EPI can be offset by losses in others. For example, in Victoria, the integration of natural resource, environment and planning functions has been achieved at the expense of the loss of momentum in agricultural and environmental policy collaboration that existed when these policy functions were separated.

Finally, in most agencies, the uptake of procedures and instruments to embed EPI has been much more limited. Few agency charters or mission statements refer to the environment, and only a minority of agencies have environmental policies (other than saving resources) or dedicated environmental units. While environmental knowledge is increasing, there is still a long way to go (Department of Environment and Conservation 2006).

Advisory and consultative bodies
Most of the states and territories have established high-level advisory and consultative bodies including industry and community representatives to advise their governments and in some cases to promote EPI. However, the aims of these bodies vary. For example, the South Australian Premier's Round Table on Sustainability operates in a relatively public manner and seeks to influence public debates. By contrast, the Western Australian Sustainability Round Table provides advice to the Premier and carries out specific projects, whereas the Victorian Sustainability Advisory Council is a relatively private body that acts as a sounding board for ministerial ideas. There has been little evaluation of Australian advisory bodies, and as with similar overseas bodies, it is difficult to assess their value with respect to EPI (Ross 2005: 137).

Many government research and development bodies carry out and coordinate environmentally relevant research, notably the Commonwealth

Science and Industrial Research Organization, the Rural Research and Development Corporations, and Land and Water Australia. There are also many ad hoc instruments that link environmental science to policy, but there is a lack of systematic coordination between environmental research and government decision making. In Australia, there is no equivalent to the powerful scientific advisory bodies found in the Netherlands and Germany. The Prime Minister's Science, Engineering and Innovation Council has the potential to play an influential role in the integration of environmental science into government decision making, but it only meets twice a year and rarely discusses environmental matters.

Decentralized administrative instruments
Much of the implementation of national and state environment and sustainable development policies and programs takes place at the regional and local level. Decentralized natural resource management involves an extremely complex set of issues and stakeholders at five different levels of administration (national, state, regional, local, community group). Regional catchment-based management bodies have been created to provide an institutional instrument linking state and local activities, using a consultative approach and supporting the activities of local groups (Curtis and Lockwood 2000: 61). However, the capabilities and hence effectiveness of these bodies and their commitment to improved environmental management have varied quite widely. Structural arrangements vary between jurisdictions, from independent statutory catchment management organizations, to state-guided coordination groups. Regional organizations often have limited autonomy and powerful traditions, and cultures within state departments constrain effective 'whole of government' integration (Farrier *et al.* 1998: 185). Funding and capacity-building commitments vary widely between catchments. There is also a risk that catchment management plans may remain unimplemented because of legal or political challenges on behalf of landholders wishing to maintain current land and water uses (Reeve 1999: 16). In this context, effective decision-making processes have to be put in place (Syme 2003: 14–15), together with improved arrangements to reconcile conflicting interests.

Experience so far illustrates the importance of clearly defining roles and responsibilities for organizations at all levels, backed by political leadership capable of ensuring diverse stakeholder participation, including regional bodies (Bellamy *et al.* 2002: xii–xiii). Implementation of catchment management over large scales in the Northern Territory has underlined the potential benefits of integrated consultative planning, cross-sector and cross-agency cooperation, engaging diverse stakeholders (in this case, pastoral and indigenous landowners), and adequate funding and time for consultation and implementation.

Greening of government operations
Federal and state departments and agencies have made more progress with greening of government operations than other processes to embed EPI. The relatively high priority given to this reflects a desire by agencies to show leadership to the private sector and the community more generally, and the fact that it is easier (though not completely straightforward) for agencies to exercise control over their operational outcomes than policy or program targets. All jurisdictions have engaged in greening of government operations to reduce the use of energy, water and paper. Generally, the framework for this has been defined on a 'whole of government' basis, with the detailed strategies and targets left to agencies. Recently, however, some jurisdictions have introduced centrally defined tasks and in some cases specific targets (see the discussion of specification of output and tasks in Chapter 3).

Green Budgeting

Australia does not posses a comprehensive green budgeting framework. Even some of the basic elements of such a framework are absent or weak. For example, government expenditure on the environment has risen rapidly in recent years, from AUS$1.8 billion in 2002–03 to AUS$3.9 billion in 2006–07 (Department of the Environment and Heritage 2006). Overall, Australia employs relatively few environmentally related taxes, and revenue from such taxes as a percentage of total tax revenue is relatively low. A survey in January 2005 showed that Australia had in place only four environmental taxes: a waste levy in New South Wales; an oil recycling levy; an aircraft noise levy; and an ozone protection and synthetic greenhouse gas levy (OECD 2006). In addition, there are a number of incentive arrangements that use a mix of voluntary commitment and market forces to encourage environmentally desirable behaviour. Australia's absolute levels of vehicle fuel taxation are relatively low. Australia's agricultural sector receives relatively little support compared to other OECD countries (OECD 1998: 134).

Australian governments have introduced financial management, budgeting and reporting on an output and outcomes basis. However, environmental assessment of government budgets and the establishment of quantitative environmental targets is not widely practised in Australia. There have, however, been moves in Victoria and South Australia to align budget proposals with state plan objectives and targets, including some environmental targets.

Strategies and/or Strategy Developing Processes

Australian jurisdictions have made substantial progress in setting directions through broad sustainable development plans and strategies, and thematic environmental strategies. The NSESD includes core objectives and guiding principles for sustainable development. The action plan in the NSESD has been overtaken by subsequent developments, but the overarching goals and principles are widely referenced and have been incorporated into many policies and pieces of legislation. There is increasing interest in sustainable development policy coordination by means of market instruments and decentralized governance processes.

In recent years, Australian states and territories have included environmental sections in their state plans, and/or adopted sustainable development strategies. While there are no national sustainable development targets or systematic monitoring of progress to provide feedback for policy development, Victoria and South Australia have included measurable environmental targets in their state plans. Western Australia, Victoria and the Australian Capital Territory have comprehensive sustainable development strategies, and in Victoria this strategy is supported by a specific budget. New South Wales has generally achieved sustainability objectives by means of environmental and land-use planning and a range of government programs. However, the 2006 New South Wales State Plan included sustainable development goals and targets. The Northern Territory has pursued EPI and sustainability through individual programs rather than any specific plan or strategy.

Both the Australian government and the states have a wide range of environmental and natural resources management thematic strategies covering topics such as greenhouse gases, biodiversity, water resources and waste management. These represent a considerable step forward towards ensuring that environmental policies and programs are internally consistent and take account of development strategies, but they are often under-resourced and not energetically followed through, especially in the sectoral ministries. Most new strategies and policy proposals are subject to some degree of consultation; efforts have been made to engage stakeholders and members of the public. For example, consultative committees are established for each major fishery, and jurisdictions have undertaken significant public consultation on natural resource management and water reform, especially via structures such as catchment management authorities in New South Wales and Victoria.

By contrast, there are few sustainability strategies or transition instruments associated with the work of the economic sectors, other than some components of the state plans governing water, greenhouse gas abatement, energy efficiency and public transport. In general, the economic sectors and their attendant bureaucracies have exhibited a relatively low commitment to EPI. Strategic economic restructuring has been constrained by fears about a loss of national economic competitiveness and jobs, and resistance from developers and sectional interest groups. The OECD found that while Australia had made progress in developing a framework for integrating environmental and economic policies, in many cases economic objectives had a higher priority than environmental concerns (OECD 2001). For example, Australia's energy structure has a strong influence on its response to climate change (OECD 2001: 145). Australian policy has been criticized for an inadequate focus on measures for energy efficiency and the potential for innovation for new technology (Papadakis 2000: 42). Some state governments have started to take independent action. For example, the South Australian Premier has announced a climate change strategy, targets of reducing greenhouse gases by 60 per cent of 1990 levels by 2050 underpinned by legislation, and a new climate change and sustainability unit in his department, charged with coordinating implementation of the strategy.

Policy Appraisal and Reporting Systems

Assessment, reporting and evaluation processes are supposed to be to be part and parcel of best-practice policy making in Australia. But at both the national and the state level, the analysis of the environmental impacts of policies and programs has been weak. This lack of commitment to environmental assessment makes it difficult to present a business case for further action to support environmentally sustainable policies and programs. An inquiry by the Productivity Commission on the implementation of ecologically sustainable development by Australian government departments and agencies concluded that:

> At the national level departments and agencies do not always satisfactorily apply existing ex ante assessment instruments such as regulatory impact and environmental impact assessment when they are formally required. Monitoring the effectiveness of policies and programs aimed at implementing ecologically sustainable development does not appear to be undertaken routinely by departments and agencies, and there appeared to be even fewer examples where the results of monitoring activities are incorporated into policy or program revisions via feedback mechanisms. A tendency to act on problems which are immediately visible together with a shortage of required data and information of long-term problems, means that departments and agencies can fail to give adequate considerations to issues likely to be a problem in the long-term (Productivity Commission 1999: xxiii).

Environmental assessment processes
Integrated analysis of environmental, economic and social impacts of policies and programs, for example in Cabinet submissions, is very limited at the national and sub-national levels. The Office of Regulation Review coordinates the preparation of regulation impact assessments at the national level, including intergovernmental regulatory activity. The guidelines for consideration of regulatory proposals have been recently redrafted to require a broad assessment of environmental impacts (Office of Best Practice Regulation 2006: 4.13). Previously, less than 10 per cent of regulatory proposals were found to have any environmental impact. Until the 2006 guidelines are fully implemented, the inclusion and treatment of social and environmental impacts of regulatory change will remain open to case-by-case negotiation between the Office of Regulation Review, regulators and parties affected by regulation. Implementation of the new guidelines provides an opportunity to move towards more systematic or consistent analysis of environmental impacts, which can contribute to greater certainty for regulators and business.

Reporting and evaluation processes
Performance assessment and reporting should enable informed debate, policy learning and, eventually, potentially better implementation on environmental matters. However, the quality of environmental and sustainability reporting in Australia remains variable. Federal and state governments publish comprehensive state of the environment reports every three to five years, and some states also produce more regular public reports, although these tend to be selective, and highlight good news. Some states have now introduced sustainability reporting linked to state plans or sustainability strategies. Only federal, Australian Capital Territory and Western Australian agencies have produced sustainability reports thus far.

Federal departments and agencies are required to report on how the activities of the organization, its administration of legislation and the outcomes specified in its appropriations accord with the principles of ecologically sustainable development. But there is little commitment to implementing these reporting requirements. In 2002–03, the Australian Auditor General (Auditor General 2003: 15, pt. 13), concluded that there was 'considerable scope for improvement in the quality of federal agencies' annual reports'. Many agencies are focused solely on the impact of their operations on the natural environment, and are yet to come to terms with the broader implications of sustainable development. Few agencies had identified their most significant sustainable development issues or targets for their achievement.

There has been limited monitoring or evaluation of sustainability structures, policies and programs such as high-level monitoring of the state plans in Victoria and South Australia. But while many jurisdictions have undertaken some research on aspects of sustainable development and on environmental problems and risks, the capacity for undertaking sustainability reviews is weak. The Victorian Commissioner for Environmental Sustainability and the Australian Capital Territory Commissioner for the Environment have relatively narrow (that is, environmentally focused) mandates, and it is too soon to assess their impact. There is no systematic evaluation of sustainable development performance equivalent to that carried out by the independent commissioners in Canada or New Zealand. Improved evaluation could be achieved through sustainable development audits by the Auditors General in all jurisdictions, or by an independent auditor such as a sustainable development commissioner (Yencken and Wilkinson 2000: 331).

Strategic Environmental Assessment

In Australia, the use of SEA is increasing but remains relatively limited. The SEA of nationally managed fisheries is required under the Environmental Protection and Biodiversity Conservation Act 1999 (sections 147–154), and the SEA of National Environmental Protection Measures is required under the National Environment Protection Council Act 1994. In the states, *ex ante* EIA is generally linked with the planning and development project approvals system. For example, Western Australia does have assessment processes for planning schemes and strategic (that is, large project) proposals and Tasmania has a process for assessing planning schemes and directives that apply to such schemes. Meanwhile, Victoria and Tasmania carry out assessments of environmental protection policies, and New South Wales assesses fisheries management schemes (Marsden and Ashe 2007).

SUMMARY DISCUSSION

A number of critical success factors, barriers and gaps could be said to have influenced the implementation of EPI in Australia. These are summarized in Table 14.1. The following paragraphs discuss the relationship between these and then draw together some concluding points about Australia's engagement with the principle of EPI.

A succession of Australian governments has chosen not to impose EPI on societal actors by using hierarchical instruments. Despite this

Table 14.1   Environmental policy integration in Australia: success factors, barriers and gaps

	Success factors	Barriers and gaps
Structural	Strong inter-jurisdictional and inter-agency cooperation; Clear roles and responsibilities for implementation of environmental policy integration; Wide consultation with affected stakeholders; Explicit recognition of different stakeholder values and interests, and processes for reconciling them.	Loss of momentum and persistence; Lack of incentives to implement resource-intensive policy integration processes.
Procedural	Well targeted communication instruments; Accessible, widely understood quantitative and qualitative assessment instruments; Connection of policy making processes with the scientific knowledge base.	Difficulty in expressing a business case for policy integration; Lack of knowledge of or access to models of implementation.
Strategic	Clear definition and direction for environmental policy; Institutional and transition instruments; Capacity to react and adapt to unanticipated international, national, legal, policy and market changes; A legislative mandate for policy Integration.	Inadequate communication and/or poor comprehension of sustainability agenda; Lack of constituency for environmental policy integration; Policy inertia owing to adverse economic impacts and inability to manage vested interests.
Leadership	High-level accessible ministerial and executive support, including prominent champions; Emphasis by ministers and executives that environmental policy integration is core business for all agencies.	Shortfall between stated political intentions, implementation and resources; Dominance of short-term perspectives.
Capacity	Effective monitoring, evaluation, audit and review processes; Adequate skills within units and agencies charged with policy integration.	Inadequate quantity or continuity of financial and human resources; Government budget procedures do not provide resources for interdepartmental coordination and action.

reluctance, a great variety of administrative instruments have been tried. Some of these have specifically aimed to improve EPI, for example by bringing together a particular range of interests. Others have reflected political priorities or personal preferences. Key success factors have included: the incorporation of clearly defined objectives and timetables; giving key agencies clearly specified roles and responsibilities; wide consultation with government and non-government stakeholders; and an explicit recognition that there are different stakeholder values and interests and that methods and processes are needed to reconcile them. Although there have been many individual examples of strong inter-jurisdictional and inter-agency cooperation, most of the high-level coordination committees have been relatively weak, task forces and teams have been relatively short lived, and no clearly preferred model for lead agencies has emerged. Coordination by first ministers and their agencies has not been a panacea either: it can increase political support for EPI, but it can also limit the EPI agenda if it increases the attention and resources devoted to upcoming environmental priorities such as climate change.

The loss of momentum arising from political and administrative changes, together with the short-term nature of the political cycle, have been major barriers to EPI. Most instances of restructuring have produced some improvements in EPI, but have also resulted in some costs, including the costs of changing from the previous arrangements. There has been little attempt to assess the costs of frequent change of organizational structures, including transaction costs, confusion about responsibilities for policy implementation, lack of policy persistence and staff and agency insecurity. These costs can outweigh the benefits of structural change. Moreover, EPI often involves expensive and resource-intensive processes, and there has been a lack of incentives and commitment to make fundamental changes, and a consequent reluctance by many bureaucrats to engage in cross-organizational collaboration.

In the context of frequent changes in policy priorities and administrative arrangements, accessible and widely understood instruments such as EIA could have played an important role in embedding EPI and sustainability objectives in decision making. They could have helped to ensure that EPI continued on a 'whole of government' basis, whatever strategies and structures were in place at a particular time. But in Australia, environmental and sustainable development policy principles have only been included in legislation and agency charters, administrative rules and codes of practice in the agencies most directly concerned with environmental policy. By contrast, industrial sectors have not been under an equivalent pressure to deliver greater EPI. Assessment instruments such as integrated policy appraisal and SEA have rarely been used in the analysis of new policies, legislative proposals or budget processes in the sectors. Sustainability analysis of government policies and programs in Australia has also been constrained by the lack of cross-government sustainability measurement and accounting frameworks which are broadly accepted and linked to existing national accounts and budget processes. This has made it difficult for environmental actors operating in and with the sectors to make a business case for EPI.

Australian jurisdictions have made substantial moves towards EPI through broad sustainable development plans and strategies and thematic environmental strategies covering topics such as greenhouse gases, biodiversity, water and waste management. In recent years, a limited number of these have included clearly defined goals and targets and apportionment of responsibilities for achieving them (for example, specification of outputs – see Chapter 3). However, the development of sustainability strategies for economic sectors, strategic economic restructuring and transition instruments have been constrained by fears about loss of competitiveness, resistance from economic interests, and lack of a strong constituency supporting EPI. There have been relatively few examples of political leadership with sufficient commitment to override vested interests. EPI has also been constrained by inadequate communication and/or poor comprehension of the complex sustainability agenda. Administrative leadership to make EPI core business has been strongest in relation to the greening of government operations, such as saving energy, water and paper.

The Australian experience indicates that the establishment of administrative instruments and sustainable development strategies is not sufficient to bring about EPI. Leadership, political and administrative culture and administrative capacity have a substantial role in determining the strength of EPI. Australian experience confirms the finding of studies conducted in other national contexts that high-level and persistent ministerial and executive support are critical to the success of EPI.

Key aspects of administrative capacity include effective monitoring, evaluation, audit and review processes, tied to adequate skills and resources to support EPI initiatives. Monitoring and evaluation are vital to provide policy feedback and allow learning. Resources need to be sufficient to support the communication, consultation and participation needed for implementing initiatives effectively on the ground. Many environmental and sustainability initiatives have failed to make much impact because they have been resourced inadequately.

Australia's experience with decentralized arrangements for natural resource management illustrates many of the above points. Some promising results have been achieved using community-based (and more recently, catchment-based) approaches to managing natural resources, but there is a number of uncertainties about their eventual outcomes. Decentralized planning and target setting have been justified on the basis of variations in regional circumstances, but methodologies and processes for setting targets and indicators are still being developed. It is also unclear whether a fair balance of interests can be achieved, or whether traditional powerbrokers and interest groups will dominate regional processes and block transition towards sustainable solutions. Likewise, the creation of markets to deal with issues such as water scarcity and salinity is turning out to be a complex legal and administrative exercise, and it is not possible to foresee the outcome. It remains unclear how much central steering and what incentives are needed to bring about effective participation and coordination. But it is clear that regional and local administrative bodies do not currently receive a strong enough mandate or sufficient resources.

Australia's decentralized and market-based approach to EPI is being severely tested in relation to the challenge of climate change. While it is true that there has been a significant amount of innovation in energy-saving and renewable technologies, the vested interests of natural resource-producing industries (such as coal and aluminium) and traditional power producers continue to dominate national policy. It seems unlikely that markets for carbon and renewable technologies can be established without stronger national political leadership and commitment, and incentives for new technologies. The national approach is fragmented, with a growing number of state government and industry initiatives taking a broader approach to climate change. It will be interesting to see if Prime Minister Kevin Rudd's 2007 decision to ratify the Kyoto Protocol significantly affects these arrangements in the coming years.

CONCLUSIONS

Australian experience suggests that there is no ideal set of structures, strategies and processes capable of driving EPI, and that leadership, cultural change and capacity building have key roles to play. Persistence, evaluation and feedback are more important than the precise model adopted. In Australia, as elsewhere, there have been many strategic initiatives and structural innovations, but effectiveness has been lost because initiatives are overtaken or abandoned before they have had time to prove themselves, or have been properly evaluated. This could be an outcome of the rapidly moving sustainable development policy agenda, but may also indicate that sustainable development has become, at least to some extent, an exercise in symbolic politics. Australian political leaders have not generally given the strong and lasting leadership needed to achieve and maintain EPI and support innovation in the face of resistance from vested interests. Australia has been a pioneer in decentralized sustainable natural resource management. It is too soon to assess fully the effectiveness of decentralized partnership-based approaches to important national issues such as natural resource management and climate change. But it is already clear that the requirements for central coordination, administrative capacity building and resources to deliver greater EPI have been underestimated.

NOTES

1. Namely, 'Policy Integration for Natural Resource Management in the Australian States and Territories', funded by Land and Water Australia. This was conducted by Stephen Dovers and Andrew Ross from the Centre for Resource and Environmental Studies at the Australian National University, in collaboration with officials from New South Wales, Victoria, South Australia, Western Australia, the Australian Capital Territory and the Northern Territory.
2. Primary industries account for over 8 per cent of national GDP, compared with an OECD average of 3 per cent, and natural resources generate 60 per cent of export earnings.

BIBLIOGRAPHY

Auditor General (2003), *Annual Reporting on Ecologically Sustainable Development*, Audit Report no. 41, Canberra: Australian National Audit Office, www.anac.gov. au/uploads/Documents/2002-03_Audit_Report_41.pdf, accessed 12 June 2008.
Australian Bureau of Statistics (2002), *Environmental Statistics Newsletter*, May, http://tinyur/.com/28njbg, accessed 27 February 2007.
Australian Government (1989), *Our Country Our Future*, Canberra: Australian Government.
Australian Government (1992), *National Strategy for Ecologically Sustainable Development*, Canberra: Australian Government.
Australian Government (2005), *Natural Heritage Trust Annual Report 2004–05*, Canberra: Australian Government.
Australian Greenhouse Office (2004), *Annual Report: 2004*, Canberra: Australian Greenhouse Office.
Beale, R. (2004), 'Reply to Evert Lindquist's presentation', *Canberra Journal of Public Administration*, 112, 24–25.
Bellamy, J., Ross, H., Ewing, S. and Meppem, T. (2002), *Integrated Catchment Management: Learning from the Australian Experience for the Murray-Darling Basin*, Canberra: CSIRO Sustainable Ecosystems.
Connell, D., Dovers, S. and Grafton, R.Q. (2005), 'An overview and analysis of the National Water Initiative', *Australasian Journal of Natural Resources Law and Policy*, 10, 81–108.
Curtis, A. (2003), 'The Landcare experience', in S. Dovers and S. Wild River (eds), *Managing Australia's Environment*, Sydney: The Federation Press.

Curtis, A. and Lockwood, M. (2000), 'Landcare and catchment management in Australia: lessons for state-sponsored community participation', *Society and Natural Resources*, 13, 61–73.

Department of Environment and Conservation (2006), *Who Cares About the Environment in 2006?*, Canberra: Department of Environment and Conservation, http://www.environment.nsw.gov.au/community/whocares 2006.htm, accessed 19 March 2008.

Department of the Environment and Heritage (2006), *Environment Budget Overview: 2006–2007*, Canberra: Department of Environment and Heritage, http://www.deh.gov.au/about/publications/budget/2006/ebo/index.html, accessed 27 February 2007.

Economou, N. (1999), 'Backward into the future: national policy making, devolution and the rise and fall of the environment', in K. Walker and K. Crowley (eds), *Australian Environmental Policy 2*, Sydney: University of New South Wales Press.

Farrier, D., Kelly, A., Comino, M. and Bond, M. (1998), 'Integrated land and water management in New South Wales: plans, problems and possibilities', *Australasian Journal for Natural Resources Law and Policy*, 5, 153–185.

Grant, R. and Papadakis, E. (2004), 'Challenges for global environmental diplomacy: Australia and the European Union', *Australian Journal of International Affairs*, 58, 279–292.

Jordan, A. Wurzel, R. and Zito, A. (eds) (2003), *New Instruments of Environmental Governance*, London: Frank Cass.

Knockenberger, M., Kinrade, P. and Thorman, R. (2000), *Natural Advantage: A Blueprint for a Sustainable Australia*, Melbourne: Australian Conservation Foundation.

Lafferty, W. and Meadowcroft, J. (2000), 'Patterns of governmental engagement', in W. Lafferty and J. Meadowcroft (eds), *Implementing Sustainable Development: Strategies and Initiatives in High Consumption Societies*, Oxford: Oxford University Press.

Lindquist, E. (2004), 'Connecting government: perspectives from Canada', *Canberra Journal of Public Administration*, 112, 15–23.

Macintosh, A. and Wilkinson, D. (2005), 'EPBC Act: the case for reform', *Australasian Journal for Natural Resources Law and Policy*, 10, 139–177.

Marsden, S. and Ashe, J. (2006), 'Strategic Environmental Assessment legislation in Australian states', *Australasian Journal of Environmental Management*, 13 (4), 205–215.

OECD (1998), *Environmental Performance Reviews: Australia*, Paris: OECD.

OECD (2001), *OECD Economic Surveys: Australia*, Paris: OECD.

OECD (2006), *The Political Economy of Environmentally Related Taxes*, Paris: OECD.

Office of Best Practice Regulation (2006), *Best Practice Regulation Handbook*, Canberra: Office of Best Practice Regulation.

Papadakis, E. (2000), 'Australia: ecological sustainable development in the national interest', in W. Lafferty and J. Meadowcroft (eds), *Implementing Sustainable Development: Strategies and Initiatives in High Consumption Societies*, Oxford: Oxford University Press.

Papadakis, E. and Grant, R. (2002), 'The politics of light-handed regulation: new environmental policy instruments in Australia', in A. Jordan, R. Wurzel and A. Zito (eds), *New Instruments of Environmental Governance*, London: Frank Cass.

Productivity Commission (1999), *Implementation of Ecologically Sustainable Development by Commonwealth Departments and Agencies*, Canberra: Productivity Commission.

Reeve, I. (1999), *Tiptoeing Round the Slumbering Dragon: Property Rights and Environmental Discourse in Rural Australia*, Institute for Rural Resources Occasional Paper, Armidale: Institute for Rural Resources.

Ross, A. (2005), 'National institutions for sustainable development: the challenge of long-term policy integration', *Australasian Journal for Natural Resources Law and Policy*, 10, 109–138.

Syme, G. (2003), Why Don't We Talk Social Sustainability When It Comes To Sharing the Water? Paper presented at the *National Water Conference*, Melbourne, 7–8 October.

Toyne, P. (1994), *The Reluctant Nation*, Sydney: ABC Books.

Yencken, D. and Wilkinson, D. (2000), *Resetting the Compass: Australia's Journey Towards Sustainability*, Canberra: CSIRO.

PART IV

Comparative conclusions

15. Environmental policy integration: an innovation in environmental policy?

Andrew Jordan and Andrea Lenschow

INTRODUCTION

The idea that 'the environment' functions as a single, integrated whole whereas the human world is divided into different parts, has been one of the guiding axioms of green thinking since time immemorial. The principle of EPI emerged as a policy response to the perceived need – forcefully expressed in the 1987 Brundtland Report (WCED 1987) – to address systematically the disconnection between the two. Were EPI ever to be implemented in the manner sought by the Brundtland Commission, it would amount to a profound innovation in the traditional orientation and structures of environmental policy making. Brundtland's ambitious vision was subsequently refined by the EEA (2005) into a series of concrete steps and an evaluation framework. But exactly how far have different jurisdictions moved to implement it?

In this chapter we shall address this question by summarizing the main empirical findings of the entire book. We begin by looking back across the empirical chapters in Parts II and III, and identify and explore the most salient trends in the way different jurisdictions have responded to Brundtland's call. This section aims to distinguish the instruments that have become a firm component of EPI processes from those that have not.

In Section 3 we once again reflect on the various meanings that have been ascribed to EPI in national and European debates. There is plenty of evidence in the existing literature which suggests that the strong interpretation of EPI (see Chapter 1) is rarely adopted. However, in what follows, we attempt to go one step further and trace more precisely the various meanings attached to the EPI concept: (a) through the entire policy- and decision-making process; and (b) in the various jurisdictions.

The conceptual meanings ascribed to EPI are – we surmised in Chapter 1 – likely to have affected the design of different policy systems. Existing studies have adopted different analytical approaches to explaining what shapes these jurisdictional designs. They commonly highlight one or more of the following: the institutional (in)compatibilities between the reforms; the level of political leadership (or commitment) in guiding and enforcing policy change; and policy makers' cognitions as a component of longer-term learning processes. In Section 4 we will revisit this continuing debate about the governance of EPI in the light of our empirical findings.

In Section 5 we shall explore what – if any – outcomes have been generated by these alterations 'on the ground' within the jurisdictions. Although an outcome perspective is not the main focus of this book, we shall begin to explore how far each jurisdiction has considered EPI from an outcome perspective, what steps (if any) it has taken to measure and evaluate outcome effectiveness, and what it has learned from doing so. Finally, in Section 6 we draw together the main findings of the whole book and look forward to the next phase of research on EPI and sustainable development.

BROAD TRENDS

Within and Across the Various Jurisdictions

The first thing to say is that the data presented in Parts II and III both confirm and further instantiate the broad phases of EPI activity identified in Chapters 1 and 2. In the early 1970s, a number of pioneering jurisdictions took innovative steps to strengthen their existing environmental policies to make them more coordinated and/or integrated with policies in the sectors. The EU – or at least the European Commission – stands out in this regard, having broadly committed itself to the principle of EPI as early as 1973 (see Chapter 8). Around the same time, Germany initiated a number of reforms including the adoption of Environmental Impact Assessment (EIA) (1975) and a wastewater levy (1976), the publication (in 1971) of an environmental programme, and the creation of a permanent committee (1972) of environmental directorates general, backed by new rules of administrative procedure. Meanwhile, the USA adopted the National Environmental Policy Act (NEPA) (requiring EIA and Strategic Environmental Assessment) and created the Council on Environmental Quality (CEQ), and the UK created the world's first integrated environmental ministry. These were innovative moves, but with hindsight they had shallow roots and were mostly focused on the 'environmental' sector, that is, environmental departments and agencies. Indeed, many owed their very existence to political campaigns mounted by environmental actors. When this pressure ebbed, the integrating instruments struggled to survive. We shall say more about their policy outcomes in a later section, but it was quite obvious from the empirical chapters in Part III that they failed to alter existing practices radically in the sectors, 'the core of [which] . . . remained largely unchanged' (Chapter 2).

In the late 1970s and early 1980s, this burst of political interest in and support for EPI subsided. The UK dismembered its integrated environmental department and the USA slashed the budget of the CEQ, blunted the radical thrust of NEPA and introduced a rival appraisal mechanism – Regulatory Impact Assessment (RIA) – to shift the emphasis back to reducing the economic costs of new regulations. In fact in Germany, this was accompanied by new instruments – 'mirror units' – whose job it was to 'reverse integrate' economic and social thinking back into the work of environmental actors.

The late 1980s witnessed the re-emergence of EPI in a number of jurisdictions, but this time in the form of an explicit policy principle harnessed to the increasingly popular concept of sustainable development. During this phase, the Nordic countries were the most ambitious pioneers. They established a number of significant policy innovations to implement EPI. For example, Norway issued a strategy on EPI (White Paper No. 46), a novel form of green budgeting (Environmental Profile of the State Budget – EPSB) and Strategic Environmental Assessment (SEA). In 1987, Sweden issued a general commitment to EPI in the form of a Government Bill. Finally, the UK created the first truly comprehensive national EPI system, which brought together new forms of appraisal and new administrative instruments within the context of an overarching environmental strategy (the 1990 White Paper). In all these examples, the publication of the Brundtland Report in 1987 proved to be an important motivating factor, a pattern which was maintained in the run-up to the 1992 Earth Summit. In the less progressive jurisdictions, the pace of reform was far slower; Australia published its first major environmental strategy statement in 1989.

This interest in and commitment to EPI continued to strengthen in the aftermath of Agenda 21 and the other international agreements adopted at Rio. In 1992, Norway adopted a constitutional commitment to EPI, supported by NEMS (a system of target setting, sectoral reporting and performance evaluation). Meanwhile, Sweden formalized its sectoral responsibility principle in law (1995) and established a new administrative instrument (National Environmental Quality Objectives – NEQOs) which, for the first time, set long-term EPI targets. Meanwhile, other actors began to behave more ambitiously, either by committing themselves more formally to EPI or establishing new and/or more effective implementing instruments. Germany, for example, initiated a system of ecological tax reform in 1999 and issued its first National Strategy for Sustainable Development (NSDS), harnessed to a suite of sustainability indicators known as 'the environmental barometer'. In 1997, the EU formally adopted a quasi-constitutional commitment to EPI (Article 6) and (in 1998) initiated the Cardiff Process of sectoral reporting and EPI target setting to put it into effect. Finally, the UK revamped its entire EPI system in 1997 (henceforth known as 'greening government') and established a system of green budgeting (1998) known as the Comprehensive Spending Review.

However, the chapters in Parts II and III reveal how in the 2000s support for EPI waned as concerns about the economic competitiveness of industry became more pronounced. Nowhere was this decline more prominent than in Norway – hitherto one of the most pioneering jurisdictions. In 2001, it discontinued its NEMS and stopped producing new sectoral environmental action plans. In the EU, the Cardiff Process tailed off and then eventually died, overshadowed by the newly emerging Lisbon Process, which aimed to boost economic growth and employment. One factor behind this shift in priorities was the perceived need to prepare the European economy for the challenges of globalization. But it also in part derived from the very logic of EPI, which encourages the sectors to share 'ownership' of environmental problems with the environmental sector. Unfortunately, the sectors responded not by strengthening, but by weakening EPI and sustainable development-related exercises such as the EU's sustainable development strategy, the Thematic Strategies and policy appraisal (or 'Impact Assessment').

Around this time, the political commitment to EPI – which had been more sharply and forcefully expressed in the 1990s – tangibly weakened, as jurisdiction after jurisdiction pledged itself to implement the somewhat broader and less explicitly environmentally focused goal of sustainable development. For example, in 2005, the Swedish environment ministry was renamed the Ministry of Sustainable Development. In both Sweden and the UK the priority throughout the 2000s shifted more towards what might be termed 'sustainable development integration'. In the UK the Green Ministers were renamed Sustainable Development Ministers and environmental policy appraisal was supplanted by RIA. The shift from a discourse of EPI to one emphasizing sustainable development was never just a semantic matter: EPI emphazizes the 'principled priority' of environmental factors in decision making, whereas sustainable development was used to suggest a process of balancing economic, social and environmental factors, which could conceivably involve weakening the last. It is telling that by the mid-2000s, the key drivers of environmental policy development at the national level in the EU were not EPI or even sustainable development-related programmes and measures, but more straightforwardly 'environmental' problems such as climate change, water scarcity and urban air quality.

Within and Across the Various Instruments

Chapters 1 and 2 identified three main types of EPI instrument: communicative, organizational and procedural. Recall that communicative instruments set out visions and longer-term objectives which are supposed to guide more detailed reform efforts, while leaving it to individual actors (for example, governments) in the targeted sectors to develop concrete operations. Examples include constitutional provisions, national environmental plans and sustainable development strategies. The chapters in Parts II and III powerfully confirmed the popularity of these instruments, while at the same time adding much greater detail to the figures presented in Chapter 2. For example, we learnt that very many communicative instruments are not used in a particularly hierarchical manner, for example, to prescribe certain minimum environmental requirements. Instead, they leave a great deal of leeway to the sectors to define these things for themselves. Using the terminology developed in Chapter 3, they therefore specify tasks to be completed (for example, to develop an EPI or sustainable development strategy), rather than outputs or fixed targets to be attained (for example, reductions in greenhouse gas emissions). Crucially, there are very few 'hard' communicative instruments that give environmental departments the power to veto sectoral policies (or even heavily amend them in policy appraisal processes to meet basic EPI requirements) or specify minimum standards required to safeguard environmental functions or resources (that is, those which normatively might be expected to receive 'principled priority').

The only two exceptions to this broad pattern are Sweden (with its NEQOs) and the UK (which has Public Service Agreements – PSAs). But even these two examples are rather open and flexible with regard to the specific outcomes expected. So, while the NEQOs appear to give force to the sectoral responsibility principle, they have never been used to elaborate more specific or binding targets to drive the performance of the sectors. Similarly, the PSAs in the UK could in principle have been a 'specification of output' (see Chapter 3), but in practice have contained very few environmental objectives. Those that have appeared tend to be couched in such non-specific (and non-constraining) terms as to be little different from mission statements.

Organizational instruments, by contrast, seek to alter the patterned context (for example, the rules and frameworks) in which policy decisions are made. Typically, these might seek to strengthen some actors (for example, environmental departments) at the expense of others, open up existing networks or even create completely new actors to push EPI forwards. Here, the existing literature refers to the amalgamation of existing departments, the establishment of green cabinets and other interdepartmental working groups. The chapters in Parts II and III confirmed that these are much less popular than communicative instruments. They also revealed that there are in fact very many different types of administrative instrument (and far more than are covered in Chapter 2 – for example, task forces, liaison officers and different types of cross-sectoral teams), but confirmed that most are barely used by any but a small minority of jurisdictions. Moreover, the chapters in Part III revealed a much fuller picture of how these and other organizational instruments are actually deployed (note their 'textbook' characteristics). For example, the green cabinets tend to have a rather broad, strategically focused role in policy making, that is, they tend not to get involved in mediating conflicts between sectors to the advantage of the environmental sector. Many are chaired by 'environmental' actors such as ministers of the environment, rather than a more hierarchically superior *primus inter pares* such as the prime minister. Similarly, the liaison officers described in Chapter 3 tend to function more as technicians (that is, providing assistance to the sectors on technical issues such as the conduct of appraisals when they request it) than 'policemen' or 'spies'. Overall, there does appear to be a marked preference for organizational instruments which are relatively quick and easy to establish (and hence to dismantle), and which give the impression that something has been done to implement EPI. By contrast, more consequential formats such as strong teams capable of identifying and resolving inter-sectoral conflicts to the benefit of the environment or powerful liaison officers are far less popular.

Finally, procedural instruments seek to intervene directly in and alter the direction of decision making so it supports EPI. Besides bureaucratic rules and standard operating procedures (for example, active information), which would be capable of significantly affecting daily working procedures in public administrations, these typically include SEA, policy-level appraisal and green budgeting (discussed in Part II). Empirically, we confirmed their relative unpopularity and noted the generally weak interpretation of EPI that they implied.

To summarize, communicative instruments have been significantly more popular than organizational instruments. With some exceptions (green budgeting in a minority of jurisdictions and SEA – which is the norm in the majority), procedural instruments have been conspicuous more by their absence in the seven jurisdictions than their presence. Of course this pattern of deployment builds a potentially important weakness into policy systems, in the sense that general framing and communicative instruments tend to work better when the issue attention cycle is swinging up, but they are easily left exposed (and hence may easily lose momentum) when it slides back down (as it has done in the 2000s).

Second, while it is dangerous to generalize too much from a sample of seven, the data presented in Chapter 2 does suggest that there is a temporal pattern in the adoption of different EPI instruments. Constitutional provisions and national environmental strategies were some of the first to be adopted and are now relatively common across the OECD. The empirical chapters in Parts II and III confirm a point (also made in Chapter 2) that a number of instruments proliferated in the 1990s and 2000s, with SEA, some administrative instruments (such as green cabinets and committees) and NSDSs proving especially popular. And yet there are several instruments mentioned in the Brundtland Report (for example green budgeting and integrated policy appraisal) that are virtually absent in many OECD states, including several amongst our sample of the supposedly more environmentally ambitious.

Third, there has evidently been – to quote Chapter 2 – 'no clear shift towards making the integration of environmental concerns a standard procedure of decision making'. Even within our relatively small sample, the number of instruments adopted by each jurisdiction varies greatly from 11 (in the UK) to just 4 (Australia). It is noteworthy that according to the data presented in Chapter 2, a number of EU Member States have very few EPI instruments, (for example, Spain (3), Ireland and Italy (4 each) and Luxembourg (1)). Moreover, most jurisdictions appear to prefer instruments that communicate the importance of EPI without developing the detailed organizational measures and procedures to put it into practice effectively.

Fourth, clear patterns are also evident in relation to the policy stage (or stages) targeted by the adopted instruments. Recall that the normative conceptual work on EPI expresses a preference for instruments that target the early stages of the policy-making cycle. In fact, some instruments (for example, green budgeting and NSDS) in principle seek to steer most (if not all) policy stages towards EPI and/or sustainable development, in an open and iterative manner. But amongst our sample of seven jurisdictions, green budgeting has only really been employed by the UK, Norway and the EU, and none of these systems addresses the very early stages of the budgetary cycle. Rather, they focus on the later implementation and/or revenue raising stages. The EU stands out in the sense that it has tried to link the disbursement of funds to the attainment of basic environmental conditions (so called 'green conditionality'), but it is the only jurisdiction to have done so. And with the exception of the EU and the UK, the systems of parliamentary oversight associated with budgeting are weak (and often entirely absent), thereby limiting the opportunities for environmental actors to exert political pressure on sectoral actors.

Broad Trends – A Summary

Having summarized the main trends, it is now possible to generate some broader conclusions about EPI – ones which we shall take up and further examine in subsequent sections. First, the jurisdictions have adopted a large number of instruments to implement EPI, but the overall pattern of adoption remains relatively uneven. In general, communicative instruments have proven to be far more popular than organizational or procedural ones. Indeed, if we ignore the data on SEA given in Chapter 2, very few procedural tools have been adopted anywhere in the world. In fact, if we remove our seven 'pioneer' jurisdictions from Table 2.1, there are virtually none! Although organizational and procedural instruments seek (at least in principle) to alter the patterned context of policy making to give principled priority to environmental issues, in practice they function much more like communicative instruments.

The second broad point that can be made is that within the OECD and amongst the environmental policy pioneers, we can further differentiate between front-runner jurisdictions and laggards. Adoption patterns appear to follow the attention cycle of environmental policy more generally. In the front-runner jurisdictions, EPI innovation has closely corresponded to a general up-swing in environmental (policy) activism. But as soon as this faded, the flow of EPI initiatives slowed too. This pattern suggests that contrary to Brundtland's hopes, EPI remains anchored in traditional environmental policy dynamics and is thus heavily dependent on environmental actors. For example, many of the most popular EPI instruments were initiated or are now closely supervised by environmental actors such as national environment ministries.

The overall pattern of deployment thus leaves some of the most strategic areas of state activity – namely budgeting – essentially untouched by EPI instruments. Similarly, the core policy planning activities in 'driving force' sectors such as industry, transport and agriculture remain mostly immune to scrutiny from policy appraisal and reporting activities, and are not really subjected to any seriously constraining environmental targets ('specification of output'). There is precious little evidence that the sectors have been willing to 'share' in the ownership of EPI (for example, via common activities like green budgeting and policy appraisal), at least in the manner sought by Gro Harlem Brundtland and Charles Caccia. Contrary to their hopes, EPI has not been a steady and progressive process of innovation; on the contrary, EPI has, to quote Chapter 2, 'been fiercely

debated, with phases of successful integration as well as phases of retreat'
and stagnation.

Third, although many instruments have been adopted in the name of
EPI, our case studies clearly revealed that they are used in very different
ways and sometimes for entirely different purposes. It is certainly very
difficult to detect much evidence that they are being applied in a systematic and coordinated manner. The UK, Sweden and Norway come the
closest to having comprehensive national 'EPI frameworks', but even here
it is difficult to detect the presence of a clear design logic. In the rest, what
we seem to be witnessing is a rather ad hoc accumulation of different
instruments which corresponds to no overall plan. For instance, in
Norway, a set of new instruments developed in the second wave were
simply 'grafted on to' those from the first wave; Hoornbeek's chapter (13)
concluded that the USA was 'backing towards' EPI; in the EU, integration strategies were said to be 'piling up'; in the UK, doubts have been
expressed about the 'fit' between particular instruments; and in Sweden
pressure has grown for existing instruments to be better harmonized,
which is rather curious given that their primary purpose is to coordinate
other things!

Finally, if we approach the same trend from an instrument perspective,
the same ad hoc pattern is evident. For example, Chapter 3 concluded that
most administrative instruments are used 'in a very superficial and ad hoc
manner, with little attention for diagnosing underlying problems'. Similarly,
Chapter 5 described most NSDSs as 'fragmented processes driven by a few
administrators who are not capable of shaping key policy decisions in line
with sustainable development objectives'. Either way, the disjunction
between the demands for coordination, integration and comprehensiveness
contained in the Brundtland Report, and the rather ad hoc manner in which
the jurisdictions have altered their policy systems to deliver them in practice
is really rather striking.

EPI: DIFFERENT CONCEPTUAL MEANINGS

The previous section revealed considerable variance in the way that the concepts of sustainable development and EPI are utilized. Underlying this is a
normative-positive gap in the meaning attributed to the two concepts individually and in relation to one another. Looking back, we notice that in
Europe, the frame of reference has moved over time from sustainable
development to EPI and (more recently) back again, whereas outside
Europe (principally in Australia and the USA) sustainable development
has been (and largely remains) the more dominant of the two.[1] These

discursive moves suggest a tension between the two concepts, which is political rather than (necessarily) in-built.

The concept of sustainable development first emerged at the global level with the Brundtland Report and in Agenda 21. Thereafter, it diffused widely as an innovative attempt to bridge the tensions between environmental, economic and social policy (Jordan 2008). The principle of EPI was not explicitly used in either of these international documents, although its importance was undoubtedly implicit in the concept of sustainable development, as noted both in various academic studies (see the work of Liberatore 1997; Lenschow 2002; Lafferty and Hovden 2003; Lafferty and Knudsen 2007) and in practitioner accounts (for example, CEC 1993; OECD 2002; EEA 2005). In tracing the conceptual development of the EPI principle, it is therefore important to search beyond the level of explicit pronouncements and also look at the operation of EPI instruments in order to understand the precise conceptual meaning given to the term 'integration'.

In the previous section we noted that EPI has usually been expressed in 'soft' law documents such as strategies, plans and programmes. Of the seven jurisdictions covered in Part III, only the EU and Norway have made a firm constitutional commitment[2] to EPI and thus moved towards potential legal clarity and enforceability. But even in these two cases, our analysis shows that the normative core of the EPI principle has remained fluid over time. Chapter 8 revealed that the EU made a relatively early and strong normative commitment to EPI which can be traced back to the dawn of its environmental policy. The Fifth Environmental Action Programme of the EU was adopted in 1993 (CEC 1993: 24). In the Treaties of the EU, EPI is not only considered to be one vital dimension (or ingredient) in sustainable development, but a policy principle in its own right, which in turn has spawned several of the policy innovations mentioned by Brundtland, namely green budgeting, integrated policy appraisal ('Impact Assessment') and programmatic planning (the so-called Cardiff Process). In the 2000s, however, a number of other initiatives were adopted that diverted attention from the Commission's focus on EPI and sustainable development. Chief amongst these was the so-called Lisbon Process, which was supposed to make the EU 'the most competitive and dynamic knowledge-driven economy' (European Council 2000), by boosting employment creation measures, reforming national economies and ensuring greater social cohesion. Only in June 2001 did the EU retrofit the Lisbon Process with an environmental dimension, in the form of a strategy for sustainable development. In so doing, EPI was effectively pursued by way of something different – 'sustainability policy integration' – which made it appear less biased towards the environment and more in tune with Lisbon's emphasis on jobs and economic growth. In an attempt to marry the two formally, the

European Council (2006) claimed that the strategy for sustainable development was in fact the 'overarching objective', although Lisbon remained the 'motor of a more dynamic economy' – a fudge that nicely revealed the politically ambiguous relationship between EPI and sustainable development in the EU's quest for a 'new economy'.[3]

If we turn to Norway, in 1992, Article 110b of the Constitution established the 'right to an environment that is conducive to health and to natural surroundings whose productivity and diversity are preserved' combined with an environmental information right for every citizen. At the level of white papers (which are relatively soft policy instruments), the reference to EPI was made more, but by no means completely explicit. The fading reference to EPI in the daily political and policy practice in Norway since 1992 (see Chapter 10), however, indicates that this commitment failed to provide sufficient normative guidance to ensure enforceability. Similar to the EU, the notion of 'prioritizing the environment' was vague in the beginning and then gradually disappeared under economic pressures.

Meanwhile, the putative 'right' to environmental protection and the prioritized treatment of environmental objectives in sectoral policy making never emerged as a constitutional issue in the other jurisdictions covered in Part III. Beneath the legal and constitutional framework (that is, at the level of political and administrative practice), Sweden and the UK stand out, however, as jurisdictions that have strong traditions and structures of integrated policy making. The UK's 'Rolls Royce' coordination system (see Chapter 12) commits all the constituent parts of the national government to meet commonly agreed objectives. Whether a high level of environmental protection becomes *the* goal of coordinated policy making depends on political leadership, however. In the absence of a legal commitment to sustainable development or EPI and, instead, the heavy reliance on the support of the Prime Minister and the central coordinating bodies, the pursuit of coordinated environmental policy in the UK has fluctuated over time. The positive commitment to EPI in Sweden appears more stable due to a generally more favourable societal attitude to strong environmental policies. As noted in Chapter 11, 'sector responsibility' has been the central policy principle facilitating EPI in Sweden. Coupled with a public management style which prefers clearly specified objectives (at national and, partly, sectoral level), and a long history of public support for strong environmental policy making, this procedural principle has aimed to ensure that the environment is routinely considered in sectoral decision making. It also implies sectoral variation, however, and no general prioritization (that is, 'principled priority' to use the terms employed in Chapter 1) of environmental protection; in practice, the 'positive meaning' given to EPI may be narrowly focused (for example, on landscape issues in agricultural policy or on the climate change implications of energy policy) or it may be completely swamped by other policy practices and/or competing integration principles (for example, regional policy integration or development policy integration) (Schout and Jordan 2007).

At the level of policy sectors, we can also identify distinct positive meanings given to EPI. Despite being one of the very first jurisdictions to push for more integrated policy making, Germany has nonetheless been bedevilled by fragmentation. Nevertheless, periodic or sector-specific niches of high EPI commitment have emerged either due to perceived problem pressure (for example, linked to the issue of climate change or, earlier, acid rain) or due to coalition politics (for example, the greening of agricultural policy under the Red–Green coalition). In both cases, we observe that sectoral policy needed to be justified in the light of environmental objectives – that is, a form of environmental prioritization. While such periods may 'lock in' EPI (in the sense that environmental measures or regulations become embedded in the sector policy practice), the lack of an overall EPI framework makes the emergence of such niches vulnerable to policy reversal once the political attention subsides and the supportive political coalitions break down.

The Downsian issue-attention cycle has also been at work in the USA. Here, the emergence of EPI practices has been mostly independent of a normative framework for integrated policy making and environmental priority setting ('backing towards EPI'), however. As noted above, a political discourse on EPI is still missing and what passes for a national sustainable development framework is comparatively weak (at least at the federal level – at the state level, things have been rather different, as shown in Chapter 13). In other words, we find no normative constitutional framework and neither has such a thing arisen 'in practice' out of the adoption of innovative policy instruments such as SEA, where the USA has adopted a pioneering role. While we notice an 'upgrading' of environmental objectives in several policy fields (by way of funding opportunities and regulatory rules), the balance between environmental, social and economic priorities has been tilted towards the economy. Some exceptions are observable, but mostly at a sub-national level: some federal states and/or American cities have taken steps towards sustainability.

This also seems to be the dominant pattern in Australia, where the dependence on natural resources (for example, water or forests) has led to strategic environmental management efforts at the level of the Australian states and territories (Chapter 14). But the creation of concrete synergy effects and 'win-win' situations is what has guided these efforts, not a normative commitment to the principled priority of environmental factors (see Lafferty and Hovden 2003; Lafferty and Knudsen 2007). The positive conceptualization of EPI, in other words, has preceded a normative one.

Different Conceptual Meanings – a Summary

To sum up, political factors and problem pressure appear to explain a large part of the (positive) conceptual meaning attributed to EPI, that is, the degree to which environmental objectives are in fact afforded priority in sectoral decision making. Even where EPI has been legally accepted as a guiding principle, the interpretation of EPI has fluctuated over time. An excellent indicator of the unsettled position of EPI in everyday political practice is the application of SEA and the policy appraisal. While these instruments may be used to drive EPI into everyday decision making, depending on political priorities, they may also be used not only to sideline the environment, but actively to prioritize economic objectives. Moreover, SEAs turn out to have had very little impact on the strategic direction of most sectoral policies. These instruments reflect the positive meaning that is given to sustainable development and EPI in daily policy affairs, more than they seem to provide operational support for a strongly environmentalist reading of these concepts.

Therefore, the political reality in the seven jurisdictions has rarely corresponded to the relatively neat normative core of EPI helpfully described by Lafferty and Hovden (2003) and further elaborated in Chapter 1. While we observe widespread political commitment to EPI at a general discursive level, at the level of day-to-day policy decisions we see controversy emerging which calls the legal forcefulness of the EPI principle even further into question. The main point of contention is precisely what level of attention (or 'principled priority') to give to environmental protection in everyday policy making in the sectors. While it is uncontroversial that EPI refers to a process of integrating environmental factors into sectoral policy making at a sufficiently early stage (EEA 2005: 13), the definition of integration (in the sense of what in practice to prioritize and to what extent) has been continually questioned and the normative debate thus continually reopened.

The politicization – and hence reopening – of the normative debate on the meaning of EPI is not really surprising, of course, to us or to Lafferty and Hovden (2003). The choice between such basic values as economic well-being, the eradication of poverty and the protection of the natural environment, constitute the very core of political contestation rather than taking place prior to it. In the usually short-term perspective of (elected) politicians, one should not expect them to take steps to protect the environment. After all, environmental protection could provide the basis for economic and social well-being in the longer term, but it is often perceived as a limiting factor in the shorter term. Hence, politicians will be much harder pressed to trade off more immediate economic and social gains for environmental protection than the normative core of concepts like sustainable development and EPI would seem to imply.

EPI AS A GOVERNING PROCESS

Parts II and III have made very clear that the normative core of EPI, namely the prioritization of the environment in decision making (see Chapter 1), has not been fully embedded into the everyday political practices of any of the seven jurisdictions. As the European states were chosen to reflect examples of environmental pioneers, this is a rather sobering conclusion. Rather, EPI seems to be given a 'positive', that is situational, meaning in different jurisdictions, in different sectors and at different points in time. In order to understand more fully under which conditions EPI is given a 'strong' or a 'weak' meaning (see Chapter 1 for details), we need to analyse EPI as a governing process that takes place inside a political system and which is characterized by the employment of different combinations of policy instruments. Analytically, institutional, political (that is, actor-centred) and cognitive approaches may be used to understand these processes. In fact, these analytical perspectives allow us to identify different aspects of the governing process.[4] Following the structure outlined in Chapter 1, this section first adopts a political system and then a policy analysis perspective.

A Political System Perspective

An increasingly dominant view in the existing literature on sustainable development and EPI perceives them as institutional problems of 'compartmentalization'. It is the norm in contemporary – that is functionally differentiated – governments to organize activities in sectoral ministries and (increasingly) even to decentralize governing activities to lower levels of government, to independent agencies, to private associations and the like (Jordan 2008). This norm leads to a demand for organizational structures and procedures that are capable of delivering more coordinated governance. As elaborated in Chapters 2 and 3, all seven jurisdictions have striven to deploy administrative instruments that link policy sectors at the mundane level of daily policy making (for example, inter-ministerial working groups or liaison offices); there are much fewer – and typically only weakly active – examples of coordination structures at the strategic level (for example, the amalgamation of ministries or the creation of green cabinets and a powerful central ministry or council for sustainable development). Coordination instruments that cross policy sectors, and specifically mainstream environmental concerns, seem altogether missing inside the legislatures. It is very hard to identify jurisdictions in which policy integration has become an everyday organizational routine (as opposed to a political objective) throughout all levels of decision making.

Nevertheless, it is possible to divide jurisdictions into groups that are prone to suffer from institutional fragmentation to a greater or lesser degree. First, the three federal systems in our sample – Germany, the USA and Australia – as well as the EU (with its quasi-federal political system) have encountered significant institutional obstacles to implementing EPI. Apart from horizontal segmentation – an enduring feature of most modern systems of governance – they are characterized by vertical fragmentation and hence (especially in the USA and Australia) a decentralization of political leadership. Here, patterns of negative integration proliferate, where compromises approach the lowest common denominator unless pay-off systems have been devised. However, those federations that leave the lower level some leeway in developing policy (that is, the EU, the USA and to some extent Australia) have also been particularly good at developing innovative EPI instruments. The EU – a political system which is still very much 'under construction' (see Chapter 8) – stands out as having been particularly responsive to new ideas. In the USA (and to a lesser extent Australia too), EPI practices have also emerged in a decentralized fashion from the bottom (that is, state-level) up.[5]

Second, in focusing on horizontal fragmentation, it is important to distinguish between political systems that feature more or less ministerial independence. Contrasting Germany and Sweden, for instance, we note that the high level of ministerial independence in Germany reinforces sectoral thinking whereas the system of 'sector responsibility' in Sweden (and, in a similar form, the UK) ensures that individual ministries or government agencies take responsibility for incorporating supposedly common objectives (such as EPI) into their operations. The system of agencies in Sweden appears particularly conducive to 'responsible' governance. In Germany, the chancellor's prerogative to define the guiding principles of governmental policy has not played an equally strong role in guiding and disciplining the sectoral ministries. Here, the prospects for ensuring EPI at the sectoral level have been heavily reliant upon the political composition of government (see below).

Third, the political system that has been the keenest to organize integrated policy is the UK. The recent trend towards greater devolution notwithstanding, it remains a relatively centralized, parliamentary-based system, whose government and legislature are politically fused.[6] Hence we find a minimum number of veto points facilitating both a decisive style of reform politics – including organizational innovation – and strong coordination mechanisms. This was confirmed in the UK chapter, which referred to the existence of a 'Rolls Royce' coordination system. Yet Russel and Jordan demonstrated that favourable institutional framework conditions have not been enough to deliver dramatically greater EPI. As with any motor vehicle (be it British, German, French or Japanese), the UK system depends on the presence of a good driver (that is, political leadership) and sufficient fuel (that is, information on the impact of policy on the environment) to find its way. In these two respects, the UK's experiences have been far less positive than one might expect from a cursory reading of its institutional components (see Chapter 12 for details).

The broader point we would like to make is that politics can be shown to have been an important factor in most of the cases discussed in this volume. There are two important parts to this point. The first is that the attention given to EPI (and the positive meaning attached to it) depends largely on the political composition of the ruling party in government. The chapters in Part III suggest that new centre-left governments tend to push the hardest for EPI whereas centre-right governments have held back or even dismantled EPI frameworks and instruments. To take one example, despite its institutionally rather unfavourable framework conditions, Germany was a front-runner on EPI matters in the late 1960s and early 1970s under Brandt's SPD–FDP government. In the period after 1998 (when a red–green coalition was in power), there was another, more 'reluctant conversion to EPI' (see Chapter 9), which Wurzel largely attributes to the size (small) and political power (relatively weak) of the 'green' coalition partner. Similarly, in the UK Tony Blair's 'new' Labour government, elected in 1997, revamped the EPI machinery by strengthening some of the existing instruments and adding some new ones.

By contrast, in the three systems that have done the most to implement EPI – namely the EU, Norway and Sweden – we have observed a reversal of earlier commitments to EPI after the political leadership changed. In the EU, the political commitment to the Cardiff Process waned in the early 2000s when the majority in the Council and the Commission turned to the right. Only after much effort did the (centre-left) Swedish Presidency of the EU manage (in 2001) to add an environmental dimension to the Lisbon Process. Thus EPI, which had appeared to be strongly embedded in political and administrative systems, became much weaker in the 2000s. Meanwhile, Norway witnessed the discontinuation of several EPI instruments after 2001, when a coalition of the Conservative, Liberal and Christian Democratic Parties was elected. And the record of the post-2006 conservative government in Sweden suggests that some of the innovations initiated by the previous government in 2004 (for example, the Ministry of Sustainable Development) have been reversed (in this case back to a ministry for the environment) (see Chapter 11). Although not explicitly linked to EPI, interest in environmental policy in the USA has fluctuated between the Democratic and Republican presidencies. And finally after 1996, the conservative government in Australia implicitly de-prioritized EPI by emphasizing the economic priorities of the country (see Chapter 14). The recently elected (2007) left-of-centre government, in turn, has begun to take environmental concerns and EPI more seriously, for example by embracing the international climate change agreement.

Second, the significance of political factors is manifest in the influence exerted by individual political leaders. *Our Common Future* (WCED 1987) cannot be understood unless some reference is made to the personal commitment of its lead author, Gro Harlem Brundtland. As this faded in the 1990s, the implementation of EPI in Norway fell away. In Germany, Sweden and the UK, the introduction of the most influential EPI instruments can also be linked to the political visions and projects of particular political leaders such as Willy Brandt (the 'modern Germany'), Göran Persson (the 'green people's home') and Tony Blair ('greening government'), respectively.

What is still missing in the systematic installation of EPI processes is any notable impact on civil society. While environmental interests have played a role in pushing specific issues (such as climate change, water or air pollution) which constituted the focal point of particular EPI activities and instruments, the general norm of EPI (or sustainable development for that matter) has not attracted much sustained public attention or support. For a start, it is difficult for environmental groups – let alone mainstream political leaders – to mobilize the body politic in defence of something as inherently abstract as EPI. Furthermore, the trade-off implications of EPI are more costly (and hence more politically contested) at the individual or small-scale level than in the aggregate. Hence the political support for EPI assumes a high commitment to the common good in the long term, as opposed to the individual good in the short term. The combination of these factors militates against running public information campaigns on EPI or sustainable development. This problem has in a sense been compounded by the rising prominence of 'environmentally' dominated media stories in the mid-2000s, such as those around climate change, genetically modified organisms and international whaling.

While a political perspective highlights the dependence of EPI on historical contingencies, a cognitive perspective alerts us to the tendency for national EPI and sustainable development practices to be rooted in particular 'frames' of thinking – for example, as a social responsibility, as a subject for technological problem solving, as a costly commitment detracting from economic growth or as a pressing governance issue. The normative core of

EPI – the principled prioritization of environmental factors in decision making – may be compatible with the prevalent frames to a greater or lesser degree at national, regional or international level, thus explaining its weak – or non-existent – acceptance in everyday policy making. Departing from such a perspective, we may come to realize that EPI may be achieved through many different means rather than one single blueprint.

Nonetheless, the cognitive context does appear to have been less suitable to EPI in some jurisdictions than others. Thus, looking at our seven jurisdictions, we may infer that the consensual policy-making style of Scandinavian countries has been particularly supportive of coordinated policy making. The joint drafting of legislation, the submission to common objectives and the exchange of information and knowledge all seem to have facilitated EPI. However, we also saw that consensual democracies are not sheltered from the influence of special economic interests (Norway) or battles over administrative turf (Sweden). The legalistic policy style in Germany and the USA, in turn, appears less suitable to an approach to EPI that relies on the emergence of a common understanding of environmental priorities. As we noted in Part III, however, these jurisdictions are very capable of arriving at some patterns of 'integrated' policy making in the sense that environmental regulation may co-determine what is deemed to be legitimate sectoral activity. A legalistically framed EPI process is predicated on there being powerful ministries of the environment, rather than joint decision procedures, task forces and commissions, which are crucial components of more consensually-based EPI systems.

Considering that we do not appear to have clear front-runners in the implementation of EPI, a cognitive approach encourages us to accept that there may be different ways of achieving integrated policy making, all of which suffer from numerous deficiencies (as noted above). Hence, EPI patterns need to be built upon existing frames and institutional frameworks. Greater awareness of the opportunities within these frames and institutions is needed, however, to establish some continuity in the EPI process, rather than hoping for political windows of opportunity which may or may not appear regularly (or strongly) enough in the future, truly to make a difference.

A Policy Analysis Perspective

A policy analysis perspective encompasses the process of policy making and its outputs (policy decisions) and outcomes on the ground. For our purposes, it is important to note that 'policy' consists of a set of measures that aim to change the process of sectoral policy making. In other words, we are looking at a 'meta' policy setting comprising structures and routines for intervening in all sectoral policies. In order to analyse this setting, we may on the one hand focus on the dimension of time and identify the points – or the system – of intervention. On the other hand, we may focus on the logic of intervention. Given the empirical focus of this book, it is important to distinguish between the different mechanisms of policy integration (and change) that are employed in the instruments of sustainable development and EPI in order to: (1) find patterns; and (2) develop an analytical perspective for evaluating effectiveness.

Focusing on the timing of EPI instruments (that is, the point of intervention in the standard policy cycle), we may distinguish between EPI instruments that: (1) aim at influencing the objectives of general or sectoral policy making *ex ante*; (2) target the allocation of resources in support of certain policy objectives; (3) focus on structuring the interaction of – or better still the coordination between – sectoral policy makers during policy formulation and decision making; and (4) monitor and evaluate the impacts of past instruments. At a general level, the agenda for EPI has been set; most jurisdictions have put in place some instruments. Read positively, the process of embedding sustainable development and EPI has started in most jurisdictions.

More critically, in Section 2 we observed that these instruments tend to be very 'soft' in the sense that they carry no legal force or normatively influential obligation to give the environment 'principled priority'. Furthermore, there are only a few jurisdictions that have really made their soft (and broad) strategies and/or plans operational. Sweden stands out in this regard with its elaborate system of indicators and environmental quality objectives which form the basis of its 'management by objectives'. Nevertheless, the discipline of preparing documents may trigger the development of administrative practices and routines of knowledge exchange and coordination. In Chapter 5, Reinhard Steurer argued that many sustainable development strategies are more than symbolic gestures; they do trigger innovative governance structures and mechanisms at the administrative level. Rarely, however, do we witness such plans and strategies receiving wider political support from the sectors or the body politic. By and large, they tend to be driven by environmental ministries and agencies, several steps removed from the driving force sectors of environmental damage – transport, energy, agriculture and so on.

The employment of soft rather than hard instruments continues when we move around the policy cycle: green budgeting is, as Chapter 4 revealed, frequently understood as 'green housekeeping' (for example, employing environmental criteria to allocate the budget for internal – administrative – spending) or 'green revenue raising' (for example, environmental taxation). Sometimes, it involves allocating budgets to more environmentally sensitive projects, but nowhere has it amounted to what Brundtland originally demanded: a long-term, strategic process of reorientating the goals and procedures of public financing towards sustainability. With the exception of the EU and possibly also the UK, from a budgetary perspective, EPI in our seven jurisdictions tends to be pursued as an 'add on' rather than as a process which challenges the underlying rationale for spending public money on unsustainable practices. Norway appeared, at least for some time, to be another notable exception in this regard, but its innovative EPSB (Environmental Profile of the State Budget), introduced in 1989, has since been criticized by the national court of auditors and the OECD.

Regarding coordination within government to facilitate EPI-conforming decisions, our chapter authors note that organizational changes tend to focus on the (lower level) administrative echelons; surprisingly few effective coordination practices have been established at the higher strategic level of the finance ministry, the cabinet or the prime minister's offices. Once again, Sweden seems to be the exception, given its tradition of collegial decision making. The UK also stands out in the sense that it has regularly reorganized government and has built a relatively elaborate (but by no means flawless – see Chapter 12) machinery of coordination. More importantly, environmental policy appraisal could have been used to expose the direction of sectoral policy making to critical scrutiny, but in practice it was used in a rather soft form (that is, few appraisals were ever very strategically focused). It follows also from Bina's chapter that the governing potential of SEA has been greatly underutilized and largely unrealized by most jurisdictions (see Chapter 7 for details).

Finally, even at the stage of monitoring and evaluation, the typically inconsequential obligation to report outnumbers the cases where parliamentary committees or courts of auditors monitor independently and may be able to exert some political pressure. Here, the UK parliamentary environmental audit committee seems to be a notable exception to the rule.

The evidence summarized above leads to a second observation. While governments have extended their repertoire of instruments to implement sustainable development and EPI, they have tended to proceed in a largely piecemeal fashion. As was already evident from our review of the major trends (see above), the handling of EPI seems to be characterized by incrementalism. Thus, despite its supposedly overarching (or meta-) nature with respect to daily policy-making processes, the introduction of EPI instruments has been both reactive (for example, adopting SEAs in response to an EU directive) and path-dependent, as opposed to strategic and innovative. Indeed, one of the most curious findings of our study is the lack of coordination between many of the very EPI instruments that are supposed to be delivering more policy coordination! Corresponding to what was already said about the weak normative embeddedness of EPI, evidently the principle of EPI has failed (in more positive philosophical terms) to shape all the stages of the policy-making process, but especially the earliest ones.

Logic of intervention

Turning now to the logic of intervention (and following the three analytical perspectives introduced above), we can distinguish between an institutional, a political and a cognitive logic. Among sustainable development and EPI instruments, institutional and cognitive measures are most prominently used, while explicitly political measures – targeting particular constellations of power – are rarely found.[7] The institutional approach rests on combining different administrative instruments in a rational and consistent way (for the available repertoire, see Chapter 3). Behind these institution-building exercises we can detect network building as an associated aim. The assumption here seems to be that actors sitting around one table or reporting to one another will eventually develop mutual understandings that favour environmental protection, and then alter their procedures and practices accordingly. Part III demonstrated that unless there is a high-level political commitment to deliver greater EPI (which cannot of course be assumed) or strong inducements to civil servants and actors in civil society (for example, in the form of career enhancements), sectoral actors are very unlikely to give priority to EPI networks or willingly adopt higher environmental standards. The study of EPI in the EU (Chapter 8), for instance, showed that following an initial period of network development and implementation in the late 1990s, the pursuit of EPI increasingly exposed environmental policy makers to demands for 'reverse integration' (that is, environmental policy taking on board the demands of the social and economic sectors), hinting that political power games were perhaps neglected or at least underestimated at the start. Hence, network building needs to be complemented by: (1) top-down legitimization; and (2) adequate incentive structures.

Of course, the strengthening of the political leadership for EPI is beyond the reach of 'policy' or 'institutional design'. Nevertheless, it is conceivable that governments may wish to empower environmental stakeholders in order to facilitate EPI. But if we look back at the evidence presented in this book, very little empowerment has in fact taken place: central ministries or committees supporting EPI and sustainable development have tended to be short-lived (depending very much on the presence of a favourable government or the absence of competing problems);[8] the procedural power of ministries of the environment has not been strengthened (for example, by giving them a veto over sectoral policy development or even a strong consultative right in joint decision). These experiences have demonstrated yet again how ambiguous has been the positive meaning attached to EPI. In fact, the contemporary discourse (which emphasizes 'balanced' policy making) could be read as a complete rejection of the normative claim that certain (for example, environmental) policy objectives should have a principled priority. The language of 'mainstreaming' may even suggest that environmental policy tasks ought to be fully decentralized to the sectoral ministries, making the environment ministries largely superfluous. Empirical evidence suggests, however, that in the absence of a prioritizing norm, EPI relies heavily on the presence of forceful and ambitious environmental ministries. But only the acceptance of a prioritizing norm will support the existence of strong – or strengthened – environment ministries, hinting at one of the most fundamental weaknesses of relying on an institutional design approach.

Finally, besides networking instruments we have found an increasing number of procedural instruments that target policy makers' cognitions. The evidence that these instruments induce learning processes is rather weak, however. Looking at sectoral strategies or plans (working with benchmarks, indicators and best practice models in some jurisdictions) as well as assessment and/or appraisal instruments, their application seems to encounter great resistance. In Norway, which appeared to have introduced a 'model' approach (NEMS), sectoral reporting is no longer conducted, a documentation system is 'on ice' and cross-sectoral analysis has been dropped altogether (see Chapter 10). Generally, we note that 'learning' or a 'change of awareness' seems to take place in response to political crises (for example, accelerating climate change) rather than the combined impact of different packages of EPI instruments.

EPI as a Governing Process – a Summary

Rather than suggesting a parsimonious analytical model to explain patterns and performance of EPI governance, this chapter has interpreted the evidence collected in this book comparatively and from various angles. Corresponding to the multifaceted nature of 'governance', we have thus approached EPI from a structural (political system) and a process (policy analysis) perspective. Furthermore, we identified institutional, political and cognitive mechanisms that have impacted on the evolution and performance of EPI 'systems' in different jurisdictions. This multidimensional perspective revealed the highly contingent and complex nature of 'policy integration'. Considering that EPI requires the 'penetration' of large parts of the political machinery throughout the entire policy cycle with a fundamental and yet unspecific norm, it is hardly a surprise that there appears to be no best practice in relation to the delivery of greater EPI. In the end, these attempts may need to respond to the prevailing institutional, political and cognitive framework, in ways that build upon the respective strengths (and compensate for the respective weaknesses) of different jurisdictions. This is, of course, a highly demanding task and one which even the more environmentally ambitious jurisdictions studied in this volume have struggled to handle.

EPI AS A POLICY OUTCOME

An Instrument Perspective

The first and most obvious point that emerges from Part II is how little is known about the effectiveness of particular EPI instruments. In fact, for many of the instruments – but chiefly administrative mechanisms and green budgeting – the existing literature is still at the much more preliminary stage of defining terms, developing typologies and simply describing existing patterns of use. The same could be said of NSDSs: Chapter 5 concluded that while 'virtually all' jurisdictions that possess them measure sustainable development at an aggregate level using indicators, most fail to say much about the effectiveness of the strategies themselves or indeed any other instrument (or package of instruments). The existing literature is only slightly more sophisticated in relation to more discrete instruments such as policy appraisal and SEA. Here, it is widely acknowledged that the potential environmental impacts of new policies are not as well covered as the economic and social ones. But above and beyond this basic point, the existing literature is – and seems likely for some time to remain – a long way short of being able to make definitive judgements about effectiveness.

It is noteworthy that where the existing literature has begun to grapple with the question of outcome effectiveness – in relation to policy appraisal and SEA for example – it has simply uncovered multiple standpoints and hence numerous evaluative criteria. Generally speaking, it tends to analyse particular instruments in isolation rather than as they appear in the real world (that is, in complex combinations). Moreover, even the underlying purpose of the instruments being analysed has been called into question. For example, in Chapter 7 we learnt that assessment specialists are still debating whether the primary purpose of SEA is to strengthen environmental policies, integrate the environment into other sectors or deliver sustainable development.

That said, some of the more procedural EPI instruments (for example SEA, policy appraisal and NSDSs) have generated some ancillary benefits such as creating new administrative capacities (for example, committees and assessment bodies) that offer environmentalists new political opportunities to green the sectors, facilitate longer-term processes of policy learning and improve the legitimacy of policy interventions by increasing transparency and public participation. In relation to policy appraisal, for example, several jurisdictions have established quasi-independent bodies to audit quality.[9] In the UK, the national Sustainable Development Commission (SDC) has been turned into a 'watchdog' charged with evaluating performance rather than simply providing impartial advice. Steps too have been taken to assess the quality of NSDSs against OECD 'ideal types' using soft modes of governance such as the OECD method of peer review. Finding ways to analyse the effectiveness of these ancillary benefits is, of course, a future research challenge.

A Jurisdictional Perspective

At one level there is a surfeit of evaluation infrastructure in place. Chapter 2 recorded that 23 of the 30 OECD states studied possessed an 'external and independent review of environmental performance'. But if we dig a little more deeply into the empirical detail presented in Part III, a slightly different picture emerges: many have very general mandates like 'overseeing sustainable development' or 'promoting environmental policy'; many are too poorly resourced and politically weak to open up sectoral policy making to critical scrutiny; the majority simply do not have the time or the resources to dig into the everyday grind of policy making. Not surprisingly, Australia and the USA scored particularly poorly here. The UK probably has the most sophisticated evaluation machinery, consisting of a parliamentary audit committee, the SDC and the National Audit Office (NAD). But aside from this, even the more environmentally progressive jurisdictions, namely Norway and Sweden, lack strong, independent and focused scrutiny bodies. Norway has advisory bodies on EPI and sustainable development, but no independent parliamentary or non-governmental auditor; Sweden has a national audit office but it does not specifically look at EPI.

Were other jurisdictions to create similar bodies, they would still need to confront another fundamental obstacle: the virtual absence of concrete yardsticks to measure the degree of EPI achieved. In the majority of jurisdictions covered in Part III (for example, Germany, the UK and Sweden), the existing performance indicators tend either to be very broadly framed (typically focused on sustainable development in the aggregate) or to have been produced by the sectors (for example, the Cardiff Process) in such a way as to be wholly unchallenging of the status quo. In Norway, evaluations of some of the component parts of NEMS have been undertaken, but there has been no systematic evaluation of the whole system. In the UK, interest in *ex post* evaluation has ebbed and flowed. The NAO and the parliamentary audit committee have produced probing assessments of individual instruments such as green budgeting, appraisal and the green cabinet, but there has been no overall assessment of the entire 'greening government' initiative. The NEQO system in Sweden is often identified as an example of best practice in this regard, but it has been plagued by poor reporting and lacks strong accountability mechanisms to pull the sectors into line.

EPI as a Policy Outcome – a Summary

If, as was argued in Chapter 1, policy outcomes are often what really matters in political life, then unfortunately we must conclude that, as analysts, we know precious little about one of the most fundamental aspects of EPI: the influence on the state of the environment and, ultimately, on the sustainability or otherwise of human development. More disappointingly, the prospect that policy makers will know more about EPI outcomes in the immediate future appears rather bleak.

Why has outcome effectiveness been such an understudied and politically unimportant aspect of the EPI story? One explanation might be that many of the instruments used (for example, NSDSs and certain types of policy appraisal) have not been around long enough to permit definitive assessments. For some instruments (for example, green budgeting) we simply do not have enough 'cases' to draw robust conclusions. Second there are very significant conceptual and methodological obstacles to measuring the outcome of procedural and organizational instruments such as appraisal, SEA and green budgeting. Finally, the lack of solid research and evaluation machinery may well also be symptomatic of some of the political dynamics noted above, namely the symbolic nature of many of the policy interventions and the relatively low profile of EPI in the wider body politic.

CONCLUSIONS

By way of an overall conclusion, it is important to reflect briefly on the more general and – we think – notable features of this book. First, in contrast to most existing EPI analyses, this book approached the analysis of EPI instruments and practices 'from their roots', that is, the principle of sustainable development. Lafferty and Hovden (2003: 2) helpfully argued that it is 'semantically inconsistent to conceive of sustainable development without successful EPI'. EPI, in turn, directly derives from the intellectual and conceptual framework developed in the 'mother document' of sustainable development: the Brundtland Report. However, it is clear from our analysis that the relationship between the framing concept, sustainable development, and its immediate descendant (or, to quote one of us, 'first order operational principle': Lenschow 2002: 6), namely EPI, suffers from a lack of direction – at least in terms of everyday political practice. Part II set out and unpacked a toolbox of potentially highly innovative instruments that could – to recall the title of this book – have been used to 'integrate the environment for sustainability'. But in terms of their application (Part III), they have tended to be used incrementally, 'softly' and in ways that are relatively weakly anchored in organizational structures and procedures.

More importantly, rather than being interpreted as the overarching concept, sustainable development seems to be seen as 'easier', less challenging when compared to EPI. In times of retreat from environmental policy integration, rhetoric tends to shift to sustainable development as a presumably more even-handed concept, with less fundamental consequences for political and institutional change. Ironically, this seemingly ever-present tendency to 'slip back' was what Brundtland was at such great pains to remove from the policy system by introducing EPI.

The weakness of sustainable development as a strong and guiding concept for EPI is related to a failure to anchor its normative core in political and institutional practice so far. The notion that the environment should enjoy principled priority (Lafferty and Hovden 2003) has remained stuck in abstract academic discourse. Politically speaking, in everyday governance processes, sustainable development is more frequently read as prioritizing economic development while 'taking into account' environmental objectives and searching for synergetic effects. Going through the empirical evidence collected in this book we may conclude that while the concept of sustainable development has given birth to the principle of EPI, the politics of sustainable development have the potential to imperil EPI by denying its principled priority or even facilitating 'reverse' integration in an open, three-way exchange with economic and social factors.

Second, this book has moved from a normative discussion of the various meanings of sustainable development and EPI to inquiring into their positive meanings as expressed in political and, above all, policy terms. In this context, we have taken a close look at the policy instruments that have been employed in various jurisdictions. This focus is still relatively novel: while we find numerous analyses of single instruments, they have rarely been linked to the 'meta-policy' challenge of EPI or, indeed, to one another.[10] Our more systematic perspective, however, brought to light: (1) various patterns that hint at the relatively soft and weak adoption of the EPI principle; and (2) the almost complete absence of a coordinated and comprehensive 'design' for implementing it in practice. From those who adopt a policy analysis perspective, this pattern of incremental policy making (a form of 'muddling through') should come as no surprise; what might surprise some readers is that so much of the – especially practically oriented – literature on EPI continues to be rooted in a strong belief in rational policy designs, informed by consistent evaluation frameworks and checklists of critical success factors. Instead, our studies point us to the crucial role of 'political support' as a powerful 'coordinator'; one that is potentially much more effective than careful design, but also more contingent and hence unpredictable.

Third and in contrast to the rationalist design perspective and the focus on EPI as a policy approach – that is, the search for the optimal policy design – our combined focus on jurisdictions and policy instruments has allowed us to adopt a more differentiated view across the field. Variations in 'design' should not immediately be read as deviations from an – as yet unknown – EPI blueprint, but they may (possibly) be adequate responses to institutional and contextual framework factors at a particular place and time. More crucial than the institutionalization of specific coordination structures or mechanisms seems to be: (1) the continuity of EPI measures through the entire policy cycle; and (2), an effective chain of communication between the apex of government and the lower echelons in the administration. In these regards, however, all the jurisdictions studied in this book have failed – although of course some more than others.

Finally, our study has shown that, like sustainable development, EPI has mostly been pursued as a political and/or administrative matter with hardly any attempt to involve the general public. Opportunities to be really innovative, by cultivating political support for EPI or opening up entirely new political opportunity structures, have not been exploited. This is curious as EPI (and sustainable development for that matter) is – at least rhetorically – often couched in terms of new or self-organizing and self-perpetuating governance. While we do indeed observe a high reliance on 'network building' – another term that is fashionable in the governance literature (Jordan and Schout 2006) – the public–private dimension is remarkable unexplored, both empirically and analytically. To the extent that successful EPI may rely (in functionally differentiated and democratic political systems) on a fundamental cognitive change, the ignorance of the general public may well constitute one of the most significant oversights of all, both in conceptual and empirical terms.

NOTES

1. But of course it is far from being *the* dominant political and legal discourse.
2. In the case of the EU (which is not a state and hence has no formal constitution), the commitment is treaty-based.

3. In this context, environmental policy makers and interest groups have been concerned about the political downgrading of environmental issues typified by the poor progress in implementing the EU's 6th Environmental Action Programme (EAP) (EurActiv 2006). The 6th EAP, comprising seven thematic strategies, was presented as a more advanced approach to EPI than its predecessor, the 5th EAP. However, due to political controversy, which was in part triggered by the new legally binding status of the programme, most of the precise targets and timetables were removed (Pallemaerts *et al.* 2006).

4. Given that our aim is to explore widely – although not systematically – the level and forms of institutionalization, we do not attempt formally to test the explanatory power of these approaches. Rather, they serve as heuristics for identifying patterns in governing processes.

5. It is still not clear, however, whether these practices then spread from the bottom upwards.

6. In the sense that there is normally a single dominant party.

7. Most institutional and cognitive measures may also have some empowering (or disempowering) potential, but their soft variants may remain rather ineffectual in this regard.

8. Recall, for example, how the UK environment ministry has incorporated and then lost the transport and agriculture portfolios several times since 1970 (see Chapter 12 for details).

9. In 2006, the EU established an Impact Assessment Board with a mandate to scrutinize and offer formal opinions on the quality of individual appraisals. However, its opinions are not binding; it cannot stop a proposal that has not been fully appraised. Ultimately it is the Commission which adopts the proposal, taking account of the assessment and the Board's opinion.

10. It is striking that the instrument chapters in Part II are mostly rooted in quite separate literatures.

BIBLIOGRAPHY

CEC (Commission of the European Communities) (1993), *Towards Sustainability: A European Community Programme of Policy and Action in Relation to the Environment and Sustainable Development*, OJ C138, 17.5.1993, Brussels: Commission of the European Communities.

EEA (European Environment Agency) (2005), *Environmental Policy Integration in Europe: State of Play and an Evaluative Framework*, Technical Report, No. 2/2005, Copenhagen: European Environment Agency.

EurActiv (2006), *Report: Environmental Policy has been 'Politically Downgraded'*, 18 May. Available at: http://www.euractiv.com/en/environment/report-environmental-policy-politically-downgraded/article-155404 (accessed on 21 November 2007).

European Council (2000), *Conclusions of the Lisbon European Council*, Lisbon, 23–24 March, Brussels: European Council.

European Council (2006), *Renewed EU Sustainable Development Strategy*, European Council Document No. 10117, 9 June, Brussels: European Council.

Jordan, A.J. (2008), 'The governance of sustainable development: taking stock and looking forwards', *Environment and Planning C*, 26 (1), 17–33.

Jordan, A.J. and A. Schout (2006), *The Coordination of the European Union: Exploring the Capacities for Networked Governance*, Oxford: Oxford University Press.

Lafferty, W. and E. Hovden (2003), 'Environmental policy integration: towards an analytical framework', *Environmental Politics*, 12 (3), 1–22.

Lafferty, W. and J. Knudsen (2007), *The Issue of 'Balance' and Trade-offs in EPI: How Will We Know EPI when We See It?* EPIGOV Working Paper, 31 January, Berlin: Ecologic.

Lenschow, A. (2002), 'Greening the European Union: an introduction', in A. Lenschow (ed.), *Environmental Policy Integration: Greening Sectoral Policies in Europe*, London: Earthscan.

Liberatore, A. (1997), 'The integration of sustainable development objectives into EU policy making', in S. Baker, M. Kousis, D. Richardson and S. Young (eds), *The Politics of Sustainable Development*, Routledge: London.

OECD (Organisation for Economic Cooperation and Development) (2002), *Improving Policy Coherence and Integration For Sustainable Development: A Checklist*, Paris: OECD.

Pallemaerts, M., D. Wilkinson, C. Bowyer, J. Brown, *et al.* (2006), *Drowning in Process? The Implementation of the EU's 6th Environmental Action Programme*, Report for the European Environmental Bureau, London: IEEP.

Schout, A. and A.J. Jordan (2007), 'From cohesion to territorial policy integration (TPI): exploring the governance challenges in the European Union', *European Planning Studies*, 15 (6), 835–851.

Index